D1555801

THE CHRIST IN THE BIBLE COMMENTARY
Volume Three

THE
CHRIST IN THE BIBLE
COMMENTARY

Volume Three

The Kings and Prophets
Psalms
Isaiah

Dr. Albert B. Simpson

CHRISTIAN PUBLICATIONS
CAMP HILL, PENNSYLVANIA

Christian Publications
3825 Hartzdale Drive, Camp Hill, PA 17011

The mark of  *vibrant faith*

ISBN: 0-87509-500-3
LOC Catalog Card Number: 92-70937
© 1993 by Christian Publications
All rights reserved
Printed in the United States of America

93 94 95 96 97 5 4 3 2 1

Cover Design: Step One Design

CONTENTS

The Kings and Prophets

Israel

Judah

Psalms

Isaiah

THE KINGS AND PROPHETS

ISRAEL

CHAPTER 1

JEROBOAM, OR SIN AND ITS INFLUENCE

And he will give Israel up because of the sins Jeroboam has committed and has caused Israel to commit. (1 Kings 14:16)

The Old Testament is a kaleidoscope of human character, revealing to us the failure of the human nature and driving us to Jesus Christ as the only remedy for man's lost condition. The story of Israel's fall is a true delineation of the roots and fruits of human depravity in every age. The text is a flashlight upon a dark life and the story that lies behind is a tragedy of curious and original wickedness. It is the picture of a brilliant man who went all wrong and set everybody else wrong too. A man who sinned and, worse than his own sin, made Israel sin—a sinful life and its more sinful influence on others. God help us to look a little at it as the pictures turn and see perhaps in some of them a mirror that will send us humble and contrite to the feet of Jesus. Not for themselves did these men fail on the shores of time, but as beacons for us, that we might receive instruction and warning and see our utter helplessness without Christ.

SECTION I—*The Story of Jeroboam*

Jeroboam was the founder of the kingdom of Israel, which for several centuries went down deeper and deeper until at last it disappeared.

The first picture is a dramatic one—a young man is in Solomon's employ in the heyday of that king's glorious reign. He is gifted and talented and Solomon puts him over the laborers who are building the supporting terraces. Suddenly an old prophet meets the young contractor one day and seizing his outer garments he tears them into 12 pieces and hands back 10 of the pieces saying, "Take ten pieces for yourself, for this is what the LORD, the God of Israel, says: 'See, I am going to tear the kingdom out of Solomon's hand and give you ten tribes. But for the sake of my servant David and the

1

city of Jerusalem, . . . he will have one tribe' " (1 Kings 11:31–32). Then he went on to say that if Jeroboam would be true to God, God would establish his kingdom and make it a witness for His name and a blessing to the world; but if he should be unfaithful, God would deal with him in judgment.

Ahijah the prophet, passes on, and young Jeroboam, with his head inflated and his soul on fire, instead of waiting for God to fulfill His part, began to concoct plans of rebellion among the jealous people of Ephraim, of whom he was one. Solomon found it out and sought his life. Jeroboam had to flee to Egypt, where he remained until the death of Solomon.

REHOBOAM

Solomon is in his grave, and his foolish son, Rehoboam, is on the throne. Rehoboam comes up to Shechem to meet the people and be crowned. Meanwhile they have sent for Jeroboam and have had a great convention, and talked it all over. They have made Jeroboam their spokesman and they tell the young king that if he will make some concessions they will serve him; but if he continues the forced labor and tribute of Solomon's reign they will have nothing to do with him.

Rehoboam takes three days to answer them and foolishly asks and acts upon the advice of some upstarts of his court and gives them an insolent reply.

THE KINGDOM DIVIDED

Immediately the standard of rebellion is raised and an impassable gulf has come between the two sections of God's people. Rehoboam's agent is stoned to death and the king is compelled to flee for his life back to Jerusalem. The tribes have separated and nothing is left of David's house but the tribe of Judah and a portion of Benjamin and Simeon. Rehoboam attempts to put down the rebellion, but God forbids it, and for once he is advised by the prophet. Jeroboam is now established upon his throne, and it is a splendid throne—the best part of Palestine, the fertile valley of Esdraelon, the beautiful city of Samaria and the vast plains and territories reaching beyond the sea of Galilee to the borders of Tyre and Sidon.

God's promises were behind Jeroboam and he might have had one of the grandest careers of the Old Testament. But he begins by building powerful fortifications, showing that he is depending upon the arm of flesh to secure his kingdom rather than upon the Lord.

POLITICAL POLICY

His next step is a move in that political policy that has in every age only brought defeat and failure. He sees that Jerusalem, being the religious capital, his people will naturally go there to the temple for worship and the observance of the feasts they have been taught to keep since the time of Moses, and thus become attached to the Southern Kingdom.

He established two new religious capitals, one at Bethel in the south and the other at Dan in the north, places at which he erects altars and begins a kind of hybrid worship more heathen than divine. The effect is to arouse the priests and Levites, and drive them to Judah, leaving him to his idolatrous and heathen worship. This was done for the purpose of saving his kingdom, but man-made religions and state churches have in every age failed.

DIVINE WARNING

God now takes more stringent measures to bring him to conviction. Just as he is opening his new altar at Bethel an old prophet suddenly appears, coming up from Judah. His name is unknown, but he denounces Jeroboam as he is about to offer incense with his own hands, and God backs up his message by cleaving the altar in two and scattering the ashes. The king reaches out to arrest the old man and instantly his arm is withered and falls by his side. He is compelled to implore the prophet to forgive his transgression and restore his useless arm. This he does and then follows the prophecy that the bones of the priests who have ministered there shall yet be burned upon this altar, and that Josiah shall come forth to avenge the insult given to Jehovah.

REPEATED WARNINGS

The prophet passes on, but on his way, through believing a false message, he is slain by a lion. His carcass is found with the lion standing guard like a very messenger from God, guarding it from insult, and yet showing that he had been slain in fulfillment of God's Word. When the dreadful story reached Jeroboam he must have seen that the God who had sent that message to him could not be trifled with. Still we are told that Jeroboam did not repent, but hardened his heart and still went on in his willfulness and sin.

Now comes the next dramatic picture. One of Jeroboam's children, a little boy, very dear to him, falls sick, and no remedies avail. In his anguish the king thinks of the old prophet Ahijah. He is too proud to be known as relenting and supplicating, so he sends his wife in disguise to the old man. But the prophet cries out as she comes in, "Come in, wife of Jeroboam" (14:6). And then he bids her go back and tell her husband that, because of his wickedness and defiance of God, this child shall be the only one of his family that shall be buried, and the moment her foot enters her palace home her boy shall die and her house shall be accursed because of the sins of Jeroboam.

THE STROKE

We cannot dwell on all that followed but the judgment came as the prophet had foretold.

A little later we read of a war between Jeroboam and the house of Abijah in which 1.2 million men were engaged. Jeroboam was defeated and half a million of his army slain, the mightiest slaughter in the history of human battles. His military prestige was broken, his army shattered and he never recovered.

Still later we are told the Lord struck him and he died and the inscription that was left on his life: ". . . the sins Jeroboam has committed and has caused Israel to commit" (14:16).

God meant that we should read it still and hearkening learn the lessons, not only of a sinful life, but of a more sinful heritage of influence upon other lives.

There is another picture that stands beside Jeroboam and is in some respects just as bad. It was Ahab, of whom we are told, "There was never a man like Ahab, who sold himself to do evil in the eyes of the LORD, urged on by Jezebel his wife" (21:25). Jeroboam made others sin and Ahab let others make him sin.

SECTION II—*Lessons Learned from Jeroboam's Life*

In the story of Jeroboam's life we see several aspects that provide valuable lessons.

PERVERTED GIFTS

1. We see a splendid mind with noble gifts prostituted by false ambition.

How the devil loves to get the best and brightest. He chooses the very cream of human intellect, the very flower of our land as his instruments. Smartness is a curse unless balanced by principle, by high moral character, by the fear and love of God.

LOST OPPORTUNITIES

2. We see a splendid opportunity thrown away.

What an opportunity! The founding of a kingdom, the shaping of a nation's destiny, a chance as great as Moses or David had! And yet how utterly wasted and perverted. The deepest lesson from Solomon and his immediate followers was this, that wisdom is not sufficient without grace, without the Holy Spirit. And the greatest lesson of these lives is not to lead men to be more prudent and self disciplined, but to lead them to see that our best wisdom is to confess our foolishness and take the "Spirit of wisdom and of understanding,/ the Spirit of counsel and of power" (Isaiah 11:2).

GOD DISAPPOINTED

3. We see again a divine calling and purpose turned aside by the disobedience of a willful man.

God called Jeroboam, gave him his kingdom and intended he should fulfill some great and useful work, but Jeroboam missed all. There is no doubt about God's purpose as announced by Ahijah, yet there is no doubt about God's disappointment. We may not put the two together, but there they both stand. Oh how often has God to cry out: "If only you had paid attention to my commands,/ your peace would have been like a river,/ your righteousness like the waves of the sea" (48:18).

Do we doubt the power of God to carry out His purposes? No, never! Do we believe that Satan is stronger than Jehovah and able to defeat Him? No, never! God always triumphs in the end.

But it is still true that God often lets you refuse your blessing if you will, and later calls another to do what you would not do and to wear the crown that you threw away.

Mordecai said to his own beloved Esther, "For if you remain silent at this time, relief and deliverance for the Jews will arise from another place" (Esther 4:14). You can step out of His will and miss His blessings, but God will go on and bring about His end. God may have great blessings for you, a high calling for you, great possibilities for you, but be careful lest you forfeit and throw them away by refusing to walk in His highest will. Remember that you have within your heart something that came to you from God and is like God—the power to choose, the power to refuse, the throne of your will.

Oh, hasten to lay it at His feet lest it should be your snare, and take Him to work in you both "to will and to act according to his good purpose" (Philippians 2:13).

THE ARM OF FLESH

4. We see the dependence of Jeroboam upon the arm of flesh instead of upon God.

The beginning of his apostasy was the building of fortifications and the raising of a mighty army. Unbelief was the secret root of all his sin. It always is. The only way to get saved is to stop everything and let Him save you. The only way to get sanctified is to cease your struggles and let Him fight the battle for you. The only way to triumph is to trust. "The one who trusts will never be dismayed" (Isaiah 28:16). While you are fretting, fussing and trying a thousand things, you have no faith.

COMPROMISE

5. His next mistake was a false political project to establish a religion for his own selfish interest.

Some people join a church to help their social influence and they join the church that will help them most. There are a thousand ways in which we can make our religious work merely a means of advancing our own interests.

Worse, it was a man-made religion. Man-made religions always end in becoming the devil's religions and it was not long before the altars of Jeroboam became the altars of Baal. And this was the outcome of Jeroboam's selfishness in daring to make God subservient to his own ambitious policy.

NEGLECTED WARNINGS

6. Then came the warnings of God and Jeroboam's proud defiance of them and his persistence in his own way.

There was the prophet at Bethel with his awful message and the sign that accompanied it; the prophet's own end the next day speaking of a God that would be true to His Word at any cost; the warning that came from Ahijah that the child must die because of his father's career of sin. All these seemed to make no impression until at last the inevitable calamity came: his army was blotted out, his power broken and the stroke of doom fell upon his own wicked head as he died under the hand of Jehovah. "Ahijah rested with his fathers" (2 Chronicles 14:1), it is said, but of Jeroboam, "The LORD struck him down and he died" (13:20), and his epitaph is, "Here lies Jeroboam who sinned and made Israel to sin."

THE BITTER FRUITION

7. Finally there is the bitter fruition of his actions and influence.

There is one word in one of the parables of Jesus that burns with a consuming flame. It is the word Abraham uses to that wretched man on the other side of the gulf, "Son, remember" (Luke 16:25). Go away into the dark abysses of the future alone with your own heart and memory. Remember how often God helped you and loved you. Remember how you refused His salvation again and again. And if in addition to memory there should come in the next world the very victims of your sins to torment you with their presence and remind you that you were their destroyer is there need for any material fire? Is there need for any hell worse than the brimstone that a wicked man and a guilty conscience carry in the recesses of their own heart?

What a picture must have come before Jeroboam at last of the splendid kingdom he had destroyed—the remembrance of the prophet of the Lord, of all that might have been, and then the awful wreck that stared him in the face too late to retrieve. Yes, and what a vision nearer home—the anguish of his broken-hearted wife, the dying boy that he loved better than his life, the curse of old Ahijah whose help he had begged in vain. These are some of the fruits of sin.

But what if he could have looked down and seen the frightful centuries that followed—Jezebel and her infamies, the murderess of the prophets of the Lord, the awful crimes that filled the succeeding years, the ruin of the 10 tribes, the coming of the Assyrians, the siege of Samaria, mothers eating their own babes, the cruel cordon around the doomed city and the going forth of all the people of the land, naked, insulted and bound as captives to the lands of the heathen, never to return, and all the awful judgments of God that came at last, as He had to cast Israel out of His sight because of the sins of Jeroboam, the son of Nebat, who sinned and made Israel to sin!

What about our influence? This is more than sin. There is an awful picture in Genesis where God met Cain and said to him, "If you do what is right, will you not be accepted? But if you do not do what is right, sin is crouching at your door; it desires to have you, but you must master it" (Genesis 4:7).

It is a fearful figure and has various interpretations, of which this is one: sin as God sees it is a crouching, wild beast. There it is gathered up ready for its fatal spring upon you. Beware how you trifle with it, for its triumph means much more than your undoing and carries in its train a curse as far-reaching as your influence, as dark as despair and as long as a lost eternity!

CHAPTER 2

AHAB, OR THE WICKEDNESS OF WEAKNESS

Ahab son of Omri did more evil in the eyes of the LORD than any of those before him. He not only considered it trivial to commit the sins of Jeroboam son of Nebat, but he also married Jezebel daughter of Ethbaal king of the Sidonians, and began to serve Baal and worship him. (1 Kings 16:30–31)

> *There was never a man like Ahab, who sold himself to do evil in the eyes of the LORD, urged on by Jezebel his wife. (21:25)*

There is something worse than original sin. There are originals in sin, and our text tells us that Ahab was one of these. He reached the climax of human wickedness, and carried off the palm for depravity and crime. "There was never a man like Ahab, who sold himself to do evil in the eyes of the LORD." And he did not do it alone. There was a woman in it. Worse, even, than his wickedness was his weakness in letting another instigate him to his crimes. "Urged on by Jezebel his wife."

When you want to find the superlative degree of sin, you must find a woman. Capable at once of the best and the basest, she reaches both extremes.

> She raised a mortal to the skies,
> She drew an angel down.

It is so natural to a woman to be good that when she flies from her orbit, she flies to the farthest limit and becomes a wandering star to whom is reserved the blackness of darkness forever. With two such, little wonder that we should find the brood of hell. The story of Ahab unfolds in a series of striking pictures.

9

SECTION I—*The Story of Ahab*

A ROYAL WEDDING

1. The first picture is that of a wedding, a royal wedding, a brilliant wedding, but a very sad one.

A gentleman called upon his minister after half a dozen years of married misery, and reproached him for having told him that his marriage would be the end of all troubles. "Yes," replied the minister, "but I did not tell you which end."

Ahab's marriage was the wrong end of all his troubles. She was the daughter of the Sidonian king, and her people represented the highest culture, civilization and wealth of ancient times. Tyre was the commercial metropolis of the world, and, doubtless, she brought with her higher styles of fashion and life, and for a time seemed a great acquisition to the simple society of the kingdom of Israel. But God's prohibition of marriage with the ungodly never fails to bring certain retribution, and Jezebel became the bane of Ahab's future life and the blight of her country and her age.

A RELIGIOUS REVOLUTION

2. The next picture is a religious revolution.

Things are soon turned upside down. She brings not only the culture of the world, but its false religion, and above all other religions the worship of the Sidonians, so vile and debasing. Baal, the male principal, and Ashtoreth, the female principal, were worshiped as the types of power by all the vile excesses known as Phallic worship, in which the lowest passions of human nature were prostituted to the service of their gods. Jeroboam had mingled a modified form of calf worship, after the example of Aaron, with the worship of Jehovah; but Ahab and Jezebel banished the worship of Jehovah altogether, and set up idolatry as the religion of the state.

A RELIGIOUS PERSECUTION

3. The third picture is of religious persecution.

Relentlessly she pursued the prophets of the Lord, and Ahab, at her bidding, hunted them down, until Obadiah, a godly member of the court, with difficulty succeeded in concealing 100 of them in the caves of Carmel from her bloodthirsty ferocity. She was the Bloody Mary, the Lucretia Borgia, the Lady Macbeth of ancient Israel, and the prototype of all that is most infamous in women in every age.

THE APPEARANCE OF ELIJAH

4. Next comes a flash of warning—the sudden appearance of Elijah

upon the scene.

First came his awful threat in the name of the Lord, that there will be neither dew nor rain for three years and six months. He disappears as suddenly as he came, and for three years the king and his servants vainly hunt for the lost prophet whom God has hidden away until the appointed time. There is something very ignoble in the picture of Ahab at this time passing up and down the land with Obadiah, seeking not supplies for his starving people, but fodder for his mules and horses. No matter who suffered, his stable must be kept in good style and his selfish luxuries pandered to at any cost.

ELIJAH'S REAPPEARANCE

5. The panorama moves, and again we have the sudden apparition of the prophet.

Before the astonished gaze of Obadiah, he stands in the way with one startling message, "Go tell your master, 'Elijah is here' " (1 Kings 18:8). With a show of courage, the king comes to meet him, and begins his harangue: "Is that you, you troubler of Israel?" (18:17). But the stern answer of the fiery prophet bows his proud head in mute obedience as he tells him, "I have not made trouble for Israel, . . . But you and your father's family have. You have abandoned the LORD's commands and followed the Baals" (18:18). Then comes the summons to the great meeting on Carmel, and the king and the prophet part.

IDOLATRY ON TRIAL

6. Next comes the vision of the scene on Carmel, that immortal picture, with idolatry on trial before an assembled nation.

Every part of the picture is intensely dramatic: the myriads of Israel; the prophets of Baal 450 strong; the king and his court; the lonely Elijah; the trial by fire, so fitting for Baal the god of fire; the vain attempt of the deluded priests all day long to bring the answering signal, while Elijah lashed them with his withering scorn, until the sunset found them pleading, panting, exhausted and beaten by their own weapons. And then comes the short and simple prayer. The altar is flooded again with water, the 12 stones reminding them of ancient covenants. We hear the solitary appeal to heaven, we see the answering flash, the hissing flame, the consuming sacrifice, the overwhelming awe of God's immediate presence, and then comes that shout like a thousand thunders from all the people: "The LORD—he is God!" (18:39).

AHAB

7. But next we see the low, gross spirit of the king in contrast with the spirit of the prophet.

"Go, eat and drink" (18:41), is Elijah's message. He knows what Ahab wants; he is hungry. And the feast is spread in the royal tent, and with eating and drinking he forgets for the time the awful days of famine. What is Elijah doing while the miserable Ahab is eating and drinking? With his face between his knees, he is travailing in prayer, bursting asunder the bars of heaven, and bidding the rains once more descend. He prays until "a cloud as small as a man's hand" (18:44) appears on the distant horizon, and soon the torrents are pouring. The prophet himself is the master of the elements and the sovereign of the hour, as he leads the van of that triumphant procession hastening to Jezreel.

JEZEBEL

8. But now the next picture brings us to a sad reaction. Jezebel was not at Carmel that day, but Ahab tells her all, and like a lightning flash her answer is hurled at Elijah. "May the gods deal with me, be it ever so severely, if by this time tomorrow I do not make your life like that of one of them" (19:2).

It was like a bomb-shell from the batteries of hell. For the time it paralyzed even Elijah. He just flew, as one might fly in the explosion of a shell, and never stopped until he sank exhausted under a juniper tree, a day's journey distant. Yes, it was very sad, but it was in God's order, for Elijah must now be withdrawn from the scene to let Ahab once more be put on trial. And so, for six years the prophet is out of sight and Ahab is on trial. Again and again God tries to bless him. He delivers Ahab from his Syrian enemies, and finally delivers up the king of Syria into his very hands. But Ahab fails to improve the opportunity, and with criminal weakness and good nature lets Ben-Hadad escape. The next message is a sentence of doom from the lips of a prophet: "You have set free a man I had determined should die. Therefore it is your life for his life, your people for his people" (20:42).

NABOTH'S VINEYARD

9. Now we come to the crisis of Ahab's crimes. Twenty-five miles from his capital, Samaria, was the charming suburb of Jezreel, where he had built his favorite palace and laid out the most beautiful estates in one of the fairest regions of the world. It was fair enough to satisfy the highest ambition; but the covetous heart is never content. As Ahab surveyed one day the fascinating view, he felt there was just one thing wanting to make his property perfect. There was one little estate that lay hard by his splendid palace which was necessary to complete the landscape. It is the property of Naboth, an old citizen, whose little villa lies adjacent to the king's domains. Of course, all that Naboth will want to know will be that Ahab needs the property. But no, Naboth does not want to sell. In fact, he does not feel that he dare sell at any price, because the Mosaic law forbids him to

alienate the inheritance of his father.

Ahab is astounded, annoyed and irritated. Jezreel has lost all its charms. He returns to Samaria sulking and will not eat, drink or sleep. Jezebel finds him in a fit of the blues. It was at just such times that she was her worst. She knew how to rule men, not by forcing their will, but by gratifying it, by making herself necessary to their pleasures and convenient for their crimes. She makes light of Naboth's objections, and has a way to settle it without further trouble: only let Ahab give her his authority and Naboth will soon be out of the way. It is a small affair of trumped up charges, a corrupt judge and jury, a lot of paid false witnesses, perjuries and lies, and in short order Naboth has been condemned for high treason and stoned to death and his family with him. The property reverts to the State for want of legal heirs. There is nobody to claim it but Ahab the king, and in the most natural way it all falls to him. How very convenient!

And so next day he slips down to his estate, congratulating himself on the splendid addition to his grounds, and gathering, perhaps, a bunch of flowers from Naboth's garden for Jezebel, his obliging queen. Suddenly an apparition stands before him that congeals all the blood in his frame, and forces from his lips the startled cry, "So you have found me, my enemy!" (21:20).

It is Elijah. It is six years since they have met, but they meet again on time. The stern avenger exclaims, "I have found you, . . . because you have sold yourself to do evil in the eyes of the LORD" (21:20). Then follow swiftly the words of doom: The dogs that have licked Naboth's blood will lick Ahab's soon, and the curse of heaven will follow his bloody house.

At last the blow strikes home. At last the proud sinner is broken. Ahab hurries to Samaria, covers himself with sackcloth and ashes, hides from Jezebel and all the court, and becomes a pitiful spectacle of remorse and humiliation. It seems like repentance; perhaps it is chiefly fear. But at least there is a break, and God sees it and gives it all the acknowledgment He can. "Have you noticed," He says, "how Ahab has humbled himself before me? Because he has humbled himself, I will not bring this disaster in his day, but I will bring it on his house in the days of his son" (21:29). Oh, wondrous mercy of God, watching for a chance to forget and forgive, "You do not stay angry forever/ but delight to show mercy" (Micah 7:18).

DOOM COMES AT LAST

10. Once again the scene changes. Three years have passed and Ahab has had a short reprieve; but doom comes at last. It comes to Ahab by willful presumption and self-deception. Jehoshaphat, the king of Judah, is visiting him at Samaria. War is on with Syria, and Ahab invites Jehoshaphat to join him in the campaign. Too hastily the good king consents, but suggests at first that they shall ask counsel of the Lord. Ahab summons his false prophets,

and, of course, their flattering words bid him go and promise victory.

Jehoshaphat begs for another voice before the final decision; and then Ahab tells him that there is only one other prophet, Micaiah, a man whom he hates because he always prophesies failure concerning him. But in deference to Jehoshaphat, he sends for him to the dungeon where he is languishing. Micaiah appears, and tells of his vision, how the Lord has shown him that a lying spirit in the mouths of the prophets has been sent forth to his ruin. The leader of the false prophets insults and smites the good old man in the presence of the king. And then Micaiah tells another vision of Israel scattered like sheep on the mountains without a king. Ahab dismisses him in anger, and bids them hold him in prison until he returns again in peace. Then Micaiah adds his final warning, "If you ever return safely, the LORD has not spoken through me" (2 Chronicles 18:27 or 1 Kings 22:28).

The die is cast. The proud king cannot well afford to retrace his steps. But evidently a deep fear and the premonition of evil have taken possession of his heart and so he enters the battle in disguise, meanly contriving to put Jehoshaphat in his place as a foil for his protection and hiding himself under false colors. The battle rages and soon Jehoshaphat, pursued by the enemy under orders to seize Ahab at any cost, is surrounded and almost captured. He is saved only when they discover their mistake about the man.

Ahab seems to be about to escape scot-free, but it is easier to hide from man than from God. What is this that comes hissing through the air, and suddenly pierces an open space in the joints of his harness, as he turns himself at that very moment to open an avenue for the deadly shaft? "Someone drew his bow at random" (1 Kings 22:34), but God aimed it. Ahab is carried dying from the battlefield, his army scatter to their homes and the dogs of Samaria and Jezreel lick up his blood as it drips from the chariot where he lies. The curse has at last come home, and his sin has found him out. Thirteen years later his wicked paramour shared a more shameful fate, and the record of two lives was stereotyped on the pages of time, "There was never a man like Ahab, who sold himself to do evil in the eyes of the LORD, urged on by Jezebel his wife" (21:25).

SECTION II—*Lessons Learned from Ahab's Life*

Two lessons follow from the story of this sinful life.

THE CLIMAX OF WICKEDNESS

"There was never a man like Ahab, who sold himself to do evil in the eyes of the LORD, urged on by Jezebel his wife" (21:25).

Wherein did Ahab's supreme wickedness consist?

1. He dethroned Jehovah as the God of Israel, and set the worship of

idols, really devil worship, on Jehovah's throne. His crime, therefore, was a direct act of treason against the Lord.

2. He persecuted the prophets of the Lord. God has so identified Himself with His servants that it is true, "He who rejects you rejects me" (Luke 10:16). He has guarded His servants by the most sacred sanctions. "Do not touch my anointed ones," He says, "do my prophets no harm" (1 Chronicles 16:22). But Ahab rejected the Word of the Lord and sought to destroy Jehovah's messengers.

3. He prostituted his power for selfish pleasure and aggrandizement. When the people were starving around him his sole object was to find fodder for his horses and mules. And when an upright citizen declined for the highest reasons to give up his patrimony he consented to his murder and the appropriation of his inheritance for his own pleasure.

4. He neglected even the opportunities that God gave him to destroy his enemies, and when Ben-Hadad was in his power, in a fit of good-natured weakness he let him go, and thus involved his kingdom in all the miseries of that monarch's later invasions.

5. He abused and despised the mercy of God. Again and again Jehovah bore and forbore, and gave him opportunity to prove his penitence, but he only used his respite to plot still deeper crimes and manifest to full maturity the depravity of his wicked heart.

6. He hated and rejected the light. The faithful Micaiah he disliked and cast into prison, and finally in defiance of God's warnings he rushed headlong to his doom.

7. He meanly sought to shield himself in the fatal battle of Ramoth Gilead by a cowardly disguise and put his generous friend, Jehoshaphat, in his place, exposing him to almost certain death in order to save himself. He was a treacherous friend as well as a cruel foe.

8. He permitted a wicked woman to make a tool of him for the basest ends, and to use his high authority for her wicked purposes. He even employed her to commit a bloody murder for his own benefit and then tried to shield himself from the responsibility for the crime by holding her guilty of the deed to which he was an accessory. There is scarcely an element of human baseness and aggravated wickedness which may not be traced in his character and life, and it seems indeed true that "there was never a man like Ahab, who sold himself to do evil" (1 Kings 21:25).

THE WICKEDNESS OF WEAKNESS

"Urged on by Jezebel his wife" (21:25). Perhaps he thought that it was rather his misfortune than his fault that he was so severely tempted by a stronger nature. But God holds him doubly guilty for yielding to her influence. It is an old excuse, as old as Adam, to say, "The woman you put here with me—she gave me some fruit from the tree, and I ate it" (Genesis 3:12).

1. Adam

Not only is it a cowardly and ungenerous thing to throw the blame upon a woman, but it avails nothing. Adam should have saved his wife from herself. But because he yielded to her temptation, God has held him guilty of the ruin of his race, and it is forever true, "For as in Adam all die" (1 Corinthians 15:22). "For just as through the disobedience of the one man the many were made sinners" (Romans 5:19).

2. Eli

Look at old Eli, a good and blameless man; but God held him guilty of the ruin of Israel and raised up little Samuel to sound the note of judgment, simply because he let his family use his power for the corruption of the nation.

3. David

And David, what have you done? Why nothing. I have been in my palace all the time. Yes, but who slew the brave Uriah in the forefront of the battle? Oh, yes, the commanding officer put him in charge of the assaulting party and he was killed, but I did not do it. Then what did Nathan mean as he thundered that sentence in his sovereign's ear, "You are the man" (2 Samuel 12:7) and "now, therefore, the sword will never depart from your house" (12:10)? And what did David mean when he cried, "Save me from bloodguilt, O God" (Psalm 51:14)?

4. Herod

And who is this that sits in the banquet while the ghastly head of John the Baptist is brought on a platter by a shameless girl and laid at the feet of her monster mother? Herod, is this your crime? Why, yes, but I had to do it because she held me to my promise. Did that excuse the murderer or abate one jot of his fearful crime?

5. Pilate

And you, master murderer of all the ages, with hands stained with the blood of the Son of God, Pilate, what have you done? Why, "I am innocent of this man's blood," he said. "It is your responsibility!" (Matthew 27:24). And they do their best to help him out. Yes, they answer, "Let his blood be on us and on our children!" (27:25). Did that save him? Then what is the meaning of that awful legend connected with Mount Pilatus where it is said this man, driven by remorse and deserted by every friend, hurled himself from the fearful cliff to go with Judas "to his own place"?

Ah, Ahab, you cannot roll over your guilt on Jezebel. Rather you shall find that your crime is only doubled by the weakness that yielded to her solicitations and involved two souls in sin and ruin.

Embezzler, it will not avail you to say you stole your employer's money to please some worthless girl. Backslider, it will not save you from perdition because the influence of some unholy friendship led you away from God. Worldling, you will plead in vain before your God that an ambitious wife, a fashionable daughter, the example and influence of your friends led you into the paths of worldliness and sin. It is through such tests that holy character is vindicated and that weakness and wickedness are unveiled.

No, it will only double your eternal remorse to know that another soul must share your misery. We are placed within the reach of temptation that we may be tested and purified. The hardest temptations often come to us from our loved ones, but we must be brave enough to say "No" to the fondest affections that would betray our Lord, and like the Levites of old, "consecrate ourselves every one upon our son and our brother" (Exodus 32:29, KJV).

BE TRUE

One of the finest of the old paintings represents a fair girl looking up into her lover's face on the eve of the Massacre of St. Bartholomew and beseeching him to let her take from his buttonhole the rosette that witnessed to his Protestant faith. She knew that on the morrow it would mean his death. But he is gently putting aside her hand and looking in her eyes with a look which seems to say "While I love you better than all on earth, I love Him best of all."

God help us to be so brave and true that we will not only refuse the temptation, but save the tempter too!

CHAPTER 3

JEHU, OR ZEAL WITHOUT GODLINESS

Come with me and see my zeal for the LORD. (2 Kings 10:16)

Yet Jehu was not careful to keep the law of the LORD, the God of Israel, with all his heart. He did not turn away from the sins of Jeroboam, which he had caused Israel to commit. (10:31)

The story of Jehu begins back of the present record. Its first chapter was that scene on Mount Horeb where Elijah received a new commission bidding him to anoint Jehu king of Israel, Hazael king of Syria and Elisha to be prophet.

SECTION I—*The Story of Jehu*

JEHU AND AHAB

The second scene falls on that memorable day when Ahab rode out from Samaria to Jezreel to take possession of his ill-gotten spoil in Naboth's vineyard. Jehu and Bidkar were his attendants that day, Jehu being the commander of the forces and Bidkar his aide. They were standing on the chariot, and perhaps driving the swift horses for Ahab, when, at Naboth's gate, the mantled prophet suddenly appeared to confront Ahab with his crime, and that cry of anger and fear was extorted from the trembling king, "So you have found me, my enemy!" (1 Kings 21:20).

That moment, doubtless, was never forgotten by Ahab's general, and many a time its memory may have suggested to him thoughts of proud ambition in connection with that throne, which was some day to fall according to the prophet's word.

JEHU'S ANOINTING

But time passes on while vengeance lingers, until at last Ahab dies, the dogs of Jezreel lick his blood at Naboth's gate, his infamous queen still lives on, and his two sons, Ahaziah and Joram, successively occupy the throne. Meanwhile, the war with Syria proceeds with scarcely an interruption, and the hostile armies are now facing each other at Ramoth Gilead, which was the key to the whole region east of the Jordan, in dispute between the two kingdoms.

Joram has just been wounded and obliged to leave the scene of battle for healing and rest at Jezreel, and Jehu the commander is in full charge of the campaign. Suddenly one of the sons of the prophets bursts in upon their council of war, and startles the assembled captains by his weird appearance and sudden message. Tradition tells us it was Jonah, who comes into such prominence a little later in the history of Israel. He was a disciple of Elijah, and perhaps not unlike him in his wild appearance. Demanding an interview with Jehu alone, they retire to the inner chamber, and there, without preface, the prophet pours the anointing oil on the head of Jehu and proclaims him king of Israel, with the solemn charge that he is to destroy the house of Ahab, even as the house of Jeroboam had been before.

The prophet leaves as suddenly as he came, and Jehu, challenged by his fellow officers, is compelled at last to deliver to them his message. Instantly they proclaim him king, spread their military cloaks as a carpet beneath his feet, and from the roof of the house in view of the camp hail him as the king of Israel. The army takes up the cry, and the revolution has been won.

THE REVOLUTION

But promptness and skill are necessary to prevent resistance. Instantly the gates of the city are closed, and Jehu with a select body of soldiers starts upon a forced march to Jezreel. Fifty miles long was the way, but swiftly did the furious driver cover it, and ere long a cloud of dust at the entrance to Jezreel proclaimed to the watchman in the tower that a cavalcade was coming. Messenger after messenger is sent out to meet them, but no answer is returned save an order to the messenger to turn and follow in the rear. At length the near approach of the party enables the watchman to identify the mad driving of Jehu.

Joram at once orders his chariot, and with Ahaziah, king of Judah, who is visiting him at the time, drives out to meet his general. Doubtless, he expects some message from the battle field. "Has Hazael been beaten? Has he made peace with Israel?" "Do you come in peace?" (2 Kings 9:18). "Is it peace, Jehu?" is the question. But Jehu's answer leaves no doubt upon the royal mind. "How can there be peace, . . . as long as all the idolatry and witchcraft of your mother Jezebel abound?" (9:22).

THE RETRIBUTION

Quickly Joram calls out to his brother sovereign, "Treachery, Ahaziah!"

(9:23) and turns to flee. But it is too late. An arrow from Jehu's mighty bow pierces the royal heart, and as Joram falls from his chariot Jehu orders his bleeding body to be hurled into Naboth's vineyard that his blood may sink into the ground in the very place where Naboth died.

Dashing on to the palace where Jezebel watches the whole proceeding he lifts up his eyes to behold her, painted and gorgeously arrayed, looking down upon him from the portico and taunting him in her defiant pride as a true follower of the assassin Zimri. "Have you come in peace, Zimri, you murderer of your master?" (9:31). She is still the untamed lioness. But the hour of her doom has come. Hurled from the window by her attendants at Jehu's command, his horses and chariot wheels pass over her mangled body, and he drives on to the banquet hall to refresh himself with food and wine after his journey. Then he pauses to give orders for the burial of Jezebel, but the messenger returns to tell him that there is nothing left but a gnawed skull and the palms of her hands and her feet. The dogs have devoured her flesh, and the word of the Lord through Elijah has been fulfilled.

THE WORK OF JUDGMENT

But this is only the beginning. Samaria, the capital, has not yet been captured, and is in the hands of Ahab's princes with 70 of his sons under their tutelage and care. Jehu sends a polite message to the princes of Samaria, bidding them select one of Ahab's sons as his heir, and let him come to meet him face to face and fight out the issue for the throne. But the princes very sensibly conclude, "If two kings could not resist him, how can we?" (10:4). And they send back a meek message that they want no other king but Jehu, and are ready to become his loyal servants. "If," replies Jehu, "you are on my side and will obey me, take the heads of your master's sons and come to me in Jezreel by this time tomorrow" (10:6).

The next morning two ghastly pyramids of skulls stood at the entrance of the gate of Jezreel like those that Assyrian kings were accustomed to rear over conquered cities. As Jehu looked at them, he shrewdly turned the blame on Ahab's princes. "It was I who conspired against my master and killed him," he says, "but who killed all these?" (10:9). Taking as a pretext for his bloody work their murder of the princes, he slays all that remains of the house of Ahab in Jezreel, his kindred and his priests, until he has left none remaining.

Then sweeping on to Samaria he meets a lot of princes from Judah on the way, belonging to the house of the wicked Ahaziah, and leaves their corpses behind him, too. His entrance into Samaria is signaled by the execution of all Ahab's courtiers and princes there, and the men that had murdered Ahab's sons but yesterday are themselves the victims today.

THE FINISHING STROKE

But yet his commission has only been half fulfilled. He is bound to extirpate the whole brood of idolatry throughout the land. And so with the deepest subtlety he calls an assembly to the worshipers of Baal at the great temple in Samaria, announcing, "Ahab served Baal a little; Jehu will serve him much" (10:18). They come from the north and the south and crowd the great assembly hall, and Jehu stands before them and offers sacrifice to Baal, and when the mocking pageant is over, his appointed soldiers fall upon the multitude and mingle their sacrifices with their blood. Then the images are brought forth and burned, and the very temple made a place for the garbage and refuse of the city to be thrown, while the historian adds, "So Jehu destroyed Baal worship in Israel" (10:28).

JEHU'S FAILURE

But how sad is the sequel! The very next sentence turns the picture over, and we read, "However, he did not turn away from the sins of Jeroboam son of Nebat, which he had caused Israel to commit—the worship of the golden calves at Bethel and Dan" (10:29). He exterminated idolatry, but he did not restore the pure worship of Jehovah, but only the hybrid religion—half heathen and half divine—which Jeroboam had established and which had led Israel into all the sins for which his house was destroyed.

Not only so. Jehu himself continued to live an ungodly life, and his own conduct contradicted the work which his zeal had begun, "Yet Jehu was not careful to keep the law of the LORD, the God of Israel, with all his heart" (10:31). And the record tells us, that while God blessed him for his fidelity to his terrible commission, yet He had to punish him and his people for his failure and his personal wickedness. "The LORD said to Jehu, 'Because you have done well in accomplishing what is right in my eyes and have done to the house of Ahab all I had in mind to do, your descendants will sit on the throne of Israel to the fourth generation'" (10:30). But two verses later we see the story of the divine retribution for the national sin. "In those days the LORD began to reduce the size of Israel. Hazael overpowered the Israelites throughout their territory" (10:32). Such is the story of Jehu. Now for some of its lessons.

SECTION II—*Lessons Learned from Jehu's Life*

THE WORDS OF GOD

1. We see an object lesson of the inevitable fulfillment of every word of God. Not one of His prophetic messages fell to the ground. To the minutest jot the words of Elijah were literally fulfilled in the death of Ahab and

Jezebel and the rule of Ahab's house. "But the word of the Lord stands forever" (1 Peter 1:25). While this is the strong security for our salvation, it is the certain warning of our doom if we presume to trifle with His great salvation and His words of warning and love.

THE CURSE OF SIN

2. We see the inexorable retribution of sin. Jeroboam, Ahab, Jezebel and Jehu all repeated the message of all history and revelation: "You may be sure that your sin will find you out" (Numbers 32:23). Even Jehu himself, the executioner of judgment upon others, became the victim and subject of God's judgment because of his own idolatry and sin. It is as inevitable as the law of cause and effect, the law which makes fire burn and heavy bodies fall, that it shall be "ill with the wicked," and "well with the righteous." Let us not try to turn God's order upside down. Judgment may linger, mercy may forbear.

> The mills of God grind slowly,
>   But they grind exceeding small;
> Though He stands with patience waiting,
>   With exactness grinds He all.

GOD USES BAD MEN

3. God uses the best instruments He can find for His providential purposes. Yet He does not always endorse the men He uses, but simply takes what He can in each life and turns it to the best account for His own righteous purposes. Then He deals individually with each man in punishment or reward, according to His individual character and work. Thus we find Him speaking of Cyrus, the idolatrous king of Persia, as His anointed, and saying of him, "I will strengthen you,/ though you have not acknowledged me" (Isaiah 45:5). Thus, indeed, He uses everyone of us in some way, either as a beacon of warning to other lives, or a lighthouse of guidance on the shores of time. Jehu was the very instrument that He needed for His present purpose of judgment, and so He called him to the terrible work of judgment. And yet He did not forget to pronounce on Jehu himself a just and righteous judgment for all his own individual sins.

GOD'S RECOMPENSES

4. God blesses men in the present life according to the good He sees in them, without reference to their future reward or punishment. God has a providential kingdom now in which He deals individually with men and nations according to this principle. He rewards diligence with success, and He punishes indolence with defeat and failure. Prudence, tact, energy,

capacity—all these are attributes of the present life and are dealt with by God on the principle of equity, according to their merit. Therefore, there is a sense in which His covenant with His ancient people is still fulfilled in a measure in present reward.

A distinguished Rabbi said the other day, with much truth, that the difference between Judaism and Christianity is that Judaism is a mortal religion, Christianity an immortal one. He meant that Judaism dealt only with the present life, Christianity was founded upon the principle of future hopes, rewards and punishments. This is true. God deals with individuals and nations now. And thus He dealt with Jehu. Because he was faithful to his commission against idolatry and the wicked house of Ahab, God promised him that his seed to the fourth generation should sit upon Israel's throne. And yet because of his failure in other respects to be true to God, Hazael, the king of Syria, was sent "to reduce the size of Israel" (2 Kings 10:32) in the days of Jehu. He and his people were receiving from another hand the punishment which he had inflicted on the house of Ahab.

His Zeal

(a) The good things in Jehu for which the Lord commended him were, in the first place, his zeal. God loves an earnest soul, and abhors the indolent, self-indulgent drone. All nature unites in thrusting out and repelling the idler; and in religious life God claims our whole heart and earnestness. "I know your deeds, that you are neither cold nor hot. I wish you were either one or the other!" (Revelation 3:15). He would rather have the infidel than the lukewarm Christian. "If the LORD is God, follow him; but if Baal is God, follow him" (1 Kings 18:21). Be one thing or the other, and whatever you are, be it with all your heart and with all your might.

His Energy

(b) Next, Jehu was a man of energy, of force, of those qualities expressed in the phraseology of today as the "strenuous" life. The two most influential men of our age, the emperor of Germany and President Roosevelt, of Washington, stand as prominent types of these qualities and are impressing their example on the young manhood of our time. These are splendid examples, and as far as they go, God approves and blesses such qualities on the purely secular plane. And He wants them on the spiritual plane in all whom He would greatly use. God give us divine enthusiasm and Holy Spirit power in the things of eternity such as men expect in their leaders today in secular affairs.

His Thoroughness

(c) Then further, Jehu was thorough in his work. He did not stop half way, but carried it to a finish. When God sent Saul to exterminate the race of Amalek, he spared Agag and saved the best of the spoil to gratify his ambition. Therefore, Saul lost his kingdom. When God sent Israel under Joshua to drive out the nations of Canaan they stopped half way, and put some of them under tribute, thinking it a good source of revenue to keep the old inhabitants to do their menial work or pay them good money. But these people afterwards became their masters and oppressors. However, Jehu was not of this stamp, and had no half measures. He never stopped until he had finished his work, and blotted out the names of Baal and Ashtoreth from Israel. These were splendid qualities, and God was pleased with them and with him to that extent, and said: "Because you have done well in accomplishing what is right in my eyes and have done to the house of Ahab all I had in mind to do, your descendants will sit on the throne of Israel to the fourth generation" (10:30). But over against these elements of strength there was failure through elements of evil and imperfection.

FAILURE DUE TO EVIL AND IMPERFECTION

5. Jehu's life was not without failure, which was due to elements of evil and imperfection. These are apparent in every human. What brings them to the surface?

Ambition

(a) Much of Jehu's zeal was the result of his own ambition. He thought it was all for the Lord, but a good deal of it was for Jehu and his throne. And so, today, many a man is building up his church very much as a business man is building up his firm. But there is great danger of allowing our personal ambitions to take the place of single-hearted devotion to God, even in Christian work. Therefore, God has sent us sometimes to fail, in order to prove that we are serving Him for love and not for the glory of success.

Temperament

(b) Much of Jehu's zeal was the result of temperament. There are people so constituted that they enjoy certain forms of religious work. They like to lead, they love to speak, they enjoy the triumphs of the orator and the public singer, they love to hold other minds in the spell of their magnetism, and much that goes for flaming zeal and lofty spiritual power may be largely the result of a glowing imagination and a natural power over the minds of men.

Personal Unrighteousness

(c) The supreme failure, however, of Jehu's life, was his own personal unrighteousness. A sinful life will neutralize the most brilliant talents and the most successful labors in any good cause. Jehu's own life was his bane. Alas, brother, is it yours? It will surely beat you in the end. You cannot stand against unrighteousness.

Negative Work

(d) Merely negative work was the fatal defect of Jehu's reformation. His work was destructive, not constructive. He rooted out the weeds, but he did not plant the seeds. He destroyed Baal worship, but he did not lead them on to the pure worship of Jehovah. This was the fault of Elijah's ministry. It was the law, not the gospel. You never can make men good by merely frightening them. You must draw them to better things by the expulsive power of love, and then the light will put out the darkness from it.

Half Way

(e) Jehu's was only a half reformation. He went half way, no further. He destroyed the altars of Jezebel, he exterminated her priests and idols, but he took up the calf worship of Jeroboam. Worship of Baal was pure heathenism. The worship of Jeroboam and the calves was a mixed religion. It was a ritualism which God had not appointed or prescribed. It was nominally the worship of God, but it was the worship of God by forbidden rites. These calves were symbols which were copied from Aaron's act just after they came out of Egypt. They were the Ritualists of the day. They thought they ought to have some symbol of God. He was too spiritual, too remote, for the mind of man to grasp. Therefore, the ox, the symbol of power, was suggestive of His attributes. It was just a human addition to the divine religion, and therein it stood exactly where Ritualism stands today.

RITUALISM

Today there are lots of people who come out of the world and turn away from the service of the devil, and then go right into this very thing. It is in these things that thousands of superficial people are expending their earnestness, their time, their means, devoting themselves to something just as bad as the calf worship of Jeroboam, instead of the pure and spiritual worship of the Lord Jesus Christ. They are playing with ecclesiastical millinery and mummery while a world is perishing, and the real work of saving souls is left to others. This is the zeal of Jehu, what Dr. Guthrie once called "laborious trifling."

SPURIOUS LIVES

How solemn is the lesson afforded by this example, showing us how easily we may be self-deceived and palm off upon ourselves a spurious piety which will never stand God's testing day. It is possible for you to be much used of God as an instrument in His hand, and yet never know the fellowship of His heart. It is possible for you to do much splendid work for God, and leave behind a record of flaming zeal, and yet in the crumble of His analysis there may be but a trace of love or holiness. It is possible for you to be a master workman in His temple, and yet never know what it is to dwell with Him in the secret place of the Most High. It is possible for you to make a great stir in your religious zeal and your busy, bustling work, and yet you be a mere imitation and an empty counterfeit.

A gentleman once constructed an automatic bee, made altogether of brass and wire and mechanical and electrical contrivances. He put it on a table and it buzzed and buzzed like a real bee, so that the bystanders shrank away for fear of its possible sting. He challenged anyone to detect the difference between his and the real insect. Another gentleman took up his challenge and brought a genuine bee. For a little while both buzzed around and looked just alike. Then the gentleman put a little honey in the center of the table and waited. Soon the real bee was busy at the honey. He was not buzzing so much, but he was loading his vessels with the precious sweetness and carrying it away to be used for others, while the first bee still buzzed and buzzed, making more noise, but no honey.

Ah, this is the test. You may buzz in your restless, driving life, and call it Christian work, but it may be little better for you at last than the trade of the politician. The true test is to know God, to find His heart, to drink the sweetness of His love, and then to carry it to others, often unrecognized, unrequited by the age, but finding it joy enough to know Him and help His children.

God help us to make the test in time. God save us from the sad story of that last character in *Pilgrim's Progress*—that man who got across the river with comfort and safety, and even found his way to the gate of Heaven, but was turned back at last and bound hand and foot by the Shining Ones, while the story ends, "So I saw that there was a way to hell from the gate of Heaven, as well as from the City of Destruction."

CHAPTER 4

THE PROPHETS OF ISRAEL

The LORD warned Israel and Judah through all his prophets and seers: "Turn from your evil ways. Observe my commands and decrees in accordance with the entire Law that I commanded your fathers to obey and that I delivered to you through my servants the prophets."

But they would not listen and were as stiff-necked as their fathers, who did not trust in the LORD their God. (2 Kings 17:13–14)

God's three divine orders in the Old Testament theocracy were prophets, priests and kings. The priests were often corrupt, and the kings, as a rule, were bad. Only three of Judah's rulers after Solomon wholly walked in the ways of David, and all the kings of Israel were corrupt. It seemed a punishment upon the nation for asking for a king, instead of accepting Jehovah as their true and only Sovereign.

THE TRUE PROPHETS

The prophets were a royal line of faithful witnesses for God, from the day of Moses, who was the first great prophet, through Samuel, who organized the schools of the prophets, and Nathan, who was a friend of David and not afraid to warn him boldly when he sinned, down to the later and darker times of Elijah and Elisha. They were the very bulwark of the nation, and a wicked king might well say of one of them: "My father! My father! The chariots and horsemen of Israel!" (2 Kings 2:12).

Still later they became God's messengers to the far distant ages, and their writings have come down to us, beginning with Jonah and covering all the later centuries of the changeful history of the kingdoms of Israel and Judah.

We will introduce this noble line by referring to the first two examples in the reign of Jeroboam. The first of these was Ahijah, and the second a nameless prophet, who came originally from Judah, but prophesied at Bethel, and afterwards perished for an act of thoughtless disobedience to the commandment of Jehovah.

SECTION I—*The Prophet Ahijah*

This venerable servant of God began his ministry under Solomon, and it was he who bore to Jeroboam the announcement of his call to be the first king of the 10 tribes.

JEROBOAM'S CALL

The incident was dramatic. Meeting the young officer of Solomon's kingdom on the open highway, suddenly, after the dramatic manner of ancient prophets, he seized his outer garment and tore it into 12 pieces, proclaiming the rending of Solomon's kingdom into 12 tribes. Handing back 10 of the fragments, he explained it by declaring that the Lord would give him these 10 tribes as his kingdom. Then, in the most solemn manner, he warned him of the blessings of fidelity and obedience and the certain retribution that would come to him and his kingdom if they disobeyed and provoked the Lord. Ahijah went his way, and in due time his prophecy was fulfilled and Jeroboam sat upon the throne of Israel, forgetting, however, and disregarding the warnings which preceded his crowning.

SIN AND JUDGMENT

Ahijah calmly waited as the years went by, and at length began to come the turning of the tide. Jeroboam's evil reign was ripening for judgment. His own family was the first to feel the stroke, and his little son was already lying on a bed of painful sickness and all human helps and hopes had failed. Then the wicked king thought of his long-neglected God and the venerable prophet that had first called him to his high position. But he dared not face him directly. So, with a cunning more offensive to God because of the insult it implied upon His all-seeing intelligence, he ventured to send his wife in disguise to wait upon the old prophet and ask him about the recovery of the child.

Ahijah was old and blind, but his blind eyes could see much farther than the brightest human vision. The moment the queen entered his presence he called her by name, and uttered the fearful sentence which had long been waiting the hour of judgment to arrive. He told her of her husband's crimes and sins, warned her of the ruin that was coming upon his house. Then he informed her that as soon as she re-entered her palace her child would die, and would be the only member of Jeroboam's house to receive even the honor of a decent burial. With what a heavy heart that wretched mother must have hurried from the prophet's chamber, dreading to cross the threshold of the palace, where her coming could only bring the knell of death. And yet she also possesses a mother's fondness, almost daring to cling to the lingering hope that perhaps the prophet might be mistaken. At last she ventures in. But the bosom upon which she throws herself is still, and the lips that meet her kiss, cold in death. The prophet is right and the hour of doom has only begun. The story has already been told how that judgment hastened in the destruction of Jeroboam's army, and finally the stroke of God upon his own head.

GOD'S TWO-EDGED SWORD

Our present purpose is to draw the deep spiritual lesson of the prophet's ministry, and surely it is this, that the same word of God may become at once our blessing or our bane. "To the one we are the smell of death; to the other, the fragrance of life" (2 Corinthians 2:16). It is the word of Ahijah that set Jeroboam upon his throne; it was the same word that sentenced him to his doom. So still, it is God's sharp two-edged sword, and woe betide everyone that trifles with it.

> Far better he had ne'er been born.
> Who lives to doubt, or lives to scorn.

OPPORTUNITY

There is a legend of a youth who started down the avenue of life with bounding step and laughing eye. As he tripped along the shining way there met him from time to time an angel form bearing upon his brow the name "Opportunity," and who, holding in his hand a vase of lovely flowers, bade the wayfarer accept them, telling him that they contained the pledge of deepest spiritual blessing. But the reckless youth hastened on, for the way seemed long and bright and he thought, "There will be other opportunities; why should I linger now?" And so the years rolled by.

A score of times the angel was passed with neglect and scorn, and only once in a while did the foolish traveler stop to notice that in his left hand the angel held a shining dart concealed under the folds of his mantle. At last the air began to grow cold and chill. The leaves were falling around the traveler's feet. The birds had ceased to sing, and many a warning seemed to say that his journey was reaching a crisis. Suddenly he found his way obstructed. Reaching out his hand, a cold gate stood across the path, and as he looked at the inscription upon it he shuddered, as he spelled out the dreadful word "Death." The end had come at last.

Shuddering and almost fainting, he sank upon the ground, when hissing through the air a dart struck him, followed by another and another. As he lay wounded and dying in agony, he noticed that these darts were flung by the angel forms that he had scorned in the years gone by. They were the opportunities he had despised and wasted, and now they were visiting him with bitter retribution.

So the same Ahijah that brought to Jeroboam the grandest opportunity of history sent him the most terrific sentence that ever fell from heaven on a single human soul. That word is living still, and still it meets each one of us with its priceless opportunities, with its eternal possibilities and with its awful responsibilities. It is for you to say whether it will be to you the word of life or the sentence of death.

SECTION II—*The Prophet of Bethel*

This incident is strange and solemn. It is the story of a nameless prophet. His very identity has not come down to us. His life seems like one of those little black crosses that stand on some of the cliffs of the Alps, marking the spot where some reckless traveler fell into the abyss below. Just a little black cross with no name upon it, but one solemn word written with mystic fingers, and speaking to us from its weird and warning front, "Beware! Beware!"

A MESSAGE FROM GOD

The story is a thrilling one. When Jeroboam was establishing his false calf worship at the shrine of Bethel, suddenly there appeared before the altar at which the king was officiating, a prophet from Judah, stern and silent. He was robed in the weird garments of his calling. The prophet publicly announced that the day would come when a king named Josiah should burn upon that altar the bones of the priests who had officiated before it. And in token of the truth of his words, he declared that the altar should be rent in the presence of the worshipers, and that the ashes should be sprinkled upon the ground. No sooner said than done, and, lo, as he stood, the altar was riven before the very face of the king and the ashes scattered at his feet. Instinctively Jeroboam reached out his hand either to strike or stop the old prophet, but the hand was stricken with paralysis and he was unable even to recall it to his side. Then his proud heart yielded, and he cried for mercy, and in answer to the prophet's prayer his withered hand was healed.

DECEIVED

He now invited the prophet to come to his palace and accept of his hospitality, but the old man had been warned to enter no household in all that wicked land, but to return in silence as he had come. On his way, however, he was waylaid by another prophet who was desirous, either from vanity or some unworthy motive, to entertain him. When the old man refused as he had refused Jeroboam, the other told him that he, too, was a prophet, and had just received a message from an angel of the Lord bidding him come and meet the servant of God and take him home to his house. The old prophet was deceived, and believing his message, went with him. Before their evening meal was ended, the Spirit of God came upon the seducing prophet, and he was compelled to declare to his guest that because he had disobeyed the voice of the Lord, he should never return to his home, but should perish through the judgment of God. The next morning he saddled his ass and stole homeward, but a lion met him in the way. After having slain the prophet, the lion stood guard over his body, touching neither his corpse nor the ass that had borne him, but standing there in silence like an angel of God, and certainly God's messenger of judgment.

THE DECEIVER'S REMORSE

When tidings came of this terrible tragedy, the prophet that had deceived him hastened to take the remains and bury them, in his own sepulchre. Then he left as his last order with his family, that when he should die they should bury him in the grave of the prophet whom he had deceived and wronged and whom, too late, he found himself unable to save. We are not told of the bitter tears he shed, of the vain remorse, of the sorrow, of the shadow that settled upon his own life and the awful sense of his having become the murderer of one of Jehovah's servants, when he had perhaps, lightly thought that he was only doing him a hospitable kindness. And so the lesson has come down to us, and surely its point is not difficult to trace and its application is just as vital today as in the days of Jeroboam.

IMPLICIT OBEDIENCE

Surely, its one message is that which God gave long ago to Joshua as the key to Canaan, "Be careful to obey all the law my servant Moses gave you; do not turn from it to the right or to the left, that you may be successful wherever you go" (Joshua 1:7). Implicit obedience! Surely, this is the mystic message that blazes from that little black cross yonder on the heights of Bethel.

BE NOT DECEIVED

Yes, we may be utterly sincere, we may not mean to disobey, we may be honestly deceived, but it does not save that ship from wreck to have mistaken the light or allowed its compass to be turned aside by some other attraction. There will be inevitable retribution both in the natural and moral world, and God has said "Do not be deceived: God cannot be mocked. A man reaps what he sows" (Galatians 6:7).

There was much that was good and glorious in the prophet of Bethel. He had been fearless and faithful in executing the divine commission against Jeroboam and his altar. He had been firm in refusing the hospitality of the king, and in this he was eminently wise, for it is vain to expect the worldly to listen to our warnings when we sit down with it at its entertainments and enter into partnership with it in its unholy gains. Especially must the ministry of God keep itself unspotted from the world and stand uncompromised with evil in every way. And he had been most godlike in his mercy in healing the penitent king and rightly representing the goodness, as well as the severity of God.

AS AN ANGEL OF LIGHT

All this was good and godlike. But all this could not excuse his weakness and incautiousness in listening to the voice of the seducer. True again, the deceiver was a prophet, but prophets may deceive, and we have no business to listen to even the most wise and eloquent words of ministers and messengers of God, unless they are according to the Word of God. It is the pulpits of our land today that are most perilously deceiving the flock of God, and no human authority or influence should have the slightest weight with us unless we find back of it in our Bibles a "thus saith the LORD." No, even though we may be told as he was, that an angel from heaven has sent the message, even Paul has told us that "even if we or an angel from heaven should preach a gospel other than the one we preached to you, let him be eternally condemned!" (1:8).

No vision, no revelation, can have any weight against the Word which God has already given to us, and by which all truth must be judged and all destiny decided. The deception was perhaps, kindly meant, but it is by mistaken kindness still that souls are often misled and forever lost. Your polite invitation to some worldly entertainment, your well-meant introduction to some ungodly friend may be the turning point for ruin in the life of someone that you love, and may yet fill your own heart with deepest sorrow.

VAIN REGRETS

Surely behind the picture of that prophet of Bethel and his seducer there is a vision which we may be pardoned for imagining. Could you have seen that broken-hearted man as he hastened to pick up the corpse of his late guest? Could you have seen him, fearless of the lion that stood growling beside it, as he gathered it up tenderly in his arms and bore it to his own burying place? Could you have heard his bitter lamentations as he cursed his own mistaken kindness? Could you have seen his overshadowed life as he went down to the grave, with but one thought, to lay his bones beside those of the man he had ruined, you would, doubtless, have seen a picture that in no way exaggerated this description. And yet such a sorrow awaits every soul that in any way allows itself to become instrumental in the ruin of another's life.

It may seem a trifling matter to lead a pure young life aside from the paths of innocence. But, oh some day when you come face to face—as you will—with the fruits of your life, when you see the anguish, the despair, the terrible ruin which you have wrought, dear friend, it will be a worse hell than your own. Oh, man of selfish and unholy pleasure, it may seem very amusing for a time to dally with temptation and lead some innocent and trusting life to take the first step in the downward course; but go down to the morgue and look upon that pale young face so cold in death. Look at the oozing froth from that mouth, and think of the anguish with which she hurled her desperate life into the oblivion she sought in vain.

> Over the brink of it,
> Picture it, think of it,
> Dissolute man:
> Lave in it, drink of it then if you can.

A few months ago at Old Orchard [a campground in Maine], I met a woman who asked me if I had not published once the incident of a young girl who had asked her mother on her deathbed to bring her the ball dress that had been given her as a bribe to keep her from joining the church after a recent revival. She had worn it once and taken the chill which ended her young life. But just before she died she made them bring it, and fondling it for a little as it lay before her, she said, "Pretty dress. Keep it and look at it every year on the anniversary of my death and remember that it cost me my soul."

The lady who asked the question then told me that this incident actually occurred at her own home in Nova Scotia, and the girl referred to belonged to a neighboring family living hard by her residence, and the facts as stated really occurred. It seemed to give a strange and fearful vividness to the story to have it thus confirmed. The anguish of that mother was greater than even the anguish of that dying child. Would the load ever be lifted from that broken heart or that accusing voice ever cease to speak, "It cost me my soul"?

Oh, think of it, mothers, when you discourage religious decision in your children. Oh, think of it, Christian friends, when you gaily trifle with serious things and dispel religious earnestness from the minds of your friends. Oh, think of it, selfish tempter, when you play with the virtue and the moral principle of your associates. Oh, think of it, companion, when you have taken some young and thoughtless friend to the unholy amusement, to the doubtful party, to the place where a sainted mother would not have one go, and remember that some day God will hold you responsible even for the sins of others, if you allow yourself to become the tempter. You may mean it in kindness, as the old prophet did, but you will curse yourself for it and perhaps your perdition will be aggravated a thousandfold by the maledictions of the souls that you sink with you to everlasting ruin. "Do not be deceived: God cannot be mocked" (Galatians 6:7). Be not deceivers, for greater even than your sin is the sin of Jeroboam, that he "caused Israel to commit" (1 Kings 14:16).

CHAPTER 5

JONAH AND HIS MESSAGE TO OUR TIMES

He was the one who restored the boundaries of Israel from Lebo Hamath to the Sea of the Arabah, in accordance with the word of the LORD, the God of Israel, spoken through his servant Jonah son of Amittai, the prophet from Gath Hepher. (2 Kings 14:25)

He answered, "A wicked and adulterous generation asks for a miraculous sign! But none will be given it except the sign of the prophet Jonah. For as Jonah was three days and three nights in the belly of a huge fish, so the Son of Man will be three days and three nights in the heart of the earth. The men of Nineveh will stand up at the judgment with this generation and condemn it; for they repented at the preaching of Jonah, and now one greater than Jonah is here." (Matthew 12:39–41)

Jonah was the first of the prophets whose writings have come down to our times. His place is, therefore, unique and pre-eminent. The story of his life was probably written by himself, and the fact that he could write a story with such humiliating disclosures, and yet with such extraordinary candor, goes far to redeem the reputation which he so sadly lost.

Jonah means "a dove." Therefore, it is not unlikely that he was constitutionally timid like Jeremiah in a later age, and for that very reason selected by God for the severest ministries, on the principle that when God has to say anything harsh He never wants a messenger who could color it by any personal severity or unkindness.

SECTION I—*The Story of Jonah*

Jonah was the son of Amittai, and a native of Gath Hepher, a town of the tribe of Zebulun mentioned in the book of Joshua. This fact gives a coloring of probability to the Jewish tradition that he was identical with the son of the widow of Zarephath, which place we know was near the borders of Zebulun, and that it was he who was raised from the dead through Elijah's ministry. Another Hebrew tradition also identifies him with the prophet sent by Elisha to anoint Jehu to be king of Israel.

UNDER JEROBOAM II

We pass, however, to the region of certainties when we come to our text, and find that Jonah was a contemporary—at least, in his later ministry—of Jeroboam II, the third of Israel's kings after Jehu, and the most powerful and aggressive of all the rulers of the 10 tribes. Under his victorious reign the coasts of Israel were enlarged to their ancient limits and the lost territories of former monarchs recovered from the nations round about. The success of Jeroboam's brilliant career is distinctly attributed to the prophesying of Jonah, who was the counselor and friend of this powerful king, and, doubtless, recognized as the religious leader of his time.

Had Jonah's life ended with this first part of his ministry his name would have gone down to posterity as one of the most illustrious prophets and honored servants of Jehovah in the whole prophetic line. But at this point his life experienced a vital crisis. A new commission summoned him to a new field, and new elements changed his whole future career and his final reputation.

NINEVEH

A mightier power than Israel was rising on the eastern horizon. It was the kingdom of Assyria, whose splendid capital, Nineveh, had become the most magnificent city of the world. Its stupendous ruins are still the wonder of the student and archaeologist. Already it was evident that this world-wide monarchy was to be a menace of Israel's future, and Jonah naturally in his selfish patriotism had thought of Nineveh with feelings only of hostility and alarm.

What a revelation, therefore, it must have been to him to receive a message bidding him to go to Nineveh as the messenger of Jehovah's mercy. Every fiber in his being rose in protest and rebellion. The idea was intolerable, and hurrying away under the impulse of the hour, he fled from the hateful task, and, as he imagined, from the presence of the Lord. The rest of the story is too familiar to need to be told in detail.

HIS FLIGHT AND RECOVERY

We all know how readily the devil's providences were found awaiting him at Joppa. How easily he sank into insensibility and lay asleep in the hold of the ship. How God's police followed close upon the fugitive until the very heathen were terrified and became his reprovers. How conscience at last awakened him, and compelled him to sit as the judge upon his own case, and condemn himself to a vicarious death to save his innocent companions. We know how mercy was tempered with judgment and the sea monster became his refuge and deliverer. How his deep penitence was at last rewarded by God's forgiving mercy and he came forth from the depths of the sea like a man resurrected from the very grave. How once more the commission was renewed and the prophet was ready to obey. How his ministry in Nineveh was crowned with a success unprecedented in all ages and the greatest revival ever known swept over a heathen empire, until from the king on the throne to the very cattle in the stall the land was covered with the sackcloth of repentance. How the mercy of God met the penitent prayer of the people of Nineveh and the threatened judgment was averted. And then how Jonah came back again to his old self-life and once more rebelled against the will of Jehovah. And finally how God met him with longsuffering patience and exhibition of His compassion that has, perhaps, no equal in any Bible scene.

HIS SECOND FAILURE

At last the story ends with the strange spectacle of the penitent and angry prophet, blaming God because He had blasted Jonah's reputation by not destroying Nineveh according to His word. Along with this is the loving Father, delighting in mercy and telling His angry child how reasonable it was that He should have compassion upon the little children and the very dumb brutes of the doomed city. The curtain falls with this sad picture of Jonah's disgrace. The only comfort left us is to go behind the scenes and see Jonah himself a little later telling the story of his own shame and magnifying Jehovah's grace. This is somewhat like Simon Peter, who tells us through Mark, in the Gospel left us by that evangelist, his secret in all the humbling details, how he had denied his blessed Master and been loved and forgiven. There is no comment, but the simple telling of the story by Peter is enough to let us know how deeply he repented. The story of Jonah is a companion picture, and we can forgive the prophet when we see the honest candor with which he puts himself in the dust that God may be glorified.

SECTION II—*Lessons Learned from Jonah's Life*

The lessons of this singular life are intensely practical.

1. A REVELATION OF HUMAN CHARACTER AND THE DEEP DECEITFULNESS OF SIN

Self-Deception

So long as everything was agreeable and prosperous Jonah was all right.

The deep self-life was hidden, as it often is, through many years of distinguished usefulness. That self-life was disguised under the appearance of lofty patriotism, and it would be most humiliating if we could only see how much that goes under the name of lofty virtue is but a cloak for some secret ambition. The heart, even of many a disciple of Christ, is deceitful above all things, and needs the deeper sanctifying grace of the Spirit to reveal and take away its hidden selfishness.

The Downward Course

We see also in the story of Jonah the alarming stages of spiritual declension. How swiftly the backsliding prophet went down the terrible incline when once he started! First, there was the impulse of disobedience. Jonah rose up. Next, the desire to get away from God, to flee from the presence of the Lord. Next, the favorable providence that smoothed his descent. He found a ship going to Tarshish. Next, the decisive committal of willful disobedience. He paid his fare. Next, the downward course. He went down into the ship. And next, and saddest of all, the deep spiritual slumber even in the midst of judgment and when all around him were aroused and filled with alarm. "But Jonah had gone below deck, where he lay down and fell into a deep sleep" (Jonah 1:5).

This is the progression of evil. Oh, let us beware of the first wrong step. It is so easy to go on and go down when once we begin.

Would Not Die

But this is not all. Through God's great faithfulness in judgment and His longsuffering in forgiving, Jonah was restored and recommissioned. And for a time it seemed as if the old self-life had died. But sin is more deceitful than the lurking viper under the beautiful bed of flowers. Scarcely had his work at Nineveh been crowned with its first blessing, when again his old self-life reasserted itself. We find Jonah as much alive as before, throwing his own shadow over his sacred ministry. He began actually rebuking God for having forgiven the penitent Ninevites, until Jehovah had to cover his work with the shadow of disgrace and leave the most successful ministry ever known under an eclipse of humiliation and failure. Let us not congratulate ourselves on our easy virtues, our agreeable services or our successful ministries, until God has tested us in the depths of our being and we have proved that we are serving God, not for our selfish honor or pleasure, but because we love to do His will.

2. A REVELATION OF THE CHARACTER AND LOVE OF GOD

Back of Jonah's selfishness and Nineveh's sin shines the sublime vision of God's grace. Jonah seems to have known this long before and rather disliked it, for we find him saying: "O LORD, is this not what I said when I was still at home? That is why I was so quick to flee to Tarshish. I knew that you are a gracious and compassionate God, slow to anger and abounding in love, a God who relents from sending calamity" (4:2).

Strange, is it not, to find a poor sinner finding fault with God for being so kind? But Jonah was a bigot, and he wanted a God that he could use on occasion to gratify his dislikes to his enemies, taking it for granted, of course, that he had a sort of prescriptive right to His favor.

Divine Mercy

But it was well for Jonah that God was so merciful. The time came when he had to fall back upon that longsuffering, and from the depths of hell cry for mercy upon his own soul, and he found it. How graciously God tempered the chastening of His disobedient child with loving kindness and tender mercy! How thoughtfully He prepared that monster to receive him when he sank amid the yawning waves! How kindly He offered him a second chance to retrieve his lost honor and accomplish the work he had refused. And oh, how gentle and surpassing the loving kindness with which he forgave repentant Nineveh!

Is there anything more touching and beautiful than the outburst of His heart when Jonah reproached Him for His mercy to Nineveh? "But Nineveh has more than a hundred and twenty thousand people who cannot tell their right hand from their left, and many cattle as well. Should I not be concerned about that great city?" (4:11). What a picture of God's compassion for the helpless children! Oh, it is these for whom His heart aches amid the horrors of heathenism. It is the children of the drunkard whom His great heart pities. And not only so.

There is another touch of exquisite pathos—His compassion for the dumb brutes in the stalls of Nineveh. God could not endure the thought of their helpless anguish. Those four words with which the book of Jonah ends shed a luster over the whole creation, unspeakably beautiful: "Many cattle as well" (4:11). Wherever there is a heart filled with the Holy Spirit and the Spirit of Jesus we shall find the same mercy toward the lower orders of creation, and the same unwillingness to inflict a needless pain upon the helpless creatures over whom God has given to us dominion in this lower world. Shame upon our humanity that we have so often abused it. The true child of God will be ever kind, and his very horse and dog will know that he is a Christian.

3. A REVELATION OF THE GOSPEL AND THE CROSS OF THE LORD JESUS CHRIST

Jonah and Jesus

Our Lord Himself has borne a conclusive testimony to the authenticity of the story of Jonah. The Higher Critics can be safely referred to the testimony of the Master. He especially honored the old Hebrew prophet as the very type of His own death and resurrection. "As Jonah was three days and three nights in the belly of a huge fish, so the Son of Man will be three days and three nights in the heart of the earth" (Matthew 12:40).

The Substitute

But we find even a finer foreshadowing of the atonement in the vivid picture given us of Jonah's tragedy when the storm was raging and the seamen were terrified and helpless. It was Jonah himself that suggested the vicarious sacrifice that alone could save them. "Pick me up and throw me into the sea, . . . and it will become calm" (Jonah 1:12). Oh, how like it was to the message of the Savior, to the men who came with swords and spears to arrest Him and His disciples. "If you are looking for me, then let these men go" (John 18:8). He was the Substitute, and when He was cast into the sea of sin, lo, the waves were still, and a lost world found peace and a haven of rest. The sacrifice of Jesus Christ is the key to the story of Jonah, as well as the story of lost humanity.

The artist Turner on one occasion invited a number of friends to see an unfinished painting. The canvas was a scene of confused tints and clouds of light and shade; but there was nothing intelligible about it. Suddenly the artist took his brush and touched the picture with a little bit of crimson, when at once the whole picture became plain. That little bit of color gave the viewpoint to all the rest and the scene was plain and striking. So the cross of Calvary has given the true interpretation to all the facts of history and all questions that affect the destiny of man.

But there is a still deeper lesson of crucifixion in Jonah's story. It was the crucifixion of Jonah himself. If we believe in a crucified Savior we must be willing to be crucified men and women. The real trouble with poor Jonah was that he was not fully crucified. If the Jewish tradition about him was true, surely he ought to have been dead enough at the beginning, for had he not been raised from the dead by the prophet Elijah? But there are people that have more lives than one, and Jonah's tenacity of life seemed boundless. It was the self-life of the prophet that met him, and rebelled against the commandment of his God, and sent him off to Tarshish in a pet. And, therefore, God had to bury him in the sea.

Very Much Alive

Jonah came back apparently dead and resurrected, but lo, the first return of success brings him back again to all his old vitality. He sits under his withered gourd at Nineveh, quarreling with earth and heaven because he has not had his own way. Therefore, the deepest teaching of the New Testament about our spiritual life is the necessity of going with our crucified Lord into death and resurrection. We have no right to sing, "May I never boast except in the cross of our Lord Jesus Christ," unless we are willing to add, "through which the world has been crucified to me, and I to the world" (Galatians 6:14).

Therefore, in the history of God's ancient people there were two chapters of death and resurrection. The first one was at the Red Sea. They passed through the floods, as a symbol of death to Egypt and the world which they left behind them. The second one was at the Jordan. They were buried once more in symbol, as the gateway by which alone they could enter the Land of Promise, Both of these types tell us of the utter need of our entering into that mystic fellowship with our Lord, which the Apostle has described in Galatians 2:20: "I have been crucified with Christ and I no longer live, but Christ lives in me. The life I live in the body, I live by faith in the Son of God, who loved me and gave himself for me."

4. A REVELATION OF GOD'S PURPOSE OF SALVATION FOR THE LOST

A Foreign Missionary

Jonah stands as the forerunner of the foreign missionary. It was not the first time God had intimated His purpose of world-wide salvation. To Abraham He had spoken of a blessing for all the families of the earth. To Moses He had sworn, "Nevertheless, as surely as I live and as surely as the glory of the LORD fills the whole earth" (Numbers 4:21).

Elisha had received Naaman, the Syrian, among the subjects of God's healing love and power, and even Elijah had bestowed his blessing on a daughter of Sidon. But Jonah was the first who definitely undertook a real mission to the heathen, and it was the most successful mission the world has ever seen. What a spectacle it was to behold an entire nation at the feet of God in penitence and prayer. God hasten the day when the message of His coming shall once more bear such instant and glorious fruit.

It is very touching to find how far the heart of God was in advance of the spirit of His own people. It was the picture of Jonah more than anything else that stood in the way of the salvation of Nineveh, and it has been the selfishness of the Church herself that has kept back the gospel from the heathen. The effect of such a spirit may best be seen in the miserable failure of Jonah. And the effect of selfishness today is, alas, but too apparent in the decay of our modern Christianity and the corrupting of her manna because she has hoarded it for herself alone.

A witty painter once drew a picture of what he called a decaying church. In the foreground stood a splendid edifice with no sign of decay about its magnificent architecture. Through the open portals the eye could see within that all was still more splendid. The spacious building was crowded with wealthy and fashionable worshipers and everything bore evidence of prosperity and popularity. But at the door was found the key to the picture. Over the costly silver plate on which the offerings of the worshipers were piled, there hung a little foreign missionary collection box, cheap and evidently neglected. On closer inspection you could see that the slot through which the coins were supposed to flow was all overgrown with spiders' webs. That was the decaying church and such a church deserves to decay.

SECTION III—*Special Lessons from Jonah's Life*

1. It reminds us of the people who are good, and even useful, so long as things suit them, but who go to pieces the moment you cross them.

2. It is a suggestive picture of the devil's providences which are ready to fit right into our sinful plans, but which we are always extremely safe in refusing.

3. It reveals to us the dishonesty of the devil, who lets us pay our fare, and then drops us in the middle of our journey into the jaws of destruction.

4. It affords us a vision of God's police. All things serve His might, and not a wind blows and not a wave flows, but is on some errand of His wise and gracious providence. God can find you and bring you back. Do not venture too far.

5. It reminds us how often even sinners put to shame God's sinful children and wake them up, as the sailors of Tarshish woke up Jonah with amazement and fear.

6. It shows us how the return of a backslider will often bring sinners to God, even as Jonah's awakening led those rude men to repentance and conversion.

7. It painfully reminds us of how people that claim to be dead are still very much alive, and how much our work for God is hindered by our throwing our own shadow over it, as Jonah did at Nineveh.

8. God often has to dishonor His servants to save them, and the work we do for selfishness will bring us no reward. Jonah did much good to others, but he lost it all himself. If you are preaching the gospel or working in the Church of God for ambition or selfishness in any way you shall not only lose your reward, but bring upon yourself at last exposure and humiliation.

9. Finally, we cannot afford to trifle with God. Oh backslider, return! Oh fugitive from duty, do come back to God! Oh worldling, playing with temptation, beware! Behold the goodness and severity of God.

A young girl one day ventured to grasp a live wire that was hanging from a post. She did it in playful fun. Instantly a fearful scream proclaimed the fact that her hand was fastened to that burning current and she was helplessly in its grasp. The other hand was quickly raised to loosen her stiffened fingers, and it, too, was caught, and there she hung in agony and helplessness. Her mother rushed to her side to pull her down, but she was flung far off by a shock communicated from the body of the girl. She seemed lost, indeed. At the last moment a young man who understood took an axe and severed the wire by striking it against the post. The current was broken and the girl fell swooning on the ground. Her life was saved, but her hands were cinders for the rest of her days.

Don't play with live wires. There is mercy, boundless mercy. You can have God's love, you can all have it, but you cannot trifle with it.

CHAPTER 6

ELIJAH, THE PROPHET OF JUDGMENT

The king asked them, "What kind of man was it who came to meet you and told you this?"
They replied, "He was a man with a garment of hair and with a leather belt around his waist."
The king said, "That was Elijah the Tishbite." (2 Kings 1:7–8)

This is the picture that has come down to us of the prophet of Horeb. Outward forms are not infrequently the figures and symbols of inward character. The very forms of the dove and the lamb prepare us for their gentleness, and one look at the hog and the tiger suggests their native grossness and ferocity. The rainbow and the sunshine are the types of loveliness and brightness, while the stormy cloud presages in its very terrors the calamity which it brings.

Elijah was true to his portrait. A rugged child of nature, wrapped in a rude sheepskin mantle, bearing upon his countenance the lines of solitude and severity, he was a fitting type of the dispensation of law and the ministry of judgment. He was at the same time a transition figure. He belonged to both the old and the new dispensations. It was his to gather up the meaning and the message of the past and at the same time introduce a better future.

His greatest work was to anoint Elisha to be prophet in his room and to accomplish that work of gentleness and grace for which he could only prepare the way by warning and judgment but which he himself could never bring.

In like manner it was also prepared that he along with Moses, twin messenger of the same law, should afterwards be chosen to introduce the Son of God on the Transfiguration Mount.

SECTION I—*The Story of Elijah*

Elijah's story is too familiar to need to be retold at length. A few rapid touches will recall the outline. Like a meteor flash in a midnight sky, he appeared from the solitudes of Gilead in the darkest hour of Ahab's reign. And like the report of the same meteor, comes the sudden announcement of his message of judgment upon the idolatrous kingdom, that "there will be neither dew nor rain in the next few years" (1 Kings 17:1).

Next we find him appropriately among the ravens by a little brook on the confines of Syria. These birds of evil omen associated with the desolating flood were to him the Lord's providers through the days of famine.

He alights next, as suddenly, in a village of Sidon far west on the Mediterranean coast, and there claims the hospitality and trust of a poor widow. Afterwards he restores to life, in recompense, her only son, said by Hebrew tradition to have been the prophet Jonah.

A little later the apparition again startles Israel and Obadiah is met on the way by the prophet with the dramatic message, "Go tell your master, 'Elijah is here' " (18:8). Then comes the summons to the great assize on Mount Carmel, the appeal to heaven, the ignominious failure of Baal, the answer by fire to Elijah's prayer, the defeat and judgment of idolatry, the execution of Baal's prophets, the return of the nation to Jehovah, the opening heavens and descending rain with Elijah himself dashing in front of Ahab's chariot amid the tempest and storm like a courier of heaven and a very spirit of the elements for more than 20 miles to the entrance of Jezreel.

Then came that terrible reaction which so often comes to human nature after some terrible tension of all its powers and even after some supreme hour of triumph. Elijah flees at Jezebel's fiery threat. Like some poor, limp, broken body that had fallen from an awful height, he lies under the juniper tree, asking only that he may die and end his discouragement and misery. We know the story, how God nursed him back and then sent him to Horeb to receive a new revelation, to learn from the wild elements of the earthquake, the whirlwind and the fire the failure of the ministry of judgment, to hear in the still small voice the true secret of power and then to go forth and commit to other hands his unfinished work—the judgment part to Jehu and Hazael, and the better work of grace to Elisha, the prophet of mercy.

Three times more we see him during the 10 years that follow. Once he appears again to Ahab, as the avenger of Naboth's murder. Next to Ahab's son, the wicked Amaziah, after he had consumed his messengers, with the announcement of his death. And then comes the last walk with his disciple, Elisha, and that final hour so unspeakably glorious when the heavenly chariots bore him to his God.

SECTION II—*Lessons Learned from Elijah's Life*

Back of his dramatic life there stand out great principles and lessons of the most practical and perpetual value and importance.

JUDGMENT

1. He was the messenger of judgment. He was the representative of law. He was the witness for righteousness and holiness in a wicked age. He stood for conviction of sin and personal repentance as the condition of forgiveness and mercy. He was like the tempest that purifies the air. He was like the winter which leads up to spring. He was like the deep plowshare that prepares the soil for the sower and the seed. He was like the geological ages of fiery convulsion which prepared the way for making this globe a habitable planet, and led on in due time to the green earth and the waving harvest field.

It was necessary that some hand must strike the blow that would wake up in Israel the voice of slumbering conscience and show the wickedness of Ahab and Jezebel in its true character. This was Elijah's ministry. In the same spirit John the Baptist came later to prepare the way for the Savior and lead men through repentance to salvation.

Still the conviction of sin is essential before the soul can understand the revelation of forgiveness; and still, in the deeper experience of the sanctified heart, there must be another conviction, not of sin, but of sinfulness, before the soul is ready to receive the Holy Spirit and the abiding presence of the Lord.

Beloved reader, have you passed through the gates of conviction? Have you seen sin as God sees it? Our milk and water age is rapidly coming to the obliteration of sharp moral lines, and it needs as much as ever the message of Elijah. God never passes by sin. It must be recognized. It must be dealt with, either in your Substitute or on your head. God give us in our hearts and in the spiritual work of our time a true ministry of conviction, of righteousness and of a quickened conscience.

GRACE

2. He was the pioneer of grace. He was permitted to fail as Moses did before him, to show that law will ever be inadequate alone to make men better, and that judgment may be destructive, but only grace can be constructive and permanent.

The three symbols of the vision on the mount, the earthquake, the whirlwind and the fire, were but symbols of the threatenings and terrors of his ministry and their failure to bring a true reformation. The prophets were dead, but their spirit was still alive. The people had shouted for Jehovah today, but they would be reveling tomorrow in the orgies of Jezebel's groves. Something deeper was needed, and that still small voice that pierced his soul and broke his heart was the type of that better ministry which Elisha was to introduce and which the Greater than Elisha, the Savior Himself, was to consummate.

And so in our experience, the earthquake, the whirlwind, the fire and the prophet of judgment must all pass, and lifting up our eyes we must see "no one except Jesus" (Matthew 17:8). It is the gentle voice of the Comforter to us, the soft wing of the heavenly Dove. It is the touch of the meek and lowly Jesus that transforms the life, regenerates the heart, supersedes the darkness by light and brings in a transformation as silent, as simple, but as glorious as the advent of the dawn or as the coming of the spring. The real power in ancient Israel was not Elijah, but Elisha. The real forces that save men are the grace of God, the love of Christ and the Holy Spirit.

PRAYER

3. Elijah's life revealed the power of prayer. That was a new era in the history of civilization when Benjamin Franklin brought from the clouds the electric spark and harnessed it to the vehicles of all our modern industrial life. That was another era when Cyrus Field found a way to carry that subtle messenger beneath the ocean waves as a submarine cable and two hemispheres could talk to each other in a moment of time. That is still a new era of progress which is giving us Marconi with his ether waves and wireless messages. But higher than all was the discovery that from this little dark planet human hearts could find a telephone to the eternal throne and talk with the almighty God in prayer. That was the ministry which Elijah crystallized into definite form and infinite power as it never had been before.

Not easily did his first great message come to him. It is not to dreamers that God speaks His great messages, but it is to men and women that have already become profoundly moved in sympathy, in sorrow and deep concern for the sons of men and in earnest efforts to vindicate the right and suppress the wrong. Therefore we are told by the Apostle James that Elijah "prayed earnestly that it would not rain" (James 5:17). It was he that took the initiative. He had been watching with a heavy heart the progress of idolatry and the power of evil. He had often pleaded on the lonely mountain side with God, and asked Him what He would do for His own great name, and it was through believing prayer at last that the commission came to the great prophet to go forth as the messenger of judgment.

And then the second time that God's hand interposed to remove the stroke, it had to come through prayer. It was no light matter to roll back those gates of brass and open the windows of heaven. Yonder on the crag of Carmel we behold him with his head between his knees bowed in agony and travail watching for the first sign of the coming storm cloud and the promised rain. Back of all this we see the working of mighty spiritual forces and we learn that prayer is to us one of the vital forces of the great economy of the universe. Could we see the spiritual mechanism of the heavens we would behold innumerable wires passing from human heartstrings to yonder throne, and then returning in mighty providential movements over all the world.

John has given us the vision of the prayers of all the saints presented upon the golden altar that was before the throne, and then the pouring back again of these prayers on earth as represented by the bowls from the altar. And then he adds, "There came peals of thunder, rumblings, flashes of lightning and an earthquake" (Revelation 8:5). Have we learned Elijah's secret? Are we using our ministry of prayer to its utmost? Are we spiritual forces in the kingdom of God? "Lord, teach us to pray" (Luke 11:1).

FAITH

4. He was the pattern of victorious faith. His whole life was a life of faith, a life that dealt with the unseen, a life that touched God by a strong hand and a holy confidence.

The first incident in his life is the story of the widow's faith. She ventured her last handful of meal on his assurance of coming plenty, and got back not only a living, but a little later the life of her boy. His splendid triumph at the altar of Carmel was a victory of faith. He made the test as hard as he could because he believed in a God who could do hard things. At a time when water was worth more than gold he found abundance of water to saturate the altar and the trenches round about, and he deluged the sacrificial pile in floods sufficient to quench all other fire but God's. It was then that the answer came and his faith was vindicated.

And so again the promise of the coming rain was not held back until the clouds were in sight, but even before he prayed on the mount he sent the message to the king, "There is the sound of a heavy rain" (1 Kings 18:41). Yes, faith can hear a voice that others cannot hear and see a form to all besides invisible and anticipate the future, calling the things that are not as though they were. Beloved, have we learned the key that unlocks the heavens? The law which is the principle of gravitation in the spiritual realm? The potency that shares the very omnipotence of God? For "with God all things are possible" (Matthew 19:26), and "everything is possible for him who believes" (Mark 9:23).

HOPE

5. He was the prophet of the future. He lived beyond his time. The double portion which he gave to Elisha was ahead of time. It was not due for a thousand years. Therefore he told his disciple that it would be a hard thing, but he claimed it in advance. His translation was more than 3,000 years ahead of time. It was like Enoch's, the prototype of the rapture of the

saints when Jesus comes. But Elijah anticipated it and entered upon it ages before it was due.

And so we like him may live beyond our age and under "the powers of the coming age" (Hebrews 6:5), saying like the great apostle, "our citizenship is in heaven. And we eagerly await a Savior from there, the Lord Jesus Christ, who, by the power that enables him to bring everything under his control, will transform our lowly bodies so that they will be like his glorious body" (Philippians 3:20–21).

GOD'S TENDERNESS

6. He was a touching example of God's tenderness with His weak and erring children. The sweetest of all the lessons of his life grows out of his one infirmity. We thank the Apostle James for the little verse, "Elijah was a man just like us" (5:17). How weak he seemed as he fled with panting breath and ran a hundred miles before he stopped for fear of Jezebel! How pitiful the spectacle of that heroic figure cringing under the juniper tree and praying that he may die, like some modern sentimental would-be suicide! And yet all that only brought out more vividly the infinite patience and tenderness of God. How gently He nursed him and fed him, not once upbraiding him with his fall. And then how graciously He released him from his trying ministry and gave him the grandest homecoming that mortal ever knew.

"I know them by their spots" was the explanation that the shepherd gave of the individual point of his sheep. "One has lost an ear, another has a broken limb, a third has lost an eye, another is always getting lost and giving me needless trouble. That is how I know them." And that is how God knows a good many of His children. It takes our failures to bring out His unfailing faithfulness.

Adam's fall was no surprise to Adam's God, but He was ready the next moment with the revelation of redemption. Gideon's broken lamps were necessary to let the light of hidden torches within shine forth. Israel's carnival of idolatry at the foot of Sinai astonished Moses, but not God; and the next thing we see is a new revelation of mercy and grace through the tabernacle and the sacrifices, with their glorious types of the grace and blood of Christ. Moses himself failed just to show how the Lord dealt with failure. He lost the Land of Promise through his own broken law. But oh, how God made it up to him as he stood over his dying bed on Nebo's heights and gently kissed away his departing spirit. With His own hands God arranged Moses' funeral and kept his body waiting until one glorious night when He brought it forth in resurrection beauty and gave him the high honor of entering the very Land of Promise and introducing the Son of God on Hermon's height.

Peter had to fail to find out the love of Jesus. It was in the experience of

Paul's darkest hours that he learned to say such words as these: "Who comforts us in all our troubles, so that we can comfort those in any trouble with
the comfort we ourselves have received from God" (2 Corinthians 1:4).

And this is our God, too. "Praise be to the God and Father of our Lord
Jesus Christ, the Father of compassion and the God of all comfort" (1:3).
Let us not willfully fail. But if we do, let us not forget that "underneath are
the everlasting arms" (Deuteronomy 33:27).

CHAPTER 7

ELISHA, THE PROPHET OF GRACE

The company of the prophets from Jericho, . . . said, "The spirit of Elijah is resting on Elisha." (2 Kings 2:15)

It is interesting to follow some noble river through its peaceful winding, through scenes of natural loveliness and commercial activity, until at last we reach its source and stand beside some little rivulet trickling over the rocks, which a child could ford and a handful of earth divert from its course. It is thus that the beautiful Hudson, the noble Mississippi and the great rivers of other lands rise and flow.

SECTION I—*The Life of Elisha*

Such a picture suggests to us the story of that illustrious life which is to form our present theme. Like some peaceful and noble river, the life of Elisha flowed through the darkest period of Israel's history for the greater part of an entire century, but its fountain was as simple as the noble streams that we have just referred to. It began in a little incident on his country farm in Abel Meholah when one day the great Elijah passed by and dropped his mysterious mantle over the young man's shoulders. From that moment life could never again be the same to the son of Shaphat. He went forth to obey his new master and at length to succeed him in his mighty work (1 Kings 19:15–21).

The call of Elisha occurred in the 10th century before Christ. Ten years later came the second crisis of his life, the parting with Elijah and the outpouring of the double portion of the Spirit upon him. With this his prophetic ministry properly began, and for the next 10 years we find him engaged in the most active service in the kingdom of Israel, with an occasional visit to Judah and even to Damascus in the north. No less than 16 great miracles are recorded in Elisha's ministry during this period. But his public ministry continued through 45 more years, of which the incidents

55

have not come down to us. However, we need not doubt that they were as actively spent as the years preceding.

His public life lasted through six important reigns, namely: Ahab, Ahaziah and Jeroboam of the house of Omri; and Jehu, Jehoahaz and Joash of the house of Jehu. His death bed was attended by the king of Israel himself, who testified with the most tender sorrow that the prophet was worth more to the kingdom than his very chariots and horsemen. And after his death his very bones seemed to possess supernatural power to quicken from the dead the corpse that touched them, and suggest to our thoughts the immortality which follows a good man's life.

SECTION II—*Lessons Learned from Elisha's Life*

The lessons of Elisha's life are intensely practical and helpful.

DECISION FOR GOD

1. He is an example of decision for God (1 Kings 19:19–21).

That scene already referred to as the starting point of all his life is a fine example for every hesitating soul at the gates of life. He has everything to hold him back—a happy home, abundant prosperity, if not wealth, a farm on which he could afford to plow with 12 yoke of oxen, and youth with all its attractions and allurements. In a moment that message came to him bidding him leave all and become the companion of the weird figure that stood before him. The man of the mountain and the desert, the man more hated and feared than any man on earth, the man whose presence and prospects had nothing to offer to youth and ambition here. Little wonder, as that mantle touched him, that the young man hesitated for a moment and asked if he might not at least go home and bid his loved ones farewell. But the old prophet saw the danger of the slightest reservation. He turned somewhat sternly away and seemed to signify, if he did not exactly say, "What have I done? It means nothing if you would have it so. God can excuse you if you wish to be excused."

In a moment Elisha saw the crisis and met it with a brave decision that never faltered again. Turning his field into an altar, he converted his plows and harrows into kindling wood and offered up his oxen and sacrificed them to God. Then turning from all his earthly prospects, he followed the stern old prophet without a moment's hesitation, and henceforth became known as "Elisha . . . [who] used to pour water on the hands of Elijah" (2 Kings 3:11).

The same story is repeated in every earnest life for God. The secret of power in our Christian experience lies at this starting point. The souls that begin, like Elisha, with unreserved devotion to God, find that all their future life bears the same character of decision, and the people that begin with half-hearted purpose are weak and vacillating to the end of the chapter. God is looking for such lives in every age, and He meets us just as we are willing to meet Him. The souls that are unreserved in their devotion to Him will find Him unreserved in His dealings with them. And "with the froward He will wrestle," and show how little it pays to be ungenerous with the Lord of Glory.

As you read these lines, God help you, if you have been halting between two opinions, to yield the last reserve and give every power of your being and every moment of your life to Him. Remember that on the cross Jesus Christ gave you both hands, both feet and every drop of His precious blood.

THE DOUBLE PORTION

2. Elisha is an example of deeper spiritual blessing.

The next crisis of Elisha's life is described in Second Kings 2:17. The experience through which Elisha passed at this time is paralleled by our experience of entire consecration to God and the baptism of the Holy Spirit. The blessing which Elisha sought at the hands of Elijah was practically the gift of the Holy Spirit in the fullness of His power. The reason that Elijah discouraged him and called this "a difficult thing" (2 Kings 2:10), must have been because in the dispensational providence of God the outpouring of the Holy Spirit was not yet due. He was asking it in advance of the time because the Holy Spirit could not come in all His fullness until after Jesus had been glorified. But just as Elijah's translation was before the time, and he was permitted to anticipate the glory which is reserved for other saints at the coming of the Lord, so Elisha, as he witnessed his master's translation, was also permitted to enter in by anticipation to the blessings of the covenant of grace that was afterwards to be revealed.

There was something audacious in Elisha's request, and just for that very reason God seems to have been pleased with it. It was not unlike the faith of that woman of Canaan, of whom we read in the story of the Gospels. The Lord Jesus had argued her down and out, and had shown her that the blessings she sought and the blessings He brought were not for such as she, but for the lost sheep of the house of Israel. But she still clung to His feet with a woman's indomitable perseverance, and believed that somehow He must have a way of helping her. So she cried, "Lord, help me!" (Matthew 15:25). She could not argue, but she could plead. Then came that last and most cruel blow by which He told her that she was not only shut out dispensationally, but morally. She was one of the dogs of the Canaan race, guilty of every shameful sin, and responsible, probably, for her daughter's curse. And then He told her that it was not meet to take the children's bread and give it to the dogs. Surely, now her faith is silenced! But, no! Again she rises superior to the trial and even wrings out of it an argument for her blessing. "Yes,

Lord," she says, "but even the dogs eat the crumbs that fall from their masters' table" (15:27). And the Master was conquered and bade her take all she would. Nothing could stand against such faith. He was delighted with her, and He is ever delighted with souls that dare to put Him to the test and venture upon His boundless power and grace.

Elisha's persistence in seeking this blessing is a fine example to those who often complain of disappointment in seeking God. His master at first seemed to want to dissuade him from his purpose. "Stay here," he said, "the LORD has sent me to Bethel" (2 Kings 2:2). But farther on Elisha was determined also to go.

So, still, the Lord loves to put us to the test and see how much we mean our prayer and how much we want our blessing. At Emmaus "Jesus acted as if he were going farther" (Luke 24:28), and compelled them to constrain Him to come in, and yet was so glad to go in when they would not let Him be excused. In the same way He often seems to hold back our blessing, only that we may call the more earnestly and wait the more perseveringly. How sad His heart must be when He finds us so easily discouraged, and how glad it must make Him to find in us the spirit of Elisha, which refused to be refused.

Separation

The various steps taken by Elisha in his journey with his master seem to be typical of actual experiences in the life of the soul. Gilgal, the starting point, was the place of Israel's separation, and it seems to stand in our lives for our separation from the world and our entire dedication to the Lord.

God

Bethel, the next station, literally means, "the House of God," and stands for the revelation of God in the life of the soul. For this deeper blessing is not merely a blessing, but it is our union with God Himself. The mistake that so many make is to seek His gifts rather than Himself. We must go to Bethel and let everything go but God before we can know and prove the double portion too.

Faith

The next station, Jericho, was the place of Israel's victory by faith, and it stands for the experience of faith in entering into our deeper life with God. It is not so much a matter of feeling, or even of earnest consecration, but of simple believing. Here, as everywhere else, the principle is invariable: "According to your faith will it be done to you" (Matthew 9:29). We may pray all our lives and yet we will get nowhere until we receive the Holy Spirit just as we received the Lord Jesus, by simple appropriating faith.

Death

The last stage, Jordan, is ever the type of death. Just as it was through the death of Moses, the symbolical death of circumcision, and the death set forth by their crossing the Jordan, that Israel entered Canaan at the first, so still it must ever be by way of the cross. We must die not only to the evil, but to the good that we possess, and learn henceforth to have no life apart from Christ alone. It is there that the revelation comes. It was there that the mantle fell upon the waiting Elisha. And it is there that we shall ever meet our risen Lord. Are we willing to meet the condition? Are we willing to pay the price?

Take Your Blessing

But we see another of the conditions of the deeper blessing strongly brought out in the story of Elisha. The mantle of his master did not fall upon him but beside him. He had to take it up with his own hands. He had to put it on himself by an act of bold, appropriating faith. Then he had to go forth and use it as he met the swelling floods of Jordan and dared to command them to part asunder while he passed over in the victory of faith.

And so we must put on the Lord Jesus. We must receive the Holy Spirit. We must take what God so freely gives. And then we must go forth and use our blessing, as Elisha used his, as we meet the first real difficulties and trials of life which God sends to prove us and see whether we really believe in our blessing or not. To such souls God ever comes in the fullness of His power. He is longing for vessels to hold His blessing. Unfortunately, most of us are made of such flimsy materials that we could not stand the dynamite of His power if it should really come.

THE APOSTLE OF GRACE

3. Elisha was the Apostle of Grace.

His very name means "God my salvation." The root of it in the Hebrew is the very name of the Messiah. And the whole character of his ministry was like that of Jesus Christ, full of gentleness, grace and love. There were only two miracles of judgment in all his ministry, and even these two were greatly modified. The familiar nursery story which haunted our infancy—of the bears that devoured the little children of Bethel—wears a very different aspect when we understand the literal meaning of the original. These were not little children at all, but young men—the roughs, the toughs of the town, the common blackguards that spend their time in sneering at good men and decent women and need to be made sometimes a wholesome example. For such people we are often thankful that there is a devil and a just and holy God. The other miracle of judgment was the punishment of Gehazi for his sneak-thieving in running after Naaman, compromising Elisha by begging of the Syrian after Elisha had so magnanimously refused his gifts. That was indeed a terrible punishment. But we seem to be justified in inferring from a later chapter, where we find Gehazi once more in the front and standing in the presence of the king of Israel, telling him of his master's power and works,—we infer from this, I say, that Gehazi must in the meantime have been forgiven and restored.

The rest of Elisha's miracles were full of grace and remind one at every step of the Lord Jesus Christ Himself and His works of love and power. They may be divided into several classes.

1. The miracles of restoration

These include the healing of the barren land by sprinkling salt upon it, and the curing of the poisoned pottage which threatened the lives of his companions.

2. The miracles of healing and physical power

These include the healing of Naaman from leprosy, the birth of the Shunammite's child and then his resurrection from the dead.

3. The miracles of material blessing

Among these were the feeding of a hundred men with bread, the supplying of water for the famine-stricken armies in Edom, the multiplying of the widow's oil and the relief of the famine in Samaria.

4. The miracles of wisdom and foresight

Among these were his announcement to Hazael that he should be king of Syria, his warning to the widow to prepare for the days of famine and his vision of the horses and chariots of fire around the mountain.

5. The miracles of supernatural power over the laws of nature

Among these was the story of the axe that was caused to swim in defiance of the law of gravity, and the floods which came without any natural cause to fill the ditches they had dug in the Valley of Edom.

6. The symbolic miracles

The arrows which he taught Joash to shoot from his dying bed were symbols of victorious prayer and divine deliverance. The oil which he multiplied for the widow's need was the type of the Holy Spirit who is still the Supply for all our need as we dare to take Him by simple faith.

7. The miracles of mercy

The most striking of these was his smiting with blindness the servants of the king of Syria when they came to capture him, and then leading them blindfolded into Samaria. After opening their eyes and showing them the greatness and the power of the city, he then sent them back to their homes with the feeling that they had been made fools of and with the sound advice to Ben-Hadad that he had better not come to a country where Elisha was its defender. The tenderness of his loving heart is shown in the tears he shed, as he told Hazael of the cruelties which he was yet to perpetrate on the innocent and helpless. His whole ministry was one of beneficence and the beautiful foreshadowing of the story of the Gospels.

RELIGION IN COMMON LIFE

4. Elisha was an example of the religion of common life.

Unlike his master, Elijah, he was always among the people. Sometimes we see him at the court of Israel, sometimes at the court of Damascus, where the king of Syria sends him such a splendid present that it took 40 camels to carry on their backs. Again we find him in the army, recognized by Jehoshaphat, the great king of Judah, as his friend and the man of God. Again we find him on intimate terms with the poor widow whose boys are about to be sold into slavery. Once again he is traveling all over the land visiting his parish and looking after the schools of the prophets, and the great lady of Shunem invites him to her villa and makes him her abiding guest, honored by his friendship. Still later we see him with his students, down on the banks of the Jordan, helping them to build a new college, and finding the lost axe when it flew off the handle. Here he is not too big to help a boy in his little troubles. And last of all we see him on his sick bed, not sick because of weakness, because he was never so mighty as in his dying hours and in his grave, but sick that he might stand closer to a sick and suffering world and be the pattern and the friend of his people like the Master. What a beautiful example of a life of consecrated manhood and the loveliness of true human kindness!

GREAT FAITH

5. Elisha was an example of lofty faith.

We see it in the way he claims his baptism and his blessing. We see it in the way he divided the Jordan in the name of the Lord. We see it in the way he announced the coming of plenty to besieged Samaria. We see it in the vision of the chariots and horses of fire, on the mountain top. We see it in the calm and almost humorous way in which he led his enemies around Samaria, and then sent them home, trusting so completely in God that he had no fear of man. And we see it finally and supremely in that beautiful scene at his dying bed, where he taught the hesitating hands of Joash to shoot the arrows of faith and prayer, and then to second the claim and the promise by striking upon the ground again and yet again. And how splendid is the noble anger of the prophet because the king had stopped so soon and had limited his own blessing when God was waiting to give so much more.

THE LIFE OF LOVE

6. Along with Elisha's faith—the keynote of his life—was also love.

It takes both to make the noblest character. President Roosevelt was asked one day by a fashionable lady caller, which he considered the greatest character of fiction, and he promptly answered, "Great Heart." The lady seemed startled for a moment, and then ventured to ask in which of the novels she could find this character. "Oh," said the President turning away with a faint smile of pity, "you will find him in the Delectable Mountains." She had evidently not read *The Pilgrim's Progress*.

Well, Elisha was one of the Great Hearts of the world. He was one of those men who had got saved clear above themselves and have no business henceforth but to help others. We meet a great many pilgrims in Bunyan's allegory, but most of them are trying to get there. Great Heart is only trying to get others there. Some people spend their lives trying to get to heaven; other people get there at the start and spend their lives taking others along. That was Elisha. Oh, that it might be you and me!

VICTORY IN DEATH

7. We see in Elisha a victorious death.

As we look on such a scene, and we see them sometimes still, we feel like asking:

Is that a deathbed where the Christian lies?
Yes, but not his; 'tis death himself that dies.

When Rudyard Kipling lay for weeks on the borders of life and death, one day his nurse saw his lips moving, and gently asked him if he wanted anything. "Oh, yes," he said, "I want my heavenly Father. He only can help me now." It was He that took the sting of the defeat from Elisha's departing, and made it an occasion for him to show the king by his bedside the resources and the power of God. God help us so to live, that even death will be part of our triumph.

IMMORTAL LIVES

8. We see in Elisha a posthumous influence.

Such men never die. After he was buried, Elisha's bones had power to bring to life the corpse that touched them. Our greatest work should follow us. Oh, that we may so live, that it may also be true of each of us, "And by faith he still speaks, even though he is dead" (Hebrews 11:4).

CHAPTER 8

AMOS, THE PROPHET OF WARNING

The words of Amos, one of the shepherds of Tekoa—what he saw concerning Israel two years before the earthquake, when Uzziah was king of Judah and Jeroboam son of Jehoash was king of Israel. (Amos 1:1)

Amos answered Amaziah, "I was neither a prophet nor a prophet's son, but I was a shepherd, and I also took care of sycamore-fig trees. But the LORD took me from tending the flock and said to me, 'Go prophesy to my people Israel.' " (7:14–15)

Therefore this is what I will do to you, Israel,
and because I will do this to you,
prepare to meet your God, O Israel. (4:12)

These words describe the humble extraction and the holy calling of the prophet Amos and pass on to us his solemn message for every soul today as well as for Israel of old.

The subject divides itself into the times, the man and his messages to our times.

SECTION I—*The Times of Amos*

He lived and prophesied in the reign of Jeroboam II, the fourth king of Jehu's line. His period was the eighth century before Christ, and his date probably a little later than that of Jonah. The one was sent of God to aid Jeroboam in his victorious career, the other to warn him of God's impending judgment for the sins of himself and his people.

Jeroboam was the most powerful and illustrious of all the sovereigns of the 10 tribes. He restored the boundaries of his kingdom almost to the limits of Solomon's splendid empire. Under his administration the nation rose to the highest prosperity, wealth and influence, and his beautiful capital Samaria became a city of architectural beauty and luxurious splendor. But, the moral and religious effects of such prosperity, as might have been expected, were all in the direction of ungodliness, oppression, idolatry and every vice.

We cannot give a better picture of the times of Amos than the following paragraphs from the scholarly volume of Dr. Geikie, most of which is really an abstract of the book of Amos itself:

THE TIMES OF JEROBOAM II

Under the reign of Jeroboam II, material prosperity rose to a height it had never previously known. Samaria grew rich from the booty of the wars and the profits of commerce and trade. Mansions of hewn stone rose on every side; the inner walls, in many cases, an imitation of Ahab's palace, covered with plates of ivory, and the chambers fitted up with couches and furniture of the same rare material. Cool houses for the hot season; others warmer, for the winter, became the fashion. Pleasant vineyards attached to them covered the slopes of the hills. But as the wealth of the few accumulated, the mass of the population had grown poorer. The apparent prosperity was only a phosphorescence on decay. Intercourse with the heathen communities around; the loose morality of armies dissolved after victorious campaigns and dispersed to their homes; the unscrupulous self-indulgence and the magnificence of the rich, prompting equally unworthy means to indulge it; and the widening gulf between the upper and lower classes, were ruining the country. Above all, the old religiousness of Israel was well-nigh gone. The ox worship of Bethel and Dan had been gradually developed into a gross idolatry; Samaria and Gilgal had raised calf images of their own, for local worship. The great temple at Bethel, at which the king worshipped, and near which he had a palace, boasted of a high priest, with a numerous staff, richly endowed; not poor, like the priests of Judea. The whole country was filled with altars abused by superstition. As time went on, even the darker idolatries of Phenicia, which Jehu, the founder of the dynasty, had so fiercely put down, rose again everywhere. A temple to Asherah had remained in Samaria, and was now reopened. The women once more burned incense before her as their favorite goddess and decked themselves with their earrings and jewels on their feast days. Silver and gold images of Baal were set up. The smoke of sacrifices to idols rose on the tops of the mountains, and incense was burned to them on the hills, under shade of sacred groves. The obscenities of heathenism once more polluted the land. Maidens and matrons consorted with temple harlots, and played the wanton in the name of religion. "Gilead was given to idolatry; they sacrificed to bullocks in Gilgal"; they "transgressed at Bethel and multiplied transgression at Gilgal."

CURSED BY PROSPERITY

The country was, in fact, spoiled by prosperity, which no healthy public morality any longer controlled or directed. Society from the highest to the lowest had become corrupt. Drunkenness and debauchery spread. Wine had taken away their understanding. The birthday festival of the king saw the most revolting excesses. "The drunkards of Ephraim" became a phrase even in Jerusalem. The very priest and the prophet reeled with strong drink at their ministrations. The judge on the bench, and the military officers, covered with medals, were equally Bacchanalian. Guests at the feast drank till the scene was repulsive. Even the women were given to their cups. The great ladies of Samaria—fair and well fed as the kine of Bashan—are described as greedy for drink. Such sensuality and profuseness led to all other vices. The passion for money became general. Corrupt judges, for a bribe, handed over honest men to slavery, as debtors, for so small a default as the price of a pair of shoes. The usurer, after bringing a man to poverty, seemed to grudge him the dust he had put on his head as mourning. Instead of restoring to the poor in the evening, as the law required, the upper garment they had taken in pledge—his sleeping robe—men spread it, as their own, over the couch on which they lay down to nightly carousals, held in the house of their gods, where they feasted on the flesh of their sacrifices, washed down with wine robbed from the helpless. Tumults, from such oppression, filled the streets of Samaria. The mansions of the great were stored with the plunder of their poorer neighbors. Their owners lay, garlanded and anointed, on couches of ivory. Their banquets were splendid. Rich music filled their halls as they feasted. Nor would the wine tempered with water—the drink of their fathers—content them. They drew it pure from the huge vessels in which their predecessors had mingled their modest refreshment. The husbandman had to make them oppressive gifts of his wheat. The great landowners used false measures and false weights in selling their corn, and claimed full price for even the refuse grain. Men had to pledge their clothes and their freedom for food.

Such was the state of things even in the earlier years of Jeroboam II, but matters grew worse toward its close, and in the years that followed his death. No truth, or mercy, or knowledge of God, we are told, was left in the land. Swearing, lying, homicide, stealing, committing adultery, house-breaking and murder till blood touched blood, ran riot. No road was safe. Bands of robbers infested the thoroughfares. Life was no longer sacred. Even the people at court and the priests were deeply compromised in the worst crimes.

Such were the times amid which Amos was called from his humble task to bear witness against a nation's sins.

SECTION II—*The Man and His Message*

He was the sole example under the Old Testament of a man in an obscure position who was called to the prophetic office. His occupation was that of a herdsman in the little village of Tekoa, near Bethlehem. When out of employment in the care of someone's flocks he eked out a living by picking and selling the wild figs known as sycamore fruit.

HIS VISIT TO SAMARIA

In obedience to God's message, he journeyed to the Northern Kingdom, and, mingling with the crowds in Samaria on the occasion of some idolatrous festival, he began after the manner of ancient prophets his public address to the little company gathered around him either in the temple court or the public street. His weird eloquence and solemn manner would soon attract a crowd, and his evident prophetic inspiration give weight and authority to his message. In the case of Amos, the style of his address was well fitted to command attention. His messages were clothed in a poetic eloquence quite out of keeping with his humble calling and apparent advantages. There are no sublimer passages in any of the prophets than many of the splendid figures which Amos draws from the constellations of heaven, the tempests of the desert, the beauties of nature and the mystic realm of pure prophetic symbolism.

A POPULAR MESSAGE

His first address was as tactful as it was eloquent. Beginning with a striking introduction, he announced that the Lord was about to thunder from Zion with a voice which should blast the verdure of the plains and wither the very forests of Carmel. And this voice was to be in judgment on Damascus and Syria, because of their cruel treatment of the people of Gilead whom they had defeated and tortured. The palaces of Ben-Hadad were to be destroyed and Syria was to go into captivity to distant Kir.

Nothing could have been more popular than such a message. Syria was Israel's ancient foe, and through all his audience there were doubtless mutterings of cordial assent and deep delight.

The prophet resumes; and now his message is against the Philistines. Upon Gaza, Ashdod, Ashkelon and Ekron, the thunders of judgment are poured forth, and still his audience listens with unmingled delight.

Next the turn of Tyre comes and she receives her sentence: "I will send fire upon the walls of Tyre/ that will consume her fortresses" (Amos 1:10).

Next comes Edom, and her cruelty is remembered, and upon Teman and Bozrah the vials of judgment are emptied.

Ammon lies hard by and her children have had their part in the atrocious cruelties of recent wars. And so the vision rises of Ammon's fall as the whirlwind of battle sweeps over Rabbah and the king and his princes go forth into captivity.

Still the torrent of judgment rolls on, and now Moab passes out in the fires of judgment, and the palaces of Kerioth perish "in great tumult/ amid war cries and the blast of the trumpet" (2:2).

The heathen nations all have had their turn, and now the people listen with wonder as Judah, their own kindred kingdom, comes in for divine judgment too. "I will send fire upon Judah/ that will consume the fortresses of Jerusalem" (2:5).

STRIKING HOME

By this time his audience must have been deeply stirred. Nothing could have pleased their national self-confidence so much as to have their rivals and enemies thus disposed of. But now, after a solemn pause, the prophet turns to his audience, doubtless with tones of sorrow, and beginning with the same formula as in the other cases, they are startled to hear him say: "For three sins of Israel,/ even for four, I will not turn back my wrath" (2:6). But the sensation deepens as he proceeds to specify his indictments and lay bare with a fearless hand the injustice, the oppression, the shameless impurity and the intemperance and vice of all classes. The chapters that follow doubtless contain portions of many addresses given at various times.

WOE TO ISRAEL

They literally burn with holy invective and scathing rebuke. "Woe to you who are complacent in Zion" (6:1), the prophet cries out, "and to you who feel secure on Mount Samaria" (6:1).

You put off the evil day

and bring near a reign of terror.
You lie on beds inlaid with ivory
  and lounge on your couches.
You dine on choice lambs
  and fattened calves.
You strum away on your harps like David
  and improvise on musical instruments.
You drink wine by the bowlful
  and use the finest lotions,
    but you do not grieve over the ruin of Joseph.
Therefore you will be among the first to go into exile. (6:3–7)

The LORD God Almighty declares:

"I abhor the pride of Jacob
  and detest his fortresses;
I will deliver up the city
  and everything in it." (6:8)

HEAVIER WOES

It would seem as if his next address was given at Bethel in the temple of idolatry there. It consisted of three startling visions. In the first he saw a swarm of destructive locusts sweeping over the land and he cried out to God to forgive and stay His hand. The prayer was heard and the scourge arrested.

Next a consuming flame appeared upon the great sea, and it sucked up the waters of the mighty deep and threatened to devour the land. Again the prophet pleaded and the judgment was stayed. In the third vision the Lord stood upon a wall with a plumb line in His hand indicating the crookedness of the kingdom. But now there was no reprieve and the sentence went forth, "I will spare them no longer" (7:8). "The sanctuaries of Israel will be ruined;/ with my sword I will rise against the house of Jeroboam" (7:9).

EXPELLED

Up to this point Amos had been tolerated by the authorities but now the high priest Amaziah interposed. The mention of the king's name and the awful threatening before the people seemed to him treasonable and dangerous, and he sent word to the king to ask what he should do. The answer came back that Amos was to be sent to his home, and with insolent language Amaziah ordered him to get out. As he turned away he told the high priest that he was nothing but a common herdsman, but that he had come at God's command; and he added as he left this awful judgment:

You say,

> "Do not prophesy against Israel
>   and stop preaching against the house of Isaac."

Therefore this is what the LORD says:

> "Your wife will become a prostitute in the city,
>   and your sons and daughters will fall by the sword.
> Your land will be measured and divided up,
>   and you yourself will die in a pagan country.
> And Israel will certainly go into exile,
>   away from their native land." (7:16–17)

PARTING MESSAGE

Amos leaves another message as he crosses the borders of Israel. It consists of two visions. The first is the vision of a basket of summer fruit so ripe as to be almost rotten, and telling of the nation's ripeness for its speedily approaching doom. The second is the vision of the Lord standing by the altar and commanding the angel to smite the altar, with the fearful threat added,

> Though they dig down to the depths of the grave,
>   from there my hand will take them.
> Though they climb up to the heavens,
>   from there I will bring them down.
> Though they hide themselves on the top of Carmel,
>   there I will hunt them down and seize them.
> Though they hide from me at the bottom of the sea,
>   there I will command the serpent to bite them.
> Though they are driven into exile by their enemies,
>   there I will command the sword to slay them.
> I will fix my eyes upon them
>   for evil and not for good.

> The Lord, the LORD Almighty,
>   he who touches the earth and it melts,
>   and all who live in it mourn—
> the whole land rises like the Nile,
>   then sinks like the river of Egypt—
> he who builds his lofty palace in the heavens
>   and sets its foundation on the earth,

who calls for the waters of the sea
and pours them out over the face of the land—
the LORD is his name. (9:2–6)

MERCY AT LAST

But now the visions change. Judgment has spent its force and mercy again rejoices against judgment. Down through the coming ages, the prophet looks and beholds God's faithful covenant love preserving Israel, though scattered among the nations and sifted like corn in a sieve, "and not a pebble will reach the ground" (9:9). Judah, also, while punished, is to be preserved. Down in the distant future is the glorious promise of the coming of the Lord and the restoration and reunion of both Israel and Judah in their own land amid blessings so beneficent that we can only quote the prophet's sublime language to describe it:

"The days are coming," declares the LORD,
"when the reaper will be overtaken by the plowman
   and the planter by the one treading grapes.
New wine will drip from the mountains
   and flow from all the hills.
I will bring back my exiled people Israel;
   they will rebuild the ruined cities and live in them.
They will plant vineyards and drink their wine;
   they will make gardens and eat their fruit." (9:13–14)

These prophecies, as we shall see later, were considered important enough to supply the substance of the first great decree of the apostles and elders in the Council at Jerusalem as they laid the foundations of the missionary work of the Christian age. Such is the story of Amos.

SECTION III—*The Lessons for Our Times*

FOR THE WORKER

1. To the Christian worker Amos is the pattern of what God can do with the most humble and illiterate instrument if only he is yielded to God in courageous obedience and filled with the Holy Spirit. Amos represented the humblest class, and yet he reached the very height of prophetic inspiration and faithful service. And so, still, it is just as true, that "God chose the weak things of the world to shame the strong" (1 Corinthians 1:27). "To nullify the things that are, so that no one may boast before him" (1:28–29).

Even if you are humble, illiterate and without talent or influence, God can use you if you will let Him have you and fill you and then be wholly obedient to His will.

FOR THE NATION

2. The second lesson is a national one. It is the danger of national prosperity leading to luxury, immorality and injustice. The sins of Amos' times are being rapidly reproduced in the social life of our republic. The wealth of this country is unparalleled, and the spirit of pride, luxury and social extravagance is growing in proportion to the increase of our wealth. Millionaires and multi-millionaires are counted today not by scores, but by thousands, and society is a competition for pre-eminence in the display of wealth, luxury and art. An English artist, who spent last summer in Newport, declared on leaving that the homes of Newport were palaces unapproachable in their artistic adornment and lavish display of wealth by those of any other age or land. The palaces of royalty in the capitals of Europe, and the splendor of ancient architecture and decoration are dwarfed before these products of American taste and riches. And the prospect grows more alarming with the amazing increase of our wealth and the expansion of our ideas of living. These are the things that have crippled our missionary activities. Modern culture has so multiplied our possible avenues of expenditure that the amplest fortunes are barely sufficient for the support of fashionable life. What the moral and spiritual effects are may be learned from the current criticisms which society itself is giving of its inner life, and the exposures of our divorce courts and our argus-eyed journalism. We have not sunk quite so far as ancient Israel, but we are on the same inclined plane, and the track seems oiled for a swifter descent to the same abyss.

Beloved, do not make wealth your ambition unless it is to spend it solely for the glory of God and the spread of His gospel. And if it has been given, do not let it tempt you from the simplicity of living into personal, domestic or social extravagancy.

FOR THE WATCHER

3. To the watcher on the towers of faith and hope, Amos is the prophet of the coming age and the blessed messenger of the Lord's return. Out of the failure and darkness of his own time, he looked on to the better age which is to come when Jesus returns. And God honored him to give the keynote to the first Council of the Christian Church and the great plan of the world's evangelization which we are carrying out today in preparation for the coming of the Lord.

"The words of the prophets are in agreement with this, as it is written:/ 'After this I will return/ and rebuild David's fallen tent./ Its ruins I will rebuild,/ and I will restore it,/ that the remnant of men may seek the Lord,/

and all the Gentiles who bear my name,/ says the Lord, who does these things' " (Acts 15:15–17).

Like Amos let us look out from the shadow of our times to the dawning of that better day, and take as our watchword for every work and hope and trial, "till the coming of the Lord" (1 Thessalonians 4:15).

FOR THE SINNER

4. To the sinner Amos is the prophet of mercy and warning. How tender the compassion that tried to save God's ancient people from their doom and still would save the presumptuous sinner from needless ruin! How fearful the retribution that came to Amaziah for rejecting the message of the Lord and how desperate the folly of those who shall dare to defy the Almighty and bring upon themselves the awful words: "But since you rejected me when I called/ and no one gave heed when I stretched out my hand" (Proverbs 1:24). "Then they will call to me but I will not answer;/ they will look for me but will not find me" (1:28). And oh, how solemn is that message which comes echoing down the centuries from the lips of Amos and has brought many a soul to conviction and salvation, "Prepare to meet your God" (Amos 4:12).

Let it bring conviction and salvation to some soul who reads these lines. Are you prepared to meet Him? Have you met Him already under the precious blood and been reconciled through Jesus Christ? Are you walking with Him in constant fellowship as a loving child; and so giving account of yourself each day to God, that for you the day of judgment is passed before it comes and the prospect of meeting Him is not only free from terror, but is as bright as the hope of heaven? Oh, beloved, "Prepare to meet your God" (4:12).

"Submit to God and be at peace with him;/ in this way prosperity will come to you" (Job 22:21).

CHAPTER 9

HOSEA, THE PROPHET OF MERCY

You are destroyed, O Israel,
  because you are against me, against your helper. (Hosea 13:9)

The word of the LORD that came to Hosea son of Beeri during the
reigns of Uzziah, Jotham, Ahaz and Hezekiah, kings of Judah, and
during the reign of Jeroboam the son of Jehoash, king of Israel. (1:1)

In the year 721 B.C., that eighth century before the Christian era, which witnessed the rise of Rome and Babylon, there happened in Samaria the saddest tragedy of the Old Testament. Amid scenes of horror, the kingdom of the 10 tribes perished, their fair city of Samaria fell under the hands of the Assyrians and Israel's tribes were carried captive into far distant lands. At the same time other captives from these lands were brought to populate Samaria; and thus, as far as it could be made humanly possible, the extermination of the nation was accomplished.

For 50 years, pious and patriotic hearts had foreseen this inevitable fate, and had forewarned this sinful people of the coming overthrow. After the brilliant career of Jeroboam II, which raised Israel for a time to her old pre-eminence, but which was but the flicker of the candle flame before it sank in darkness, the story of Israel's kings was an unbroken record of anarchy and assassination.

God's time of love is always the hour of man's emergency. Just as Elijah and Elisha came to Israel in the dreadful days of Jezebel, and Jeremiah hovered like a guardian angel over Jerusalem two centuries later when she fell, so God sent His messengers again and again to Israel to plead against their reckless crimes, and avert, if possible, their threatened judgment. We have already seen how Jonah was the counselor and friend of Jeroboam, and how Amos came up from Judah to warn him and his people against the coming peril.

73

But above all others, there was one man who for more than 60 years stood as the protecting angel between them and their fate. He lived and prophesied from the time of Jeroboam to the time of Hezekiah, a span of a good deal more than half a century. His beautiful name, the same as Joshua, Jesus and Messiah, signifies "salvation" or "savior." By a striking coincidence, the last king of Israel bore the same name as the last prophet. Both were Hosea or Hoshea. Both had the same significance; but the one, the king, had stood for the best that man can do to save, while the other, the prophet, stood for the salvation of the Lord. Thus God was pointing forward, as if by a living parable, to the greater Savior that was in due time to come to deliver His people, not only from their calamities and enemies, but from that which was the root of all their trouble—their sin.

The life and writings of Hosea, when considered in connection with his place in the tragic history of his time, present the most pathetic picture, perhaps, of the Old Testament. Let us first look at the man, and then at his message to his own people and to our times.

SECTION I—*The Man*

A MINISTRY OF SUFFERING

Like Ezekiel and Jeremiah, and like the greater Prophet to whom his life pointed forward, the Man of Sorrows, he was early baptized into a ministry of suffering. His own life became a sort of object lesson of the story of his country and the message of God to His people. He was commanded by Jehovah to marry a woman of bad reputation, like so many of the women of her time, as a divine picture of God Himself, stooping to take to His heart the vile sinner whom He so strangely loves and saves. Three children were born of this ill-mated union, and as one by one, each little babe lay in its cradle, it also became a living picture of the mournful story that was so soon to be enacted. The firstborn was called Jezreel, meaning, "I will punish," and he was thus made a living prophecy of the judgment that God was so soon to send. The second was a daughter, and her name was Lo-Ruhamah, meaning, "no longer show love," and she forewarned her people of the fact that God's mercy for them soon should end. The third was a son, and his sad name was Lo-Ammi, meaning, "not my people." This expressed the last stage of the impending calamity, when they would be cut off, not merely from God's mercy but from God's covenant, and He should drop them utterly.

After all this there came a second trial to the prophet. The wife of his bosom, whom he had reclaimed from shame and made the mother of his children, went back once more to her old life of sin and forsook her husband and sought her lovers. All this was symbolic of Israel's turning from God after He had called them and saved them. Then follows the story of the reclaiming of the unfaithful wife; but now she is not received back fully at first, but for a time is placed on probation. "You are to live with me many days," is the contract, "and I will live with you" (3:3). This long interval was intended to foreshadow Israel's centuries of waiting through the times of the Gentiles, until God's set time shall have come, and then the restoration will be complete, and they shall be betrothed to Him in faithfulness, never to wander again.

Thus the prophet's whole history was a parable of his ministry, and his own secret soul went through all the sorrows which his people were to experience, and his own life was a sort of miniature of the greater story of their destiny. Is it not true that every worker for God must pass through the experience of his work first in his own soul? It is only that which we have deeply felt that we can make others feel. This is the very essence of our Savior's priesthood, that He "is [not] unable to sympathize with our weaknesses" (Hebrews 4:15).

This was the secret of Paul's great power to help and bless. "Who is weak, and I do not feel weak? Who is led into sin, and I do not inwardly burn?" (2 Corinthians 11:29) was his sympathetic testimony. "I fill up in my flesh what is still lacking in regard to Christ's afflictions, for the sake of his body, which is the church" (Colossians 1:24). Beloved, are we willing thus to bear His cross and to carry His burdens for His suffering ones?

SECTION II—*His Message*

HIS FAMILY TRAGEDY

The book of Hosea begins, as we have seen, with a sort of autobiography, the story of a family tragedy: the prophet's marriage to a licentious woman, the birth of his three children, her unfaithfulness afterwards and her return and probation, with the final reconciliation and the application of all this to the history of Israel. This occupies the first three chapters.

NATIONAL SIN

The chapters that follow contain reports of a large number of addresses and messages given by the prophet from time to time, and thrown together, not perhaps in any exact logical or chronological order, and yet as a fair expression of the various stages of his ministry and its treatment by the people. The fourth chapter contains an indictment of the nation for its crimes, and an awful picture of their bloodshed, murder, stealing, idolatry and shameless impurity. He charges the priests with being the leaders of the people in vileness, and the very matrons and maidens with consorting with temple prostitutes, and even sharing in their wickedness in the shameless orgies of their idolatrous worship.

In the fifth and sixth chapters their punishment has already begun. The Assyrians are upon their border, but instead of turning to God they resort to diplomacy and deceit. They play alternately with Egypt on the one side as an ally, and then Assyria on the other, and their dishonesty is punished by losing the friendship of both. At last God turns away and exclaims, "Then I will go back to my place/ until they admit their guilt./ And they will seek my face;/ in their misery they will earnestly seek me" (5:15).

The very next verse finds the vacillating people crying, "Come, let us return to the LORD./ He has torn us to pieces/ but he will heal us;/ he has injured us/ but he will bind up our wounds" (6:1). But, alas, it is all transitory. "What can I do with you, Ephraim?" He cries, "What can I do with you, Judah?/ Your love is like the morning mist,/ like the early dew that disappears" (6:4). "They do not turn to the Most High;/ they are like a faulty bow" (7:16).

And so he gives them up again to punishment and judgment. "The days of punishment are coming" (9:7). "They sow the wind/ and reap the whirlwind" (8:7). "My God will reject them" (9:17). "All your fortresses will be devastated—/ as Shalman devastated Beth Arbel on the day of battle,/ when mothers were dashed to the ground with their children" (10:14).

DIVINE COMPASSION

But once more God's merciful heart recoils from the strange work of judgment. Looking back over their past history, He remembers, "When Israel was a child, I loved him,/ and out of Egypt I called my son" (11:1). "It was I who taught Ephraim to walk,/ taking them by the arms;/ . . . / I led them with cords of human kindness,/ with ties of love" (11:3–4). "How can I hand you over, Israel?/ How can I treat you like Admah?/ How can I make you like Zeboiim?/ My heart is changed within me;/ all my compassion is aroused./ I will not carry out my fierce anger,/ nor will I return and devastate Ephraim./ For I am God, and not man" (11:8–9).

But mercy was wasted on their unworthy, deceitful nature, and the sentence had at last to go forth. "So I will come upon them like a lion,/ like a leopard I will lurk by the path./ Like a bear robbed of her cubs,/ I will attack them and rip them open./ Like a lion I will devour them;/ a wild animal will tear them apart" (13:7–8). "The guilt of Ephraim is stored up,/ his sins are kept on record" (13:12). "The people of Samaria must bear their guilt,/ because they have rebelled against their God./ They will fall by the sword;/ their little ones will be dashed to the ground,/ their pregnant women ripped open" (13:16).

THE LAST APPEAL

But now there seems to come a pause in the movement of this drama of sin and judgment, and a voice is heard pleading in strange tenderness in the closing chapter: "Return, O Israel, to the LORD your God./ Your sins have been your downfall!/ Take words with you/ and return to the LORD./ Say to him:/ 'Forgive all our sins/ and receive us graciously' " (14:1–2). And there comes in response, like the voice of a mother's tenderness, "I will heal their waywardness/ and love them freely,/ for my anger has turned away from them" (14:4).

And then follows that magnificent picture drawn from all the richest imagery of that luxuriant land—from the sparkling dew of the morning and the blossoms of the fertile plain, and the forests of mighty Lebanon and the verdure of the olive on the mountain side and the waving harvests of grain, and the sweet fragrance of the mountain and the plain—all blended in one supernal picture of gentleness and grace, as God pours out the fullness of His heart and the promises of His grace. And the last scene in the drama is the penitent resolve of Ephraim, "What more have I to do with idols?" (14:8), and the last answer of Jehovah, "your fruitfulness comes from me" (14:8). Ephraim has come back to God and God has betrothed His bride to Him forever in faithfulness.

SECTION III—*Lessons Learned from Hosea*

SIN

1. The first lesson deals with the aggravations and effects of sin. The sin of Israel was the type of all sin, for sin is the same in every age. As we have already seen, the sins that grew out of Israel's luxury and ungodliness are repeating themselves once more in these last days of luxury and pride. And they can only bring the same result. Hosea's proverb expresses it more forcibly than any other language can express: "They sow the wind,/ and reap the whirlwind" (8:7). The consequence will be the same as the cause, but immeasurably greater. The whirlwind is but the wind in another form, but the wind multiplied 10 thousandfold. Let us take care as we trifle with the gentle zephyr of passion and of sinful pleasure. It fans your cheek today, it breathes its fragrance upon your senses, but tomorrow it will sweep like the desolating blast.

INSINCERITY

2. The second lesson deals with half-hearted service. The Israel of Hosea was the picture of a large part of the Church today. "Ephraim is a flat cake not turned over" (7:8). Is there anything more disgusting than half-cooked food? And so the Church is full of people who have had a touch of fire—at the altar today, at the theater tomorrow; thanking God today, grumbling tomorrow; singing today of a Savior's love, and tomorrow squeezing the last

cent out of some hapless victim. Again, what is more expressive than Hosea's figure: "Your love is like the morning mist,/ like the early dew that disappears" (6:4).

Inconstant purposes, ebbing and fading; love and faith, faltering and stumbling; obedience, halting and compromising. Oh, how sad the end of our good beginnings and the blighting of our morn's fair promise! "He who stands firm to the end will be saved" (Matthew 10:22). Hosea's people were like the Laodiceans, to whom John bore the message of the Savior: "Because you are lukewarm—neither hot nor cold—I am about to spit you out of my mouth" (Revelation 3:16).

THE BACKSLIDER

3. The third lesson is God's mercy to the sinner and the backslider. We have already traced the pathetic figure and utterance which express the divine love for sinful Israel. This love is still the same for the sinner and the backslider. It is not a mere sentimental love which trifles with sin. With inexorable faithfulness it deals with transgression and aims to bring the erring one to true repentance. But how gladly it welcomes the penitent and freely forgives and fully heals his backsliding and his sorrow! The prophecy of Hosea has been well called the Old Testament parable of the Prodigal Son. It is just like it in its deep pathos and overflowing love.

THE GOSPEL

4. It is a picture of the gospel. "I will . . . love them freely,/ for my anger has turned away from them" (Hosea 14:4) suggests immediately to the thoughtful mind the ground of that free and full forgiveness, and the cross of Calvary by which the anger was turned away. There is a passage in the sixth chapter where penitent Israel exclaims, "After two days he will revive us;/ on the third day he will restore us,/ that we may live in his presence" (6:2). This is obviously an allusion to the three days of Christ's death and burial and the resurrection on the morning of the third, and also to the spiritual fact that the believer also must die with Christ and rise with Him into new life, in order to receive the fullness of divine grace.

ISRAEL

5. Hosea is the prophet of Israel's restoration. He tells us that the time is coming surely when they shall sing again in the mountains of Samaria and the heights of Zion, and the fearful curse of ages shall be wiped away in God's eternal favor and His everlasting covenant.

> Yet the Israelites will be like the sand on the seashore, which cannot be measured or counted. In the place where it was said to

them, "You are not my people," they will be called "sons of the living God." The people of Judah and the people of Israel will be reunited, and they will appoint one leader and will come up out of the land, for great will be the day of Jezreel. (1:10–11)

> I will plant her for myself in the land;
>   I will show my love to the one I called "Not my loved one."
> I will say to those called "Not my people," "You are my people";
>   and they will say, "You are my God." (2:23)

Afterward the Israelites will return and seek the LORD their God and David their king. They will come trembling to the LORD and to his blessings in the last days. (3:5)

THE RICHES OF GRACE

6. Hosea gives us a most attractive picture of the riches of God's grace to His own. All the beauty and glory of nature are called into requisition to express in eloquent figure and expressive phrase His gentleness and grace. "I will be like the dew to Israel" (14:5). How it speaks of the hallowed influences of the Holy Spirit. The beauty of the lily, the luxuriance of the olive, the strength of the cedar, the abundance of the grain, the fragrance of the vine, the sweetness of the wine of Lebanon—all these proclaim the infinite grace and overflowing blessing which God is waiting to pour into the hearts that can receive it. "Men will dwell again in his shade" (14:7), tells us of the higher blessing which He will make us give to others after we ourselves have been blessed, and then His grace is guaranteed to keep us faithful. "O Ephraim, what more have I to do with idols?/ . . . / your fruitfulness comes from me" (14:8).

In the second chapter there is a magnificent series of metaphors rich with the suggestion of His abundant grace. He says, "I will betroth you in righteousness and justice,/ in love and compassion./ I will betroth you in faithfulness,/ and you will acknowledge the LORD" (2:19–20). And as he calls us from the lower plane of the servant to the closer intimacy and higher dignity of the bride, He adds: "you will call me, '[*Ishi*] my husband';/ you will no longer call me '[*Baali*] my master.' " (2:16).

Then, too, He tells them the blessings of His providence will follow close upon the riches of His grace, and all nature will be made tributary to the purposes of His love. "I will respond to the skies,/ and they will respond to the earth;/ and the earth will respond to the grain,/ the new wine and oil,/ and they will respond to Jezreel" (2:21–22).

What a beautiful chain of second causes all leading up to God! The people call to the grain and the wine, and they in turn call to the famished earth, and the earth cries to the brazen heavens. But all are in vain until the heavens cry unto the heart of God, and then the showers come, the fruits spring, the earth is covered with verdure and abundance and the wants of the people are supplied. And it is still as true as ever that all things wait upon the soul that walks with God, and "we know that in all things God works for the good of those who love him, who have been called according to his purpose" (Romans 8:28).

While we learn from these lurid visions the certainty that justice and judgment are the habitation of His throne, yet how sweetly we also learn that mercy and truth shall go before His face. In the abundance of His grace we may well add, "Blessed are those who have learned to acclaim you,/ who walk in the light of your presence, O LORD./ They rejoice in your name all day long;/ they exult in your righteousness" (Psalm 89:15–16). Sinner! Backslider! Return to this loving Father. And child of His love and bride of His heart, walk softly and closely with Him. "Who is wise? He will realize these things./ Who is discerning? He will understand them./ The ways of the LORD are right;/ the righteous walk in them,/ but the rebellious stumble in them" (Hosea 14:9).

JUDAH

CHAPTER 10

REHOBOAM, OR THE PERIL OF UNGODLINESS AND PRIDE

He did evil because he had not set his heart on seeking the LORD. (2 Chronicles 12:14)

Something like the great convocation held once on the plains of Delhi to proclaim the sovereignty of the Indian emperor, was the convocation which had been summoned to meet at Shechem in the time of Ephraim for the purpose of crowning Rehoboam as the successor of David and Solomon, the king of Israel. Rehoboam had consented to this arrangement as special compliment to the powerful family of Joseph and tribe of Ephraim. And doubtless, preparations had been made for a pageant worthy of so great an occasion, and for a scene of Oriental magnificence and splendor in keeping with the glory of Solomon's kingdom.

SECTION I—*The Story of Rehoboam*

AN INTERRUPTION

But there is a sudden interruption of the program before the procession can move or the coronation ceremony begin. There is a deputation which insists upon an interview with the king. And to add special significance to it, the leader of the deputation is a young politician named Jeroboam, who has just come back from Egypt. He had fled to Egypt to escape the wrath of Solomon, when suspected, some years before, of plotting to secure for himself the throne. He has been patronized by the Egyptian Court, and meanwhile has kept in touch with the disaffected leaders in his own and other tribes. They have summoned him back for the coronation, and many a caucus has been held, no doubt, to arrange the policy with which they are to meet the future king.

Rehoboam receives the deputation and listens with astonishment to their demands. "Your father put a heavy yoke on us, but now lighten the harsh labor and the heavy yoke he put on us, and we will serve you" (2 Chronicles 10:4). That seemed most moderate and reasonable. There was nothing insulting or unduly insistent in their terms. The taxes which Solomon had imposed for his vast improvements had been oppressive; and still more obnoxious had been the burden of forced labor by means of which the temple and his gorgeous palaces and luxurious parks had been constructed. The delegation simply asked for some letting down of these oppressive impositions.

A REASONABLE DEMAND

Rehoboam asked three days to consider their demands and, meanwhile, consulted with his advisers. First, he called the old men to him that had been the counselors of Solomon and knew the condition of the people and the kingdom. Their advice was eminently wise. They urged him to conciliate the people and thus win their lasting confidence and loyalty.

Then he called to him his boon companions, the young men of the court, and he received what might have been expected—some hot-headed, insolent suggestions. The idea of his conceding anything was preposterous to these young aristocrats. What were kings for but to own and control their subjects? And what were subjects for but to minister to their will? These young braggarts advised, "Tell the people who have said to you, 'Your father put a heavy yoke on us, but make our yoke lighter'—tell them, 'My little finger is thicker than my father's waist. My father laid on you a heavy yoke; I will make it even heavier. My father scourged you with whips; I will scourge you with scorpions' " (10:10–11).

A BLUNDER

Rehoboam was delighted with this advice. He saw at once that this would give him the true dignity of a real king. And so he met the deputation again after three days and with lordly and defiant air began to repeat the little speech of folly which his boon companions had dictated. But he had not got more than one-half through when there arose that old, terrible cry which twice before had been the signal for a national rebellion: "What share do we have in David,/ what part in Jesse's son?/ To your tents, O Israel!/ Look after your own house, O David" (10:16).

Too late, Rehoboam realized what he had done and tried, as weak men do, to compromise. He sent Adoniram, tribute officer, to negotiate with them, but in a moment he fell under a shower of stones. Rehoboam instantly sought safety in flight and returned to Jerusalem, barely escaping with his life. As well might one have tried to stop the rising of the tide or the raging of the storm! The little spark of his folly had kindled a conflagration which would not cease to burn until it had consumed both parts of the now-divided kingdom and covered his name with a dishonor that should never pass away.

A WRECK

The splendid kingdom of David and Solomon was rent in twain. One section would maintain a precarious and ungodly throne for two centuries and then pass out in seeming extermination. The other, which lingered a little longer, would disappear into exile for a time at least, and its future be overshadowed for 2,000 years, with deepest gloom.

Such was the heritage of shame and sorrow which one reckless moment brought upon his people and his throne. All that is left to him now is to gather up the fragments that remain and make the best of his stupendous blunder.

A KINGDOM LOST

How much was lost! The splendid and fertile plains of Samaria and Galilee; the coasts of the Mediterranean; the luxuriant pastures of Gilead and Bashan; the vast regions stretching northward to the Orontes and eastward to the Euphrates, the richest part of Israel's inheritance, all gone; and five-sixths of its people under the banner of Jeroboam and the 10 tribes! And how little was left! A territory about 50 by 80 miles in extent, not much larger than two or three counties in some of our states. A population at the most of two or three million and a lost prestige among the surrounding tribes and nations, which would soon bring upon him the rebellion of the Philistines and Edomites and the neighboring people and cut him off from the maritime trade which his father had secured to the south. The chief possession that was left him was ancient Jerusalem, its holy sanctuary the temple and the dynasty of David and Solomon.

His first impulse was to fight for the kingdom and to put down by force the rebellion, and he immediately levied an army of 180,000 for this purpose. But the message of a prophet forbade this second folly, and so he set himself to work as best he could to safeguard what was left of the kingdom. Fifteen cities surrounding Jerusalem were strongly fortified, especially on the south toward Egypt, their most formidable rival. For a while he showed some zeal and wisdom in arranging the civil government of the nation.

AN UNGODLY RULER

But the fatal defect of Rehoboam was his own character and his lack of real principle and godliness. The text betrays the fatal secret of his life. "He did evil because he had not set his heart on seeking the LORD" (12:14). And so it was not long before the character of the king began to reflect in his government and policy. Evils of all kinds were permitted in the moral, social and religious conditions of the State. Idolatry was even established by sanction of the king, and men and women of the grossest character encouraged, and even appointed in the worship of the groves (1 Kings 14:22–24).

The second chastisement soon came in the form of an invasion by Shishak, known in history as Sheshonk, king of Egypt. With a vast army of horses, chariots and countless soldiers from among the cave-dwellers of Ethiopia, he swept overland, crushed the cordon of fortifications which Rehoboam had vainly provided and invested Jerusalem itself with a vast, besieging army. Doubtless, this invasion was, in part at least, suggested and encouraged by Jeroboam in order to weaken and destroy the southern kingdom.

HUMBLED PRIDE

The Egyptians were bought off only by giving them the entire treasure of the city and temple—the vast stores of gold and precious stones that David and Solomon had accumulated for the house of the Lord, amounting to billions of dollars' worth. All this was stripped from the helpless captive, and Rehoboam was left with but the shadow and mockery of his royal state. The country was placed under tribute to Egypt. God did not utterly destroy them because they humbled themselves before Him, but He sent them this message: "I will not destroy them but will soon give them deliverance. . . . They will, however, become subject to [Shishak], so that they may learn the difference between serving me and serving the kings of other lands" (2 Chronicles 12:7–8).

Poor Rehoboam still tried to keep up the show of his kingly state. Instead of shields of gold which Solomon had made to carry before him when entering the temple, he had shields of brass made. But the real glory had departed, and the remainder of his 17 years he just lived out the empty form of royalty and at last passed to the sepulchers of his fathers, leaving behind him the memory and the heritage of having wrecked the grandest empire ever committed to mortal hands and having brought upon his successors an entail of more shame and sorrow than any other king of David's line.

SECTION II—*Lessons Learned from the Life of Rehoboam*

The lessons of his life are the more significant and profitable to us because he had some good even in his imperfect and blundering life. Had he been one of the great originators of wickedness like Ahab or Athaliah, men might have said that his example did not apply to ordinary lives. But the fact was that he was just like other young men of today—a man with some good in him. But since he had enough conceit and recklessness to make him dangerous, and to wreck his life and the lives of others, makes the picture the more timely, and the lesson the more intensely personal to the men— and especially to the young men of today.

RECKLESSNESS AND PRIDE

1. His life teaches us of the folly and danger of rashness, vanity and pride. One hasty word is like a spark in a powder magazine and the Apostle James may well say, "Consider what a great forest is set on fire by a small spark" (James 3:5). Pride brought Nebuchadnezzar to his fall. It led to Peter's denial of his Master. It brought Pharaoh's doom, and it always brings deepest humiliation and punishment, for "God opposes the proud/ but gives grace to the humble" (4:6). Let us ask God to keep our temper and our tongue.

EVIL COUNSELORS

2. His life teaches us of the danger of evil companionship. When Rehoboam's sinful life is described it is emphatically added: "His mother's name was Naamah; she was an Ammonite" (2 Chronicles 12:13). He had a bad mother, a heathen and idolatress, no doubt. How could the issue have been different? How cruel the crime of Solomon to make an idolatress the mother of his son and successor. And his wife was no better. The granddaughter of Absalom, she was probably as beautiful as her grandfather, but she was also as sinful, for a little later in the story of Asa we read that when he came to the throne he put her aside from being queen dowager because of her idolatrous influence (2 Chronicles 15:16). And yet she was Rehoboam's favorite wife. Little wonder that with an idolatrous mother and a wife who was also an inveterate idolatress his life was all wrong.

We all depend to a great extent on the influences that environ us. Weak natures take the coloring, chameleon-like, of their surroundings, and to a greater or less degree it is true of us all, "He who walks with the wise grows wise,/ but a companion of fools suffers harm" (Proverbs 13:20).

LOST OPPORTUNITIES

3. Rehoboam's life teaches us the value and the responsibility of opportunity. What an opportunity Rehoboam had, but what an awful responsibility! For one moment it was in his power to save or to destroy the noblest kingdom of the earth, and once done his act was irrevocable. So to each of us opportunity comes with its far-reaching possibilities of weal or woe and lingers not for our convenience. The decisive word must be spoken; once done—the issues are eternal. There are opportunities of personal salvation; there are opportunities of useful work. There are opportunities for spiritual blessing; there are opportunities for blessing and helping others which come

to us all. Over each is inscribed one burning message: "Making the most of every opportunity, because the days are evil" (Ephesians 5:16).

GOD'S OVERRULING PROVIDENCE

4. One reason why our responsibility is so great is because there is a divine purpose behind our actions. The message of the prophet to Rehoboam when he purposed, by force of arms, bringing back the rebellious tribes was this, "Do not go up to fight against your brothers. Go home, every one of you, for this is my doing" (2 Chronicles 11:4). God had told Jeroboam through the prophet, Ahijah, many years before, that all this should come to pass and that he should be king of 10 tribes. And yet He allowed it all to come about by human agency and held the agents responsible for their individual actions; but when their acts were finally decided upon they became links in the inexorable chain of God's fixed purposes. There was a time during which Rehoboam was free to act and by his action save his kingdom, but once having acted he could not play with God's plans and change the course of events which he himself had determined. Back of his willful, wicked conduct God was overruling his folly for some final purpose of His providence. This made life very solemn.

How forcibly the Apostle Peter expressed it when, charging the rulers of Israel with having murdered the Son of God, he said, "You, with the help of wicked men, put him to death by nailing him to the cross" (Acts 2:23). It was their act, their crime, and they were held responsible for it. But at the same time he tells them, "This man was handed over to you by God's set purpose and foreknowledge" (2:23). God had planned it all, knowing their wicked hearts and how they would act, and had determined to overrule it all for the salvation of men and the purposes of His own glory and yet hold them to the effects of their sin.

And so we must ever remember that, while we are acting according to our own caprices and preferences, we are unconsciously fitting into a great chain of causes and effects which God is overruling for some great purpose of His own. Each link that we forge passes into the hands of the Divine Architect and is henceforth beyond our control and yet we are eternally responsible for its power for good or evil. What an awful sacredness this gives to every human act! How carefully we should use the freedom of choice that God has given. What a responsibility rests upon every decision and action of our lives! What would Rehoboam have given to recall that foolish word at Shechem! But it was too late! All that was left him was to meet the inevitable consequences and make the best of what remained.

Dear friend, remember as you pass through life that you are touching every moment live wires and the currents of influence you set in operation will soon pass beyond your own control and will influence your own and other lives through all eternity.

WRONG AT HEART

5. The impossibility of a bad man living a good life. Our text gives us the key to Rehoboam's failure, "He did evil because he had not set his heart on seeking the LORD" (2 Chronicles 12:14). He had a bad heart and the outcome inevitably must be a bad life. Men are always making a mistake trying to do good without the necessary spiritual resources. God does not ask us to do better. He asks us to let Him make us better in our nature and then the doing will take care of itself. A good tree cannot bring forth bad fruit, neither can a corrupt tree bring forth good fruit. Let the fruit alone, get the right sort of tree. It is a new heart you need, not better rules and principles. It is the power of Jesus Christ and His Holy Spirit alone that will make it natural and spontaneous for you to love and serve.

Rehoboam's fault was that "he had not set his heart on seeking the LORD" (2 Chronicles 12:14). Notice, it does not say "to serve the LORD." It was not better service that God asked from him, but a disposition to seek and obtain divine grace and help. Oh souls that are struggling in vain to make the crooked straight—the tiger, lamb-like—when will you learn God's better way: "You must be born again" (John 3:7)?

NOT WHOLLY BAD

6. Rehoboam stands as an example of a man that was not bad, who had some good in him, but who was constantly under divine chastening and in the hand of God for judgment and discipline. One is in the heart of God, and the other is in the hands of God. "It is a dreadful thing to fall into the hands of the living God" (Hebrews 10:31).

Some people never seem to get out of that fearful place. They are always getting into condemnation and compelling God to deal with them in a judicial way. All sweetness is out of their lives, and they seem to have just enough religion to make them miserable. God does not wish to deal with us thus. We are not under law, but grace. Let us come into the place of sonship, of confidence and of loving obedience where through His grace we may ever say, "The one who sent me is with me; he has not left me alone, for I always do what pleases him" (John 8:29).

THE TWO SERVICES

7. Rehoboam is an illustration of the difference between the two services, the service of the Lord and the service of the world. There is a remarkable statement in Second Chronicles 12:8, "They will, however, become subject to him, so that they may learn the difference between serving me and serving the kings of other lands." That is to say that God allowed His people for a

time to be tributary to Egypt that they might find out for themselves how much easier it was to be the servant of God than of the world. Some Christians get very tired of God's will and long for freedom to live like the world. Sometimes God lets them have it and they find to their sorrow that it is a bitter bondage. For a time the pleasures of the world may fascinate, but in the end they are more bitter than death. Often their votaries and victims find, like Solomon, after his wasted life, that "everything is meaningless" (Ecclesiastes 1:2); and that the only true freedom and lasting happiness are found in His service, who has said, "Come to me, all you who are weary and burdened, and I will give you rest. Take my yoke upon you and learn from me, for I am gentle and humble in heart, and you will find rest for your souls. For my yoke is easy and my burden is light" (Matthew 11:28-30).

THE WORLD A CHEAT

I remember a beautiful woman in my early ministry whom I tried in vain to turn aside from the sinful world. She was a professed Christian, but her answer was, "I just love the world and cannot live without it." Vainly I tried to tell her that the world would cheat her in the end, but she would not listen. The day came—and came, alas, very soon—when she returned to me for counsel and comfort. Her cry was, "I hate the world. I find no interest or pleasure in the things that used to charm me. I care for nothing, my heart is like stone." It seemed impossible to comfort her, and a few days later her poor little body was taken out of the waters of the river where she had sought oblivion from her bitter disappointment. As I stood by her bier with a deep, unutterable sorrow, that chills the heart even yet to remember, it seemed as if those cold and silent lips were saying, "Do not love the world or anything in the world. . . . The world and its desires pass away, but the man who does the will of God lives forever" (1 John 2:15–17).

CHAPTER 11

ASA, OR THE FATAL FAILURES
OF A WELL-MEANING LIFE

*Asa did what was right in the eyes of the LORD, as his father David
had done. . . . Although he did not remove the high places, Asa's heart
was fully committed to the LORD all his life. (1 Kings 15:11, 14)*

In Rehoboam we saw the portrait of a bad man with some good in him. In
Asa we have the converse picture, a good man with some mingled spots of
infirmity and failure.

SECTION I—*The Story of Asa*

Jeroboam was still upon the throne of Israel when Asa succeeded his
father, or more probably his brother, Abijah. The fact that Maacah, the wife
of Rehoboam and his favorite queen, is called the mother of Asa and was
specially deposed by him on account of her notorious idolatry, would seem
to indicate that she must have been his own mother and not his
grandmother. Abijah's reign had been a brief one, lasting less than three
years, and with but one bright spot in all its dark record of sin. And Asa
came to the throne in the midst of precedents and conditions little favorable
to a reign of piety or prosperity.

His reign occupied 41 years and was contemporary with no less than seven
of the kings of Israel, namely, Jeroboam, Nadab, Baasha, Elah, Zimri, Omri
and Ahab, in the earlier years of Asa's reign. He must have ascended the
throne while still young, perhaps less than 20 years of age.

A GOOD BEGINNING

His bright and promising beginning was therefore the more to his credit
and honor. He immediately instituted the reforms in temple and state so

greatly needed, and restored something like even the best days of his father, David. He put away the groves of Baal, the unhallowed priests and priestesses that ministered at their altars and the whole system of idolatry which Rehoboam had countenanced. He even deposed his own mother because she had set up a shameful shrine and an obscene image in one of her idolatrous groves. The temple worship was reestablished in Jerusalem, and "he commanded Judah to seek the LORD, the God of their fathers, and to obey his laws and commands" (2 Chronicles 14:4).

WISE ADMINISTRATION

Not only so, his public policy was as wise and sagacious as his personal character was upright. He erected fortresses throughout the land and drilled an army of no less than 580,000 men, including probably almost all the males able to bear arms in Judah and Benjamin. He did not do this in a spirit like that of Rehoboam, of human self-confidence, but in dependence upon Jehovah, who had given them the opportunity to take these wise precautions. "Let us build up these towns," he said, "and put walls around them, with towers, gates and bars. The land is still ours, because we have sought the LORD our God; we sought him and he has given us rest on every side" (14:7).

None too soon did he make these prudent preparations, for suddenly there burst upon his kingdom the most terrific invasion it had ever known. Zerah, the Cushite, known in history as Usarken, the third in descent of Egypt's kings from the famous Shishak, or Sheshonk, who had captured Jerusalem in the time of Rehoboam, with an army of a million and the usual accompaniment of chariots and cavalry, came up from the south with all the military power and prestige of Egypt to conquer his kingdom and enforce the tribute which probably had been discontinued after Rehoboam's death.

FAITH AND DEATH

With wise strategy and heroic faith, Asa promptly met the invader. He marched his little army in front of the walled cities which he had forfeited, and thus had his base protected in case of retreat. But he did not count upon defeat, nor even upon his strategy nor his army, but upon the living God. "LORD," he said, in language never to be forgotten, "there is no one like you to help the powerless against the mighty. Help us, O LORD our God, for we rely on you, and in your name we have come against this vast army. O LORD, you are our God; do not let man prevail against you" (14:11). Not in vain did he claim this high and divine resource. Victory crowned his fight of faith. The Egyptian army was defeated and routed, and so completely overthrown that it was centuries before they ever dared again to cross the Judean frontier. Enormous spoil was recovered, and even the Arabian allies of Egypt, far to the south, were smitten by Asa's hosts, and vast spoil and herds of sheep and cattle and camels captured and carried back to Jerusalem.

Asa's splendid victory was followed by a public act of national consecration and a solemn league and covenant to serve the Lord with all their heart, and to cut off all who refused to do so.

The result of all this was a long period of peace, righteousness and great national prosperity.

EVILS OF PROSPERITY

But few men and few communities can enjoy long continued prosperity. A silent process of disintegration was meanwhile going on in the heart of the king and the spirit of the people and in the 26th year of Asa's reign an incident occurred that brought to light this baleful process. Baasha, the energetic king of Israel, began a movement against Asa's kingdom, by building powerful fortifications at Ramah on the border in order to cut off all communication between the two countries, and prevent the tide of immigration that had been setting in toward Judah from the tribes of the northern kingdom. There was also, no doubt, the hint of more direct hostilities as well.

THE ARM OF THE FLESH

Asa immediately took alarm and instead of turning to God, as he had in the more formidable invasion of the Egyptians, he resorted to diplomacy and sent an immense bribe, which he took from the treasures of the temple, to Ben-Hadad, king of Syria. Asa proposed to him that they should enter into an alliance and that he should attack Baasha and draw off his invading army from Ramah. Asa's policy was immensely successful for the time. Ben-Hadad attacked and captured a large number of important towns in the northern kingdom and Baasha withdrew his forces from Ramah, while Asa captured the stones that had been intended for its walls, carried them away and built two powerful fortresses for himself.

But it was a costly victory in the end. The prophet Hanani was sent to rebuke the king for turning away from God, who had given him such a glorious deliverance in the former and great invasion, and turning to the arm of flesh in his present need. But Asa, instead of accepting the divine reproof, went from bad to worse and became angry with the prophet, threw him into prison and vented his bitter animosity not only on him but on many of his subjects. The spirit that had once been so trustful and holy became soured and malignant, and the good and benignant ruler threatened to become a cruel oppressor.

THE PHYSICIANS

Before long a more severe trial came to show the depth of his spiritual declension, and at the same time to give him an opportunity of profiting by the divine discipline. A severe illness came upon him, some form of disease in his feet, perhaps gout or rheumatism. It continued through two whole years, affording him abundant opportunity to learn his lesson and turn to God. But the sad story still moves on in its downward trend. "Even in his illness he did not seek help from the LORD, but only from the physicians" (16:12).

Egypt in these days had a very high order of medical science, and the museums of Cairo contain many a surgical instrument worthy to be compared with the advanced science of today. This high culture had even reached Judah in the days of Solomon, but hitherto God's people had not turned back from their ancient trust in the arm of Jehovah. As Dr. Geikie well says, the very fact that Asa's resorting to physicians is commented upon with such strong disapproval only shows how high the standard of faith still was even in those degenerate times.

The issue of Asa's trouble was just what might have been expected. Very gently he is let down into his humbling grave. Very generously does the record bear witness to his splendid funeral and his high record as a king, but none the less was it a failure, defeat and the grave. "Asa died and rested with his fathers" (16:13). But all the delicacy of the historian, and all the gentleness of the inspired penman cannot hide the mournful fact that one of the best of Judah's kings had fallen from his high estate, and over his tomb invisible fingers had written, "The glory is departed."

SECTION II—*Lessons Learned from the Life of Asa*

FAITHFULNESS

1. The first lesson is that of faithfulness to God in a place of high trust and hard trial. He ascended a lofty throne in his immature youth with three bad examples before him—his grandfather, his father and his brother—and with an established condition of idolatry and unrighteousness on every side. It was no easy task for a youth to set himself against the powerful current of depraved human nature strengthened with the evil bent of half a century of tolerated sin. Worse than all else, his own mother, the most potent social influence in the realm, was herself the patroness of idolatry, and had no doubt done her best to instill into his own mind her pernicious principles. But in the face of all this young Asa was true to God. With loyal purpose and powerful energy he succeeded in stemming the tide of evil, in turning it backwards and reestablishing the worship of Jehovah and the righteous government of which his ancestor David's was his lofty example. Let this not be forgotten even when we have to deplore the sad and humbling declension of his later years. God did not forget it, and Asa deserves to stand very high

in the roll of Judah's best kings. God help each of us to be as true in the places of responsibility and trial to which he calls us.

PRUDENCE

2. Another lesson is that of prudence and preparation in times of prosperity for days of danger. Asa prepared himself while his realm was at peace and his subjects were at leisure for the emergencies that the future was sure to bring. And so the wise man will look forward and husband the resources of today for the needs of tomorrow.

Even the ant prepares its food in summer. Likewise, prudence is one of the instincts with which God has armed us against the vicissitudes of life. The highest confidence in God need not prevent us from anticipating the future and "lay up treasure for themselves as a firm foundation for the coming age" (1 Timothy 6:19). Frugality and economy in the practical affairs of life are Christian graces as well as natural virtues. Every young man and woman with even the most limited income should endeavor to save a little not merely for future needs, but for future possibilities of wise advancement even in the business of life. In the spiritual world we can store the heavens with prayer and the day will come when the answer will be poured upon our heads in blessed help and abundant service. We can store our minds with truth and by diligent preparation become fitted for higher usefulness in the work of God.

CONFIDENCE

3. Asa displayed confidence in God in a time of great trial and emergency. The crisis came for which Asa had wisely prepared; and when it came he did not depend upon his half a million trained militia, nor his carefully established line of fortifications, but upon God. "In your name," he cried, "we have come against this vast army. O LORD, you are our God; do not let man prevail against you" (2 Chronicles 14:11).

Faith can never rise to simpler, sublimer confidence than these words express. It was God's battle and God vindicated His servant's trust. This is the true spirit in which to meet our difficulties and our enemies. Let us make God responsible, and He will not fail us in our time of need.

CONSECRATION

4. The next lesson is the consecration of our blessings. After Asa's victory, instead of boasting in his own skill and triumph, we find him gathering his people to an act of solemn recognition of Jehovah as the God of the nation. Asa leads them into a league and covenant of fidelity to Him, and swears that whosoever should not seek the Lord should surely be put to death. This does not mean that we are to murder everybody who does not come up to

our idea of consecration, but that we are to put to death everything in ourselves that does not answer to God's supreme claim.

The question is pertinent to us. How have we used our blessings? Have we consecrated them to God? What have you done with the means that He gave you as you asked Him to prosper your business? Have you put Him off with some trifling tithe or even less? Or have you given Him all and recognize yourself as but a steward, holding and using everything for His service and according to His will? This is true consecration.

What have you done with your health which He gave you back? Have you given it to Him and are you using it sacredly for His service and according to His will, or selfishly for the enjoyment of life or the amassing of riches? God help us to consecrate our blessings. How sad the record of Hezekiah, that he rendered not again according to the benefit that he had received, but turned his blessing into vainglory and display, and brought upon himself and his country the displeasure of God and the despoiling hands of the Chaldeans.

WATCHFULNESS

5. Still another lesson is the failure that comes through prosperity without watchfulness. The splendid record of Asa's first 26 years was sadly dimmed by the later portion of his reign. The king that would despise a million Egyptian soldiers and go forth in faith to overcome them, became alarmed by a little threat from Baasha of the possible invasion of his country, and immediately turned to the arm of flesh and his heart departed from the Lord. Alas, how hard it is for many of us still to stand even God's best blessings without forsaking the fountain of living waters and turning to broken cisterns that can hold no water.

REPROOF REFUSED

6. His worldliness soon led to sin. The prophet that came to reprove him was rejected and persecuted, and the man that had been so devout became the oppressor of his people. His sweetness was turned to malignity and moroseness, and his whole character became embittered.

FAITH UNDERMINED

7. But unfortunately the evil progression did not stop there! The worst thing about our failures is that they disarm us for the next conflict and leave us to more disastrous failure in some fatal crisis. So it was with Asa. And when sickness came and his health and life began to break down under the lingering pressure of chronic and incurable disease, the same unbelief that had turned from God to the Syrian league for help turned again from God to the physicians of Egypt for healing. We have already seen the inevitable

result and mourned his dishonored tomb. But let us not forget the lesson that the failure of today is going to unfit you for the victory of tomorrow. Every time we yield to the enemy, we become disarmed and dismembered for the next test of faith.

Dr. Livingston tells of the ant lion of the desert that digs a little hole in the sand the shape of an inverted cone, and, sitting at the bottom, waits for its prey to tumble over the edge. Some foolish traveling ant draws near and, with a curiosity more natural than prudent, ventures to look over the edge of this strange pit, when suddenly the ground gives way and down it plunges headlong on the sloping crumbling incline. The moment it reaches the bottom the sharp scissor-like fangs of the ant lion with a click have cut off one of its feet. With a start of terror and agony it begins to climb back to the top, but just as it reaches the edge again the sand gives way, and again another limb is severed. This continues until at last it falls into the den of its destroyer the mutilated and helpless victim of his devouring jaws.

So, too, the devil begins the process of destruction in many a thoughtless life. God help us to "watch and pray so that [we] will not fall into temptation" (Matthew 26:41).

CHAPTER 12

JEHOSHAPHAT, OR A GOOD MAN IN THE WRONG PLACE

Should you help the wicked and love those who hate the LORD? Because of this, the wrath of the LORD is upon you. (2 Chronicles 19:2)

W e have just studied two companion pictures in the story of Judah's kings. We saw Rehoboam, a bad man with some good in him, Asa, a good man with some faults and now in Jehoshaphat we have a good man without personal faults, but who made the mistake of associating himself with bad men. He was good himself but became smirched by the foul odor of his companionship. This is a picture worth looking at, for it contains a lesson worth learning.

SECTION I—*The Story of Jehoshaphat*

Jehoshaphat came to the throne of his father Asa and his ancestor David at the age of 35, in his full manhood. He reigned for a quarter of a century, passing away at the age of 60, and leaving behind him a memory fragrant of good works and wise administration. He had seen enough of the mistakes of Asa to learn the lesson, and had so studied the character of David as to understand that he could not follow him blindly, but he walked in the "first ways" (17:3, KJV) and thus escaped the later dangers of both David's and Asa's lives.

AN UPRIGHT RULER

Jehoshaphat's name means "God is Judge," and he was true to its high spiritual significance. He walked in the clear light of God and he himself endeavored to judge as the representative of God. His reign began with the wisest and most vigorous administration. He thoroughly equipped his military establishment and had an army amounting to more than a million thoroughly drilled and equipped. He also had a chain of fortifications reaching up into the mountains of Ephraim beyond the borders of Israel, guarding the large frontier which his father had won from the northern kingdom. It would seem as if every adult male was in the army, for the entire population could not have exceeded six or seven million. Jehoshaphat used his resources to the utmost and kept them all in hand.

He looked after the civil administration of the state. He appointed courts of appeal with a supreme court in Judah at Jerusalem. He gave the strictest charges to the judges over them to administer their functions as in the very sight of God, for "with the LORD our God there is no injustice or partiality or bribery" (19:7).

A GODLY KING

He looked still deeper and higher and knew that "the fear of the LORD is the beginning of wisdom" (Proverbs 9:10), and he took pains to instruct his people in the law of God. The Higher Critics say that the law of God was not in existence until the days of Jeremiah, several centuries later. But we find it here in good shape and it had been there ever since the days of Moses, notwithstanding the Higher Critics. Jehoshaphat appointed princes and Levites representing the highest people in the land as a sort of educational bureau. They went all over the country reading the law of the Lord and instructing the people in the principles of righteousness and truth, and thus laying the foundations for true, solid national character. He put aside the vile Asherahs, and banished from the country the images and exterminated the worship of the groves with their obscene forms. In every possible way he reformed his kingdom and established the ordinances of civil government, and the worship of Jehovah.

No wonder "great wealth and honor" (2 Chronicles 17:5) came to him, and the fear of him was upon the nations round about, so that they came no more against him, with but one or two exceptions. National dignity and far-reaching influence followed the high principles which he exemplified and according to which he established his temporal throne.

WEALTH AND POWER

Jehoshaphat was a contemporary of the worst kings of Israel. He ascended the throne when Omri was king, and he reigned all through the time of Ahab, and for the first years of his son Ahaziah. He lived in the darkest age of the northern kingdom. He was also contemporary with the prophet Elijah, although he seemed not to have met him. But he was the intimate friend of Elisha, and we find this great prophet in his camp on one of the most important occasions in the history of his reign.

FRIENDSHIP WITH AHAB

A friendship grew up between the two courts of Ahab and Jehoshaphat, and his chief fault was an intimacy which led to almost all the evils of succeeding years. Three great wars occurred during his reign. The first, resulting from a foolish alliance with Ahab, inveigled Jehoshaphat to fight with the Syrians at Ramoth Gilead. He yielded in a moment of good nature to Ahab, and took his army to the battle. Treacherously Ahab got Jehoshaphat to wear his royal robes while Ahab hid to save his own life. Jehoshaphat was sorely pressed and almost lost his life. But he cried unto the Lord in the hour of his extremity and God saved him. He got no honor out of the battle, but God taught him a very solemn lesson. He sent a prophet to say to him, "Should you help the wicked and love those who hate the LORD? Because of this, the wrath of the LORD is upon you" (2 Chronicles 19:2).

BERACAH

The next great campaign was the one of which we read in Second Chronicles 20—that great conflict in the Valley of Beracah. There remains to us to the present day one of the most remarkable monuments of ancient times. It is known as the Moabite stone. It tells the full story of Moab during the reign of Jehoshaphat. It is the story of the king of Moab told by himself, how he invaded Israel and captured city after city from the old frontiers of the kingdom of Israel, and followed his victories by the usual cruelty of Oriental conquerors. It was after his northern invasion that, flushed with victory, laden with spoil and with a throng of auxiliary armies from the cities he had conquered, he suddenly appeared just at the edge of the Dead Sea, a little south of Jerusalem, at En Gedi. There were myriads upon myriads of these Moabites and Ammonites, and the crisis hour had at last come. We know the story well of that old battle of faith, where they had not to strike a blow, but sent out the white-robed singers to lead the charge. As they praised the Lord, and as Jehoshaphat stood in the front saying, "Have faith in the LORD your God and you will be upheld; have faith in his prophets and you will be successful" (20:20), the great fight was won and the story of Jericho's walls was paralleled once more, and the Lord sent disaster upon their enemies.

The historical explanation is that the Moabites got jealous of their allies on account of the spoils, and when Jehoshaphat got there he found they had killed each other, and there was nothing to do but to gather the spoil. It was a typical victory of faith. The Lord fights for us when we trust Him.

A FOOLISH ALLIANCE

The third campaign resulted from another foolish alliance with Ahab's son. He allowed himself to be drawn into it with a view to recover what

Mesha had captured before. The combined armies marched seven days into the desert and found a worse foe than the Moabities, the peril of a water famine, from which their noble army was in danger of perishing. Then the wicked king of Israel gave up, saying, "What! . . . Has the LORD called us three kings together only to hand us over to Moab" (2 Kings 3:10).

How different the spirit of Jehoshaphat even when he is in the wrong place. "Is there no prophet of the LORD here, that we may inquire of the LORD through him" (3:11)? And, lo, Elisha was in the camp. They brought him to the presence of the kings, and with scorn and contempt he turned from the king of Israel and said, "If I did not have respect for the presence of Jehoshaphat king of Judah, I would not look at you or even notice you" (3:14). But as the harpist played, the prophetic message came, bidding him to make the valley full of ditches. And then came the flooding of the ditches. In the morning the enemy supposed, from the shadows of the mountains and the crimson tints of the morning skies, that the ditches were filled with blood. They thought the enemy had slain one another, and started for the spoil. They found, however, the armies ready to meet them, and were repulsed with terrific slaughter, and driven back within the walls of their capital. The siege was raised only by the fearful tragedy of a human sacrifice, the only son and heir of Moab being the victim. As the armies of the allies witnessed this horrible sight on the walls of Kir they withdrew in dismay, and Moab was saved from extinctions. This was the last of Jehoshaphat's campaigns.

A BAD PARTNERSHIP

A little later he entered into a business partnership with Ahaziah, a great maritime trust. They built a commercial navy at Ezion Geber, Solomon's old haven on the Persian Gulf. But before their plans were consummated, Jehoshaphat received another rebuke from the prophet of Jehovah for his compromise with Israel's wicked king, and the intimation that his enterprise would end in disaster. The result was that "the ships were wrecked" (2 Chronicles 20:37), and the forbidden partnership ruined, and the story of his life closes under the cloud of God's displeasure.

SECTION II—*Lessons Learned from the Life of Jehoshaphat*

FAITHFULNESS

1. The first lesson involved the picture of a faithful servant in a place of high responsibility. He was the servant of the Lord and he recognized himself not as a king for his own benefit, but as a trustee for the nation and for the Lord. Faithfully he served his generation as a king.

There is nothing finer in human legends than the old motto of the German and English knighthood, "*Ich dien.*" Handed down to us from the days of chivalry, it has about it a true ring of both human nobility and Christian fidelity—"I serve." Each of us is a servant. In the constitution of human society no man can be independent. The king upon the throne is the servant of his people. The statesman at the forum is a public servant. The manager of that great corporation alike with the humblest clerk or laborer is a servant of society, and every one of us, whatever our station or calling, is called to serve.

Christianity does not change our circumstances, but introduces a motive and a principle which elevates and consecrates every occupation and action and links it with heaven. The sacred talisman which we find over and over again in the New Testament epistles is that little phrase, "in the Lord." Whether you are a husband or a wife, a parent or a child, a master or a servant, the key to all your actions is your relation to Christ. And the principle which dignifies and dedicates the humblest ministry is this:

> Whatever you do, whether in word or deed, do it all in the name of the Lord Jesus. . . . Whatever you do, work at it with all your heart, as working for the Lord, not for men, since you know that you will receive an inheritance from the Lord as a reward. It is the Lord Christ you are serving. (Colossians 3:17, 23–24)

Beloved, are we thus serving our Master and our generation, and winning the glorious guerdon by and by: "Well done, good and faithful servant! . . . Come and share your master's happiness" (Matthew 25:23).

FAITH

2. Jehoshaphat's life serves as an example of sublime faith in God in the most trying situations.

What can be finer than the picture in Second Chronicles 20 of the pious king of Judah, forgetting all about his great army of more than a million soldiers, and like a helpless child turning to his heavenly Father with the appeal, "For we have no power to face this vast army that is attacking us. We do not know what to do, but our eyes are upon you" (20:12). And then leading forth his hosts behind the white-robed choir of singers to the charge, while he exhorted them, "Have faith in the LORD your God and you will be upheld; have faith in his prophets and you will be successful" (20:20). That victory of faith and that Valley of Beracah have become the pattern and the inspiration of countless triumphs to the children of faith in every age.

Perhaps the most inspiring feature of Jehoshaphat's faith was the fact that in nearly all his situations of difficulty and danger he was himself to blame for his misfortunes. But this did not in the least diminish his confidence in God. Like a simple-hearted child he went straight back to the Father he had offended and threw himself upon His mercy and grace. No child of God ever did this in vain.

When pressed by the Syrians at Ramoth Gilead he had no business to be there. But none the less "Jehoshaphat cried out, and the LORD helped him. God drew them away from him" (18:31). Again his alliance with the armies of Ahaziah and the Edomites was all wrong. He had no business to be there. But God had anticipated his foolish act and sent the prophet Elisha to be on hand for the emergency. And while the wicked Ahaziah could see nothing but the vindictive purpose of the Lord watching for an opportunity to destroy them, the good Jehoshaphat immediately thought of resorting to his God for "grace to help . . . in . . . time of need" (Hebrews 4:16), and the help came.

The difference between the good man and the ungodly comes out in the hour of trial. The one sinks into sullen despair, the other rises to a higher confidence notwithstanding even his worst mistakes. The finest chapter in David's life was when he saw his crimson crime and yet could say, "Wash me, and I will be whiter than snow" (Psalm 51:7).

Will we accept the beautiful and comforting lesson to trust Him at all times, and even in the hour of our deepest failure to "approach the throne of grace with confidence, so that we may receive mercy and find grace to help us in our time of need" (Hebrews 4:16)?

A GOOD MAN IN THE WRONG PLACE

3. Jehoshaphat is a picture of a good man in the wrong place.

This is a most practical lesson. We may be faultless ourselves and yet neutralize much of our influence for good by evil associations and forbidden situations.

Condoning Their Sin

1. Jehoshaphat's first mistake was his friendly visit to Ahab and the court of Samaria. He must have known the utter wickedness of Ahab and Jezebel, and yet we find him feasting in their palace on terms of equal and intimate friendship.

This is all wrong. We cannot sit at the table of the wicked and accept their hospitality and their confidential friendship without being almost compelled to share, or, at least, condone, their sins. It was almost impossible for Jehoshaphat to receive the royal welcome of Ahab and then refuse his reasonable request for help against the enemy. "Have nothing to do with the fruitless deeds of darkness, but rather expose them" (Ephesians 5:11).

Reckless Compromise

2. Jehoshaphat's second mistake was his off-handed and impulsive consent to enter into alliance with Ahab and involve his kingdom and army in

an unholy war for the sole benefit of that wicked king. There is something very charming in the easy, generous good nature with which he met the request of Ahab, "I am as you are, and my people as your people" (2 Chronicles 18:3). He reminds us of many another generous fellow whose good nature is his bane. "Hail fellow, well met" is what the world calls it. But the sacred dignity of the child of God does not permit us thus to throw down all the bars of our separation and consecration in reckless compromises with the world. We are not as they are nor our people as their people, and we may not share their fearful responsibilities. Such compromises never pay.

In every instance Jehoshaphat was the loser and narrowly escaped losing everything. And it will always be true, "He who walks with the wise grows wise,/ but a companion of fools suffers harm" (Proverbs 13:20).

Forbidden Bonds

3. The intermarriage of his son and heir with the wicked house of Jezebel was the immediate result of Jehoshaphat's visit to Samaria. We may escape the tiger and fall into the hands of the tiger's cub. The bloody Athaliah became the frightful link that transferred the curse of Jezebel to the kingdom of Judah and led to the cutting off in the next generation of all Jehoshaphat's house except the infant Joash, who was saved by little less than a miracle.

God has forbidden such intermarriages between His people and the ungodly, and no minister of the Lord Jesus Christ has a right to celebrate such forbidden bonds. And no Christian girl or man is justified in running the risk of disobedience no matter how plausible the pretext may be.

I saw the beautiful Arve flow down from the spotless snows of the Alps into the muddy Rhone. For a few hundred yards it kept its crystal current clear, and then it was lost in the foul waters of the larger river. So I have seen a pure young life meet a worldly partner and a godless family. There was a short, brave struggle, and then, alas, the old story was once more proved true, "Bad company corrupts good character" (1 Corinthians 15:33). The testimony was quenched, and the very soul well nigh sunk in the dark floods of this present evil world.

Business and Social Ties

4. A business partnership was the last form of Jehoshaphat's compromise. Once already had he repeated his foolish mistake of forming a military alliance with Israel. He had joined Ahaziah, the son of Ahab, in the campaign against the Moabites already referred to, and had paid dearly for his error in the narrow escape he had from the water famine in the wilderness. But now he enters into a business partnership to reestablish the commercial navy of Solomon on the Persian Gulf. God sent a prophet to say to him, "Because

you have made an alliance with Ahaziah, the LORD will destroy what you have made" (2 Chronicles 20:37).

Many Christians think that, while intermarriage with the ungodly and intimate social fellowship may be unwise, "business is business," and it is nobody's business who are your partners in secular affairs. This is not so. The New Testament distinctly forbids all partnership between God's people and the ungodly. "For what do righteousness and wickedness have in common? Or what fellowship can light have with darkness? What harmony is there between Christ and Belial? What does a believer have in common with an unbeliever?" (2 Corinthians 6:14–15). You may not always lose your ships in these unholy partnerships, but you may lose your peace, your spiritual life and your children's souls.

What a solemn lesson does this good king teach us! How searchingly should the question come home to each of us: *Are we in any false position, forbidden connection or wrong place?* The enemy of your soul is the god of this world, who wants nothing so much as to have the credit and countenance of God's people. He will give a free ticket to any of his excursions for the benefit of your presence and the advertising value of your name, but you will lose much more than your fare. What a solemn prayer is that of the Psalmist: "Do not take away my soul along with sinners" (Psalm 26:9)! What a dreadful thing for the Lord to find you at His coming among His enemies!

Once, it is said, in a police raid in New York City, a modest and beautiful young lady, evidently of unblemished character, was found among the women arrested in a disorderly house. She was deeply humiliated and almost ready to die with shame, begging the officers on no account to divulge her name. In a short time she was able to secure the most unquestionable testimonials to her character, and it was very evident she had no sort of likeness to the women among whom she found herself in the police court. This was the explanation: Through an advertisement in the public papers and through the plausible deceit of the runner for this disorderly house, she had taken a room in a most innocent way, in what she supposed to be a respectable building. Before she discovered the character of the other tenants, the police raided the building and without making any inquiry about her she was dragged away in the common net. She ultimately secured her release and narrowly saved her reputation, but it was a very close chance, and there was infinite pathos in her distress and anguish when she found herself in the company of these lost men and women.

Even if you yourselves escape defilement, how terrible it would be for the Lord to find you among His foes! Should we not constantly send up to Him the cry, "Do not take away my soul along with sinners" (26:9)? And in order to cooperate in its fulfillment, let us not only shun evil, but "avoid every kind of evil" (1 Thessalonians 5:22).

CHAPTER 13

JOASH, OR THE BAD END OF A GOOD BEGINNING

Joash did what was right in the eyes of the LORD all the years of Jehoiada the priest. (2 Chronicles 24:2)

J ehoshaphat died at the age of 60 amid the peace and honor which his lofty character and righteous reign had so well earned. But he left to his family and his kingdom, through his weak and foolish compromises with wicked men, a heritage of sorrow. He sowed the wind and left them to reap the whirlwind.

SECTION I—*The Background of Joash*

JEHORAM

Jehoshaphat was succeeded by his son Jehoram at the age of 32. Already this young prince with his father's consent had allied himself with the wicked house of Ahab by marrying Athaliah, the daughter of Jezebel. True to her influence he signalized his ascension to the throne by murdering his six brothers and thus leaving himself without a rival.

He next proceeded to undo all the good work of his father's reign and re-establish the vile worship of his wife's family, and restore the altars of Baal and the groves of Asherah with their obscene rites all over the land, so compelling the men and women of Judah to minister at the impure altars of the Sidonian religion.

ELIJAH

It was in this connection that the prophet Elijah for the first time interposed in the history of the southern kingdom. He sent what the chronicler calls "a writing" to the wicked king, rebuking his daring impiety and announcing to him the judgment of God upon his kingdom and also upon his own person in the form of a loathsome and fatal disease. It was not long until the judgments of God began to materialize. First the Edomites revolted and regained their independence. And next the Philistines and Arabians invaded Judah, captured Jerusalem and carried off his treasure, his wives and his sons, leaving only the youngest son, Ahaziah, to continue the dynasty.

Soon after the final tragedy came, and by a hideous living death, his miserable life was ended, and his body literally fell to pieces as Elijah had predicted. His funeral was as ignominious as his reign, and even his own subjects refused to bury him in the sepulcher of the kings.

AHAZIAH

His youngest son, Ahaziah, succeeded and was the mere puppet and tool of the queen mother, Athaliah, during the one short year of his infamous reign. He went with Ahab's son to fight the Syrians at Ramoth Gilead, and while resting at Samaria to be healed of his wounds he fell into the hands of Jehu when he was executing his terrible judgments upon Jezebel and her house. Along with Jehoram, king of Israel, he was slain as well as a large company of the princes of Judah, who were at the same time on a visit to the northern court.

ATHALIAH

Athaliah, his mother, infuriated by the destruction of her family, seized the opportunity to usurp the throne. To make her possession the more secure, she murdered the entire royal seed of her own family. At least she thought she had. But in this she was mistaken, for another woman was raised up by God to counteract her wicked policy and save the house of David from extinction. Jehosheba, the wife of Jehoiada, the priest, and herself the daughter of King Jehoram, though not by Athaliah, was used of God to save the infant Joash from the wholesale assassination.

She hid him first in the storeroom of the palace among some clothes. Afterwards she smuggled him into the temple, where for six years he was brought up under the care of herself and her husband. There they trained and prepared Joash for his future destiny.

Meanwhile, during those six years, Athaliah held a carnival of idolatry and crime. Doubtless this carnival of revelry was one of God's providential instruments in preparing the way for her final overthrow by producing a growing reaction against her own daring wickedness.

SECTION II—*The Life of Joash*

THE REVOLUTION

At length the crisis hour came for which the faithful leader had long been preparing. On a certain Sabbath morning a large company of princes, priests and Levites, whom Jehoiada had taken into his confidence, were armed and stationed within the temple courts. At the appointed moment the little king was brought forth from his hiding arrayed in the royal robes and placed on an elevated dais in sight of all the people, where he was solemnly anointed and crowned. The scroll of the sacred law was placed above the crown upon his head as the sacred symbol of his authority and the law of the kingdom. At the same time the shout was raised and taken up by the great multitude outside, "Long live the king" (23:11), until the ominous sounds reached the ears of Athaliah in her palace.

Startled but not afraid—true to the audacious courage of her brilliant but wicked mother—she immediately hastened to the scene attended, according to Josephus, by her military guards. But the guards of Jehoiada were already posted and armed at the temple gates and she was compelled to enter alone. The moment her eye fell upon the coronation scene she took the situation in and made a wild appeal for popular sympathy, crying, "Treason! treason!" (23:13). But there was no response. The revolution was too well planned for failure. Jehoiada immediately ordered that she be carried from the sacred precincts of the temple to the horse gate in the rear, where baggage and beasts of burden entered, and there slain. And so without a note of sympathy or a hand raised to help her she fell in her own blood, rendering blood for blood for the murders and outrages that have so well entitled her to be called the "Bloody Mary" of her time.

THE GOOD BOY KING

Joash was now established upon his throne without a rival or a challenge. Under the wise and venerable counsel and cooperation of the good Jehoiada, the first part of his reign, covering perhaps about 25 years, was worthy of the best traditions of Jehoshaphat and David. It was indeed a unique and beautiful spectacle to see that boy king of only seven years zealously and loyally restoring the sacred temple that had been the shelter and home of his early years.

THE CHANGE

But after the death of Jehoiada there came a melancholy change. That grand old man lived to the extraordinary age of 137, so that he must have been over a century old when he led the brilliant *coup* that dethroned Athaliah and restored the dynasty of David. He was buried like a king in the sepulcher of Judah's kings, and his character and influence had held the nation loyal at once to Jehovah and Joash to the very close of his venerable life. But when he was gone it was soon apparent how little of the character of Joash was his own and how much but the reflected goodness of his teacher and foster father.

FASHION

The young king began to court the society of the aristocracy of the kingdom, and these had always been the patrons and friends of idolatry. Judah and Israel got their fashions and their fine arts from the splendid commercial capitals of Tyre and Sidon. And along with their fashions and their culture came their idolatry.

RITUALISM

The old and simple faith of Judaism seemed dull compared with the splendid ritual and the mystic philosophy of the Oriental faiths. And just as today the intellectual conceit of our times is running after such fads as Christian Science and Theosophy, so it was then, and Joash's unstable mind was soon carried away by the popular fashion and the old altars were established and the groves of Isis and Asherah were again swarming over all the land.

REPROOF REJECTED

Then God sent the prophet Zechariah to reprove the sinful king. Instead of humbling his heart he murdered the prophet. The blood of the first martyr of Israel stained the sanctuary of the Lord and left such an awful shadow upon his name that Christ Himself refers to the "blood of Zechariah, who was killed between the altar and the sanctuary" (Luke 11:51) as the climax of Israel's crimes.

THE SAD ENDING

After this pronounced and aggravated step Joash's iniquity ripened fast and judgment followed swiftly. Hazael, the king of Syria, with a small army invaded Judah. But the sacred narrative adds with strange emphasis, "Although the Aramean army had come with only a few men, the LORD delivered into their hands a much larger army. Because Judah had forsaken the LORD, the God of their fathers" (2 Chronicles 24:24). Jerusalem was captured and despoiled of all its treasure and the princes of Judah carried captive. Joash himself was left on a bed of painful sickness. The climax of the tragedy soon came when two of his own servants, doubtless representing the anger and disappointment of the people at their terrible defeat slew him upon his bed, and his dishonored body, although buried in the city of Jerusalem, it was refused a place in the sepulchers of Judah's kings.

Could there be a contrast more pitiful and terrible than that between the child king of seven years with his fresh and glorious crown upon his radiant brow, as he began his reign amid the benedictions of heaven and the shouts of his people's acclamation, and the ignominious grave of the same king after 40 years of failure, disobedience and divine judgment? It reminds one of the familiar story of Raphael's painting of John the Beloved and Judas Iscariot, for which the model in each case was the same, the first a radiant youth in the beauty of innocent manhood, the second the same man 12 years later when sin had set its awful mark upon his disfigured face and debilitated frame. How tragic the story! How solemn the lessons!

SECTION III—*Lessons Learned from the Life of Joash*

JEHOSHAPHAT'S MISTAKES

1. The first lesson relates to the misery that follows the mistakes of a good man. Jehoshaphat little dreamed of the heritage of woe he was bequeathing to posterity when he celebrated the marriage of his son and heir to the daughter of Jezebel. Just as many a Christian father and mother would not believe even if they were told by an angelic vision of the sin and ruin they are preparing for some loved child long after they have gone to heaven by introducing them to the pleasures and temptations of the world.

THE POWER OF A WOMAN

2. We see the power of a woman for good and for ill. What could be more bitter than the awful blight that Athaliah brought on all she touched! But what could be more blessed than the wise and beneficent goodness of that other woman whom God raised up to counteract her influence and save young Joash from her bloody hand? If woman can be the worst of transgressors and tempters she can also be the best of our earthly blessings. Oh woman, how great are the possibilities of your destiny!

A CHILD

3. We see the value of a child. How beautiful the light this story sheds on childhood. A little babe of one year old was the sole link that saved the dynasty of David and the very lineage of Jesus Christ. "Only a child"—never say it again. That child may carry in its bosom the destiny of a nation or a world.

MOTHERHOOD

4. Another lesson deals with the sacredness and influence of motherhood. The value of that child is the measure of your responsibility to teach him or to save him. Never think it a trifling task to train the future teachers, preachers and statesmen of our land. The first five years of human life strike the keynote of all later life. The mother, the nurse or the teacher that can seal these earliest impressions upon the child's mind, is the most potent influence in every human life. And if perchance you have no children of your own to train, like Jehosheba, play the part of motherhood to some of His

lambs who are wandering without a shepherd, or worse, with motherhood which brings nothing but a curse.

A BRIGHT EXAMPLE

5. Joash stands as an example for every child. This is a message not only to parents and teachers, but to children themselves. What fairer picture could be set before you than this little child king devoting himself to the house of God? The house of God stood not only for the Church today, but for the cause of God. Children should be taught to love the services of God's house. The Sunday school is not a substitute for public worship, and childhood is just the time to receive and seal those spiritual impressions which form the religious character of men and women. Thank God for the little hands and hearts like Joash that are building the temple of the Lord and sending forth the gospel to a perishing world.

LEANING ON OTHERS

6. The story of Joash also shows us the danger of leaning on others. After all the good things we have said about the foster parents of Joash, they proved to be—at least in a measure—his bane from the fact that he had leaned too much on them, and did not possess those elements of personal character and fixed principle without which the best examples can be of no permanent value to us. There are plenty of people who easily absorb, chameleon like, the colors that surround them. They can repeat glibly the spiritual phrases they have heard until they have learned to think they have a corresponding experience. But when they come under different influences they take on the next color just as readily.

Joash was like Jehoiada as long as the old priest was near. But he was just as ready to absorb the ideas and imitate the vices of the cultured people who surrounded him after Jehoiada was gone. It was the old story of Joshua and the next generation. As soon as Joshua was gone they relapsed into their old ways. So how often we find the families of Christians and ministers going into every excess of worldliness and sin after the best examples have been given and even the best beginnings have been made. Rest in nothing less than personal character and conviction. Hereditary religion cannot avail you. Do not accept the faith of your fathers because you were born in it, but get your convictions from your Bible and in your own heart; and when "the rain descends, and the winds blow" you will find your house is on a rock.

PUBLIC MEN

7. This story provides a noble example for public men. The story of Jehoiada is a splendid pattern for the statesman of today. The curse of our modern political life is selfishness and timeserving. This grand old man had

no end but to honor his Master and help his king to be good and glorious. He lived for his God. Oh, the politicians that have twisted and writhed under all the contortions of political compromise to gain the highest offices, and ended their careers in bitter disappointment! God save the young men of today from selfish ambition! It will always defeat itself, and uprightness, honesty and sincerity always win.

PROGRESSION IN SIN

8. We see the bitter progress of sin. How swift and terrible was the fall of Joash! Beginning in the company of the worldly and wicked, it led on fast to idolatry and irreligion. Who could imagine that fair boy, with the crown upon his brow and the Word of God as a bright diadem upon his head, a child of Cain, with the blood of the first prophet's murder upon his hands? Oh friends, if some of you could see your future as God sees it and the lengths to which your wicked heart will carry you yet and from which His grace is trying to hold you back, you would cry out with agony and say, "Lord, save me from myself!"

RETRIBUTION

9. Joash provides us a lesson in the inexorable law of retribution. "Whatever he has done must be done to him" (Leviticus 24:19). This old aphorism is as true as the law of gravity, and our lesson is full of its illustrations. Jehoram, Ahaziah, Athaliah and Joash all found it true. "Whoever sheds the blood of man,/ by man shall his blood be shed" (Genesis 9:6). The dart you hurl will come back to you and "you may be sure that your sin will find you out" (Numbers 32:23).

GRACE

10. Finally, it is a delight to find back of the story of Joash one of the most glorious revelations of the grace of God. For it was in the reign of Joash that the first of Judah's prophets arose and left us his beautiful message in writing. It was the prophet Joel. It was when this backsliding king was bringing on his country every calamity that Joel stepped forward and called for a national fast to avert the threatened judgments, and in response to the repentance of the people uttered those sublime prophecies and promises which have been the keynote of later prophets and even of many of the apostolic messages. It was he who taught them the coming of the Holy Spirit who would put into our poor, helpless, human nature a power which the law could never give—to keep God's commandments and be steadfast in His ways.

There is a humorous story of a little girl who was set at a tedious task by a Puritan aunt who required of her the hemming of a lot of napkins. The little fingers stood it for a time and at last grew tired and resolved to strike. With a quaint fancy she determined to stop at the 101st stitch, and under no condition would she make "the 102th [sic]." Very slowly did she carry out her stern resolve, for she felt it meant a great crisis. The last two or three stitches were held back long and gravely, but at length the fatal number struck and the napkin was thrown aside with its unfinished task. The punishment was inexorable; no food until the work was finished. But the little will was as resolute as the Puritan aunt's, and supper passed and the night rolled on with no relenting.

The story is told in much greater detail than would suit our purpose to repeat. Suffice it to say that it was pathetic to see the little hungry girl watching the chickens eat their corn and wondering how it tasted. It was still more heartrending to watch her as she slept and dreamed that night, and see the suppressed sob and hear the half-uttered sentences that told of the feasts that were passing before her slumbering mind. At last the aunt could stand it no longer. She went to her minister for advice, but the minister's wife gave her little comfort and suggested some sharp things about the spirit of the gospel rather than the law, which must have had their effect. The good lady broke down, awakened the slumbering child and told her to hurry and dress and come down for supper. You may be sure this did not take very long, and when they met in the dining room and looked at that laden board with plates for two, it turned out that good auntie, with a better heart than she had been given credit for, had fasted too. The little child, before she sat down at the table or touched the viands for which she was famished, flung herself into her auntie's arms and cried, "Auntie, I took the 102th stitch before I came downstairs."

Yes, friend, that is the old story of the gospel of Jesus Christ and the face of God. That is the only thing that can break the heart and change the life. That is what the Holy Spirit has brought. You cannot do it, but you take Him and then He will do it for you. Oh, accept His grace and receive the Holy Spirit!

CHAPTER 14

JOEL AND HIS TIMES

The word of the LORD that came to Joel. (Joel 1:1)

As a lighthouse is planted on the storm-beaten shore and shines in the midnight darkness, so God's lighthouses all along the shores of time are placed amid the darkest scenes of human history.

It was when Ahab and Jezebel were deluging Samaria with martyr blood and idolatrous iniquity, that Elijah was sent with his heavenly messages and holy fire. It was when Israel was sinking to her long night that the prophet Hosea came with his message of mercy for God's prodigal people. It was when Jerusalem was passing into the shadows of the tragedy of the Babylonian captivity that Jeremiah hovered as a guardian angel over her darkening night. And so it was in the days of Joash, after the good child king had become the cruel oppressor and had brought upon himself and his country the judgments of heaven, that Joel was sent as the first in that illustrious series of sacred prophets which includes Isaiah, Jeremiah, Ezekiel, Daniel and other honored messengers of God's prophetic will.

The name Joel is the same as Elijah, only inverted; it means "one whose God is Jehovah." It is a revelation at once of the greatness and goodness of the Lord, and Joel's message is true to the meaning of his significant name.

THE TEXT OF LATER PROPHETS

Joel's little book, which would just about fill a column in one of our modern daily papers, contains the keynote and the kernel of the most important messages of the later prophets. Amos begins his longer message with a direct quotation from Joel as a sort of text for his whole book. Isaiah expands the thoughts which Joel uttered into the larger and loftier message of his pen. Peter, on the day of Pentecost, quotes the prophecy of Joel as the very foundation of the outpouring of the Holy Spirit which had just occurred, and which was to continue through the whole New Testament age.

And even the great Apocalypse of John is but a larger unfolding of the promise of the Lord's coming, which Joel gave in brief outline. Thus our prophet becomes the pioneer of all Judah's prophets and the forerunner of the gospel of the New Testament, and the very Advent of the Lord himself.

Let us briefly glance at the outline and plan of this prophetic volume.

SECTION I—*A Vision of Judgment*

It begins with a vision of judgment. Primarily, it is a visitation of locusts, one of the most fearful plagues of Eastern countries, but this is but a type of the greater judgment referred to again and again throughout the book as the "day of the LORD."

LOCUSTS
Joel 1:2–12, 2:1–11

The picture of the locust army is most vivid and dramatic. The sound of their wings is like the distant rumble of the chariots of a mighty army amid the mountains. Like clouds of darkness they cover all the heavens and the sun and moon grow dim and the stars withdraw their shining. Over every barrier they march resistlessly on, everyone in his place like disciplined soldiers, and swords and spears are powerless to turn them aside.

Up the city walls, over the houses, in through the crevices of the windows, everywhere they swarm and everything is destroyed before them. The cattle perish on the blighted fields, the vintage is blighted on the mountains, the fertile valleys are like a withered desert. And the very offering of the temple is impossible, because everything has been devoured. The locusts themselves at last become their own destroyers, as they perish of starvation on the land which they have stripped of vegetation, and their corrupting bodies cover the land from the Dead Sea to the Mediterranean, until the stench fills the air and brings pestilence to the people.

A TYPE OF FUTURE JUDGMENT
Joel 1:13–20

In this terrible visitation, the prophet saw the type of God's final judgment on the wicked. The heaven and the earth are full of flaming symbols and pledges of that one day at which the scoffer laughs in vain. Yonder lake of brimstone in the valley of the Jordan remains to this day as a fragment of the hell that infidelity derides; while the earthquake that so often shakes our planet, and the flaming star that disappears in a cataclysm of fire are other witnesses to this same truth. All these are but pointers to that great day for which all other days were made, "The day of the LORD," which draws nearer as the story of human history hastens to its consummation.

SECTION II—*A Call to Repentance*

Joel brings us a call to repentance. In view of this visitation of judgment which is darkening their priests and the people to individual and national repentance. "Return to me," he cries in the name of the Lord, " 'with all your heart,/ with fasting and weeping and mourning.'/ Rend your heart/ and not your garments./ Return to the LORD your God,/ for he is gracious and compassionate,/ slow to anger and abounding in love,/ and he relents from sending calamity" (Joel 2:12–13).

The people are to gather from their homes, the children and their mothers are assembled in the great congregation, the bridegroom and the bride are commanded to weep between the porch and the altar, and the whole nation bows prostrate and pleading at the feet of their King.

THE MINISTRY OF JOHN

In all this we have the echo of God's ancient law and the picture of the ministry of John the Baptist, which was soon to be ushered in with its message of repentance.

And while this is not the whole gospel, it is the foundation of the gospel. Its place is primary and necessary. Without a deep and thorough conviction of sin there can be no true appreciation of the atonement and grace of the Lord Jesus Christ. And without a similar and deeper conviction, not merely of our past sins, but of our deep sinfulness of nature, we cannot pass on to the higher experience of sanctification and a mature spiritual life.

Yes, and it is also true that before great public blessings can be poured out upon the Church of Christ and the work of God there must be the same profound preparation as in Joel, by humiliation and waiting upon God for his mercy and blessing.

SECTION III—*A Promise of Mercy and Restoration*

Joel proclaims a promise of mercy and restoration. Not in vain did they wait upon their God. "Then the LORD will be jealous for his land/ and take pity on his people" (2:18). "Be not afraid, O land;/ be glad and rejoice./ Surely the LORD has done great things" (2:21).

MERCY AND DELIVERANCE

First comes His mercy and forgiveness. He is still the same. He delights not in judgment. He waits to be gracious. He loves to forgive and save.

Next, He delivers from the temporal judgment that was impending. He removes the destroyer from their midst. The same God still says to us, "But if we judged ourselves, we would not come under judgment" (1 Corinthians 11:31). Chastening may be averted by repentance and obedience.

THE PAST RECOVERED

But best of all, He promises to make up for what they have lost. There is no more precious promise in all the Bible than Joel 2:25: "I will repay you for the years the locusts have eaten—/ the great locust and the young locust,/ the other locusts and the locust swarm—/ my great army that I sent among you."

There is a false theology of hopeless fatalism which tells people that although their past may be forgiven and their future assured, yet they must reap the consequences of their follies and pay the penalty in the life of their errors and sins. This is not the gospel. Jesus Christ has borne all our curse and the life that fully trusts Him may claim His restoring, as well as His redeeming grace, and the undoing of all that our sin has done.

Augustine found himself a physical and moral wreck, yet he arose from the ruin of his youth and fortune to live to an old age of vigor, honor, happiness and worldwide blessing to millions. His life is but a sample of what God is doing today in the bodies and the families and even the fortunes of many a man and woman who has been snatched as a brand from the burning, and used as a torch to light the darkness of other lives.

Is there anyone reading these lines whose life is a wreck, and whose crimes have ruined others along with you? Listen to the message that comes back to you from the man whose God was Jehovah: "I will repay you for the years the locusts have eaten" (2:25), and you, too, may become a monument to the fact that

> Nothing is too hard for Jesus,
> No man can work like Him.

And not only shall your past be undone, but your future shall be filled with overflowing blessings. "You will have plenty to eat, until you are full,/ and you will praise the name of the LORD your God,/ who has worked wonders for you;/ never again will my people be shamed" (2:26). God is able to satisfy every need of the human heart and even of our mortal frame, and the life that was as dark as despair may be as bright as heaven.

SECTION IV—*The Coming of Jesus*

Next, there is the promise of Jesus Christ. Joel's prophecy passes on to a higher plane, and next it reaches the coming of the Savior Himself and His incarnation as "He appeared in a body" (1 Timothy 3:16). "Then you will know that I am in Israel,/ that I am the LORD your God,/ and that there is no other" (Joel 2:27). This sublime promise is more than deliverance, more than the coming of blessing, prosperity and happiness. It is the coming of their God to dwell among them.

It is the fulfillment of that lofty dream which we find in ancient poetry and mythology, and which was embodied in the idolatrous systems of Greece and Rome and breathed out in the ancient books of India. It was the cry of an embodiment and incarnation of God Himself. It was the cry of Philip, expressed a little later in the New Testament, "Lord, show us the Father and that will be enough for us" (John 14:8). And God has answered that cry. "In the past God spoke to our forefathers through the prophets at many times and in various ways, but in these last days he has spoken to us by his Son" (Hebrews 1:1–2).

THE VISITATION OF GOD

The gospel begins with the visitation of God Himself. The Babe in Bethlehem's manger was no mere child of mortal mother. His high and glorious name, Immanuel, meant, "God with us" (Matthew 1:23). The prophet that announced Him could literally say: "Praise be to the Lord, the God of Israel,/ because he has come and has redeemed his people" (Luke 1:68).

It is no small or trifling matter that the hands into which God has committed the eternal salvation of your soul and mine are more than human hands, even the hands of the everlasting God. This is the fundamental fact of Christianity; God has come into our nature and our planet and He is God and none else.

SECTION V—*The Outpouring of the Holy Spirit*

Pentecost

Joel tells of the outpouring of the Holy Spirit. This is Joel's next and greatest message. It was this that Peter quoted on the day of Pentecost. It is this that has given character to our age—the Holy Spirit as a divine enduement for life and work. Let us note a few points in this promise of the Spirit:

Afterwards

(a) It was to be "afterward," that is, it did not belong to the Old Testament dispensation, but to the New. The Holy Spirit was to be the gift of Christ and to come after His earthly ministry had been finished (Joel 2:28).

Poured Out

(b) God was to "pour out" (2:28) the Spirit. It was to be an abundant and boundless bestowment. Under the former dispensation the Spirit was limited to a few persons and special occasions, but now the Holy Spirit is given without measure to all who can receive Him.

Upon All People

(c) He was to be poured out upon "all people." Former visitations of the Spirit were limited to the Jewish people, but this was to be a universal and worldwide blessing.

All Ages and Classes

(d) All ages and classes were to receive His influences and there was to be no distinction of men or women, old or young, lord or slave, but the humblest and most illiterate were to be as competent to receive His gifts and work for His cause as the most cultured and lofty minds.

Supernatural Signs and Wonders

(e) It was to be accompanied by supernatural signs and miraculous powers, such as marked Christ's personal ministry, in the healing of the sick, the casting out of demons, etc. These are still manifested wherever the Holy Spirit is fully recognized and we fully claim His working.

Continuous

(f) The outpouring of the Spirit and the effects of his presence were to continue up to the very close of the age and down to the coming of the Lord. Joel distinctly declares in this prophecy that the supernatural signs are to lead up to the coming of that great and terrible day of the Lord. The promise of Pentecost was not a temporary, but a permanent one, and the Church of Christ has a right to expect the same divine presence as in apostolic times. Indeed, this was the reason why the Lord Jesus claimed to perform all His miracles, not through His own personal deity merely, but by the Holy Spirit. And so the very same Agent who wrought the miracles of Christ is still present in the body of Christ to work through His name as of old.

Widespread Salvation

(g) The Pentecostal blessing was to be accompanied with a widespread work of salvation. He adds, "And everyone who calls/ on the name of the LORD will be saved" (2:32). The presence of the Holy Spirit produces power in the ministry and conviction in the hearts of the people. It is the only secret of soul winning. If we want to see more saved today we must seek the same Source of supernatural power and meet the conditions which He Himself has given for the enduement of His Church and people with "power from on high" (Luke 24:49).

ISRAEL'S REMNANT

Along with the salvation of multitudes, there is also a special promise of the salvation of the remnant of Israel. The translation here is a little faulty. A literal rendering of Joel 2:32 is: "And in the remnant, such as the LORD shall call." By the remnant is meant the children of Abraham, who are in the world today and who are blinded for the present to their true Messiah, but in due time shall have the veil taken away and receive Him as their King. Meanwhile, however, the apostle says: "So too, at the present time there is a remnant chosen by grace" (Romans 11:5). That is, some of the children of Israel are even now being led to accept Christ, as well as the great multitudes from among the Gentles who receive Him. We are, therefore, to expect the conversion of Jews in our day, not in large numbers at present, but as a remnant, a little sample as it were, of the whole nation which is yet to crown Jesus as their King.

Let us be true to this part of the gospel of Jesus Christ. Let us seek for the lost sheep of the house of Israel, and thus be carrying out the purpose of the Holy Spirit, the plan of the Lord Jesus and the preparation of His second coming.

SECTION VI—*The Day of the Lord*

Joel proclaims the coming of the day of the Lord. This is the climax of Joel's vision.

(a) It is to be preceded by preternatural signs. "The sun will be turned to darkness/ and the moon to blood/ before the coming of the great and dreadful day of the LORD" (Joel 2:31).

(b) It is to be ushered in by war and tumult. "Prepare for war!/ Rouse the warriors!" (3:9). "Beat your plowshares into swords/ and your pruning hooks into spears" (3:10). "Let the nations be roused;/ let them advance into the Valley of Jehoshaphat,/ for there I will sit/ to judge all the nations on every side" (3:12).

(c) It is to be accompanied by the angels of heaven. "Bring down your warriors, O LORD!" (3:11). These are the mighty angels who are to accompany the final appearing of Jesus Christ.

(d) It is to end in the overthrow and destruction of the ungodly nations.

> Swing the sickle,
>   for the harvest is ripe.
> Come, trample the grapes,
>   for the winepress is full
>   and the vats overflow—

so great is their wickedness!

Multitudes, multitudes
in the valley of decision! (3:13–14)

This is the same figure that John uses in the book of Revelation, where the "winepress of God's wrath" (14:19) is used to describe God's final judgment upon the wicked nations.

(e) It is to be also accompanied by the revelation of God in His glory. "The LORD will roar from Zion/ and thunder from Jerusalem;/ the earth and the sky will tremble" (Joel 3:16).

(f) It is to be a day of salvation for His own people. The Lord "will be a refuge for his people,/ a stronghold for the people of Israel" (3:16). Literally, this means the "harbor" or place of refuge on that awful day. When the heaven and the earth will be dissolved the only place of refuge in all the universe will be the Rock of Ages, the bosom of Jesus. Let us make haste to make it our refuge now.

(g) All this is to close with the personal reign of Jesus Christ on earth. "Then you will know that I, the LORD your God,/ dwell in Zion, my holy hill" (3:17). Israel shall be restored, the earth itself shall be reconstituted, "the mountains will drip new wine,/ and the hills will flow with milk;/ all the ravines of Judah will run with water./ A fountain will flow out of the LORD's house/ and will water the valley of acacias" (3:18). (That is, the desert where the acacia always grows).

This is a little foregleam of that glorious day which is soon to dawn upon our dark and wintry world. Not always will Israel's tribes be scattered and despised. They shall yet "sing in the heights of Zion" and "sit under [their] own vine/ . . . and fig tree" (Micah 4:4). Not always will the stormy winter, the yawning ocean and the devouring grave blight this sin-cursed earth, but some day earth will be a summerland of love. "There was no longer any sea" (Revelation 21:1). "There will be no more death or mourning or crying or pain" (21:4). "For the Lamb at the center of the throne will be their shepherd;/ he will lead them to springs of living water./ And God will wipe every tear from their eyes" (7:17). "Come, Lord Jesus" (22:20). Come quickly!

CHAPTER 15

MICAH AND HIS MESSAGE

Micah of Moresheth prophesied in the days of Hezekiah king of Judah. He told all the people of Judah, "This is what the LORD Almighty says:

> *'Zion will be plowed like a field,*
> *Jerusalem will become a heap of rubble,*
> *the temple hill a mound overgrown with thickets.'*

Did Hezekiah king of Judah or anyone else in Judah put him to death? Did not Hezekiah fear the LORD and seek his favor? And did not the LORD relent, so that he did not bring the disaster he pronounced against them? We are about to bring a terrible disaster on ourselves!" (Jeremiah 26:18–19)

This brief reminiscence, a century and a half after the days of Micah the prophet, throws an interesting light upon his writings and ministry, and shows us the high place of respect and honor that he held in the estimation of his country.

SECTION I—*The Life and Message of Micah*

Micah was the second, in order of time, of the prophets of Judah whose writings have been preserved to us. His period was perhaps a century later than that of Joel, whose life and writings were our last theme. The powerful impulse given to the spiritual life of the nation through Joel's ministry survived him for more than 100 years. The great revival that he had inspired continued to bear fruit through the reign of three successive kings, and the prosperity and blessings which God had given them in connection with that revival were abundantly fulfilled during the succeeding century.

AMAZIAH

Amaziah, the successor of Joash, began his reign well, but ended like so many of his dynasty, in a sad declension from God, and brought upon his kingdom grave calamities.

UZZIAH

But Uzziah, his successor, raised the dignity and power of Judah to a higher plane than any of his predecessors since the days of Solomon. For more than half a century he carried the victorious arms of Judah against all the surrounding enemies of his country. He again brought under tribute the Philistines on the west, the Arabians on the south, and the Ammonites on the east. He fortified Jerusalem and other places with the strongest defenses, and the latest military engines of his time. He organized a powerful army of more than 300,000 men and established the prestige of his name among all the surrounding nations.

The record in Second Chronicles speaks in the most emphatic terms of his power and prosperity: "As long as he sought the LORD, God gave him success" (26:5). "Because he had become very powerful" (26:8). "His fame spread far and wide, for he was greatly helped until he became powerful" (26:15). His end, however, was like the others, overshadowed by a dark eclipse. The spiritual vitality of even the good kings of Judah did not seem sufficient to outlive their natural life. Like some tree rotten at the heart, which decays and falls before its time, so most of them ended their career with a record of humiliation.

DESTROYED BY PROSPERITY

With Uzziah it was his very strength that at last destroyed him. In his presumptuous willfulness, he insisted upon entering the Holy Place and offering incense at the altar where only priests might minister. The high priest, with 80 of his assistants, tried in vain to withstand him. As Uzziah pushed his way through, the hand of God smote him with a withering leprosy. And Josephus tells us that in the same hour an awful earthquake shattered the temple and rent the ceiling, so that a gleam of sunshine poured through the breach and disclosed the white face of the stricken king, who himself was only too glad to escape from the awful Presence that he had insulted. God's blessings, however, continued to be manifest even through the reign of his son and successor, Jotham, who was a good king, and whose 16 years of sovereignty were summed up in the honorable mention of Second Chronicles 27:6, "Jotham grew powerful because he walked steadfastly before the LORD his God."

But all the while the leaven of wickedness had been working in secret even in Jotham's time. It is said, "The people, however, continued their corrupt practices" (27:2). The death of Jotham was the signal for the outbreak of the malignant disease that had been slowly developing.

AHAZ

Ahaz, Jotham's successor, was perhaps the worst of all Judah's kings, and only the difference of a single letter in his name distinguished him from Ahab of Israel. They both reached the climax of royal iniquity. Not only did Ahaz yield to all the public tendencies of the corrupt people, but in every way he endeavored to promote idolatry and ungodliness. He sold his country to the new Assyrian power which had risen up on the Euphrates under the famous Pul or Tiglath-Pileser. He despoiled the temple of its precious jewels and gold to pay tribute to the Assyrian king and secure his help against other adversaries. And while visiting Damascus his artistic fancy was struck by a beautiful altar which he immediately copied and had set up in the temple at Jerusalem, and there he himself ministered as a priest in the idolatrous ceremonies which this altar represented. The house of God was apparently closed to the worship of Jehovah. The vile and obscene rites of the Baal worship were reestablished all over the cities and the land. And he even offered one of his own children as a human sacrifice on the altar of Moloch.

He seems to have been a special devotee of fine art, and proved, as has so often since been proved, that aesthetic culture has no connection with moral purity or spiritual uplifting. So inveterate did his wickedness become, that the only standard of comparison left for the biographer is himself, and one sententious phrase sums up the black record of his crimes, "Thus did that king Ahaz."

MICAH

It was during the reigns of Jotham and Ahaz that Micah's ministry began. It seems to have reached its climax in the early days of Hezekiah, who followed Ahaz after that monarch's miserable reign of 16 years and found the kingdom a heritage of shame and peril. One single incident is left us in the book of Jeremiah respecting the results of Micah's testimony in connection with Hezekiah.

HEZEKIAH'S CONVERSION

It would seem as if he had the high honor of being the instrument of Hezekiah's conversion, even as the prophet Isaiah had afterwards of being the teacher and counselor of the same glorious king. Word had been brought to Hezekiah that Micah was uttering loud and fearful denunciations against the kingdom, and even proclaiming the utter destruction of Jerusalem, and that "Zion will be plowed like a field" (Micah 3:12).

This was looked upon as a dangerous and perhaps seditious agitation, and men like Joash and Ahaz would have speedily ended it by the prophet's arrest and perhaps execution. But Hezekiah was of a different mold. He heeded the terrible warning, humbled himself before God, summoned the people to repentance, averted the curse and brought upon himself and his kingdom the glorious days of blessing which made his reign the brightest epoch of Jewish history after the days of Solomon. This incident gives our prophet a very high place of importance and distinction, and entitles his message to our most careful consideration.

HIS PERSONALITY

The personality of Micah is not left to vague conjecture. His own writings give to us a most vivid picture of the man. In contrast with the courtly Isaiah and the polished Elisha, who were the companions of kings, Micah was a typical Oriental prophet. He came from a country village on the borders of the Philistines, and seems to have been not unlike the great Elijah in the quaintness and weirdness both of his dress and his gestures and expressions. While speaking, perhaps on some street corner or in the temple to the assembled multitudes, very much as a street preacher would address the crowd today, his gestures and tones would become wild and violent. Stripped to the waist, until he seemed almost naked, with his tangled hair streaming behind, and with violent gesticulations and cries of anguish, he would depict the horrors that were coming on the land, as though enacting the very scenes in a sort of pantomime. Describing his own manner in Micah 1:8–9, he cries, no doubt as he had cried while uttering his message before the crowd, "Because of this I will weep and wail;/ I will go about barefoot and naked./ I will howl like a jackal/ and moan like an owl./ For her wound is incurable;/ it has come to Judah./ It has reached the very gate of my people,/ even to Jerusalem itself." And then looking down to his old home and the villages of his childhood, he cries out as he sees their destruction passing before him in vision, "Tell it not in Gath;/ weep not at all./ In Beth Ophrah/ roll in the dust./ Pass on in nakedness and shame,/ you who live in Shaphir" (1:10–11). "Those who live in Maroth writhe in pain,/ waiting for relief,/ because disaster has come" (1:12). "Shave your heads in mourning/ for the children in whom you delight;/ make yourselves as bald as the vulture,/ for they will go from you into exile" (1:16).

The name of Micah is quite suggestive; it means "Who is like God?" And it is the basis of one of the finest passages of his prophecy. In Micah 7:18 the prophet makes a play upon his own name: "Who is a God like you,/ who pardons sin?" It is beautiful thus to have the man identified with his message and the name will suggest to us the practical lesson of impersonating our own sermons and making our messages the echo of our lives.

SECTION II—*Micah's Message for Our Times*

In studying the writings of these ancient prophets we must ever remember that most of what they said was of special local and temporary interest, arising out of the circumstances that called forth their message; then continuing with some special prediction for future times. The prophets of Israel were the counselors of their age, the moral and spiritual teachers of their times, and therefore we must not seek to find in all their messages some special vision applying to our age.

The moral and spiritual lessons are of permanent value, but much of the colorings belong to local and temporary conditions. At the same time, interspersed with these immediate messages, we find ever and anon some glorious vision that reaches out to coming ages and contains the substance of some larger prophecy of later times.

Let us gather out of Micah's remarkable little message of less than 4,000 words, about the length of an ordinary sermon, his special messages for our times.

JUDGMENT

1. First there is God's judgment against sin. The searchlight falls upon the scene and what a picture do we behold of the secret thoughts and even dreams of sinful men. "Woe to those who plan iniquity,/ to those who plot evil on their beds!/ At morning's light they carry it out/ because it is in their power to do it" (2:1). How solemn to think that God sees us in the darkness of the night and even in the dreams of our slumbering hours, as we live over our thoughts and perhaps our sins.

Next we have a message of judgment against the rulers of his people:

> But as for me, I am filled with power,
> with the Spirit of the LORD,
> and with justice and might,
> to declare to Jacob his transgression,
> to Israel his sin.
> Hear this, you leaders of the house of Jacob,
> you rulers of the house of Israel,
> who despise justice
> and distort all that is right;
> who build Zion with bloodshed,
> and Jerusalem with wickedness.
> Her leaders judge for a bribe,
> her priests teach for a price,

and her prophets tell fortunes for money.
Yet they lean upon the LORD and say,
  "Is not the LORD among us?
  No disaster will come upon us."
Therefore because of you,
  Zion will be plowed like a field,
Jerusalem will become a heap of rubble,
  the temple hill a mound overgrown with thickets.
    (3:8–12)

This was the message which led to the conversion of Hezekiah and the awakening of the people to a sense of their sin and danger.

The searchlight falls again and now we have a view of the desk of the dishonest merchant and the contents of his safe and the ungodly methods of the trust and syndicate which may well speak words of warning to our own selfish and grasping age.

Am I still to forget, O wicked house,
  your ill-gotten treasures
  and the short ephah, which is accursed?
Shall I acquit a man with dishonest scales,
  with a bag of false weights?
Her rich men are violent;
  her people are liars
  and their tongues speak deceitfully.
Therefore, I have begun to destroy you,
  to ruin you because of your sins.
    (6:10–13)

Next there rises before us the godless home, where confidence is destroyed, affection blighted and selfishness and distrust destroy the very shrine of national virtue and honor.

Both hands are skilled in doing evil;
  the ruler demands gifts,
the judge accepts bribes,
  the powerful dictate what they desire—
  they all conspire together.
The best of them is like a brier,
  the most upright worse than a thorn hedge.
The day of your watchmen has come,
  the day God visits you.

Now is the time of their confusion.
Do not trust a neighbor;
    put no confidence in a friend.
Even with her who lies in your embrace
    be careful of your words.
For a son dishonors his father,
    a daughter rises up against her mother,
a daughter-in-law against her mother-in-law—
    a man's enemies are the members of his own household.
        (7:3–6)

Such are samples of Micah's messages of warning which are as timely today as they were 2,700 years ago.

RIGHTEOUSNESS

2. Micah presented the true way of righteousness. In chapter 6, we have an incident recorded from the lost history of Balaam and a little dialogue of Balak, king of Moab, which does not appear in the story given us in the book of Numbers. There we find Balak asking about the way of acceptance with God and inquiring whether those human sacrifices so horribly real in the bloody idolatry of the Moabites were acceptable to heaven.

Micah gives us the answer:

My people, remember
    what Balak king of Moab counseled
    and what Balaam the son of Beor answered.
Remember your journey from Shittim to Gilgal,
    that you may know the righteous acts of the LORD.

With what shall I come before the LORD
    and bow down before the exalted God?
Shall I come before him with burnt offerings,
    with calves a year old?
Will the LORD be pleased with thousands of rams,
    with ten thousand rivers of oil?
Shall I offer my firstborn for my transgression,
    the fruit of my body for the sin of my soul?
He has showed you, O man, what is good.
    And what does the LORD require of you?
To act justly and to love mercy
    and to walk humbly with your God.
        (6:5–8)

Can anything finer in the definition of divine ethics be found than this? What does God require of us? Just three things: The first is practical righteousness towards our fellow-men, "to act justly" (6:8). The second is a kind heart, more than righteousness, even love and beneficence, "to love mercy" (6:8). And the third is the higher world of the spiritual life that knows God, loves God, reverences God, obeys God, walks with God, "to walk humbly with your God" (6:8). There is the whole story of a true life, and the principles of morality and piety can make no advance on Micah's definitions.

CHRIST

3. Micah's message foretold of the coming Savior. Micah goes far beyond the role of a moral reformer. He was a gospel minister and his messages and his vision pointed forward with clear supernal light to the coming of Jesus Christ. Indeed, it was his message that localized the birthplace of the Babe of Bethlehem and enabled the Scribes and Pharisees to tell the Magi where they should find the Holy Child. Here is Micah's ancient message:

"But you, Bethlehem Ephrathah,
    though you are small among the clans of Judah,
out of you will come for me
    one who will be ruler over Israel,
whose origins are from of old,
    from ancient times."

Therefore Israel will be abandoned
    until the time when she who is in labor gives birth
and the rest of his brothers return
    to join the Israelites.

He will stand and shepherd his flock
    in the strength of the LORD,
    in the majesty of the name of the LORD his God.
And they will live securely, for then his greatness
    will reach to the ends of the earth.
    And he will be their peace.

When the Assyrian invades our land
    and marches through our fortresses,
we will raise against him seven shepherds,
    even eight leaders of men.
        (5:2–5)

How simple and sublime the picture of Jesus Christ: the Babe of Bethlehem and yet the Everlasting One whose goings forth have been of old, even from everlasting; the Shepherd of Israel who shall feed His flock; and the King who shall rule and defend them and be the Prince of Peace to protect them from their enemies. All other helpers should fail them and he would give them up until "she who is in labor" (5:3), that is, the Virgin Mother, should bring forth Israel's true King and man's Redeemer.

THE COMING KINGDOM

4. Micah presented the millennial vision. Micah passes far beyond the cradle of Bethlehem and the Shepherd of Israel, and he gives us the substance of that glorious vision of the reign of righteousness and peace, which runs through all the later prophets. Isaiah quoted literally from this passage and made it the text of one of his earlier messages:

In the last days

the mountain of the LORD's temple will be established
as chief among the mountains;
it will be raised above the hills,
and peoples will stream to it.

Many nations will come and say,

"Come, let us go up to the mountain of the LORD,
to the house of the God of Jacob.
He will teach us his ways,
so that we may walk in his paths."
The law will go out from Zion,
the word of the LORD from Jerusalem.
He will judge between many peoples
and will settle disputes for strong nations far and wide.
They will beat their swords into plowshares
and their spears into pruning hooks.
Nations will not take up sword against nation,
nor will they train for war anymore.
Every man will sit under his own vine
and under his own fig tree,
and no one will make them afraid,
for the LORD Almighty has spoken.
(4:1–4)

What is this mountain of the house of the Lord that is to rise above the tops of the mountains and be the light and the glory of the coming age, and the metropolis of the millennial world? What can it be but the new Jerusalem which John describes in the book of Revelation, which is to come down from God out of heaven and overhang this earth during the reign of Jesus and His saints, and from which like a glorious city from the skies, He and His saints shall govern the earth below for 1,000 years of peace and blessing. We may well bless Micah for the bright and prophetic vision and pray and labor to hasten its coming.

ISRAEL

5. Micah brings a message that tells of Israel's future. He does not forget his own country in his prophetic vision. Micah sees notwithstanding their judgments and calamities, that even out of the Babylonian captivity and other trials, there is yet to come a destiny of surpassing glory when Israel shall be the queen of nations and the Lord shall reign over them in Mount Zion, forever.

> "In that day," declares the LORD,
>
> "I will gather the lame;
>   I will assemble the exiles
>   and those I have brought to grief.
> I will make the lame a remnant,
>   those driven away a strong nation.
> The LORD will rule over them in Mount Zion
>   from that day and forever.
> As for you, O watchtower of the flock,
>   O stronghold of the Daughter of Zion,
> the former dominion will be restored to you;
> kingship will come to the Daughter of Jerusalem."
>   (4:6–8)

> The day for building your walls will come,
>   the day for extending your boundaries.
> In that day people will come to you
>   from Assyria and the cities of Egypt,
> even from Egypt to the Euphrates
>   and from sea to sea
>   and from mountain to mountain.
> The earth will become desolate because of its inhabitants,
>   as the result of their deeds.

Shepherd your people with your staff,
 the flock of your inheritance,
which lives by itself in a forest,
 in fertile pasturelands.
Let them feed in Bashan and Gilead
 as in days long ago.

"As in the days when you came out of Egypt,
 I will show them my wonders."
  (7:11–15)

SALVATION

6. Micah presents God's mercy to His erring and sinful people.

Who is a God like you,
 who pardons sin and forgives the transgression
 of the remnant of his inheritance?
You do not stay angry forever
 but delight to show mercy.
You will again have compassion on us;
 you will tread our sins underfoot
 and hurl all our iniquities into the depths of the sea.
You will be true to Jacob,
 and show mercy to Abraham,
as you pledged on oath to our fathers
 in days long ago.
  (7:18–20)

This passage, which we have already said is a play on Micah's own name, gives us a striking and most comforting revelation of God's infinite mercy and grace—so ready to forgive, so reluctant to destroy, so compassionate in His pity, so mighty to subdue as well as pardon all our iniquities, so faithful to His promises in all His blessings. Such is our God, and well may we say, "Who is a God like you?" (7:18).

What a wonderful Savior is Jesus, my Jesus,
What a wonderful Savior is Jesus, my Lord.

WARNING

7. Micah also presents the danger of neglected warnings. Notwithstanding

all the infinite mercy of such a God, the story of Micah teaches us the folly of neglecting and despising His warnings. Our text reminds us that his ministry began with the most severe denunciation of the people's sins and that it was through heeding these warnings that Hezekiah, the king, was himself saved and enabled to become the savior of his people. This incident was turned to account 150 years later, when the foolish king of Judah was threatening Jeremiah with death because he dared to warn them of God's coming judgment. He was reminded of the wisdom of his ancestor, good Hezekiah, in turning at God's reproof and averting the impending judgment.

Let us likewise learn the solemn lesson. As well might you strike back at the forked lightning of the skies, as try to trifle with God's unchangeable word. You never can turn it aside, but you can turn aside from its path and escape its stroke. Jeremiah sent to the king of Judah a scroll of warning, and the insolent king took his penknife, cut it into shavings and threw it into the grate. Had he destroyed it? Far from it. The next day there came back to him a second edition of the prophet's scroll, rewritten and written larger, with judgment added to judgment and curse to curse, and the awful message that in his insolent pride he should perish for his sins and be buried like a donkey (Jeremiah 22:19). Nor was it long till this daring rebel against the word of God met his awful fate. Outside of the walls of Jerusalem, his body fell in a vain conflict with the Chaldeans and his unburied remains were hustled away like the body of an old beast of burden, while tradition whispered that on his brow was stamped an awful mark, the name of the demon that had misled and destroyed him.

On the other hand Hezekiah listened to the prophet's message and, turning aside from the stroke of judgment, found instead the loving welcome of a forgiving Father and a beneficent Friend. So you will find, if you heed His message and turn at His call. Listen to Him as he cries, "If you had responded to my rebuke,/ I would have poured out my heart to you" (Proverbs 1:23). Listen again as He pleads, " 'As surely as I live,' declares the Sovereign LORD, 'I take no pleasure in the death of the wicked, but rather that they turn from their ways and live. Turn! Turn from your evil ways! Why will you die, O house of Israel?' " (Ezekiel 33:11).

Three centuries ago, two lads in Germany were strolling musicians and both ungodly. Suddenly one day one of the boys was struck by lightning and his companion gazed with horror upon the spectacle of his lifeless friend. He heard in it the warning voice of heaven, he turned immediately to God and that little German lad became Martin Luther, the great reformer who gave to us the Bible.

A century ago two young men, graduates of a New England college, and both skeptics, were off on a revel in a country inn. After a night of debauchery they lay down together to sleep. The next morning one of them awoke to find his companion beside him cold and dead. Springing up with horror, he recalled the last night they had spent on earth: the reckless and godless way they had talked and lived; the holy teachings and examples of his father and mother and the prayers they had offered in vain. And in this stroke he saw God's last message of warning to him. He listened; he repented; he hastened to his home to begin a new life. That awakened student became Adoniram Judson, the man whom God honored as the pioneer of American missions and the gospel in Burma. Today hundreds of thousands of souls bless his name.

Oh, careless one, stop and think! God has often warned you. Your father, your mother, your Sunday school teacher, your pastor, many a message that you can recall, many a warning voice that comes back to you, even from the graves of friends that died to awaken you from your indifference—these are the voices that are calling to you. And perhaps the touch has come yet closer to you in your own very body when sickness laid you low, or some sudden accident brought you within a hair line of eternity and God said to you, "Go thy way for this time." Perhaps the words you are reading now may be God's last warning voice to you. Oh! heed then and turn at His reproof, lest it should be true of you, "A man who remains stiff-necked after many rebukes/ will suddenly be destroyed—without remedy" (Proverbs 29:1).

CHAPTER 16

HEZEKIAH, THE BEST OF JUDAH'S KINGS

Hezekiah trusted in the LORD, the God of Israel. There was no one like him among all the kings of Judah, either before him or after him. (2 Kings 18:5)

This is very high praise that the Holy Spirit gives to good King Hezekiah, placing him higher than even David or Solomon. Doubtless he deserved this lofty tribute, for while he was not free from blame, his faults were less than theirs; while his confidence in God and his faithfulness to God's great trust were worthy of comparison with the highest examples that had gone before him.

HIS AGE

He lived in a stirring time, like the age in which we are living today. The 20th century is not more intense in its forces and bearing upon future ages than was that age before the cross. It was an epoch age of human history. It reads like a thrilling drama. It looks like a game on a great chessboard with an invisible hand moving the pieces. It was the age of Babylon and Rome, the founding of those great empires, that were to rule the world in succession as the "wild beast" powers. It was the time when the Assyrian was in all his glory and cruel power, and Sargon, Shalmaneser and Sennacherib and other names that have been written deep upon the history of the world and upon their own tablets, were making the earth tremble with the shock of battle and the tread of their victorious armies.

Hezekiah lived as the contemporary of these great events and had a very prominent and honorable part in them. God brought him to the front and used him as His instrument to humble the pride of the world's greatest masters.

We can only understand the book of Isaiah as we read it in connection with the reign of Hezekiah and the story of his crimes. Hezekiah was the son of the worst of Judah's kings, the wicked Ahaz. He came out of the densest darkness into the brightest light, and the glory that shines upon his reign is all the brighter because of the disadvantages that preceded it, the difficulties that environed it as he began his reign.

SECTION I—*The Story of Hezekiah*

HIS CONVERSION

1. Hezekiah's conversion was through the ministry of that strange weird figure, Micah the prophet. Suddenly he appeared in Jerusalem in one of the street services held by ancient prophets. In his grotesque dress and with wild gesticulations and striking pantomime, he was going through the very scenes of the siege of Jerusalem and the captivity of the people. They brought word to Hezekiah of this agitator that was disturbing the people. Unlike other kings, who might have silenced him with a shower of stones, Hezekiah listened to him, heeded his message and turned his own heart to God in deep humiliation. Hezekiah called upon his people to repent and humble themselves before Jehovah and, if possible, avert the terrible judgments of which they had been forewarned.

God heard their prayers, gave to Hezekiah the true spirit of penitence and godliness, and for the remainder of his reign, shed upon his kingdom the richest glory and blessings. Thus, Hezekiah's conversion occurred through the faithful message of an obscure prophet, a humble and somewhat singular man. But he did not allow his prejudices or his pride to prevent his receiving God's message from the humblest source.

So let us be willing to hear God speak, no matter through what sort of voice. Most of our blessings are hidden in disguise and the devil puts up a scarecrow wherever there is a cornfield. You never see a scarecrow in the woods. Whenever you see anything that appeals to your prejudices, look out for the corn. Don't miss the blessing and be cheated by your own pride out of the blessing God has for you. Hezekiah listened to Micah and got his blessing and spent his life transmitting it to his kingdom.

HIS ADMINISTRATION

2. Hezekiah brought about the reformation of the kingdom. He found it in a dreadful condition. Ahaz had closed up the temple of God, filled it with heathen altars, covered the city and country with shrines of Baal and Ashtoreth, built up the high places and the groves devoted to obscene idolatry and made the temple of Jehovah almost a stable. Hezekiah immediately set a large force of men to work, and in a fortnight had restored the temple and made it fit for its ancient worship. Then he summoned his people from all Judah and from the tribes of the Northern Kingdom, which had already

been scattered by the fall of Samaria, and the captivity of Israel under Shalmaneser. He sent messages by post to every corner of the land and invited them to Jerusalem. They responded and for a week they held the ancient Passover. The blessing was so great they resolved to hold it another week, and the blessing deepened and the presence of God was made manifest. The heart of the nation was turned back again, and they renewed their covenant with Jehovah and He with them.

The sacred historian concludes the record of this wonderful convocation and sums up the narrative by the emphatic statement, "There was great joy in Jerusalem, for since the days of Solomon son of David king of Israel there had been nothing like this in Jerusalem. The priests and the Levites stood to bless the people, and God heard them, for their prayer reached heaven, his holy dwelling place" (2 Chronicles 30:26–27).

Hezekiah's religious reformation was followed by a radical reorganization of the entire administration of both the secular and religious affairs of the kingdom. The idolatrous images were broken to pieces and the groves and high places throughout Judah were abolished, the old Levitical system of tithes was reestablished and ample provision made for the public services of divine worship. Public improvements for the supply of the city with water so that it could stand a siege, storehouses for the increase of grain and wine and oil and large estates with flocks and herds and great wealth are added to the record of his enterprise and prosperity. The character of the man is finally summed up by the author of the book of Second Chronicles in several striking sentences: ". . . doing what was good and right and faithful before the LORD his God. In everything that he undertook in the service of God's temple and in obedience to the law and the commands, he sought his God and worked wholeheartedly. And so he prospered" (31:20–21). The writer of the book of Second Kings uses equally strong language: "There was no one like him among all the kings of Judah, either before him or after him. He held fast to the LORD and did not cease to follow him; he kept the commands the LORD had given Moses. And the LORD was with him; he was successful in whatever he undertook" (18:5–7).

HIS POLICY

3. Hezekiah's policies were in conflict with the spirit of his age. The book of Isaiah gives us the inner side of Hezekiah's life and reign. Isaiah was his intimate friend and trusted counselor, and in their long and strenuous conflict for the honor of God and the independence of their country they stood heart to heart and hand in hand. Hezekiah's greatest opposition in his work of reform came not from hostile nations but from the politicians of his own country. Generations of moral corruption and spiritual declension had corrupted the principles of the most influential among the people.

The men of wealth and rank as a rule were out of sympathy with the high religious principles and the lofty views of Isaiah and Hezekiah. They believed in what would be called today, "political expediency." They had little faith in anything directly supernatural, and their creed might fairly be expressed by the popular proverb: "God helps the man that helps himself." Therefore they laughed at the idea of looking directly to Jehovah to interpose in any practical form for the help of their nation in the political dangers that were thickening around them. And they insisted that the king should avail himself of every political "pull" that could be used to advantage against the encroachments of the powerful Assyrian king that was every day becoming more and more the menace and terror of the Western nations.

The nations of Palestine, Syria and Northern Africa had formed a confederacy to resist the Assyrian conqueror. Egypt, the oldest and most powerful of these nations, was the fomenter of these political intrigues, but in the critical moment Egypt had shown that she was utterly unreliable and very likely to leave her allies to their own resources and look out for herself. The Egyptians at Jerusalem were constantly insisting upon the Egyptian alliance and Hezekiah and Isaiah stood firmly against it. Many of the most impressive chapters in the book of Isaiah, such as the 30th chapter, have specially referred to this conflict.

The Spirit of the Age

It was only an older form of the irrepressible conflict that is still going on between God's true witnesses and the spirit of "the present evil age" (Galatians 1:4). We find it today as much as in the days of Hezekiah. Its watchword is "compromise." Its ethics may be summed up in a few popular maxims: "Don't be extreme;" "Don't be righteous overmuch;" "Go with the majority;" "Keep in the popular current;" "Don't make too much of what you call your 'principles';" "Meet the world half way in order to lift it to your plane;" "All is well that ends well;" "Let us do evil that good may come;" "Don't be too particular about the means employed if you are accomplishing a desired end;" "Don't give offense by preaching too closely to the prevailing sins among the fashionable and wealthy members of your congregation;" "Be moderate, be prudent, be politic." And so the Church today has gone into the arms of the world and lost the presence and power of her Lord, and every true follower of the Lord is called upon in some way to face this public trend, and to stand often with the keenest anguish and the loneliest sorrow in the minority, even against the religious world, with his rejected Lord.

But it was this isolation of Judah through Hezekiah's faithfulness that saved her at last, when the Assyrians swept over the land and fell like an avalanche on the other members of this Egyptian league, and Judah was spared the ruin that overwhelmed them. Then, when the crisis came to her, God proved Himself better than all the cavalry of Pharaoh and mightier than all the power of Sennacherib.

HIS HEALING

4. A closer test of his faith is now pressed upon him. Suddenly in the midst of his great reforms and his splendid reign, a strange message comes to him from God, which seems to sound the knell of all his hopes and plans: "Put your house in order, because you are going to die; you will not recover" (2 Kings 20:1). There seems to have been no reason for this in his own life. We hear so far no censure of his conduct, and in his own confession, written after his healing, we find no consciousness of sin. Perhaps he says too much about the uprightness of his life when he tells the Lord, "I have walked before you faithfully and with wholehearted devotion and have done what is good in your eyes" (20:3). But at least it reveals a good conscience and a heart that had no condemnation for itself. And yet the message came to him and came from God that all his plans and aspirations must be buried in an early grave, for as yet he could not have been 40 years of age.

A Hopeless Case

The king was stunned by this sudden and terrific blow, and it is not strange that for a little while he sank in discouragement and turned his face to the wall in the gloomiest despair. But right here let us quickly grasp the precious lesson that comes to us from his experience. Do not turn your face to the wall, no matter what the discouragement may be. Do not give up your faith and hope lightly if all within you and all around you, and even all above you, seem to combine in one black shroud of despair. There is no reason that you should give up your confidence.

A humble heathen woman once came to Christ only to meet repeated refusals from Him, until at last she lay helpless at His feet, not only rejected but insulted and reminded that she was only a dog. But not for a moment did she give up her trust. Indeed, she even wrung a plea from His refusal. And the Lord was so pleased with her faith that He surrendered and told her she could have whatever she wanted.

There is another case. It is the story of Paul. There had come to him a terrible affliction and his physical strength was crushed out, so that he despaired even of life. And when he went to God about it in prayer, he tells us that the answer he got was death, but did he give up to death? No. But he tells us his trust was in "God, who raises the dead" (2 Corinthians 1:9), and he claimed a deliverance as mighty as even an act of resurrection. He rose up in victory and tells us that He "delivered us from such a deadly peril, and he will deliver us. On him we have set our hope that he will continue to deliver us" (1:10).

The Victory of Faith

So, after awhile Hezekiah's tone changed and his attitude also. From looking at the blank stone wall he began to look up, and immediately his prayer changes and he cries, "But what can I say?/ He has spoken to me, and he himself has done this" (Isaiah 38:15). Already the steps of Isaiah are heard at the threshold of his chambers, and the message comes from God, "I have heard your prayer and seen your tears; I will add fifteen years to your life" (38:5).

Hezekiah has left us the diary of his illness and it is interesting to go with him through the first wailings of his unbelieving prayer; it sounds very much like many of our useless prayers.

> I said, "In the prime of my life
>   must I go through the gates of death
>   and be robbed of the rest of my years?"
> I said, "I will not again see the LORD,
>   the LORD, in the land of the living;
> no longer will I look on mankind,
>   or be with those who now dwell in this world.
> Like a shepherd's tent my house
>   has been pulled down and taken from me.
> Like a weaver I have rolled up my life,
>   and he has cut me off from the loom;
>   day and night you made an end of me.
> I waited patiently till dawn,
>   but like a lion he broke all my bones;
>   day and night you made an end of me.
> I cried like a swift or thrush,
>   I moaned like a mourning dove.
> My eyes grew weak as I looked to the heavens.
>   I am troubled; O Lord, come to my aid!"
>   (38:10–14)

But the moment he begins to talk about looking "to the heavens" and turns to God in simple trustful prayer, God meets him in the spirit of his prayer. And so He still waits to be gracious even in the darkest hour to all who can trust Him.

A Preparation for His Work

Doubtless Hezekiah needed this experience of a stronger grasp on God in preparation for the great conflict which was yet to come to him as the leader of his nation in a severer test of faith. The experience of divine healing through which God brings His people is not an end, but a means to something higher. God was preparing His servant Hezekiah for a great public service, and He brought him through this vivid personal experience of God's all-sufficiency, that he might remember it as an inspiration to his faith when the graver crisis of his country came. And so God's leading in your life and mine is designed to show us His all-sufficiency and prepare us for higher ministries in helping others, and trusting Him in the supreme emergencies which come to every good cause.

TEMPORARY FAILURE

5. But now there comes a brief eclipse of this glorious sunrise—a temporary failure. The writer of the book of Chronicles puts it very briefly but emphatically. "But Hezekiah's heart was proud and he did not respond to the kindness shown him; therefore the LORD's wrath was on him and on Judah and Jerusalem. Then Hezekiah repented of the pride of his heart, as did the people of Jerusalem; therefore the LORD's wrath did not come upon them during the days of Hezekiah" (2 Chronicles 32:25–26).

The extraordinary deliverance and the supernatural sign that accompanied it, had excited the profoundest interest and wonder throughout the world, and ambassadors came all the way from Babylon to congratulate him. Then it was that his heart became lifted up and he showed the ambassadors the treasures of his palace and brought upon himself the terrible threat that these treasures should yet be taken by these very Babylonians and carried away to Babylon.

There was one merciful reprieve, namely, that the judgment would be deferred until after his days and should come in the time of his successors. But he rose above this failure through sincere repentance and God restored him to His favor and blessing, and enabled him to reach the supreme climax of the life of faith before the chapter ended.

It is so delightful to find one life that did not close in disaster, one sun that went down "largest at its setting," to prove that God is "able to save completely" (Hebrews 7:25), and to keep to the end those that truly trust in Him.

SENNACHERIB

6. The supreme trial and triumph of his faith came in his dealings with Sennacherib. At last it came, the terrible Assyrian invasion. Again and again it had been warded off, but ever and anon it returned. Shalmaneser had swept over the land in the early part of his reign, and had blotted out Samaria and carried captive the tribes of Israel. Sargon had followed him and covered the Western world with terror in his conflict with Egypt and the surrounding nations.

At last Sennacherib came. Once and again he passed by Jerusalem. On one occasion he was bought off by an immense bribe from Hezekiah and marched away without assaulting the city. The second time he brought the army up to its gates, and sent an insulting message and demanded its surrender. But, encouraged by Isaiah, Hezekiah refused his demand and God sent "a rumor" as Isaiah had predicted, that filled him with alarm, that the Egyptians were marching against him with a powerful army.

A third time he sent a more insulting message, for now the Egyptians had been defeated and there was nothing between him and his prey. In the most offensive manner, the Assyrian ambassador shouted his blasphemous message in the hearing of the army, telling them of their helplessness, inciting them to mutiny and despair and laughing to ridicule the idea of their God protecting them against the gods of the Assyrians who had already triumphed over all other nations and divinities; and promising clemency if they but yielded the city up to his demands. It was indeed as the king expressed it in his message to Isaiah, "a day of distress and rebuke and disgrace" (2 Kings 19:3). But he and Isaiah together took the insulting letter of Sennacherib and quietly "spread it out before the Lord" (19:14), and then in a simple prayer reminded Jehovah that the battle was His, and the insult against Him, and besought Him: "Now, O LORD our God, deliver us from his hand, so that all kingdoms on earth may know that you alone, O LORD, are God" (19:19).

God's Answer

It was not long until the message came to Isaiah that God had accepted the challenge of the impious king, and that He would answer him. The message of God is sublime in its majesty. He recognizes that Sennacherib has been His instrument and scourge, but now that he has overstepped his limits and defied the God that used him as a tool, he shall find his helplessness and his doom. "Therefore this is what the LORD says," the message concluded, "He will not enter this city/ or shoot an arrow here" (19:32). "By the way that he came he will return" (19:33). "I will defend this city to save it,/ for my sake and for the sake of David my servant" (19:34).

The Destroying Angel

As sublime in its simplicity is the record that follows: "The angel of the LORD went out and put to death a hundred and eighty-five thousand men in the Assyrian camp. When the people got up the next morning—there were all the dead bodies! So Sennacherib king of Assyria broke camp and withdrew. He returned to Nineveh and stayed there" (19:35–36).

It is not often that secular poetry so nearly approaches the very spirit of the inspired record as does Lord Byron's picture of the Assyrians overflow:

The Assyrian came down like the wolf on the fold,

And his cohorts were gleaming in purple and gold;
And the sheen of their spears was like stars on the sea,
When the blue wave rolls nightly on deep Galilee.

Like the leaves of the forest when summer is green,
That host with their banners at sunset were seen;
Like the leaves of the forest when autumn hath blown,
That host on the morrow lay withered and strown.

For the Angel of Death spread his wings on the blast,
And breathed in the face of the foe as he passed;
And the eyes of the sleepers waxed deadly and chill,
And their heart but once heaved, and forever grew still.

And there lay the steed with his nostril all wide,
But through it there rolled not the breath of his pride;
And the foam of his gasping lay white on the turf,
And cold as the spray of the rock-beating surf.

And there lay the rider, distorted and pale,
With the dew on his brow and the rust on his mail;
And the tents were all silent, the hammers alone,
The lances unlifted, the trumpet unblown.

And the widows of Asshur are loud in their wail,
And the idols are broke in the temple of Baal;
And the might of the Gentile, unsmote by the sword,
Hath melted, like snow, in the glance of the Lord!

This stupendous miracle left its impression not only on Hezekiah, but on later times. Several of the Psalms seem to have been specially written and chanted in connection with it, especially the 46th, 48th and 76th.

SECTION II—*Lessons Learned from the Life of Hezekiah*

1. The hardest places and the darkest times need not discourage us, but may become occasions for the highest faith and the noblest lives. Hezekiah the Good came as the successor of Ahaz the Infamous. And so your life may be linked with the most opposite and uncongenial surrounding, and these may be but a foil against which God will bring forth the very trophies and triumphs of His grace.

2. Each of us is being prepared for our victories on the public stage of life and service by our personal experiences and triumphs. It was Hezekiah's healing that fitted him to understand God's all-sufficiency and prepared him for the great emergencies which afterwards came to His country. And so God is bringing us to our personal tests not that we may be crushed by them, but that we may get strength from them for some grander service yet in store. Are you triumphing on the lonely battlefield of your own heart and preparing to lead others in the future in some high service?

3. We can rise above our failures. Hezekiah failed even after his healing, but the eclipse did not continue, the shadow passed and a brighter radiance returned to his life. Do not let your faults discourage you any more than your sicknesses and trials. Learn to rise above yourself and in the strength of God be avenged upon your worst failures and your saddest memories. This is indeed to defeat the devil and turn his weapons against him.

4. Hezekiah teaches us to put the whole strength of our being into everything God calls us to undertake. Always let us be our best. There is nothing finer as a watchword for our young manhood that talks so much about the "strenuous life," but often does so little. "In everything that he undertook, . . . he . . . worked wholeheartedly. And so he prospered" (2 Chronicles 31:21).

5. Finally, the supreme distinction of Hezekiah's life was his faith in God. He trusted in the Lord God of Israel, so that, "there was no one like him among all the kings of Judah, either before him or after him" (2 Kings 18:5). That was the secret of Hezekiah's faith and prosperity! It was not his wisdom, his uprightness, his earnestness, but it was his faith. And the reason that faith is so important an element in every true life is simply because it links our nothingness with God Himself. Works stand for the best that we can do. Will we learn this lesson, and, losing ourselves in true humiliation, find ourselves in simple faith? Then every hard place that faces us, every trial that confronts us, every impossible situation that defies us, will be but another opportunity for revealing God and showing that He is the "El Shaddai," the All-Sufficient One. The watchword of our life will be, "Thanks be to God, who always leads us in triumphal procession in Christ" (2 Corinthians 2:14). In other words, it is God's business to fight the battle and win the victory and it is ours to follow and say, "Hallelujah!/ For our Lord God Almighty reigns" (Revelation 19:6).

CHAPTER 17

MANASSEH, A MIRACLE OF MERCY

I will make them abhorrent to all the kingdoms of the earth because of what Manasseh son of Hezekiah king of Judah did in Jerusalem. (Jeremiah 15:4)

This was God's estimate of Manasseh 100 years after his wicked reign. This was the testimony of Jeremiah the prophet after a century had passed, and the impartial scales of time had weighed the man's life and character.

Notwithstanding all the crimes of later kings it was Manasseh's wickedness that primarily brought about the captivity of Judah and the ruin of Jerusalem.

SECTION I—*The Story of Manasseh*

Manasseh was the son of Hezekiah and Hephzibah, the wife whose name is so fondly mentioned in the prophecies of Isaiah as the type of God's own beloved bride. Doubtless she was a good woman, and Jewish tradition even connects her with the prophet Isaiah, as his own daughter. The name was given to Manasseh probably out of compliment to one of the leading tribes of the Northern Kingdom, which had so recently been broken up and carried into captivity, and whose remnants Hezekiah had endeavored to gather around the old standard at Jerusalem. There can be little doubt that Manasseh's education and training up to the death of Hezekiah were all that the influence of his own parents and the good Isaiah could throw around him. His father died while he was yet a lad, and, at the early age of 12 years, the boy king found himself suddenly raised to a throne. Judah had its good child kings, such as Joash and afterwards Josiah, but in Manasseh she was to find a ruler who, both as boy and man, was utterly and inveterately bad.

BAD INFLUENCES

From the very beginning, Manasseh took his stand with the aristocratic party, who had always favored idolatry and had maintained a suppressed but unceasing protest against all the reforms of Hezekiah. In those days, Nineveh, Babylon and Tyre were the great centers of culture and fashion, and their religious ceremonies were observed on a scale of impressive splendor, beside which the simple and spiritual worship of the temple at Jerusalem seemed crude indeed and utterly unfashionable. There were about ancient idolatry, with all its grossness, certain sensuous attractions which appealed to the tastes and passions of the human heart. All the accessories of art and music were added to its attractiveness. The objects of worship included the sun, the moon, the stars and the most impressive and beautiful objects of nature. Its places of worship were the mountain, the grove and the lofty roofs where the heavenly bodies could be seen and worshiped in all their majesty.

It is said that when Pompey, the great Roman general, visited Jerusalem, he was amazed at the simplicity of the temple, which was just an empty sanctuary, containing no statuary, paintings or works of art, but was a magnificent solitude. He could not understand that Divine Presence which filled those sacred courts with a higher majesty than earthly ornaments of art. So Manasseh and the idolatrous party in Jerusalem despised the old and obsolete religion of the past age and went in without restraint for the newest thing in religion.

The temple of Jehovah was soon filled with heathen idols and obscene images. The groves and high places with their carnival of license were reestablished. The worship of the host of heaven and all the mummeries of spiritualism were publicly recognized, and even the horrid rites of Moloch and the human sacrifices that accompanied them were instituted in the Valley of Hinnom. Manasseh himself afterwards set the example of offering his own children in living sacrifice at the horrid shrines. Not only so, but idolatry soon became aggressive and the religion of Jehovah, which had been at least tolerated in the worst reigns that had preceded, was now placed under the ban of a bloody persecution.

It is thought by many that Psalm 79 is a description of the horrors of this persecution.

> O God, the nations have invaded your inheritance;
>   they have defiled your holy temple,
>   they have reduced Jerusalem to rubble.
> They have given the dead bodies of your servants
>   as food to the birds of the air,
>   the flesh of your saints to the beasts of the earth.
> They have poured out blood like water
>   all around Jerusalem,
>   and there is no one to bury the dead. (79:1–3)

In this awful persecution the prophet Isaiah himself is said to have perished, and it is to him that reference is made in Hebrews 11:37: "They were stoned; they were sawed in two." Jewish tradition affirms that the venerable prophet was placed inside a hollow tree, and by the orders of the cruel king, his body was literally sawed to pieces with the tree.

This fearful carnival of cruelty and idolatry was permitted to run its terrible course for 50 years. The worst of the reigns of Judah was also the longest, and this prodigy of sin actually ruled, or misruled, God's heritage for no less than 55 years.

CARRIED TO BABYLON

At last retribution came. More than once during his reign had the Assyrians invaded Palestine. In the tablets that have come down from the reigns of Esarhaddon and Sardanapalus, perhaps the two greatest Assyrian monarchs, we find Manasseh himself among the tributary kings who were represented as paying their tribute to the great conqueror in one of his Durbars. But at last the divine vengeance closed around him. Jerusalem was captured and the king himself was taken in chains to Babylon, which was now one of the capitals of the Assyrian empire. The story in Chronicles states that they "took Manasseh prisoner, put a hook in his nose, bound him with bronze shackles and took him to Babylon" (2 Chronicles 33:11). This expression literally means by a hook in his mouth with a chain to grit, and leading him like a wild beast, while his limbs were loaded with fetters. This custom is represented on many of the Assyrian monuments. The same Hebrew word is used in Job 41:2, about the hook in the mouth of the great leviathan: "Can you put a cord through his nose/ or pierce his jaw with a hook?" And so at last the end had come to this long and sinful career.

FOUND MERCY

And yet even for Manasseh there was mercy. There is nothing in the whole Bible more wonderful and touching than the account of his repentance and forgiveness. "In distress he sought the favor of the LORD his God and humbled himself greatly before the God of his fathers. And when he prayed to him, the LORD was moved by his entreaty and listened to his plea; so he brought him back to Jerusalem and to his kingdom. Then Manasseh knew that the LORD is God" (2 Chronicles 33:12–13).

We know that the Assyrian king about this time released another royal captive, Necho, king of Egypt, and sent him back to his kingdom under a covenant, that he should be the loyal servant of Assyria against the rebellious parties of his country. The same wise policy may have dictated Manasseh's release. But Manasseh at least fully understood that it was to the Lord he owed his deliverance.

LAST YEARS

When the blessing came, he did not forget to show his gratitude and faithfulness. The last years of his reign appear to have been spent in an honest effort to undo his former crimes. He reorganized the civil and military government of the kingdom. He put away the idols from the temple and the city, and restored the worship of Jehovah throughout the land. And it did seem that the ancient worship was fully reestablished, with, however, the exception that the high places remained and became the scenes of the worship of God, instead of the ceremonies of idolatry. But it was impossible for him to effectually turn back the tide that he himself had so fully set in motion. After his death at the age of 67 we find his son Amon plunging headlong into the same sins and crimes in which his father had so long set the example, and, even worse than his father, refusing to be warned, but defying heaven and leaving this fearful record against his short and shameful career: "But unlike his father Manasseh, he did not humble himself before the LORD; Amon increased his guilt" (33:23). Amon's name is an Egyptian one and was given him doubtless in his father's evil days, as a compliment to the Egyptian idolatry. The son proved true to the evil associations of the name and succeeded in undoing even the better work of his father's last days, by which he had sought to atone for a wasted and destructive life.

SECTION II—*Lessons Learned from the Life of Manasseh*

1. It teaches us that goodness is not hereditary. Manasseh had the best of parents, but this did not make him a good boy or a righteous man. God permits these sad misfits in family life to teach the young as well as the old that they cannot depend upon the piety of others but that each soul must stand alone with God and know Him for itself.

2. "Even a child is known by his actions" (Proverbs 20:11). Manasseh at 12 years of age was the father of the man that afterwards developed in all his monstrous cruelty. The tendencies of character begin early to show themselves. The Lord Jesus was only 12 years of age when he was found sitting in the temple "about his Father's business" (Luke 2:49, KJV). And Nero, who afterwards developed into a monster of crime, spent his childhood tearing off the legs and wings of flies, and graduating in the school of juvenile cruelty. Let the boys and girls who read these lines remember that the habits and tendencies you cultivate or allow today are going to last through life and determine your future good or evil. And let parents and teachers remember that the issues of life for most people are determined in the first 12 years of existence.

3. Manasseh teaches us of the power of bad men to undo the work of the good. The saddest thing about Manasseh's life was that he spent it tearing

down all that his good father, Hezekiah, had built up. How sad it is that "one sinner destroys much good" (Ecclesiastes 9:18).

A child can burn up the building or the papers that a lifetime has been spent in preparing. Many a man has brought into his home, through an ungodly wife or the tolerated sins of his children, the forces that are to render futile all the work for God in which his own life has been spent.

4. The crime of causing others to sin. It was the aggravation of Jeroboam's bad life, that he not only sinned, but "caused Israel to commit [sin]" (1 Kings 14:16). The same terrible charge is recorded against Manasseh: "But Manasseh led Judah and the people of Jerusalem astray, so that they did more evil than the nations the LORD had destroyed before the Israelites" (2 Chronicles 33:9). Dear friend, are you reproducing your sinful life in other lives? Are you planting seeds of evil which will blossom and bear fruit when you are moldering in the dust?

Someone has said about moths that "they have no teeth, but they have children that have teeth." And so there are lives that do not reach their full fruition until they themselves have passed beyond the scene and left others to carry on the sad results of their influence. Have you started some other life on a wrong career that will continue after you, perhaps, have been saved from your follies and crimes?

5. There is the lesson provided by the rejection of light. "The LORD spoke to Manasseh and his people, but they paid no attention" (33:10). This is the worst aggravation of sin: to commit it in the face of light; to know the right and do the wrong; to refuse the warning voice of God and recklessly trample on all the appeals of His love and the very mercy that would save you from yourself.

You know how it would irritate you for some child or servant to coolly ignore your call and walk on in insolent silence. How must God feel when He calls us again and again and we trifle with His authority and His love? "This is the verdict: Light has come into the world, but men loved darkness instead of light" (John 3:19). Dear friend, is this your condemnation?

6. "Be sure that your sin will find you out" (Numbers 32:23). Man is often baffled in tracing human crimes, but God has an automatic apparatus that always finds its way to the guilty. It is said that a French gentleman having been frequently robbed by his own servants, at length by the advice of a detective, placed a lot of gold coins as a bait in their way, and covered them with a chemical substance which would afterwards leave a stain upon the hands of the thief. Soon afterwards he called the household together with the detective, and after all had denied, the officer insisted that they should show their hands. Sure enough, the guilty tint had already begun to appear upon the fingers of one of the pages, and seeing with horror the telltale traces of his crimes, which even he had not noticed before, he confessed

the whole series and begged for mercy.

Yes, in God's unerring economy each of us is carrying our own judgment with us, and there will be no need for other evidence than the sensitive records of our own conscience and the imprint of our own acts upon ourselves. Manasseh's punishment came at last. It does not always come in this life to every sinner, but come it will, and many a lost soul would have been thankful if it had come to him in time to save from eternal exposure and punishment.

7. Manasseh's life shows us the infinite mercy of God. Even Manasseh's judgment was but a stepping stone to his salvation. Was there ever a more wonderful object lesson of God's forgiving love? He hearkened to the cry of this wretched man, who repented only when cornered by his own crimes, and forced to give up the struggle. There was nothing noble in his surrender. There was nothing that would appeal to human mercy. But God heard even Manasseh's cry and God will hear the sinner's cry, even when there is nothing to plead for him but his utter worthlessness and misery. And the infinite mercy of Jesus Christ never thinks any case too hard, even Manasseh's.

8. There is the lesson of the sediment of sin. Manasseh repented and was forgiven, but alas, he could not blot out all the effects of his wretched life. He tried to reform the nation, but they only came back half way. Doubtless he tried to reform his own son, but Amon refused to follow his father's later steps and persisted in the sinful career which that father himself had taught him a little earlier, and he outran even Manasseh's example and died in open rebellion against God. If Manasseh could have looked down from heaven upon the next generation, he would have seen his people under the leadership of his own boy drifting back into the old current of his own sinful career, and reaping the fruits which he had sowed.

Joseph Cook used to say that the question of the future is not a question of eternal punishment, so much as of eternal sin. If men are not going to stop sinning here, what likelihood is there that they will stop sinning under the worse influence of the hereafter? And eternal sin must ever mean eternal suffering. Amon stands before us as a type of something even sadder than Manasseh. It is the soul that will not cease sinning. It is the hell which begins on earth and only needs the atmosphere of a lost eternity to develop into the worm that never dies and the fire that shall never be quenched.

Let us take care how we trifle with sin. It is the most fearful thing in the universe of God, and it carries its own retribution along with it. Someone asked a poor old black saint how it could be possible for God ever to find brimstone enough to make the hell which the Bible talks about, and the old saint silenced the skeptic by an answer that deserves to be well pondered: "Oh, honey, dey'll carry dere own brimstone wif dem."

The difference is that in this life it is possible to get the brimstone out, but there it will be too late.

PSALMS

CHAPTER 1

THE IDEAL MAN

Psalm 1

I t is usual to put a frontispiece in the beginning of a book, and if the book is a biography, the frontispiece is usually a portrait. The first psalm is the frontispiece of the Psalter and the portrait of the man described in the course of these inspired psalms. The perfect fulfillment of the ideal is only to be found in that Man of men, the Son of man, the Lord Jesus Himself. So it is not out of place among the Messianic Psalms, among which it was classified by the most spiritual of the Christian fathers.

It has another title to a gospel place. The word "blessed" with which it opens is the keynote of the New Testament and of the gospel of Jesus Christ. When He opened His mouth on Mount Hattin (traditional location of the Sermon on the Mount) to proclaim the righteousness of the new kingdom, His first word was "blessed," and He repeated it again and again until He had laid the foundations of New Testament righteousness in eight beatitudes. When He went away from earth, His hands were extended in blessing; and when He closed the revelation of His love in the Apocalypse of John, its last whisper was a benediction. So this word "blessed" brings the first psalm down to gospel times and up to gospel heights. Indeed, the book of Psalms is a wonderful anticipation of the spirit of Christianity.

This beautiful psalm contains the portrait of a righteous man.

SECTION I—*By Way of Contrast*

In the distance is the figure of the ungodly man sinking into the darker, deeper shadows of the scorner. The course of the evil man is described in a very dramatic way by three climaxes which express the downward descent of evil.

1. We have the three words—ungodly, sinner, scorner (KJV). These are

155

three very different stages of wickedness, three very different kinds of men.

The ungodly man is remarkable rather for what he is not. He is a man of the world, perhaps a moral and respectable man, but he is ungodly; he has no supreme love for God; he has no interest in divine things; he is not saved; he is not consecrated; he is not living for God.

But the sinner is a very different character. The progression has deepened; the ungodly man has become the sinner; the man without God has become evil; he is now a wrongdoer, a transgressor, a man positively evil, speaking, acting, thinking, living unrighteously and in contravention to God's holy will and law. He may be a dishonest man, an immoral man, a profane man, a selfish man, a false man; but it matters little, for all sin is of the same kind if not of the same degree.

But there is a deeper gradation, the scorner. This is the reckless, presumptuous, abandoned, profane and utterly reprobate man who has given up God, conscience, fear, hope, everything holy, sacred and divine; who has sinned against the Holy Spirit, and has swept out on the awful current of infidelity and defiant wickedness. He is past feeling; he is given over to a reprobate mind; his heart is hardened. He despises the things of God, and he is waiting for his doom.

2. But there is a second climax, marked by the three words, counsel, way and seat. The counsel of the ungodly is simply their example, their principles, their conversation, their ideas of things. But the way of sinners is their actual conduct, their deeds, their works of evil. The man has now come to perpetrate them, to share them, to do as they do.

But there is still a deeper descent, and that is the seat of the scorner. A way is something from which a man may turn back, but a seat is that in which he has sat down and made himself comfortable. He has committed himself to his evil course and does it without compunction, distress or any sense of reproof or condemnation. He is a lost, willful man; and if a miracle of grace does not interpose, he is irrevocably lost.

3. There is still another climax: walk, stand, sit. The first describes an unsettled course of life. He has not yet committed himself to these principles, but is allowing himself to be thrown into contact with them.

But the next expression describes a more settled condition. He stands. He has become settled in his evil course; he continues in it; he is determined in his spirit; he has taken his stand for evil.

But the third term is still more positive—sit. It describes a man who has become at ease in his evil course, who has made himself comfortable in wrongdoing, who has fixed himself and settled himself forever in unbelief and sin. He has said to God: "Leave us alone!/ We have no desire to know your ways" (Job 21:14), and God has left him to himself, a poor self-castaway, awaiting the hour of judgment when his eyes will open with amazement and horror, and see the folly and madness of his sin.

These are the progressions of evil. Truly, the sinner cannot stand still. The descending avalanche gathers volume as it rolls. "Evil men and impostors will go from bad to worse, deceiving and being deceived" (2 Timothy 3:13). It is an awful thing to begin to go down. You reach a point where you cannot stop. Like the poor driver in California who had been accustomed to drive the stagecoach up and down the tremendous declivities of the mountains, and knew so well how to stop the wheels by pressing on the brakes; but as he lay one day upon his dying bed, conscious that he had oft neglected the great salvation, and indeed had rejected the Savior, he cried with bitter agony: "I am going down the mountain and cannot get my feet upon the brakes!" He could find no stopping place.

Oh, brother, if you are on the downward road today, stop! It all begins with neglecting the great salvation. The second step is rejecting, and the third step is despising. Brother, stop now, and the hand of infinite love will grasp you and lift you up to righteousness and salvation.

SECTION II—*The Righteous Man's Positive Characteristics*

CONFORMITY

1. "His delight is in the law of the LORD" (Psalm 1:2); his life is in conformity to the will of the Lord; his character is founded upon God's revealed will. The law here does not mean the Ten Commandments, but the whole Mosaic revelation. The Hebrew word *torah* means instruction.

The only true foundation of any life is righteousness. Nothing else can bring blessedness. There are mechanical and material laws which cannot be violated; and if you try to build your wall off the plumb line, it will certainly crumble in ruins about your head and leave you overwhelmed and crushed. Just as vain as it is for you to attempt to build your spiritual house on unholy principles. The slightest deviation from spiritual righteousness will bring failure, danger, perhaps destruction. God expects men to be right; requires them to be right; enables them to be right. He has given us a perfect standard, and He is able to bring us up to it. Let us not try to lower it to accommodate God's will to ours, but let us hold it up in its high, imperial grandeur and claim the grace to enable us to rise to meet it.

The New Testament is not less righteous than the Old. The very foundation of the redemption of Christ and the cross of Calvary is God's holiness, justice and eternal righteousness. Nowhere does God's will shine more conspicuously than in the cross of Calvary. The very death of Christ was but a testimony to it. Even to save men God would not violate one tittle of its terms, but required the exaction of its utmost penalty and the fulfillment of its minutest precept. Christ has come not to excuse us from the righteousness of the law, but to deliver us from the penalty of the law, and then so to deliver us from the power of sin "in order that the righteous requirements of the law might be fully met in us, who do not live according to the sinful nature but according to the Spirit" (Romans 8:4).

DELIGHT IN THE LAW

2. The second characteristic of this man is his delight in the law. Some men obey the law because they must; this man, because he wants to. Two little words express the high condition of two dispensations: the one is *have* to, the other is *love* to. The blessedness of the Christian life is that we love to do right, to be right. We delight in the law of the Lord. God writes it upon our inward parts. That service which we render without the heart's full consent is not right service. That righteousness which does not spring from the depths of our being is not complete or satisfying to the great heart of God.

He wants to make us so pure that we shall love the right and hate the wrong, and every instinct of our being shall choose the will of God, and cry, "I desire to do your will, O my God;/ your law is within my heart" (Psalm 40:8). Nothing but the infinite grace of Christ can give us this spirit. Here the Old Testament picture fails, and the New Testament Christ must come to realize the ideal only as His heart is in our heart.

FRUITFUL AND USEFUL

3. This man is a man of practical fruitfulness and usefulness. He is not a man of theories and experiences only, but he lives in the great world of living men and women, and busy events and things, and everywhere and always his life is a benediction. "He is like a tree planted by streams of water,/ which yields its fruit in season/ and whose leaf does not wither./ Whatever he does prospers" (1:3).

A tree is not only a beautiful thing with its luxuriant verdure, but it is a most useful thing, especially if it is a fruit-bearing tree and yields its fruit in season. This man lives for others and for God, and makes the world his debtor. The age in which he lives, his country, his church, his home, his business, are all better for him. He is not a one-sided man, but he fits into all situations, and is faithful and fruitful under all circumstances. He "yields [his] fruit in season" (1:3).

Is he a business man? He carries his religion into his business. Is he an old man? He lights up the winter of age with the torch of faith and love and holy gladness. Is he a young man? He is bright, manly, enterprising, buoyant, a young man among men, but a man of God and a blessing to everyone he touches.

Is she a mother? She brings forth the fruit of her holy life among her children, and generations call her blessed. Is she a maiden? She adorns her youth and beauty with the loveliness of Christ's spirit and character, fresh, beautiful, springing, youthful, simple-hearted, child-like as a girl, yet sacred, white-robed, separated from the world and dedicated to God, making men and women to feel as she moves among them as if an angel had passed by.

Is he or she a suffering Christian? There is fruit appropriate to the hour of sorrow, the time of temptation, the hard conflict, the hour of misunderstanding, loneliness, disappointment, desertion. All this is recognized but as an occasion to glorify God and show the loveliness of the Christian life.

Is it a time of prosperity? There is also appropriate fruit for this: the spirit of cheerfulness, usefulness, unselfishness and remembrance of the claims of God and the needs of men. There is fruit for childhood days, for the morning of youth, for the meridian of life, for the twilight of age, for the shadows of sorrow and death, for all possible situations, circumstances and places; and the man whose roots are planted by the streams of water finds in God support and strength for every possible condition.

PERMANENCE

4. The next characteristic of this man is permanence. "Whose leaf does not wither" (1:3). His life is not a spasm of well-meaning effort, dying in weak reaction, but a steady, onward movement of constant and victorious power, his path shining more and more unto the perfect day. Of such a man the Master has said, "You did not choose me, but I chose you and appointed you to go and bear fruit—fruit that will last. Then the Father will give you whatever you ask in my name" (John 15:16).

Such are the characteristics of the godly, the righteous, the ideal man. Oh, who can meet the lineaments of the picture? Who but He, of whom the world's proud, heartless ruler had to say, "Here is the man" (19:5), and of whom the Father proclaimed, "This is my Son, whom I love; with him I am well pleased" (Matthew 3:17).

SECTION III—*The Blessedness of This Man*

The Hebrew introduction to the Psalm is very full and expressive. Literally it may be translated, "Oh, the blessedness!" There are many blessednesses in this life. It is always blessed, blessed in every way.

1. He is blessed in what he escapes: the wretched lot of the ungodly, the sinner and the scorner. For, surely, the way of the transgressor is hard, and he is happy indeed who shuns it.

2. He is blessed in the spontaneousness of his life. "His delight is in the law of the LORD" (Psalm 1:2). Anything is happy in life if we can enjoy it and take pleasure in it. The hardest cross is a joy if it is our delight. The

blessedness of the spiritual life consists in this, that it is not an effort, a struggle, a painful constraint, a burden of law. It is a delightful freedom, a springing impulse, a spontaneous overflow, an artesian well rising ever from exhaustless depths, a great current of water to swim in, bearing us upon its bosom, and making all duty, and even trial, a luxury of joy, a luxury of love.

Oh, do you not long, heavy-laden ones, for the life in which it will not be *have* to but *love* to? For a life in which you shall always have your own way because you delight in God, and He gives you the desires of your heart? For a life that will fulfill His own sweet promise, "Take my yoke upon you and learn from me, for I am gentle and humble in heart, and you will find rest for your souls. For my yoke is easy and my burden is light" (Matthew 11:29–30)? For life in which you shall run in the way of His commandments when He has enlarged your heart? This is the life of the godly. This is the life of the first Psalm. This is the life of the New Testament saint. This is the life of Christ. This is the life of the Holy Spirit. This is the well of water which Jesus gives, to be within us, springing up into everlasting life. Oh, the blessedness of such a life!

3. The blessedness of such a life springs from the indwelling of the Holy Spirit. This is what is meant by the "streams of water" (Psalm 1:3) where he is planted. These streams refer to the blessed influences of the Holy Spirit. It is not one stream but many, the manifold streams that flow with all the fullness of the Holy Spirit as the Spirit of peace, of love, of joy, of holiness, of wisdom, of power, of prayer. This is the source of all blessedness. It is this that makes his life so spontaneous and his lot so easy. A power from above, a power from within fills all his being and divinely enables him to fulfill all the will of God.

He walks in the comfort of the Holy Spirit. He lives in that blessed kingdom which is "righteousness, peace and joy in the Holy Spirit" (Romans 14:17). He is a tree in the garden of the Lord whose fruit is love, joy, peace. He is drinking of the fountain which is the source of the blessedness of God and the raptures of heaven. Blessed is the man who is "planted by streams of water"!

4. He is blessed because "whatever he does prospers" (Psalm 1:3). His life is not in vain. He accomplishes what he undertakes. His work succeeds. He may not be rich or great or prosperous in the sense in which the world understands and esteems. He may have many troubles and what the world calls failure, but no real evil comes to him. All things work together for good to him. God turns everything that comes to him into real blessing, and surely this is prosperity in the truest sense.

5. He is blessed because of God's approval. "For the LORD watches over the way of the righteous" (1:6). This is enough to make any life happy and successful, for God to set His heart upon it and to take delight in it. The

word "knoweth" (KJV), according to a familiar Hebraism, means "to approve." The Lord does set His heart upon His people. He takes pleasure in them as a mother in her child. He looks with complacent delight upon their consecrated service and holy purposes to glorify Him. He loves to bless them. He says: "I . . . will assuredly plant them in this land with all my heart and soul" (Jeremiah 32:41).

In His favor is life, and His "love is better than life" (Psalm 63:3). Oh, the blessedness of the man who walks in the light of His countenance, who walks in His favor! Oh, the happiness of "those who have learned to acclaim you,/ who walk in the light of your presence, O LORD" (89:15). What can harm those whom God loves, chooses and uses? "The eyes of the LORD are on the righteous/ and his ears are attentive to their cry" (34:15). "If God is for us, who can be against us?" (Romans 8:31).

6. He is blessed because of the future issues of his life in contrast with the ungodly, for there is a day coming when all lives shall be tested, and the transient prosperity of the wicked shall fade away like the chaff before the wind. Oh, then shall we know the blessedness of the righteous life, and truly appreciate what it meant to choose God as our God and to know His great salvation!

> When this passing world is done;
> When has sunk yon glorious sun;
> When we stand with Christ on high,
> Looking o'er life's mystery;
> Then, Lord shall we fully know—
> Not till then—how much we owe.

In conclusion, where shall we look for the realization of this glorious picture? Who can fill up in his own life these perfect lineaments? Listen to the sad cry of God through the ages of the past! "I looked for a man among them . . . but I found none" (Ezekiel 22:30).

But at length the Son of man appeared, and as He stood upon the banks of the Jordan, the Father was satisfied. Humanity had reached its bloom and fruition and there was the Man on earth at last who met all the conditions of ancient prophecy and inspired Scripture. It was Jesus. But what avail is this to us? Can we imitate His holy character any more than we can fulfill the first psalm? No! Teaching and example are alike unequal to the task of transforming man. We know the right but cannot rise to it. Thank God, there is a better way!

Here is a beautiful rose. How we wish we could copy it. The painter takes his brushes and he tries, and lo, there appears a very wonderful imitation. But you put it to your face, and there is no fragrance. It is a lifeless pigment.

Or perhaps some gentle fingers carefully shape from wax or some finer fabric the exquisite petals, and tint them like the beautiful forms of nature. As you hold it in your hand, it looks like a rose; but, still, it is dead, and you throw it aside dissatisfied. It is not your rose. Ah, there is a better way!

Cut a little graft from that rose and put it in the warm nursery; or take one of its seeds and plant it in the ground. In a little while, opening its fragrant bud and breathing its sweetness into your nostrils, you have the offspring of your rose! It is identical because it was born of it. It is its own very self reproduced. Ah, that is the secret of the first psalm! To imitate Christ and His example is but a painted or imitation rose; but to take the living Christ and let Him be born in your heart and reproduce Himself there, so that it is not you but Christ who lives in you—that is the living rose. That is why He lived and died and rose again, that He might come into every open heart and become its life and purity, its love and joy, its righteousness and salvation.

CHAPTER 2

THE COMING KING

Psalm 2

The Messianic character of this psalm is established beyond all others by the frequent references to it in the New Testament in direct connection with the Lord Jesus Christ. To none but Him could its strong language be applied without the wildest extravagance. It contains three striking pictures.

SECTION I—*The Earth Picture*

It is a vision of the world in rebellion against God and His Son, Jesus Christ. The first element in the picture is the restlessness of the nations. "Why do the nations conspire (rage, KJV)?" (Psalm 2:1).

To the Psalmist's mind, humanity is like the heaving ocean, like a troubled sea which cannot rest. The stormy deep is frequently employed as a symbol of human passion, and of the troubled, restless masses of humanity. Along with this, the psalm expresses the idea of vanity, of unrest and strife. "Why do . . . the peoples plot in vain?" (2:1). They are like the ocean, ever fretting but never accomplishing anything by its unrest, beating against the shore in futile rage, and rolling back again into its own restless tides, rising and falling, but never any fuller.

"Meaningless! Meaningless!" (Ecclesiastes 1:2) indeed. Oh, how little has come out of all the world's ambition and mighty endeavor! What is Pharaoh today but a withered mummy in a glass case? What is Caesar but a particle of dust that makes up old Rome? What has become of Nebuchadnezzar's grandeur or the very site of his splendid city? Well might the great Frenchman say as he gazed on the splendid pageant of the review of the Grand Army under the Pyramids, "Nothing is lacking here, nothing but permanence." Oh, how the smallest fragment of all that which came from God lives in immortal glory while the mightiest monument of human greatness passes away in oblivion!

Pharaoh is gone, but Moses remains. Nero is forgotten, but Paul is more illustrious today than when he died under Nero's hand. Nebuchadnezzar is but a dream, but Daniel's prophecies are only today reaching their grandest fulfillment. Pontius Pilate and Tiberias Caesar have disappeared, but Jesus Christ, their contemporary, is rising every day, every century, into still more prominence.

On the front of a Muslim mosque, centuries ago, was traced in gilt letters the name of Mohammed, but underneath the plaster that bore the inscription, the Christian architect secretly cut in the solid stone the name of God and a verse of His holy Word. This was the verse: "Your kingdom is an ever-lasting kingdom,/ and your dominion endures through all generations" (Psalm 145:13). Ages passed on, the superficial stucco crumbled from the front of the mosque and left the stonework exposed to view, and then the inscription of God's holy Word came out in all its bold relief. Today it stands before the eyes of every passer-by as a memorial of the imperishable glory of the things of God, and the transitoriness of all man's boastful pride. How vain, how transient, how futile all the selfishness, ambition and strife against God!

But the figure tells not only of the restlessness and vanity, but also of rebellion. "The kings of the earth take their stand/ and the rulers gather together against the LORD/ and against his Anointed One./ 'Let us break their chains,' they say,/ 'and throw off their fetters'" (2:2–3). This is the spirit of lawlessness which in every age has resisted the authority of God and is culminating today, as never before, in a thousand forms of license and lawlessness, and which is to reach its full development in the coming of the Lawless One. We see it in its most extreme forms in the anarchy and socialism of our age and the revolt of men against every form of government and religion.

We see it next in the democratic tendencies of our time. We see it in the bold antagonism of many to the authority of the Christian religion, and the popular demand for a freedom that ignores the Lord's day, the laws of marriage and even the restraints of morality sometimes. We see it in the insubordination of the young, the precocious freedom of the children of our land, the dissolution of parental authority and control, and the irreverence and self-will of the young.

We see it in the spirit of freedom that is entering the Church of Christ and lowering the standard of Christianity: the spirit of compromise with the world, the laxity of Christian life, the rejection of the authority of the Scriptures, the tendency to reduce even God's Word to the standard of human reason, the refusal of the human heart to submit to God's requirements of personal holiness on the part of His people, the ungodliness and unrighteousness of professing Christians and the refusal to believe that God requires personal holiness on the part of all who claim to be His people and His followers. We see the two classes even in the Church of God: Those who accept God's holy will in all its requirements, and those who do "that which [is] right in [their] own eyes" (Judges 17:6, KJV).

The age is rapidly drifting into license and lawlessness, and we need not wonder at the bolder forms that the daring infidelity and wickedness assume, in defying the very authority of heaven and claiming that man is able to be a god unto himself. We shall yet see greater things than these. The world is hastening to its Armageddon, "for the battle on the great day of God Almighty" (Revelation 16:14).

SECTION II—*The Heaven Picture*

How different is all on the heaven side!

1. How calm and tranquil is Jehovah amid the raging of His foes! He is "enthroned in heaven" (Psalm 2:4). He is not agitated; He is not oppressed. He is not even doing anything, but calmly waiting till they have spent their force in vain, like the fretting billows against the rockbound coast.

2. He despises all their petty and futile hostility. "The One enthroned in heaven laughs;/ the Lord scoffs at them" (2:4). How foolish must seem to Him all the efforts of His enemies to defy Him! How ridiculous the attacks of infidelity upon the Bible, and how vain the fiercest assaults of human and hellish hatred against the cause of Christ! How God loves to confound His enemies by little things, and to laugh to scorn their vain attempt to resist Him.

Once in England, it is said, a bold and blatant infidel had amused and overawed a crowd by his defiance of God to strike him dead; and after again and again appealing to heaven to prove if there was anything in Christianity, without any apparent effect, he turned to his audience and ridiculed the God who was powerless to harm him. Some were influenced by his audacity, but God was waiting. On his way home, apparently in good health, he suddenly fell from his horse, and in a few moments expired. A medical examination was held; it was found that the cause of his death was a little insect no larger than a sand fly, which he had inhaled. This smallest of insects was sent against him to show how contemptible all his strength and opposition were, and how easily God could confound and destroy him by the feeblest of His creatures.

So, again and again, has God turned into contempt the wrath of His enemies. The very place that was once used as a meeting place for infidels in London became an office of the British and Foreign Bible Society, and the very arguments that infidelity has turned against Christianity have been found afterwards to be the strongest evidences of the truth of the Bible.

3. At length God's hour will come, and His mighty voice will speak in anger and His glorious arm be raised in judgment. "Then he rebukes them in his anger/ and terrifies them in his wrath" (2:5). God's judgments have already fallen upon a sinful world, and the bowls of His wrath are now preparing for the days of tribulation. So daring has human wickedness become and so audacious human pride, that

> The purging fires must soon begin,
> And judgment end the curse of sin.

4. God's supreme remedy for all the evils of humanity is His own dear Son, Jesus Christ. Not judgment, but Jesus, is the provision of heaven for rebellious men. So we come to

SECTION III—*The Christ Picture*

1. We see the divine King. "You are my Son;/ today I have become your Father" (2:7). Earth's true King is no less than God's eternal Son. That which should be recognized as the height of honor has been the one object of the world's fiercest opposition. The Lord's parable has been fulfilled. "Last of all, he sent his son to them. 'They will respect my son,' he said. But . . . they said . . . 'This is the heir. Come, let's kill him and take his inheritance' " (Matthew 21:37–38). But He shall have His inheritance in this little world, the high and eternal honor of having as its King, the Creator of all worlds and the highest of all beings.

2. He is the King of Zion, the King of Israel Himself. On the cross the inscription was by the order of an overruling providence: "THIS IS JESUS, THE KING OF THE JEWS" (27:37), and this shall yet be verified in the fulfillment of history. Christ is the only living Heir to David's throne, and on that throne He shall yet sit in glory and majesty.

3. He is the King of His Church. Men have tried to govern the spiritual kingdom of God, but Christ is the only Head of His Church, and all her work and worship should be subject to His authority and dedicated to His glory.

4. He is the King of Nations. "Ask of me,/ and I will make the nations your inheritance,/ the ends of the earth your possession" (Psalm 2:8). All earth's nations are yet to be subject to Him, and all her tribes and tongues are to have a part in the redemption song of which He shall be the theme. But let us not forget how this kingdom is to come to Him. It is to be given to prayer. "Ask of me" (2:8). Is this to be His prayer alone, or is it to be His prayer in unison with the Church as inspired by the Holy Spirit? Is this not

our high calling, to be the voice with which He shall ask, the priesthood through whom His prayer shall be breathed to heaven, and the world evangelized and brought to His feet?

This is the great force, dear friends, through which the gospel is to be spread among all nations. This is the mightiest force of Christianity today: believing prayer prompted by the Holy Spirit. This is the mightiest missionary lever. And this is something that every Christian may wield if he will, in the power of the Holy Spirit. It will be found by a reference to the history of missions, that all the great triumphs of the gospel have been in answer to prayer. It will bring money; it will bring men; it will bring openings for the gospel; it will bring millions to accept it. Let us mention two simple illustrations.

A few years ago, two or three earnest women were led to ask in united prayer that God would lay it upon the hearts of some men of wealth to give largely to foreign missions. In the town where they held their little prayer meetings, there was a very rich man who was opposed to foreign missions and had often spoken of the folly of giving so much to the heathen when there was so much need at home. After a time this man died; and when his will was probated, it was found that he had left many thousands of dollars to foreign missions, and that the will was made at the very time these ladies were praying about this matter. God had quickly answered their prayer and touched his heart, without his knowing whence the impulse came.

Again, in a little town in Ohio, an old minister had received the baptism of the Holy Spirit and spent his last days in continued prayer for the world's evangelization. It was customary for him to write his prayers in his diary, and this he did with systematic order, going around the world and covering in turn every mission field. It was found after his death that in the very order of his prayers God had poured out His Spirit upon each one in the form of missionary revivals, leading to the conversion of many souls. Thus God had answered his prayers with such literal exactness as to encourage us in claiming definite results.

Oh, do we realize how much Christ depends upon us to give completeness to His intercession? He is but the Head in heaven, we are the body on earth. And He needs us to fill up the unity of the prayer and make it the cry of the whole body—not only the Head in heaven but the Bride on earth, with the Holy Spirit inspiring her cry. Beloved, do you realize that your Master needs your prayers? You have prayed much for yourself; do you ever pray for Jesus? He is asking you today, "Will you pray for Me and My kingdom?" It is one of the promises of the 72nd Psalm, "May people ever pray for him" (72:15). How much are you praying for Him? How much have you been delivered from selfish prayers? What fruit are you claiming in heathen lands which you may never see?

5. "He is . . . King of kings" (Revelation 17:14). "Therefore, you kings, be wise;/ be warned, you rulers of the earth./ Serve the LORD with fear/ and rejoice with trembling" (Psalm 2:10–11). How marvelously God has put His hand on earth's kings and shown His ascendancy over all human power! How easily He came to the house of Pharaoh, through the infant Moses, and used a child to humble the monarch! How quickly He came to Babylon, through the three Hebrew children, and by their victorious faith compelled Nebuchadnezzar to proclaim the true God through all His dominion! How easily He stepped into the palace of Xerxes, and by the influence of a Hebrew maiden controlled the mighty monarch of the world and saved a whole race from destruction!

How manifest His providence in the career of Alexander and his successors, and the minuteness with which He made them fulfill the prophecies of Daniel and Zechariah to the letter! How easily He arrested the career of the great Napoleon and caged him on a lonely isle when He had accomplished His purpose through him! How quickly He humbled the pride of the Papacy in the very hour in which it claimed infallibility with impious audacity! How mightily within the last few decades His hand has moved upon all the nations and shaken all the thrones of earth, and how easily some day He will cause them all to crumble before His touch and give way to Messiah's throne!

Oh beloved, let us take hold in mighty prayer for earth's kings and governments. There is a promise in the book of Proverbs which we may claim for the evangelization of the world: "The king's heart is in the hand of the LORD;/ he directs it like a watercourse wherever he pleases" (21:1). Our King has sent us forth not merely to the people of this world, but to its nations and sovereigns. "Therefore go and make disciples of all nations" (Matthew 28:19) is His royal commission. Like ambassadors of a great king, we go forth to take not only individuals but nations for our Lord.

How much depends upon the attitude of the governments of the earth to the gospel, and we can control this by the ministry of prayer. Let us claim the hearts of the earth's rulers for Christ, the King of kings.

6. He is the King of love and grace. So far the picture has been one of majesty and, in some degree, of terror; at least, of power and judgment. But suddenly it all changes, and an appeal of infinite and surpassing tenderness closes the whole wonderful drama.

It reminds one of the scene toward the close of our Savior's life when He had just been honored and worshiped as the King of Israel, and, amid the plaudits of the multitude, was marching into Jerusalem. But suddenly, on the side of Olivet as the city burst into view, His whole demeanor changed, and the procession paused at His command. For a moment He gazed at the city at His feet and, bursting into a flood of passionate weeping, cried: "O

Jerusalem, Jerusalem, you who kill the prophets and stone those sent to you, how often I have longed to gather your children together, as a hen gathers her chicks under her wings, but you were not willing" (Matthew 23:37).

He could not enjoy the grandeur of the spectacle before Him. He saw not the enthusiasm of the multitudes and the glory of the city and the temple. He could see only the gathering legions of Rome, soon to encompass the beleaguered city, the famine and the terror of the doomed inhabitants, the streets running red with human blood, the pillage and horror that were soon to follow, the captives going forth unto all nations, the ashes of the temple and the desolation of the city for nearly 20 centuries. All this He saw; and, as if He would save them even yet from its horrors, He poured out His heart in one last appeal of tender compassion and love.

Such is the picture of this psalm. Suddenly all the figures of royal majesty are changed, and, bending from His throne, the Savior reaches down His lips of love to rebellious men and, offering the kiss of reconciliation, cries: "Kiss the Son, lest he be angry,/ and you be destroyed in your way" (Psalm 2:12). It is mercy in the midst of majesty. It is love triumphing over judgment.

He sees the coming tribulation. He sees the iron hand that will break rebellious men like a potter's vessel. But He would save us from it. He would gather us to His bosom and shelter us in the coming storm if we would accept His love. He would spread out His wings for the little birdlings and shield them from the cruel hawk and the angry tempest if they only would. His highest prerogative is mercy. His dearest attribute is love. His most kingly glory is to forgive and save.

These are expressed by this beautiful figure: "Kiss the Son" (2:12).

SUBMISSION

1. It speaks first of submission. The kiss is the Oriental token of absolute submission; and so our first attitude toward Christ must be surrender. He will lead us into a closer union and lift us to a higher friendship, but we must begin with submission and unconditional surrender; then shall we find that He will welcome us with tenderest love and lift us up into His royal favor.

Bunyan has given us in the allegory of the Holy War, a picture of the surrender of the town of Mansoul to King Immanuel. Long it held out against Him and tried to resist His authority. But at length it was forced to surrender unconditionally and its citizens compelled to march in single file into His presence, with ropes around their necks, acknowledging themselves as worthy of death, and submitting themselves to His sovereign will. But then, to their astonishment, as they lay prostrated at His feet, He caused the herald to proclaim the decree of forgiveness to all the transgressors, through

His clemency and mercy. The herald was also to add that King Immanuel had not only forgiven the rebellious town of Mansoul, but had also determined to bestow signal honors and privileges upon the city that had submitted to Him, and make it henceforth His capital and home, and lavish upon it the highest privileges of His kingdom, accepting its citizens as His own personal children, and sharing with them all the riches of His glory. He requires of them that they shall yield unreservedly to Him, and then He rewards them with His richest blessings and fondest love.

RECONCILIATION

2. The figure expresses reconciliation. It tells of friends divided, meeting in love and forgiveness. It recalls the picture of Jacob and Esau falling upon each other's bosom in the embrace of mutual love. It tells us of the prodigal and his father meeting in each other's arms with the kiss of reconciliation. It tells of the Savior waiting to forgive and ready to receive the poor sinner to a higher place than Adam lost or angels ever knew. He, at whose feet holy angels fell in adoring awe, bends His lips to kiss the vilest sinner.

Once at the door of a police court a refined lady met a poor abandoned girl in the hands of the police. The poor creature looked so dejected and ashamed, that the lady threw her arms around her and kissed her lips, with some tender words of compassion. The girl was so overwhelmed that she burst into tears and said: "You are the only one who has kissed me since I left my mother. How could you do it?" And that kiss saved her precious soul and brought her to receive her Redeemer's love.

Down in a police court in New York City, a man was on trial. His wife had testified against him, and the judge was about to pronounce a very severe sentence, when the babe in the mother's arms caught sight of its father in the prisoner's dock, and began to cry and to reach out its little hands to go to him. The mother allowed it to climb over the railing. The father took it in his arms. The little one was overjoyed, and in the presence of the court began to caress him in a very tender manner, putting its arms around his neck and kissing him with childlike love and freedom. The court was deeply moved.

The judge even felt the tender appeal, and, after a moment of silence and deep feeling, he said to the man, "You may thank that child for your freedom. I was about to punish you severely for your inexcusable conduct, but the kiss of that little child has saved you from a long term of imprisonment. A man that can be so loved by a pure child cannot after all be utterly hopeless." So, dear friends, there is One who bends from heaven and offers you the kiss of His love. "God's holy Child Jesus" will stand between you and your doom, and the Judge upon the throne will spare even the vilest sinner who accepts that kiss of reconciliation. Oh, do not refuse such love.

How easy it is to come back to God in that simple way! How easy it was for you as a little child to go to your father and your mother and by a kiss of reconciliation know that all was forgiven.

Some years ago a minister was called to see his boy die, as was supposed. He was a young man just out of his teens, but did not know the Savior. The father was told as he entered the hospital that the boy could not live many hours, and that if he had anything to say, it must be said quickly. He entered the chamber and took the cold hand of his child with deep emotion. The son looked up and said: "Father, they tell me I am dying, and I know I am not saved. Tell me in the fewest words you can just how to come to Christ, and tell me as if I had only five minutes to live."

What a responsibility for a father's heart! But he sat down and quietly said, "My boy, my dear boy! You remember once when you were a child how you grieved and disobeyed me. I had to treat you with severity and refuse to let you come to me as you used to, and sit on my knee and put your arms about my neck. You saw that it hurt me to be stern and distant as much as it hurt you, but that I had to do it for your good. But you remember how at last you could not stand it any longer, and you came to me, threw yourself into my arms, and said: 'Papa, forgive me. I am sorry. I will try never to do it again.' You remember how quickly I forgave you without a word, and just took you in my arms and loved you more than ever, and it was all right between us. Just one kiss settled all the trouble. That is all, my dear boy, that you have to do with your Savior. Just as you came to me, go to Him, and He is more willing than I was to take you to His love and make you know it."

"Is that all, Father?" the son answered. "Then pray for me, and I will do it." He covered his face, closed his eyes, and all was still for a few minutes. Then there was a little sob. He threw the covering from his face, opened his eyes, and, with a cry of joy, said: "It is all right, Father. He has received me, and I know that I am saved." That was all, but it was enough. The soul passed from hell to heaven, from sin to salvation forever, and so blessed was the effect of the transition that it lifted him above the power of disease and death. In a few days he was recovering and became one of the most prominent devoted Christian men of this country, not ashamed to tell others the wonderful story of his simple conversion. Oh, who is there that, as he reads these lines, will "kiss the Son" (2:12) and come into the love of God, of a God who waits to be gracious, with more than a father's love?

FRIENDSHIP AND LOVE

3. But the figure means more than reconciliation. It tells of intimate friendship and tender love. So Jesus is calling us into the inner circle of His friendship. Soon He is coming in His glory, and the world will see Him as a mighty King. But He wants us to know Him as a tender, welcome Friend.

Clad in his war-like armor, Ulysses met his child. It cowered and fled from his father. The old hero could not stand it. Tearing the helmet from his head and the breastplate from his bosom, he clasped the little one in his arms and said, "Darling, you must not fear me." Then it looked in his face with smiles of joy and said, "Papa, I am not afraid of you now because I know you."

Will we meet Him in the armor of His might and the glory of His majesty, and cry to the rocks and mountains to "hide us from the face of him who sits on the throne" (Revelation 6:16)? Or will we meet Him with the loving confidence of happy children; and as we look up to that majestic throne, will we catch the glance of a loving welcome that will seem to say, "I have summoned you by name; you are mine" (Isaiah 43:1)?

It will be a dreadful day for those to whom He shall say, "I don't know you" (Luke 13:25). Job could say in blessed contrast, "I myself will see him/ with my own eyes—I, and not another" (Job 19:27). He is longing to know you now and to take you into the inner circle of His friends, so that when that day shall come, you shall look up with rapture and say: "Surely this is our God;/ we trusted in him, and he saved us./ This is the LORD, we trusted in him;/ let us rejoice and be glad in his salvation" (Isaiah 25:9).

Yonder is a steamer reaching the dock. I see two persons on board. But, oh, with what different feelings they view the landing! One is a prisoner in the charge of an officer. On that dock are standing officers of justice who are to carry him to the gloomy prison to bear the punishment of the crimes for which he has been arrested, and brought from far-off lands. Oh, how he dreads that landing!

But another is standing near. It is a daughter returning home. Her father and mother are waiting on that pier. Her husband also stands there with smiles of welcome, and many loving friends are waving their handkerchiefs and sending their welcome across the narrow space as the ship draws to the shore. Oh, what a different meeting!

So it will be when Christ comes again. Some will meet Him with horror and dismay; some, with rapture and delight. To some it will be a day of judgment and an everlasting prison; to others, it will be the Bridegroom, the wedding, and the homecoming.

> Oh, shall we be found of Him in peace,
> Spotless and free from blame?
> Shall we meet Him with loving confidence,
> Or with tears of grief and shame?

CHAPTER 3

THE HEAD OF HUMANITY

Psalm 8

What a wonderful page is the blue firmament of heaven! Always beautiful, it is the most beautiful of all in the glorious East as David gazed upon it often on the plains of Bethlehem, and Persian sages studied it with eager search for truth and God. Oldest pages, grandest of records, graven with the finger of God, punctuated with burning stars of light! All else beneath those old skies has changed, but the skies are still the same. The same constellations are hanging in the blue vault which the Magi studied and which David wrote about in this beautiful psalm.

But how the page has grown since David's day, in another sense, through the deeper insight which human science has given to the vision and the mind of man. Under the telescopic lens, how much more those skies reveal than David saw, and with what deeper meaning and profounder feeling the intelligent astronomer, or even the well-informed and developed student of natural science, can read these ancient words: "When I consider your heavens,/ the work of your fingers,/ the moon and the stars,/ which you have set in place,/ what is man that you are mindful of him,/ the son of man that you care for him?" (Psalm 8:3–4).

SECTION I—*The Majesty of Nature*

We have here a view of the majesty of nature. Majestic and glorious as the heavens are to the natural eye, they are incomparably grander when seen with the eye of science and under the magnifying lenses of the telescope of the astronomer. Man has been able in the progress of the human mind to weigh these mighty orbs, to span that vast immensity, to tell how far those worlds are hung from our little planet, and how long their light has been traveling across the mighty spaces of immensity.

The facts of astronomy are so stupendous that the mind reels under the weight, and the brain almost sinks in the effort to realize their magnitudes and distances. So we first think of their vastness.

We know something of the dimensions of our globe. It is a pretty large sphere, especially when we begin to travel across the continents. But our globe is but a pygmy among the planets of our system.

Yonder crystal star that shines in the evening—our noble planet Jupiter—is hundreds of times bigger than this globe; and yonder sun that whirls us around his center once a year is 350,000 times the size of earth. It would take 350,000 earths to make one sun. But the sun is by no means the vastest of the worlds in space. While he is the king of light in the planets of our system, yet there are other suns in yonder firmament that look to us like little stars, far vaster than he.

Beautiful Sirius, the brightest of the fixed stars—that shines like Venus all night long in our heavens—is 63 times as big as the sun. Yonder Pole Star, that you have to search for in the heavens because of its comparative insignificance, is 86 times the size of the sun. Arcturus, of which Job sang so long ago, would make 500 of our suns; and Alcyone, which twinkles in the Pleiades—the beautiful seven stars, so-called, which you can see any evening directly above your head—could be divided into 12,000 pieces, and each piece would be as large as the sun.

The comet of 1680 covered a space four times the distance between us and the moon, and its tail was long enough to reach from here to the sun, and then nearly as far beyond, or about 130 million miles.

Shall we look next at the distance of these vast orbs? Our nearest neighbor is yonder silvery moon that seems to us so much greater than the stars because so near. She is 240,000 miles away, or about 30 times the diameter of our globe. The sun is about 400 times farther distant than this, or 95 million miles. This seems an enormous distance, and yet light, which travels about 186,000 miles in a second, could reach us from the moon in a little more than a second. From the sun it takes about 10 minutes for the light to come; that is to say, after the sun rises in the morning, it takes about 10 minutes for its light to reach us, swiftly as it flies across the intervening spaces.

But yonder Pole Star is three million times as far as the moon, and the light which takes only 10 minutes to reach us from the sun would be 60 years in reaching us from Polaris. That is, if it had been destroyed 60 years ago, it would only now disappear from the sky. But what is that compared with distant Andromeda, one of the stars of yonder nebula, so far away that it would take seven million years for its light to reach our globe!

Look up some night in the southern heavens, and you will see a faint light upon the sky. When looked at with a powerful telescope, it is a great bank of suns, each standing out distinctly. How wide, do you suppose, is that space of stars? How far from the one extremity to the other of that little circle of nebulous light? It would take a ray of light, traveling 186,000 miles per second, 30,000 years to sail across that little speck.

Do you begin to realize the immensity of the universe? In that one little cloud of light there are suns upon suns, systems upon systems, worlds upon worlds.

But again, think of their numbers. We can count a few thousand stars upon the sky at night. How many do you suppose astronomers have found in our firmament? Eighteen million, and these are all suns, each of them with its train of worlds around it like ours.

There are about 300 worlds in the solar systems. Suppose there should be as many in each of these 18 million systems, how many worlds, do you suppose, belong to even our firmament? The mind is lost in trying to count. But they say there are millions of other firmaments besides ours, and each has its new stars which we have never seen. No wonder that we labor in vain to grasp the realization, and cry, "What is man?" (8:4).

Shall we think of their movements and velocities, the satellites revolving around their planets, the planets around their suns, and each sun with its planet revolving around some great center, and each of the suns revolving around some still greater? And so on, wheel beyond wheel, until we reach the satellite systems, the solar systems, the cluster systems and the great universe systems, where all the stars of yonder heaven seem whirling around mighty Alcyone in the distant Pleiades, beyond which there may be still vaster wheels circling away through the realms of immensity.

This earth itself is spinning around yonder sun at the rate of 70,000 miles an hour, or 20 miles a second, and yet there is not even the vibration of the mighty express train as it sweeps through space. But the mighty comet of 1680 flew around the sun at the rate of 200 miles a second; and yet with this immense velocity, so vast was its orbit that it would take 30 centuries to complete its year. Surely, this is too high for us to comprehend, too vast for us to measure, and yet we can realize it sufficiently to sink into our littleness and to rise from our nothingness into the conception of our Father's majesty and unsearchable glory.

But not only are these heavenly bodies vast and majestic, but they are beautiful beyond expression. Looked at through our modern instruments, some of yonder suns are brilliant green; some, like the Pole Star, a gorgeous yellow; some, a heavenly blue; some, like the Southern Cross, the color of drops of blood, while other stars are variegated, combining all the colors of the rainbow and looking like great bouquets of light in the heavens. Oh, what will they seem when we shall be endued in the new creation with all the physical powers which science is now anticipating, and faith is foretasting, and we shall know as we are known (1 Corinthians 13:12)!

Such are some of the facts of this material universe. Surely "the heavens declare the glory of God;/ the skies proclaim the work of his hands./ Day after day they pour forth speech;/ night after night they display knowledge./ There is no speech or language/ where their voice is not heard./ Their voice goes out into all the earth,/ their words to the ends of the world" (Psalm 19:1–4).

SECTION II—*The Insignificance of Man*

"What is man that you are mindful of him,/ the son of man that you care for him?" (8:4). Surely at first sight man seems to be a strange contradiction as heir of all this mighty universe. His body, how weak and frail, the prey of disease, the victim of even the animal creation, and at last the food of corruption and the worm; his mind so weak and enfeebled even to understand this mighty world; his spirit so oppressed by sin and sorrow, and led captive by evil influences and unhallowed beings! How touching Job's description of the littleness of man who dwells in a house of clay, whose habitation is in the dust, who is crushed before the moth, whose days are as a handbreadth, and his life like the withering grass of the field!

And yet in the great purpose of God, man has an importance that we can scarcely comprehend. Sometimes a very insignificant being has a singular value. Sometimes a little child is worth more than a whole kingdom. Sometimes it is the question of relationship. If that child is the child of a king, an empire's destiny is wrapped up in his life. Little Moses in the Nile was more important than the pyramids of Egypt. Humble David in his sheepfold was more important than all the sons of Saul. So man, little as he may be, sustains a relation to the Creator of this universe which is unspeakably intimate and glorious. Into our nature has come the very Son of God Himself. The eternal Creator has called Himself our Brother. Our human form is worn by Him who sits upon the throne. Our strange race, fallen though it is, has been chosen as the one eternal link between the Creator and the creation; and to latest ages, as angel after angel shall come, and inhabitant after inhabitant shall find his way to the great metropolis of the universe, he shall still find seated upon the throne, supreme above all those glorious worlds that we have just been viewing, a Man.

This it is that makes our race so important, that it is related to God Himself, and has been chosen to be the eternal embodiment of Deity. This is the mystery of godliness: "He appeared in a body,/ was vindicated by the Spirit,/ was seen by angels,/ . . . was taken up in glory" (1 Timothy 3:16).

But again, importance is sometimes determined by a question of principle. A single human life has become important because it decided a principle. Six or seven Englishmen imprisoned in Abyssinia were important enough to bring on a war between Great Britain and that land. Nay, a single American subject, unjustly treated by a foreign nation, would involve this whole nation in war, if necessary, for his vindication. The little field of Waterloo was of no importance until a certain day when it became the scene where the destinies of Europe were to be decided and the greatest despot of the 19th century was to be broken forever.

And so man is linked with the greatest principle in the universe, the achievement of redemption, the settlement of the question of sin without inflicting punishment, the salvation of a lost race in harmony with the justice of God.

The question of sin, so far as justice was concerned, had been settled long before when Satan and his legions had been hurled from heaven because of their disobedience and rebellion.

But now another question has come up. How can sin be met in any other way—not by judgment, but by mercy—and yet the holiness and justice of God be vindicated? Nothing less than the infinite wisdom and love of God met the issue. His own Son undertook the amazing mission, and, clothed in human form, bore the penalty of a guilty race, and now is working out for them the wondrous transformation by which the effects of that atonement become applied. And they are brought back not only from all the effects of sin, but to a place infinitely higher than the race ever could have enjoyed before—to be the sons of God, the partakers of the divine nature, the heirs of all the glory of which we have just now been speaking.

This gives to man an importance of which he in himself is altogether unworthy. This little planet has been chosen as the theater for working out the greatest problem of the ages, and it is yet to become the scene of the triumphant march of the King of kings and the Conqueror of Satan, over which all the stars shall wave their torches, and all the spheres shall sing in concert with cherubim and seraphim: "Worthy is the Lamb, who was slain,/ to receive power and wealth and wisdom and strength/ and honor and glory and praise!" (Revelation 5:12).

SECTION III—*The Honor Bestowed upon Man*

"You are mindful of him/ . . . you care for him./ You made him a little lower than the heavenly beings/ and crowned him with glory and honor./ You made him ruler over the works of your hands;/ you put everything under his feet" (Psalm 8:4–6).

This is high honor. God is mindful of man notwithstanding his insignificance. God has devoted His highest, wisest thoughts to the welfare of man. We are the supreme objects of the attention of Jehovah. How precious are His thoughts! This glorious Bible is the record of some of them, but they are more than can be numbered, and the ages to come shall "show the incomparable riches of his grace, expressed in his kindness to us in Christ Jesus" (Ephesians 2:7).

But further and higher: He has not only been mindful of us, He has visited us. He has made this world His residence. He has tabernacled among us, and He is coming back again to dwell upon it through the coming age, and for a thousand years this little planet will be the center of the universe and the metropolis of all other worlds. Not distant Alcyone, but little Earth, will be the proud and happy capital of the realms of the air, and wondering angels shall hover round it, and often say, perhaps, as they come from yonder blazing worlds, "What is man that you are mindful of him . . . ?" (Psalm 8:4).

Not only so, "You . . . crowned him with glory and honor" (8:5). Made a little lower than the angels, he is raised above them, for it is clearly taught here that he is to receive the supreme place in creation; for even this psalm declares that this is to be taken rigidly and literally, and that "In putting everything under him, God left nothing that is not subject to him" (Hebrews 2:8b). He is yet to rise to the supremacy of the universe, higher than those 18 million suns, more glorious than all the satellites and stars, more mighty than all the forces of nature and more honored than the highest archangel that bends before the throne.

SECTION IV—*Man's Failure to Realize This*

This does not come out of the Psalm, but it does in the New Testament commentary of it. Speaking of it in the second chapter of Hebrews, the inspired writer says: " 'What is man that you are mindful of him,/ the son of man that you care for him?/ You . . . put everything under his feet.'/ In putting everything under him, God left nothing that is not subject to him. Yet at present we do not see everything subject to him" (2:6–8). Oh, how true this is! We do not see this proud empire of man. We see human conquerors trying to gain this crown of universal dominion, but becoming themselves the slaves of sin and passion, enslaving others under them, and sinking at last beneath the dominion of the grave, while their empires fade away like the snowdrifts or the autumn leaves.

Man's place, as a fact, is still that of a poor, sinning, sinking, sorrowing creature. With every pulse beat, another and another is passing to the grave, and up to heaven evermore is rising from this sad world one ceaseless groan of agony amid the spheres of space in a little black cloud of unbroken gloom. Even we who have begun to receive our kingdom are yet struggling with forces that often seem too strong for us. Sin, Satan, sorrow and sickness press us, and all things are not yet put under our feet. A few have sprung into victory, but it is only moral and spiritual. Material things still hold us down, and we are shut in from our great inheritance by the limitations of mortality, and can only claim our crown in foretaste, in hope and aspiration. But, thanks be to God, the problem is solved, the paradox is explained. "We do not see everything subject to him. But we see Jesus" (2:8–9a).

SECTION V—*The Head of Humanity Crowned*

We see Jesus, the Head of humanity, crowned already as the pledge that we shall share His crown and inherit all His glory. The race is not yet victorious, but the Head of the race is; and where He is, we shall be; as He is, so shall we be like Him! Glorious hope! We have not the victory yet in all its fullness, but we have the Victor, and "both the one who makes men holy and those who are made holy are all of the same family" (2:11).

He is not there for Himself, but for us, "head over everything for the church, which is his body, the fullness of him who fills everything in every way" (Ephesians 1:22–23). Glorious vision! Glorious forerunner! Glorious guarantee! It is enough! Man is crowned! Man is crowned in the Son of man; and all His spiritual seed are following hard after Him and soon shall be by His side. Oh, as we see our failings and shortcomings, our limitations and disappointments, let us look up! One has reached yonder heights, and we are following Him. Invisible cords bind us to His heart. We can never be separated from Him. Not as a solitary and selfish Conqueror does He sit yonder, but as our Brother and Helper. From His heart there come to our hearts the cords of love and power that are drawing us to Him to share His dominion and to partake of His glory.

This was the meaning of the cherubim that God placed at the gate of Eden in the hour of man's shameful fall. The faces of the lion, the ox, the eagle and the man were typical of the glory of the Son of man, to which we, His redeemed posterity, are yet to rise. When the picture of man's primeval innocence had been blighted and broken, God hung up the picture of man's redeemed and far surpassing glory, that man might see from the beginning his future destiny, and that it might lift him to high and glorious hopes.

Not the cherubim now at the gates of Eden, but the loving Christ at the gospel gates, standing before us as the Pattern of our perfect humanity, the Inspiration of our hopes, and the glorious Head of our redeemed race. Let us claim the realization for ourselves. Let us see Jesus. Let us take Jesus. Let us rest short of nothing that He has given us in Himself, and amid all the discouragements, depressions and defeats of life, let us look up, let us press on, let us sing:

High is the rank we now possess,
  But higher we shall rise;
Though what we shall hereafter be
  Is hid from mortal eyes.
Our souls, we know, when He appears
  Shall bear His image bright;
For all His glory full disclosed
  Shall open to our sight.
A hope so great and so divine
  May trials well endure,
And purge the soul from sense and sin
  As Christ Himself is pure.

CHAPTER 4

THE ASCENDED CHRIST

Psalms 16, 24, 68

These three beautiful psalms give us the combined picture of the risen and ascended Christ. The 24th comes in central order after the 22nd and 23rd. The 22nd is the psalm of crucifixion; the 23rd, the picture of blessings that follow to us; and the 24th, the ascension of the Lord and His glorious reign at God's right hand. The logical order begins with Psalm 16: "Therefore my heart is glad and my tongue rejoices;/ my body also will rest secure,/ because you will not abandon me to the grave,/ nor will you let your Holy One see decay./ You have made known to me the path of life;/ you will fill me with joy in your presence,/ with eternal pleasures at your right hand" (16:9–11).

SECTION I—*Descent into Hades*

This is the inspired picture of what is known in the ancient creeds as the Lord's descent into Hades. That the Psalm refers to our Lord directly is evident from Peter's application of it in his sermon on the day of Pentecost. Peter says it cannot refer to David, whose sepulchre is with them, and whose flesh has seen corruption. Therefore, it must refer to Jesus, who had been raised from the dead by the power of the Father.

But what is meant by His descent into Hades? For the apostle says in Ephesians: "What does 'he ascended' mean except that he also descended to the lower, earthly regions?" (Ephesians 4:9). The Apostle Peter has given us the strongest light on this subject of any New Testament writer: "He was put to death in the body but made alive by the Spirit, through whom also he went and preached to the spirits in prison who disobeyed long ago . . . in the days of Noah while the ark was being built. In it only a few people, eight in all, were saved through water" (1 Peter 3:18–20).

This forms the battleground of Bible exposition. It is not necessary that we should even state all the views that have been held and advocated. It is enough to give the two which are most approved by evangelical teachers. The old conservative view is that it refers to Noah preaching through the Holy Spirit to the antediluvians, who are now "the spirits in prison" (3:19), because they were disobedient when he preached to them. In other words, and freely paraphrased, it might be rendered thus: "Jesus is put to death in the flesh, but is quickened, or raised from the dead by the Holy Spirit, which in the days of Noah, and through Noah, preached unto the unbelieving men of that age, who are spirits in prison." In fact, it is a bungling attempt to make the Bible meet a preconceived opinion; and even though it is a good opinion, it is a profanation to wrest Scripture, even with the best intent.

The central meaning of the passage is, that Christ died in His body, but not in His spirit; but, on the contrary, that spirit was quickened into more intense life the moment of His death, and in the disembodied state His spirit went and preached to spirits in prison; that is, to the inhabitants of the world of the dead. The Old Testament represents departed spirits as dwelling in a region called Sheol or Hades.

This seems to have had two sections, one for the lost and one for the saved. The latter is the Paradise of the dying thief, the bosom of Abraham where Lazarus went, the place where Abraham was gathered to his fathers, a sweet and restful place where the redeemed ones waited for the great redemption. It was not heaven, for heaven was not yet opened.

There was another section to this region where the spirits of the wicked passed, represented by the rich man in the parable, far away from the unsaved, and yet in view of them, even across the great gulf. Now, it was to this region of the dead that the spirit of Jesus passed.

In order truly to die, it was necessary not only that His body should hang lifeless on the cross, but that His spirit should go down into the regions of the dead. But how did He go? Not as others had gone before, as victims of death, but as Conqueror and Witness, to preach the consummation of redemption. Even to the unbelieving dead, it was proper that He should announce the accomplishment of those promises which they had rejected. Even to the devil himself and all his angels, it was right that the Son of God should proclaim that Satan was defeated at length, and that his last desperate blow had been turned against himself in the very death of the Lord.

But to the saints of the past how peculiarly fitting it was that He should preach the great truth that He had come and died for their complete salvation, and that the gates of their prison were about to be opened and they were to follow Him in a few days as He ascended heavenward to take His place with them at His Father's side. This is the sense in which He went to preach to the spirits in prison. That He went to proclaim a second probation, another chance of salvation, we do not believe; and there is no semblance of evidence anywhere in the Scriptures to prove, or even imply it. This is the time of men's probation; this is the day of grace; and when it shall be passed, he that is unjust shall be unjust still, and he that is righteous shall be righteous still (Revelation 22:11).

SECTION II—*His Resurrection*

"You will not abandon me to the grave,/ nor will you let your Holy One see decay./ You have made known to me the path of life" (Psalm 16:10–11).

Not long did He remain among the dead. On the morning of the third day the fetters of the tomb were burst asunder, the stone rolled away, the spirit returned to the uncorrupted clay and the body sprang to life in all the fullness and glory of immortality, and Jesus became the firstborn from the dead. Others had been raised from the dead, but He was the first raised to die no more. Even the saints that were raised in connection with His crucifixion did not come out of their graves until after the resurrection of their Lord. This glorious fact of the risen Christ is the general theme of the apostolic testimony; it gives eternal greatness to the whole gospel; and in proportion as we realize it, it uplifts and glorifies our whole Christian life.

The difference between the religion of the New Testament and Judaism on the one hand, or Romanism on the other, lies right here in the conception of a living Christ. It is the great evidence of Christianity. It is the mighty inspiration of spiritual life. It is the pattern, both of our spiritual resurrection now and our future glorification in His fullness when He shall come again.

That path of life which He has shown has become the shining way to a mighty multitude, who pass from mortality to immortality, from the race of Adam to the race of our second great Head of humanity. "For as in Adam all die, so in Christ all will be made alive" (1 Corinthians 15:22). "The first man Adam became a living being; the last Adam, a life-giving spirit" (15:45). "As was the earthly man, so are those who are of the earth; and as is the man from heaven, so also are those who are of heaven. And just as we have borne the likeness of the earthly man, so shall we bear the likeness of the man from heaven" (15:48–49).

But we pass on from this theme, which has been so often unfolded, to the third question.

SECTION III—*His Ascension*

This is described in Psalm 16, and more fully in the others. "You will fill me with joy in your presence,/ with eternal pleasures at your right hand" (16:11).

This, undoubtedly, is an allusion to Christ and the ascension at His Father's right hand. Psalm 24, however, expressly refers to this glorious event. It is the responsive chorus of the saints and angels who attend the Son of God as He ascends. "Lift up your heads, O you gates;/ lift them up, you ancient doors,/ that the King of glory may come in" (24:9), is the shout of the approaching procession as it mounts the sky and nears the heavenly portals.

"Who is this King of glory?" (24:8) is the answer of the heavenly chorus that wait at yonder gates. And then the answer is returned from the approaching throng: "The LORD strong and mighty,/ the LORD mighty in battle" (24:8). "Lift up your heads, O you gates" (24:9), again they shout, "lift them up, you ancient doors,/ that the King of glory may come in" (24:9). Once again the heavenly hosts answer, "Who is he, this King of glory?" (24:10). And once again the chorus around the King sends back the cry as they reach the gates, and both companies unite in the swelling refrain, as it echoes to the confines of the universe, "The LORD Almighty—/he is the King of glory" (24:10).

It is something like the mighty scene which John presents, the whole creation in earth, and in the heaven, and in the sea, away out to the uttermost parts of the universe, waiting with the saints and angels to echo, "Then I heard every creature in heaven and on earth and under the earth and on the sea, and all that is in them, singing: 'To him who sits on the throne and to the Lamb/ be praise and honor and glory and power, for ever and ever!' " (Revelation 5:13).

To apply this sublime Psalm to the ascension of the ark to Mount Zion would be unworthy of its lofty character. For there were no everlasting doors; but the gates through which Jesus passed shall never be shaken or removed. The throne to which He ascended can never pass away. The glory which He has inherited can never decline.

The New Testament has given us the earth view of this glorious event. Out to Bethany He has led them. Perhaps for a moment they have entered that loving home and taken a last farewell of its dear inmates; perhaps they have accompanied the disciples and the Lord from the door to the little eminence on which He stands; and now, with hands outstretched in blessing, He is speaking to them—perhaps praying with them—when, suddenly, they behold Him rising and disappearing.

Often in these 40 days had He vanished from them, but now His attitude is different; He does not disappear, but fully in their view He begins to ascend. His hands are still stretched out toward them with tenderness and love as higher and higher He rises into the clear, blue heavens, while they gaze intently as if they would follow if they could. Higher and higher He rises, still blessing, still spreading those hands above their heads, until a cloud intervenes, and they see Him no more. Perhaps it was a cloud of angels; angels, we know were there—multitudes of angels, and multitudes of saints.

Upward and upward still He arose, beyond the nearest of the stars, beyond the distant constellations, beyond the nebulous clouds which form the great invisible worlds, beyond the vision of the eye, to the one central spot, somewhere in this immensity where stands the metropolis of the universe, the throne of God and the home of the redeemed. "Far above all rule and authority," the apostle has said, "power and dominion, and every title that can be given" (Ephesians 1:21). Far above all heavens, that He might fill all things. Then it was that the glorious chorus of the 24th Psalm begins, and the King of glory enters in and takes His seat at the right hand of God.

But the New Testament picture has one little addition, sweeter than all the rest. Just at that moment, when all heaven was prostrate before Him, and when the echoes of those songs were resounding through the universe, His loving heart was turned backward to the earth He had just left; He was thinking of the 11 loving hearts, whose eyes were still straining upward and trying to pierce the little cloud that hung between Him and Bethany. Quickly, therefore, does He send back from the heights of glory two angel messengers, to bear to them His last word of comfort and of love: " 'Men of Galilee,' they said, 'why do you stand here looking into the sky? This same Jesus, who has been taken from you into heaven, will come back in the same way you have seen him go into heaven' " (Acts 1:11). How beautiful! How loving! How comforting! It was as if He sent them back a miniature photograph of His own face and had written at the bottom, "The same yesterday and today and forever" (Hebrews 13:8). Blessed be His name forever for those three little words, "this same Jesus" (Acts 1:11).

Oh, how things change! But how sweet to know there is One who is the same forever! I have read somewhere the sweet poem of an old man who addresses the companion of his life after 60 years of sojourning together, and tells her that to him she has still the same face that he knew when she was a little child. Others see the wrinkles and the gray hair, the stooping form and the faded cheeks, but he ever sees only the bright young face of 60 years ago. To him, to his love, her youth is immortal. Her girl-face is stereotyped forever upon his heart, and she can never grow old. This is, in a sense, true of all loving memories. We see the ideals of things rather than the things themselves, and our imaginations sometimes picture those we love as they have been rather than as they are.

We thank God sometimes for those who are not. To us their faces can never change. That beautiful child is forever young. Others grow old and are scarred with sin and wrinkled with care, but there are some who live in our love and memory in immortal youth and beauty. Thank God that it is forever "this same Jesus" (1:11). We may change; He changes not. Circumstances may change; He changes not. As He loved you then, He loves you still and will love you forever. Oh strange, changeless heart of Christ, we praise Your changeless love. We cannot understand it fully, but let it draw us to be worthier of His love.

Why did He ascend?

1. That He might enter upon His reward. "So he became as much superior to the angels as the name he has inherited is superior to theirs" (Hebrews 1:4).

2. That He might assume the kingdom and government of the world which the Father had put into His hands, as mediatorial King; for now power was given Him in heaven and in earth, and He is Head over all things for His Church. His ascension has put all things under His feet, and He sits in calm repose and mighty omnipotence, from henceforth expecting until His enemies are made His footstool.

3. That He might become our Great High Priest, and at God's right hand represent us in heavenly places, meeting for us every question of sin, temptation and need, presenting our petitions to the Father and keeping us by His intercessions forevermore.

4. To take possession in our name of our inheritance, and to prepare a place for us when He shall have finished for us our life work and called us home.

5. That we may now ascend with Him and live in heavenly places through the power of His ascension. There is something higher than resurrection life; we may live an ascension life above our trials, anticipating already our heavenly calling, and feeling and acting as we shall when earthly things shall have passed away forever.

SECTION IV—*The Effects of His Ascension*

These are described more fully in the 68th Psalm. "When you ascended on high,/ you led captives in your train;/ you received gifts from men,/ even from the rebellious—/ that you, O LORD God, might dwell there" (Psalm 68:18).

1. "You led captives in your train" (68:18). This undoubtedly refers to the multitudes who ascended with Him from the regions of the dead. The captivity which He led captive is just a Hebrew expression for the captives that He liberated and took with Him to heaven.

Up to the time of Christ's ascension, as we have already seen, the spirits of the sainted dead were not in heaven, but in Paradise or Hades. But when Jesus ascended, He opened the gates of heaven to all believers, and took with Him these ransomed prisoners from the abodes of the dead. And now these gates are ever open, and day by day our friends are passing through, passing in. Stephen looked up from the murderous stones of his persecutors and the blood that was streaming from his face, and saw heaven opened and Jesus standing at the right hand of God, waiting to receive him. And Paul could say, "I desire to depart and be with Christ, which is better by far" (Philippians 1:23). And the Epistle to the Hebrews tells us we "have come to . . . the heavenly Jerusalem, . . . to thousands upon thousands of angels in joyful assembly, to the church of the firstborn, whose names are written in heaven. You have come to God, the judge of all men, to the spirits of righteous men made perfect" (12:22–23).

2. "You received gifts from men" (Psalm 68:18). Into His hands the Father gave, on His ascension, all things.

All that had been included in the covenant of redemption between the Father and the Son was now handed over to Jesus to dispense to His people: pardon for the penitent; power to become the sons of God through the regenerating work of the Holy Spirit; grace to keep, to sanctify, to sustain; all the fullness of Jesus, the all-sufficiency of His love and life, especially the greatest of all gifts—the Holy Spirit, Representative of Christ, the Executive of God, and all the ministries which He endues and directs.

When He ascended on high, "he . . . gave some to be apostles, some to be prophets, some to be evangelists, and some to be pastors and teachers, to prepare God's people for works of service, so that the body of Christ may be built up until we all reach unity in the faith and in the knowledge of the Son of God and become mature, attaining to the whole measure of the fullness of Christ" (Ephesians 4:11–13). Like a king at his coronation, He has received the power and might to give whatever He wishes; and ever since His ascension, He has been pouring out the riches of His love and grace, and saying to sinful man, "Ask and it will be given to you" (Matthew 7:7).

3. The third effect of Christ's ascension was the proclamation of the gospel of reconciliation to lost and rebellious men.

A great prince rising to the throne usually signalizes his advent by some distinguished act of amnesty. When Alexander of Russia visited Napoleon at Toulon, the French Emperor gave his illustrious visitor the privilege of liberating any one of the prisoners in the galleys. The Emperor went among the men and asked them concerning their lives and their crimes. But none of them was willing to acknowledge his guilt. One said he was unjustly convicted; another, too severely punished; another, persecuted by the officials; but all were virtuous and innocent.

At length, he found one man who was thoroughly penitent and humble and could only blame himself for his sufferings. The Emperor was so pleased that he said, "I have been looking for a sinner all this day, and you are the first I have been able to find. Now, because you are a sinner, you are pardoned and free. Go and use your liberty for his honor to whose clemency you owe it."

So Jesus at God's right hand has received authority to pardon even the rebellious and save the most unworthy and lost, on the simple condition that they will acknowledge their sin and accept His free and sovereign grace.

Oh, the gifts He has to pour out upon the sinful and unworthy: the gift of eternal life, the gift of peace, the gift of grace to stand and overcome, the gift of His Holy Spirit—all as the gifts of His grace, without money and without condition, to all who will receive them by faith and use them for His glory.

4. The presence of God in the hearts of His people. "That you, O LORD God, might dwell there" (Psalm 68:18). This is the crowning glory of Christ's ascension. It has brought God down to man in a new relationship. God was *with* men under the Old Testament. He is *in* them under the New. Christ has been glorified that man might be glorified in Him and raised up to union with Him. Born as an Adamic race, we may be newborn into a divine nature.

He has gone up to yonder throne that He may send the Holy Spirit to dwell in our hearts and unite us to Himself. Henceforth God's home is to be the human heart. Strange as it may seem, His going up has really brought Him down! So high above us, He has really come so much closer to us than He could have done had He remained on the earth in human form.

How finely the apostle presents this in the lofty Epistle to the Ephesians! He presents Christ in the first chapter as going up, far above all principality and power, and might and dominion. And then in the third chapter he presents Him as coming down to dwell in our hearts by faith, and bringing us to know "how wide and long and high and deep is the love of Christ, and to know this love that surpasses knowledge—that you may be filled to the measure of all the fullness of God" (Ephesians 3:18–19).

Beloved, do you know this mystery of love and life divine, "Christ in you, the hope of glory" (Colossians 1:27)? He is waiting now to make your heart His home.

> This is my wonderful story,
>   Christ to my heart has come;
> Jesus, the King of Glory,
>   Finds in my heart a home.

CHAPTER 5

THE SUFFERING SAVIOR

Psalm 22

T his is the Holy Spirit's picture of the suffering Savior. It is the *Ecce Homo* of the Psalms. The Gospels have given us the outward picture; this is the inner one, the Holy of Holies of the Redeemer's anguish when He trod the winepress alone.

Well does it precede the 23rd Psalm. That is the picture of the Shepherd in the fold, but this is the Shepherd in the night, in the desert, in the wilderness, among the wolves, with bleeding feet and broken heart, seeking for the sheep that went astray. May the Holy Spirit engrave the picture upon our hearts!

SECTION I—*Christ's Sufferings*

THE FATHER'S DESERTION

1. The first element in it is the Father's desertion. The opening verse is the wail of Calvary: " '*Eloi, Eloi, lama sabachthani?* '—which means, 'My God, my God, why have you forsaken me?' " (Mark 15:34).

Have you ever felt a sense of God's displeasure or desertion? Do you remember your first conviction of sin and your cry for pardon? Then you know something of the suffering of Christ when He stood in the place of a sinner under the judgment of God and suffered the penalty our sin deserved.

For the first time in His existence He felt the withdrawal of the Father's love. Never had the Father's face been clouded before. But now it is turned away. Nay, it is turned against Him. "It was the LORD'S will to crush him" (Isaiah 53:10). "Therefore, I have begun to destroy you" (Micah 6:13). We can scarcely understand it. But it was strangely, awfully true. For one day God dealt with Jesus as He will deal with sinful, rebellious men. All other agonies could not compare with this. This was the dregs of the cup of woe—

the desertion, the wrath of God.

> The Father lifted up His rod.
> O Christ, it fell on Thee!
> Thou wast sore smitten of Thy God;
> Thy bruising healeth me.

THE CRUELTY OF MAN

2. The second ingredient in the bitter cup was the cruelty of man. How vividly is it all portrayed! The mockery around the cross: "All who see me mock me;/ they hurl insults, shaking their heads:/ 'He trusts in the LORD;/ let the LORD rescue him./ Let him deliver him,/ since he delights in him' " (Psalm 22:7–8). The cruel crucifixion: "They have pierced my hands and my feet./ I can count all my bones;/ people stare and gloat over me" (22:16–17). The weakness and agony: "I am poured out like water,/ and all my bones are out of joint./ My heart has turned to wax;/ it has melted away within me./ My strength is dried up like a potsherd" (22:14–15). The awful thirst: "My tongue sticks to the roof of my mouth" (22:15). The approaching dissolution: "You lay me in the dust of death" (22:15).

It was the most painful and shameful form of public execution. Then, added to the torture of the cross were the insults of the men who mocked Him. How easily could He have silenced them! How easily could He have sprung from that cross and made them fall at His feet in terror! How easily could He have shown the power they doubted! But that would have forfeited our salvation. It was true, " 'He saved others,' they said, 'but he can't save himself!' " (Mark 15:31).

Thomas Carlyle tells of a Scotsman who once, when ascending a coal shaft of a mine in the bucket, found the strands of the rope giving way. One had already snapped, and the other was breaking. There was another man in the basket, but the rope would not hold both. In a moment his purpose was formed. He was not afraid to die. He turned to his companion and quickly said: "Goodbye! You are not ready, and I am; meet me in heaven!" and he dropped from the basket to the bottom of the shaft. He saved another, himself he could not save. There was room only for one life. So the Master "died to save us all," and bore the jeers and taunts of men that they who mocked Him might not die, but be saved by His very sacrifice.

THE SATANIC HATRED

3. The third element in the Savior's cup of suffering was Satanic hate and demonic rage and cruelty. Around Him there gathered in that dark hour, not only the cruelty and hate of men, but all the wrath of hell. "Roaring lions tearing their prey/ open their mouths wide against me" (Psalm 22:13)

is the strong language of the inspired picture. "Rescue me from the mouth of the lions" (22:21). "Deliver my life . . . from the power of the dogs" (22:20). Like wild beasts they seemed to Him in their ferocity and hideousness. And so indeed they have often seemed to many of God's dear saints in the dark hour of spiritual conflict.

Some of us have passed through the valley of the shadow of death. Amid the hosts of hell we have spent nights and days that seemed to be infested with dragon forms and fiendish shapes. Our very cheeks could feel the fire, and our ears could almost hear the hissing of the serpent; and even the smell of the pit was in our nostrils as we passed along, or stood in the evil day in desperate conflict with the powers of darkness. In such an hour Martin Luther actually believed he saw the devil, and threw his ink bottle at him in the reality of the conflict. The dying and unsaved soul has often been known to realize the vision of that dark and evil world, even as the departing saint has seen the opening of the gates of glory and the angel forms that wait.

Oh, if we have ever known the anguish of spiritual conflict and the awful pressure of Satan's power upon our spirits, we can have some conception of what our Master suffered on that day on Calvary. There is no pain so keen, except the wrath of God, as that which comes from the fiery touch of Satan. But all the fury of the pit was concentrated upon the Savior in that day, in that hour. Man had determined to take His life, but Satan was determined to have His soul. Oh, if Satan only could have seized the precious spirit of the Son of God and trampled beneath his feet the deeper life of the Sinless One, hell indeed would have triumphed and heaven would have been lost forever.

Like packs of wolves, Satan's hordes crowded around, blotting out the light of heaven with their dragon forms, piercing His spirit with their fiery darts, filling His soul with darkness and agony, and trying in vain to defile Him with their wiles, or betray Him into some word or thought or feeling of impatience, or distrust, or sin. Could they but for one instant have tempted Him successfully, could they have compelled Him to doubt His Father, to complain of His sufferings, or to resent His injuries, a shout would have gone up from their dark abodes that would have shaken the walls of heaven and filled the eyes of angels with tears they never shed before. He knew all this, and the strain of that awful conflict was infinite and indescribable. But not for one moment did He yield. Not one whisper of murmuring escaped His lips. Through all their hosts He passed in triumph, and even Satan had to acknowledge Him Conqueror. They could only torment, they could not tempt the sinless Son of God. But, oh, the torment, what tongue can tell, what heart can understand!

There is a strange and beautiful Hindu legend that sheds a sweet vividness on the Savior's sufferings, and especially His sufferings from the hand of Satan.

It is said that a human spirit was once pursued by the demon of vengeance. When about to be overtaken, it cried to the goddess Vishnu, who changed it into a dove so that it was able to rise above the serpent's reach. But now the serpent prayed to his god and was changed into a hawk, and soon swooped down upon the dove. He was about to seize his prey when the dove again cried to the goddess; and now Vishnu opened her bosom and took the frightened fugitive under her protecting wings. But the hawk demanded his prey, and claimed the rights of justice.

Vishnu did not dispute the claim, but said: "You cannot have the dove, but I will bare my bosom to your beak and talons, and you may tear from my flesh as much as will satisfy you for your lost prey." And then, the legend tells us, the demon sprang upon her breast and tore from her bosom as much as would be equivalent for the rescued dove. So heathenism has blindly pictured the mystery of the atonement and the strange substitution whereby we are saved.

Jesus gave Himself up for a season, even to the devil's hate. Oh, can we ever love Him enough for all our life has cost Him?

DEATH

4. The next element in His cup was death. For Him there was no release. Down to the dark abode of Hades His spirit must descend. There is something in death which tells its own story of dread and agony. Naturally, and apart from the gospel, it is indeed the king of terrors. Truly has it been said:

> The worst
> That age, ache, penury, and imprisonment
> Can lay on nature, is a Paradise
> To what we fear in death.

True, to the Christian this has been changed; the sting has been extracted because it has already been borne. But it was not thus that death came to Him. To Him it came under the law and with all the bitterness of the curse. To Him it came as it comes to the sinner—not only with all its natural bitterness, but with a sense of penalty, a consciousness of sin and condemnation. He *tasted* death for every man (Hebrews 2:9). The emphasis is on that word "tasted." He drank the dregs of the cup, and now for us the bitterness of death is past. But what it was to Him can be understood only by the combination and concentration of all that it has ever meant to sinful, dying men.

HELPLESSNESS

5. Helplessness is another element in this cup of woe. There was no escape. In our darkest hour, for us there is hope of release; but for Him there

could be none. From the beginning He knew that He must tread the winepress alone till the last; that He must drink the cup to its uttermost dregs; that there could be no reprieve; that it could not pass from Him, and that no one could help Him in it. He was utterly alone and inevitably doomed by His own act. He had chosen that dreadful place of substitution, and He could not now retrace His steps. Not for a moment did He wish to; but that utter loneliness, desolation and unutterable woe was terrible even to imagine. What must it have been to realize and endure?

SECTION II—*The Silver Lining*

These were some of the dark shadows of the cross, but the Psalm does not close without the brighter silver lining on the awful cloud. Four things are especially noticeable, in contrast with Christ's sufferings, as described in this Psalm.

THE CONCIOUSNESS OF INNOCENCE

1. There is the consciousness of innocence. Nowhere through the entire Psalm is there a single hint of any iniquity on the part of the Savior. It cannot, therefore, be a mortal man whose distress is here described. The best of men in their afflictions have been conscious of some lesson to be learned and some imperfection to be acknowledged; but this Sufferer has no consciousness of sin. It must have made the burden lighter, while at the same time it made it stronger. He was suffering wholly for others, for He "committed no sin, and no deceit was found in his mouth" (1 Peter 2:22). He suffered, the just for the unjust (1 Peter 3:18), that He might bring us to God. His sinlessness was essential to make the substitution adequate. With nothing to answer on His own account, all the merit of His sacrifice is imputed to the sinner and settles the claims of God against us.

THE SPIRIT OF FAITH

2. We see the spirit of faith. Even when He cries, "Why have you forsaken me?" He can say, "My God! My God!" (Mark 15:34). Again we find Him fighting the good fight of faith, as His children often do, by re-echoing the promises of God and the faithfulness of His love and care. "In you our fathers put their trust," He cries; "they trusted and you delivered them./ They cried to you and were saved;/ in you they trusted and were not disappointed" (Psalm 22:4–5). "Yet you brought me out of the womb;/ you made me trust in you/ even at my mother's breast./ From birth I was cast upon you" (22:9–10). "But you, O LORD, be not far off;/ O my Strength, come quickly to help me" (22:19). "Save me from the horns of the wild oxen" (22:21).

Here we see His spirit trusting in God just as we must trust Him today. It is a glorious example of faith resting on the promises and faithfulness of God in the dark hour. We are apt to forget the perfect humanness of Christ in His life and death. It was as a man that He trusted and triumphed in the strength of God. He was ever dependent upon His Father just as we are dependent upon Him.

It was not through His exalted divine nature wholly that He was able to endure His sufferings, but He was in all points tempted like we are, and sustained even as we are—not from Himself but from His Father's supporting strength. And so He is for us the Author and Finisher of our faith. He who fought this battle once, comes still to fight it in our hearts. He who believed for Himself, now believes in us, and sustains in us the spirit of trust and victory.

This is our weapon in the hour of suffering—to believe God and trust His faithfulness and promises. "Who among you fears the LORD/ and obeys the word of his servant?/ Let him who walks in the dark,/ who has no light,/ trust in the name of the LORD/ and rely on his God" (Isaiah 50:10). Let us go forth unto our trials in the spirit of His faith, and, like Him, we shall triumph, too.

THE SPIRIT OF LOVE

3. We see the spirit of love. His sufferings were not for Himself. Very beautifully is this thought brought out in one of the obscure passages of the Psalm (22:20, KJV): "Deliver my soul from the sword; my darling from the power of the dog." What is His "darling"? The usual interpretation of this is "His own soul," and the Hebrew word does mean my "only one." But is it not sweeter and loftier to apply it to His beloved Church, His dear Bride, His people, for whom He died, and between whom and destruction He was standing in that awful hour? Dearer even than His own soul was your soul. He was covering you from the destroyer and holding you to His bosom while He sank to protect you from the fate He would not flee.

On a Scottish moor the shepherds found one morning, beneath a snowdrift, a slumbering babe on the naked breast of a lifeless mother. The little babe was wrapped in its robes and the mother's outer garments. As the numbness of death crept over her, she had wrapped her mantle around her babe. Death to her was less terrible when she knew her babe was safe. She was saving her darling from the power of the storm. So He sheltered us that dreadful day from the power of the dog. He bore the cruel blow—nay, gave His life itself, and we live because He died. Strange if that child could ever forget its mother's love! Years afterwards, it is said, the remembrance of that story brought that child to God.

Oh, let the memory of our Redeemer's sacrifice bind all our hearts by cords of everlasting gratitude to Him, who loved us and gave Himself for us!

THE RAY OF HOPE

4. Hope was the last bright ray upon this cloud of sorrow. Bright, indeed, it is; so bright that in its glory all the darkness has passed away forever. In a moment the cries of anguish are changed into songs and shouts of praise. As soon as He passes the gates of death, lo, all the regions of the dead resound with the announcement of His victory. "I will declare your name to my brothers;/ in the congregation I will praise you" (22:22). And then the vision brightens till it covers all the future, till it takes in all the generations of the ransomed, and till it rises to the glory of the millennial world. He sees His ransomed people enjoying the fruits of His sorrow. "The poor will eat and be satisfied;/ they who seek the LORD will praise him" (22:26). He sees the gift of eternal life coming to poor lost sinners, and He cries, "may your hearts live forever!" (22:26).

He sees all the ends of the earth remembering and returning to the Lord. He sees all the kindred of the nations worshiping Him. He sees the kingdoms given to the Lord, and the nations bowing beneath His scepter. He sees the proud kings of the earth submitting to His throne. He sees a seed serving Him, and a generation born from His own bosom to love and serve Him. He hears age after age reechoing the story of His redeeming love. He sees you, poor sinner, burdened with your guilt, sinking in your woe, helpless and despairing, and His heart is glad to know that you have found in Him a Savior; and your tears of penitence, your songs of grateful praise, and your service of love are recompense enough to repay even Calvary.

He sees the heathen world rescued from its idolatry and wretchedness through His precious blood shed for it. He sees that innumerable company that no man can number, of all nations, and kindred, and people, and tongues, standing before the throne, with white robes, and palms in their hands; and the distant echo of their shout, "Worthy is the Lamb" (Revelation 5:12), takes away the sting of death, lights up the darkness of the tomb, and enables Him, for the joy set before Him, to endure the cross, scorning its shame (Hebrews 12:2).

Oh, shall we not join to give Him His recompense by bringing others to know Him, and sending the good news of His death and redeeming love to all mankind? It was for them He died as much as for us. They are His joy and crown as well as we. His heart bleeds at their sorrow and peril. Oh, let us rouse ourselves to do our best for their redemption, and to haste that day when He shall be crowned with the crown of all the world and enter into the joy which comforted Him to anticipate in the hour of His agony.

Let us go from the study of this psalm imbued with the spirit of missions and of service. It was the dying thought of Jesus to save the world. The great work in which we are now uniting all our energies was the work on His heart in the last conscious moment of His life. It was also the thought next to His heart when He was leaving the world and bidding farewell to His disciples on Olivet. Let it be our deepest, highest, latest thought.

When they told Dr. Backus, of Baltimore, that he was dying, he said: "Lift me from the bed and put me on my knees." There for the last two hours of his life he poured out his strength and soul in prayer for the heathen world. It was his last thought, his dying prayer. Like his Master, he entered into the eternal world in the spirit of missions. Oh, let it be our spirit while we live, and in it Christ shall see of the travail of His soul and be satisfied!

Can we ever bear to let one drop of that precious blood be lost? Can we bear to let one soul perish that it might save? Shall we not say, like the lepers of old, when they found the camp of the enemy full of spoil, and the city they had left was dying of famine, "We're not doing right. This day is a day of good news and we are keeping it to ourselves" (2 Kings 7:9). Oh, let us not hold our peace with such a gospel, but give it to the world, the whole world,

> [Till] every kindred, every tribe
>   On this terrestrial ball,
> To Him all majesty ascribe,
>   And crown Him Lord of all.

CHAPTER 6

THE FOLD AND THE FAMILY

Psalm 23

This beautiful psalm deserves to stand as the gateway to the Palace Beautiful of the Messianic psalms. It has been written on the hearts of many generations and many pilgrims to the heavenly home. It has furnished green pastures and still waters to God's flock through all ages, and has spread a table in the midst of their enemies for millions of God's redeemed.

Go to the walls of martyr prisons; look at the records of the sainted dead; recall the echoes of Christian deathbeds; look back upon your own memories and associations, and you will find nothing more sweet, or spiritual, or tender, than this psalm of psalms.

It has two great themes, two central figures running through it. The first is the Shepherd and His flock, and the second, the Father and His family. In this respect it recalls the 15th chapter of Luke and the two most precious of our Savior's parables: the Good Shepherd and the Prodigal Son. This is the same picture that we find in the 23rd Psalm.

SECTION I—*The Shepherd and His Flock*

No one but an Oriental can fully understand the vivid force of this beautiful figure. The shepherd of the East is not only a property owner, but he is a lover of his flock, and a friend and a father to every member of his fold. He knows them all by name, he lives with them, sacrifices everything for them, and loves them with tender affection. In short, he stands between them and everything. Of all creatures the sheep is the most defenseless, helpless and foolish; it cannot help itself. And so the child of God is absolutely helpless amid the elements surrounding him, especially the consecrated child of God. They who have wholly yielded themselves to Christ, and not to their own strength and sufficiency, are peculiarly defenseless when they wander from their Lord; they have not the strength of other men to stand alone, and they do not need it if they abide in Him. The safest place is that of utter helplessness and utter dependence.

The trouble with most of us is that we try to be our own shepherds. We forget that the Lord is our Shepherd, and our business is not to trouble ourselves, but to let Him keep us, and to trust and follow Him.

The emphatic words are the two smallest in the sentence: "my" and "is." The first expresses the appropriating faith which claims Him. It is not enough to recognize Him as a Shepherd, but we must put ourselves under His protection and claim Him as our own by personal appropriation and trust. And we may do this. He allows us thus to claim Him, and He undertakes the everlasting care of all who do. "My sheep," He says, "listen to my voice; I know them, and they follow me. I give them eternal life, and they shall never perish; no one can snatch them out of my hand" (John 10:27–28).

The other word is the very emphatic "is." David's confidence is without a doubt. So we must trust our Shepherd.

It is not because the sheep is worth so much in dollars and cents, nor the value of its flesh, that it claims the Shepherd's care; but because He bought it and owns it. It is His and He belongs to it, to care for it as much for His own sake as for its sake. So the Lord allows us to claim His love and life because we belong to Him, and He has given Himself to us. Has He not justified our confidence? Has He not come to seek us when we were lost? Has He not given us His life to save us? Has He not given us His wonderful promises and His more wonderful love and care? Let us take Him at His word and answer back, "The LORD is my shepherd" (Psalm 23:1).

"I shall not be in want" (23:1). This covers every possible need of human life—every proper desire and want, whether it be for soul or for body, for this world, or for the world to come. We can claim the fullness of His supply and say, "My God will meet all your needs according to his glorious riches in Christ Jesus" (Philippians 4:19). "The LORD bestows favor and honor;/ no good thing does he withhold/ from those whose walk is blameless" (Psalm 84:11). This is the state of utter content, thankfulness, and joy. It is the cry of the heart that has no pining, but can see nothing but blessing and goodness in its lot and in its future. So infinite is its Shepherd's love, so vast His resources, so kind His care, that it can think of nothing that He will not supply.

Have you this unbounded confidence in God? Are you taking thus from Him of His fullness? Are you honoring Him thus by your testimony and your praise, or are you reflecting upon your Shepherd by miserable discontent and meager, thankless lives?

"He makes me lie down in green pastures" (23:2). This is the testimony of His rich provision for our needs. Not one pasture, but many are supplied, and they are all green. He does not feed us on the stale bread of past experiences, but He gives us fresh supplies every day, like the morning dew and the morning light. And so abundant are they that we lie down among them for very satiety. We lie down because we cannot hold any more, even as we have seen the beautiful herds in the English meadows lying down amid the tall, green grass for very fullness. This is the picture of a happy, joyful, victorious Christian life. He "is able to do immeasurably more than all we ask or imagine" (Ephesians 3:20).

"He leads me beside quiet waters" (Psalm 23:2). Rather it should read, "the waters of rest." Here again it is not one stream, but many; they are "waters." This is the picture of the Holy Spirit and tells of the divine Comforter as He brings us into the deepest rest of Jesus: the peace that "transcends all understanding" (Philippians 4:7), peace like a river, and righteousness like the waves of the sea. But it is only when we follow His leading that we can have this peace. In our own paths we shall not find the waters of rest; but as we follow Him, taking His yoke upon us and learning of Him who is "gentle and humble in heart," we will find rest for our souls (Matthew 11:29).

"He restores my soul" (Psalm 23:3). In the Hebrew this might mean "my life," and thus expresses His physical redemption and healing love and life. He is the constant Quickener of our life, for the body as well as for the soul. It may also mean His restoring mercy when we go astray or stumble in the way. How often this is realized in our experience! How often we need our Shepherd's tender, restoring mercy, and how tenderly and gently He does arrest the erring and bring back the lost one! How different God's dealings with sin from the devil's, and even from men's! How tender and patient His mercy! Look at Him as He meets Elijah on his running away, and tenderly rests him, feeds him, pleads with him, and then restores him! Look at Him as He looks on Simon Peter and melts his heart to penitence, and then gives him back more than he has lost! Listen to His tender words to the erring and the weak, and never, never fly from Him again, whom we have even offended, but

> Go to His bleeding feet, and learn
> How freely Jesus can forgive.

"He guides me in paths of righteousness" (23:3)—that is, the right paths. Not only does He rest, but He sanctifies. He cleanses; He keeps; He leads into the land of uprightness. He "is able to keep you from falling and to present you before his glorious presence without fault and with great joy" (Jude 24). For His own name's sake He does all this.

This is the way He becomes our Sanctifier. It is Christ Himself who does it all. We do not deserve it; we cannot accomplish it. We can only receive it as the gift of His mercy, through the blood of Jesus Christ and His exceeding great and precious promises "for his name's sake" (Psalm 23:3). "It is not for your sake, O house of Israel" (Ezekiel 36:22), He says. We cannot claim any credit for our holiness. It is a free gift of His suffering grace, and we can only wonder and adore as we think of the love that does so much for us so undeservedly.

"Even though I walk/ through the valley of the shadow of death,/ I will fear no evil,/ for you are with me" (Psalm 23:4). This is because of our wandering. This is the way back from the forbidden paths, from the dark wilderness. It does not necessarily mean death itself, but any dark vale overshadowed like the grave. After we have wandered from God, we do often find such dark and lonely passages. It is also true that, after we have become fully the Lord's, we are often called to pass through the darkest trials, and are tested in the most painful ways, drinking a cup more bitter, often, than death itself. Thus it is that the promise becomes so precious.

How much comfort there is in this verse! First, we go through the valley. We do not fall in the midst of it, but ever before us we can see the light at the farther end, the opening vista of the larger place that lies beyond. Again, we are saved from fear. This is often worse than any other evil. If we have no dread, we can have no harm. And He has said, "Whoever listens to me will live in safety/ and be at ease, without fear of harm" (Proverbs 1:33). How sweetly the Master's presence can charm away our fears and whisper comfort and rest in the darkest hours!

Next, we have His promise, "For you are with me" (Psalm 23:4). This is the spirit of nearness and safety. Notice now how beautifully the grammar changes. Up to this time he has been speaking of his Shepherd in the third person, as "He"; but now it all changes and becomes "You." The reason is obvious. The promise has become nearer; the Shepherd is no longer at a distance; he is not talking *about* Him any more, but talking directly *to* Him. Going through a deep tunnel one day, my little child drew close to me and held my hand. When we were on the other side and in the bright light, he was not afraid to sit away at a distance and play; but in the dark and narrow place he wanted to feel my touch every moment. So He lets us draw close to Him in the valley, and hold His hand and hear Him say, "So do not fear, for I am with you" (Isaiah 41:10).

Again, even His rod comforts us. Even the thing that hurts us so is shown to us to be for our good, and we can say: "It was good for me to be afflicted" (Psalm 119:71). "Before I was afflicted I went astray,/ but now I obey your word" (119:67).

Again, "You . . . knew the anguish of my soul" (31:7). Oft has the suffering Christian sung:

Trials make the promise sweet;
  Trials give new life to prayer;
Trials bring me to His feet,
  Lay me low and keep me there.

A daughter of the East has told this beautiful story of the Oriental shepherd. Sometimes when his sheep would wander and would not answer to his call or come back to the fold, he would take his sling and a little stone and hurl it through the air. Lo! the wandering sheep is stricken, perhaps on one of its foolish feet, and falls wounded to the ground, to pick itself up again, to hobble back with its suffering member, but to escape the perils of the wilderness through its wound. So He wounds to heal and smites to save, and pains us only that He may save us pain.

But, again, not only does His rod comfort us, but His staff comforts us still more. It is not all chastening, but more blessing, and, "Just as the sufferings of Christ flow over into our lives, so also through Christ our comfort overflows" (2 Corinthians 1:5). God has two hands; the one presses us down, the other presses us up. Thank God, it is the right hand that holds us up, for He says: "For I am the LORD, your God,/ who takes hold of your right hand/ and says to you, 'Do not fear' " (Isaiah 41:13).

How beautifully these two hands are described in the First Epistle of Peter: "Humble yourselves, therefore, under God's mighty hand" (5:6). This is the hand that presses us down. But he adds very soon, "Cast all your anxiety on him because he cares for you" (5:7). That is the hand that holds us up; that is the staff that comforts us when the rod has smitten us. It is like the mother eagle, who stirs up her nest and hurls her young ones in mid-air, and leaves them to fall, screaming, earthward. But soon her mother-heart flies to the rescue, and swooping under them, she spreads abroad her wings and bears them up again in safety and repose, telling them, doubtless, in strange speech, that she has only done it all in order to teach them to use their little wings and learn to fly themselves. So God lets the pressure of trial come, and then upholds us in it with His everlasting arms and bears us as on eagle's wings.

This is the trial that comforts us. His precious promises—oh, how they cheer the sorrowing heart! How sweet they grow in trial, until the heavens glow with stars of hope we never realized before, for

Sorrow touched by God grows bright
  With more than beauty's rays,
As trials show us worlds of light
  We never saw by day.

SECTION II—*The Father's House*

The figure now changes. There is, perhaps, a spiritual gradation here. Trial and deeper experience, as we have already discovered, may bring us into a closer place with God; and so we have the Father's house next. It is not the fold and the shepherd, but the family circle meeting at the table, the child dwelling in the house forever.

The first feature of the picture is danger; there are enemies. "You prepare a table before me/ in the presence of my enemies" (Psalm 23:5). We never know the real force of spiritual conflict until we come into a closer place in the life of God. But the victory is so complete that we are not fighting now. He does all the fighting for us, and surrounds us with a wall of fire so wide and secure that we sit in the center, happy, fearless children, eating and drinking at the festal table as though there were no foe in sight. What a perfect picture of security! Eating and drinking in the midst of our enemies! Like the great apostle, on the tossing ship in the Adriatic storm, bidding his companions eat and drink because they were safe under the promises of God (Acts 27:33–34). This is no longer the picture of the wilderness, but it is the prepared table of the feast where all the fullness of His love is freely given to us; and we sit down and partake of the riches of His bounty until our cup overflows in the full measure of our blessing and our joy.

Beloved, is this our place? Are we so victorious that, like our Master, we sit down expecting until all our enemies are made our footstool (Hebrews 10:13)? Are we so full that our "cup overflows" (Psalm 23:5) and we can hold no more, so that we have ceased to think of ourselves and our blessings in the overflow with which we bless others?

"You anoint my head with oil" (23:5). This is the figure of the Holy Spirit. This is the spirit of the overflowing joy. This is the symbol of healing, of gladness, of sweet fragrance. In the East, when a traveler comes in from his journey, travel-stained and wet from perspiration, his feet are washed to take away the dust of the road; his head is anointed with oil, and the sweet perfume removes the odor of heat and perspiration; and he sits down all sweetened and restored at the table of his host. So He anoints our head with oil, fills us with His gladness, sweetens us with His fragrance and brings us into the innermost chambers of His love.

Provision is made for the future. "Surely goodness and mercy (KJV) will follow me/ all the days of my life" (23:6). Not only is the present abundantly supplied, but it is all right beyond. Goodness covers every temporal need; mercy, every spiritual need. Goodness includes every gift of His love; mercy, every provision for our sinfulness. Not only will He love us and care for us as His dear children walking in holy obedience, but His mercy will keep us holy and guard us from even our own unworthiness.

The "house of the LORD" (23:6) in which we shall dwell in His presence. We are in it now and never shall be withdrawn. But surely it looks forward to His glorious coming, to the house made without hands (2 Corinthians 5:1), which is awaiting us when He shall appear.

I cannot withhold a personal testimony. On the first night of a new year, after I had retired and fallen asleep in very close communion with the Lord, I had one of those rare dreams which leave behind them an impression of the voice of God. In my dream I was gazing into the heavens at night, looking at one of the brightest constellations, when suddenly there appeared among them a wonderful star as bright as Venus at its brightest. As I gazed upon it, wondering at its strange beauty in that quarter of the heavens, I became conscious that it was rapidly growing larger every moment. In a few moments I was aware that it must be swiftly approaching; so fast did it enlarge that it seemed to be literally rushing earthward, and my whole being was stirred with the consciousness that some stupendous event was happening.

Then there passed over my spirit a distinct consciousness that the Lord was coming; that this was the Morning Star and that He was just behind it. The best part of the dream was that it brought only rest and joy. Startling as was the appearance and the certainty of the coming King, there was no fear, but a sweet consciousness that all was right; that I was glad He was coming; that I knew in a few moments He would be here. Although I saw no one around me, I had the quiet assurance that all was right for them, too; it was all right for those I loved as well as for myself. Just at that moment I awakened with the quiet sense that God had spoken to my heart with a personal message respecting what His glorious coming would be to me. Oh, that we all may so live each moment that "when he appears we may be confident and unashamed before him at his coming" (1 John 2:28)!

There is one thought more in this psalm. The grammar changes once again to the third person, and the Psalmist is talking not *to* but *about* God. It is the voice of testimony to the world. It is the call which we should echo to those who know Him not as their Shepherd and their Father. Is there any such lonely lost one reading this message? Oh, let this little psalm that has led so many to heaven lead you to God!

Down in a southern hospital a soldier was dying; he was a Scotsman and an infidel. A Christian worker stood by his cot, but he would not listen to the gospel; he covered his face with the bed cover and turned away in pride and scorn. Noticing that the patient was Scottish, and knowing, himself, the sweetness of the old Psalms to the Scottish ear, the worker sat down a little way off and began to sing the 23rd Psalm in the old Rousse version:

The Lord's my Shepherd, I'll not want;
He makes me down to lie
In pastures green; He leadeth me
The quiet waters by.

He sang on quietly, tenderly. Before he was half through the psalm, the patient was trembling from head to foot and sobbing aloud. He threw the covering down and asked, "Why did you sing that psalm? My mother taught it to me by her knee, and it was her last message to me when she died." The ice was broken; the heart was open to the truth; tenderly the seed was sown, and the soul was saved.

Two days afterwards the worker returned, but the Scotsman had passed through the gates. The nurse told him that the night before, as she was passing down the corridor, she heard him singing that verse about the dark valley, and before he got through it, he began to choke with exhaustion. Then he gave a great cry, and said, "Mother! Mother! Mother! I'm coming! The Lord's my Shepherd, too!" The nurse hastened to his side, but he no more needed the care of human hands. He had been saved by the 23rd Psalm.

I venture to add another incident which illustrates the preciousness of this psalm for the living as well as for the dying. A well-known Scotsman in New York, a man of great influence and high Christian character, was lying in the stupor of apparent death. A Scottish minister, also widely known, was leaning over him trying to recall his attention from the sleep of approaching death. At last he began to repeat to him the 23rd Psalm; and when he got to the second verse, the dying man roused from his stupor and began to follow him, repeating the words after him until the psalm was finished. The effect on the sinking man was electrical; he was completely aroused and began to talk with those around him. From that moment he grew better and lived for many years, well and happy, a useful Christian, saved from death by the 23rd Psalm.

Blessed watchword for both worlds! May the Lord make it gloriously real to us, and may we all be truly able to say with its closing refrain: "Surely goodness and love will follow me/ all the days of my life,/ and I will dwell in the house of the LORD/ forever" (23:6).

CHAPTER 7

A PSALM OF INSTRUCTION

Psalm 32

The title of this psalm is *Maschil.* It is a Hebrew word signifying instruction. It touches very deeply the whole experience of the child of God, from the first to the highest stages of life.

SECTION I—*Instruction Concerning Sin*

Nowhere do we learn so much about sin in a few words as in the four terms here applied.

TRANSGRESSION

1. The first is *transgression* (32:1). This means to go beyond. It denotes the actual violation of the law of God by an act in contravention of a divine command. It represents positive disobedience. It includes all the overt acts of sin; all the deeds, words and thoughts of men which they have committed contrary to God's precepts and commands. This alone is enough to form an awful account against the sinner in the divine impeachment, but this is only the beginning of sin.

SIN

2. The word *sin* is next used (32:1), and it describes the converse of this; namely, the coming short of God's will and law. The word here used means *to miss the mark*, to fail to reach our aim, and it includes that large and often overlooked class of evils, which we might call sins of omission. Little do we realize how much they mean, and how immense will be the account when we stand in the judgment of the Lord: all we might have been, all we might have done, all we might have said, all the sorrow we might have assuaged, all the sin we might have prevented, all the good we might have done, all the

souls we might have saved. Oh, what will it be to look at this some day, as God will show us the picture of the possibilities of life, and we shall feel we have lost it forever?

Here are two men passing into judgment. Both have had equal opportunities, equal talents, equal wealth, equal length of life. They have perhaps lived side by side and often passed each other on the path of life. The one goes home with his hands full of sheaves. He has spent his fortune for God and for holy usefulness. He has used his time to do good. He has often denied himself some special pleasure to save a soul, or to comfort a sorrowing one. At the gate of heaven he meets not only the smile of his Judge, but his works do follow him, and glorious trains of happy spirits welcome him. How many there are to greet him as their deliverer, their comforter and the instrument of their salvation! What a large place in heaven is filled by the fruits of his love! What eternal and infinite horrors have been saved by his self-denial and his loving life service. All this has come out of one consecrated life.

And now the other meets his future. There is nothing to greet him. No happy spirits welcome him as their dearest friend. No white-robed saints lead him up to the throne as the one who led them to Jesus. But before him rises the vision of just such a heaven as his brother has received; just such a multitude as he, too, might have saved. But where are they? Down in yonder pit of darkness. As he sees what might have been in the light of what actually is for another, he awakes to realize what life meant; what it was not to do, not to sacrifice, not to serve the Lord. Oh, it will be an awful thing for such a one to meet his Judge, and see in the first flash of eternity's light all that he might have saved and kept forever; but it is all forever lost!

Oh saint of God, if you could blot out the precious fruit of your life, would you for a million worlds? But that is what every sinful man and selfish woman is doing. That is the meaning of sin: the things you have not done, the love you have not given, the faith you have not exercised, the service you have not rendered, the reward you have not won.

INIQUITY

3. The word *iniquity* (32:2, KJV) also has a distinct meaning. Literally, it signifies something twisted, perverted, turned aside from its divine intention, and so it represents the perversion of human nature from its high and holy purpose. Man has perverted everything. That thing which God gave for the noblest uses has been prostituted for selfishness and evil. Man's own body, created as the vehicle of the soul and its instrument of high and holy service, has been turned into the means of gratifying every unholy lust. The human mind, a ray of the divine and created to glorify God, has been used to glorify man, to worship the creature, to dishonor the Creator.

The very gifts of God and His infinite goodness have been abused as an encouragement to sin; and even religion itself has been turned aside from its sacred intent, and been used to serve the devil and promote the wicked selfishness of men. Surely men "have gone in search of many schemes" (Ecclesiastes 7:29). "We all, like sheep, have gone astray,/ each of us has turned to his own way" (Isaiah 53:6).

But the word iniquity has a more general meaning. It is used to express, in a general way, the whole depraved nature of man. It represents the deep fountain of corruption from which all transgressions and sins proceed; far worse than the streams of evil that have filled the history of humanity is the deep fountain of sinful human nature from which all have sprung. Fetid and foul may be the fog that rises from the marsh, but far deeper and far more foul are the slimy waters of the unclean things that lie beneath the surface, from which these fogs are only exhalations. This is iniquity.

It is the vile human heart of which God says: "The heart is deceitful above all things/ and beyond cure./ Who can understand it?" (Jeremiah 17:9). And "every inclination of the thoughts of his heart was only evil all the time" (Genesis 6:5). This is the real cause of human ruin. Our acts might be forgiven; our omissions might be overlooked; but our nature is ruined and only capable of continued evil, waxing worse and worse forever. Unless it be radically changed, it is incapable of happiness or holiness, and would turn heaven into hell, even as a leper's body would infect and poison a whole community. There is nothing to be done with this wicked human heart but to destroy it.

DECEIT

4. There is still another term for sin—*deceit*. This is the subtlest and most hopeless of all the characteristics of sin. It is utterly false, crooked, dishonest. We have often felt, in dealing with sinful man, that there was hope for the most abandoned and depraved, if we could only feel that the man was true and sincere; that he really was ready to acknowledge his sin without palliation or excuse, and truly longed to be right. There is hope for such a man. But when you feel a man is not honest and true, and that he is only deceiving you, playing with you, and using the cloak of religion for some mean and sordid motive, you feel that you can do nothing with him. He is irretrievably lost.

It is this double heart in man, this lack of uprightness and sincerity which makes his case so desperate. And this is the case with all men naturally, for the old serpent, the father of lies, rules in the children of disobedience, and makes them like himself, deceiving and being deceived.

Oh, what a category of evils: transgression, sin, iniquity, deceit! If you have ever seen your heart as God sees it, you may well cry, "God, have mercy on me, a sinner" (Luke 18:13).

SECTION II—*Instruction Concerning Salvation*

God has four provisions to set over against these four names of sin.

FORGIVENESS

1. The first is *forgiveness*. This has to do with our acts of evil. They render us liable to punishment; and when God forgives us, He acquits us of all charges, conceals the judgment against us, delivers us from guilt and punishment, and treats us as if we had not sinned. This is the purchase of Christ's blood; this is the offer of the gospel to all who will sincerely repent and accept the Lord Jesus Christ.

Beloved, to all of you who read these lines, "through Jesus the forgiveness of sins is proclaimed to you" (Acts 13:38). "If we confess our sins, he is faithful and just and will forgive us our sins and purify us from all unrighteousness" (1 John 1:9).

COVERED

2. The second provision is covering. "Blessed is he/ . . . whose sins are covered" (Psalm 32:1). This is fuller, deeper, and more definite. It tells us of the great facts and principles that lie back of the forgiveness. Something had to be done to purchase this forgiveness, to provide for this settlement, to make right the relations between the sinner and the law of God. There had to be a covering.

Go back with me to Eden. See that guilty pair cowering with shame. It is not that their forms are naked. They, poor souls, are conscious of being exposed to the holy eye of God. Their sin is uncovered, and they cannot bear the exposure. So they take the fig leaves and sew them together, and put them on their persons. The searching eye of God has found them out, but His compassion provides a better covering. He bids them take those spotless lambs that stand before them, and doubtless, confessing their sins with their hands upon their heads, He slays the victims as sacrifices for their guilt. Then He takes the skins from their bleeding bodies, all dripping with crimson drops, and He puts them on their persons as a covering of blood, reminding them of the great Sacrifice that was yet to come, and by His blood make expiation for their guilt, and then by His righteousness cover their souls with spotless robes.

This was the meaning of the lid of the ark in the ancient tabernacle. It was the covering all sprinkled with blood which hid the broken law from the eye of Him who looked down from between the cherubim. The word *propitiation* means *covering*, and this word is applied to Christ. "He is the atoning sacrifice (propitiation, KJV) for our sins" (1 John 2:2); that is, the *covering* for our sins. When the poor publican smote upon his breast and cried to heaven for mercy, his prayer was "God be the propitiation for me a sinner." He saw that there must be a covering.

This was the meaning of the blood upon the doorposts of Israel's tents when the destroying angel passed by. Jesus, the Great Sacrifice, in this beautiful type, was covering them from the wrath of the avenger. Are your sins not only forgiven, but covered, canceled and forever put away through the blood of Jesus Christ which cleanseth from all sin?

NOT COUNTED

3. The third provision is that our sin is not counted (Psalm 32:2). This word literally means *not to think*. It not only describes the judicial act of God in acquitting the sinner and dismissing the charge against him, but it means still more: it means that He forgets as well as forgives, and thinks of us no longer in the light of our sin, but treats us and loves us as if we had never sinned. He puts it quite out of His heart, and never again upbraids us with its faintest suggestion.

This is the wonderful part of God's forgiveness; it is so generous, so affectionate, so ennobling, that He takes away every sense of shame from the poor, guilty, shame-faced criminal cringing at His feet, and lifts him up into His confidence, and gives him the self-respect and dignity of a prince and a child. There is something wonderful about this in God, and yet some of us understand it in our human relations. We want to trust those we love, and we must trust them perfectly. We know what it is to be unwilling to lose confidence in a friend, and to cling to that confidence even when we might suppose that it was not deserved. How the parent continues to trust his child, and refuses to doubt him even though he knows him to be wrong, until at length his noble confidence has ennobled its object! God is unwilling to lose confidence in us; and when He justifies us, He determines to trust us, and begins to treat us as if we were worthy of perfect trust; and indeed He makes us worthy by His confidence and by His grace.

How beautifully this comes out in some of His words respecting His people! "No misfortune is seen in Jacob,/ no misery observed in Israel" (Numbers 23:21). There was plenty to see, but He would not see it. "He said, 'Surely they are my people,/ sons who will not be false to me'; and so he became their Savior" (Isaiah 63:8). They would often lie, but He would not believe it, but resolved to love them into goodness. He has been loving us and ennobling us by His love, and holding fast to us in His strong purpose of full salvation, and every moment He looks upon us in the light of that loving purpose as we shall be when we shall "shine like the sun in the kingdom" (Matthew 13:43) of our Father.

Oh, how wonderful this confidence of God! But how good and kind He is to exercise it toward us. How we love Him for it! He has "sworn not to be angry" with us and "never to rebuke" us (Isaiah 54:9). This draws us to His bosom and makes us love Him and love to please Him. "Blessed is the man/ whose sin the LORD does not count against him" (Psalm 32:2), and against whom He will not even think one thought or shadow of his former self.

EXPULSION OF DECEIT

4. Finally, there is the expulsion of deceit. "In whose spirit is *no deceit*" (32:2). God not only refuses to think a thought of evil against us, but He actually takes the evil away by putting in us the true heart, the honest will, the new spirit and the single eye to choose and please Him. He drives out the evil to bring in the good. So we have the fourfold salvation over against the fourfold sin: forgiveness, atonement, love and cleansing. All this is for us in the finished and perfect work of Christ. For "if we confess our sins, he is faithful and just and will forgive us our sins and purify us from all unrighteousness" (1 John 1:9). Oh, the blessedness of the man who receives this full salvation! All our sorrows come from sin, and in full salvation we find our perfect joy. Do you know all this in its fullness? Is the blessedness of this great salvation even now filling all your being with the glad amen of praise to God?

SECTION III—*Instruction Concerning Trouble and Sorrow*

We have two kinds of sorrow in the next verses. One is the trouble of the impenitent sinner trying to override his conscience and be happy in his sins. But the Psalmist could find no peace this way. "When I kept silent,/ my bones wasted away/ through my groaning all day long" (Psalm 32:3). Oh, the misery of a guilty conscience and a hidden sin! But, oh, the relief that comes to the penitent heart! "I said, 'I will confess/ my transgressions to the LORD'—/ and you forgave/ the guilt of my sin" (32:5).

We have also the picture of the sorrows of the saint, but they do not touch him. "Surely when the mighty waters rise,/ they will not reach him" (32:6). And then he sends up his shout of triumph: "You are my hiding place;/ you will protect me from trouble/ and surround me with songs of deliverance" (32:7).

How free! Our spirit springs above all care and sorrow when we enjoy the love and peace of God. How light the burdens of temporal distress when the heart can spring and sing in the triumph of the Lord's great love! Only let us see His gracious face and know that He is pleased, and we can sing above the darkness and the storm,

Let cares like a wild deluge come,

And storms of sorrow fall;
May I but safely reach my home,
My God, my heaven, my all.

SECTION IV—*Instruction about Guidance*

"I will instruct you and teach you in the way you should go;/ I will counsel you and watch over you" (32:8).

1. We have God's instruction. The forgiven and saved soul needs to be taught, and how graciously He teaches and opens up His Word!

But more than instruction is needed. Direction also in practical duty is required. "I will . . . teach you in the way you should go" (32:8). This is more than knowledge; this is wisdom. And this He gives by His Holy Spirit to the sanctified judgment, and makes us know what we ought to do.

2. "I will guide thee with mine eye" (32:8, KJV). This is more than being taught in our mind. This is something finer, more delicate, more divine. I have seen a drillmaster stand before a class of hundreds of young children, and by a glance that I could scarcely detect, direct every movement of their hands, and feet, and faces, with the utmost precision. But how closely they watched him! He was guiding them with his eye. Is this the meaning of the verse? Does it teach us that we are to keep our eyes so constantly fixed upon God that we shall catch His every movement, and always know His will by the smile of His approving countenance? Yes, it is true, and it may be the meaning of the verse. But it seems to us there is still a closer meaning.

It seems to us that He offers in this verse to put His own eye in us, and enable us to see with His eyes, and not with our own. There is a great difference in these two things. Looking at people with your eyes, you get narrow, selfish views. Looking at people with Christ's eyes, they seem so different. You can love and bless them. He is willing to put His mind in us, to let us think His thoughts, to see all things even as He sees and knows. But in order to do this, we must renounce our wisdom; we must subject our judgment to His; we must crucify our opinions and thoughts, and be willing to be fools that we may be wise.

In order to have the divine guidance in this blessed way, we must be yielding and obedient. "Do not be like the horse or the mule,/ which have no understanding/ but must be controlled by bit and bridle/ or they will not come to you" (32:9). The horse and the mule cannot be guided by intelligent sympathy with the driver. And so many Christians have to be held by the Lord with a strong hand, because they will not let God draw them near enough to guide them with His eye.

Oh, let us not be servants but friends, of whom the Master can say: "For everything that I learned from my Father, I have made known to you" (John 15:15).

Finally, this psalm contains instruction about joy. "Rejoice in the LORD and be glad, you righteous;/ sing, all you who are upright in heart!" (Psalm 32:11). Let the Lord bring them into the sweet place of trust and guidance, and they who know the blessedness of this full salvation may well rejoice and shout for joy.

Blessed is the man that is forgiven, but more than blessed is the man who lets God guide him with His eye.

Let us not be behind the spirit of these ancient psalms. Three thousand years nearer the throne than they, oh surely we should have a louder, sweeter song. Let us rejoice in the Lord evermore.

CHAPTER 8

THE ROYAL BRIDEGROOM

Psalm 45

A little bit of broken glass is sufficient to reflect the full glory of the sun; so human love, a poor fragment at best, helps us to rise to that love divine of which it is the feeble type, the earthly foretaste of the marriage of the Lamb.

The Bible is a love story, and the great objective point to which it moves forward is the rapture of the Bride and the marriage supper before the throne. In the beautiful story of Adam and Eve, the wooing and wedding of Rebekah, the sacred idyll of Ruth and Boaz, the exquisite poem of the Canticles, the parable of the virgins, the marriage of the king's son and the beautiful vision of the Apocalypse, we find it running like a golden thread. The earthly figure is only the shadow. The reality is the union of the whole Church with her glorious Lord and Head.

This is the theme of the 45th Psalm. It is the story of the heavenly Bridegroom and His Bride, the Church. There are three points in the prophetic picture on which we shall dwell: the Bridegroom, the Bride and the offspring.

SECTION I—*The Bridegroom*

This is a picture combining the elements of strength and sweetness, so seldom found together in any human character. Some people are strong without being gentle; others are sweet without being stable. This picture combines both elements in perfect harmony, like the solid mountains with their ribs of adamant and their covering of moss, verdure and bloom.

THE STRONGER QUALITIES

1. The first of these is righteousness. "You love righteousness and hate wickedness" (45:7). There can be no permanent love for one unless it is

founded on esteem, and that esteem based on the sterling qualities of uprightness and moral worth. We cannot permanently love an unrighteous person. This glorious Bridegroom comes to us in all the attractions of perfect purity, uprightness and infinite holiness. We can rest with implicit confidence upon His infallible integrity, and know that He is always right.

Truth is also essential to the confidence of love. We must be able to rest on the word of the one we love; not only upon his word, but upon his absolute sincerity, honesty, frankness and faithfulness. We must know that he is thoroughly consistent and unchangeable in his love. Our Bridegroom is the embodiment of faithfulness. He is called True and Faithful (Revelation 19:11). His lightest word will be fulfilled. His very thought is absolute fidelity. He is "the same yesterday and today and forever" (Hebrews 13:8). Even "if we are faithless,/ he will remain faithful,/ for he cannot disown himself" (2 Timothy 2:13). Has He given us a promise? We can rest upon it forever. Has He given us a right to trust Him anywhere? He will never change. Has He encouraged us to lean upon Him? We may lay our whole weight upon His faithful breast and know that He will never fail us. Others may change, but He is changeless, our truehearted and everlasting Friend.

Victorious power is another quality. He rides forth as a Conqueror amid His enemies and ours. There is none can stay His hand from working. There is none can resist His will. Other friends may want to help us, but they are not able. There is nothing that He cannot do for His Bride. He could speak worlds into existence for her if necessary, and His lightest command would banish in a moment all her adversaries. He is her Vindicator and Defender, and none can dispute His will. His friendship means eternal safety, eternal victory. All power is given unto Him in heaven and in earth. Those who are the objects of His love can never have cause to fear. Who would not have such a Friend? And, oh, who would refuse to be His bride?

He has kingly and sovereign power. He has supreme authority. He has the right to exercise His power without resistance. The eternal Father has invested Him with all authority and dominion. His will is supreme above all this vast creation, and all shall yet crown Him "King of kings and Lord of lords" (Revelation 19:16). This is the Bridegroom that offers you His love.

HIS GENTLER QUALITIES

2. The first of these is His beauty. "You are the most excellent of men" (Psalm 45:2). There are fair faces and noble forms among the sons and daughters of men, but He is fairer than them all in the loveliness of His spirit, and even in the beauty of His person.

If His very name can thrill the heart with such delight, what must His person be? All beauty of human loveliness came originally from His hand and must somehow be in His person. All that is beautiful in the sunshine and the stars, the loveliness of nature and the beauty of art, is but the reproduction of something which was originally in Him. A photograph can combine in one face the beauty of 20, so that the single picture expresses the charm of each different face combined in one. Ancient art sometimes gathered up in one single form the loveliness of man or woman in its Venus or Apollo; but, oh, what must that beautiful face be that can combine all the beautiful faces of earth lighted up by the glory of Deity!

Sometimes we catch a glimpse of the radiance that streams from it, but that face itself we have not seen except through the revelation of the Spirit as He brings the full conception of its loveliness to the heart. Then, language is too poor to describe the view of Jesus which the heart sometimes catches even here. A poor dying retarded man caught a glimpse of its glory, and for weeks he could only cry amid his wandering thoughts as his face every few minutes would light up, "Yon lovely Man; I want to go to yon lovely Man." The great and good Dr. Anderson, of Boston, Secretary of the American Board of Foreign Missions, often said for weeks before he died, "I have such a longing to see the face of Jesus." Some day we shall see it, and it will be ages before we shall want to look away to any other.

Another quality is His gracious words. "Your lips have been anointed with grace" (45:2). What a singular beauty there is in the words of Jesus, even if there were no deeper reality behind them! When did poetry frame such sentences as some of the promises that fell from the Master's lips? "Come to me, all you who are weary and burdened, and I will give you rest" (Matthew 11:28). "Do not let your hearts be troubled" (John 14:1). There is music in their very sound, and their sweetness can never die. But how much sweeter when they are spoken to the heart by the Holy Spirit! Oh, how the memory lingers on some of these gracious promises whispered to us in some hour of sorrow, turning all our darkness into day and lifting us up into praise and victory!

"In your majesty ride forth victoriously/ in behalf of truth, humility and righteousness" (Psalm 45:4). This is more than beauty. This is grandeur, sublimity, loftiness, glory. But, notwithstanding, there is nothing in it that overawes or repels, for it is all so blended with meekness and gentleness that it attracts and rests us. How often we see these elements combined in the character of God: "Our Father," the gentleness; "in heaven," the majesty (Matthew 6:9); "a Lamb," the meekness; "standing in the center of the throne," the almightiness (Revelation 5:6). He is a glorious King. He is a mighty Conqueror. He is the majestic God. But He is our Beloved, our Husband and our Friend.

Sometimes we look at some distinguished man, or meet with some lofty personage, and yet we wonder at the freedom and simplicity with which we can think of him, because we know him as a friend is known. A little child can lie in the bosom of a queen and forget the monarch in the mother. And so the Bride can rest upon the heart of the King, and know that to her He is only her beloved. And so Christ will let us come as near, and even amid His transcendent majesty, see only the Savior who died for us and the Friend who loves us.

Another one of His gentler qualities is gladness. "Therefore God, your God, has set you above your companions/ by anointing you with the oil of joy" (Psalm 45:7). There are some natures that are so joyous and radiant that we love to be with them. Their very presence sheds gladness all around them. Jesus, our royal Bridegroom, is full of gladness, and to be in His presence is to have fullness of joy. They who dwell in His presence are ever happy and triumphant.

In our darkest hours, could we but see His face, it would be lighted up with victory and rest, and we would wonder at our own fears and cares. There is nothing more beautiful in the picture of His life than the radiant gladness that ever shone upon His face, and lighted up His spirit even in the most trying hours. When all around seemed dark and threatening, He could rejoice in spirit, and, forgetting all His sorrows, could say, "Do not let your hearts be troubled" (John 14:1). Even on the cross His joy triumphed over pain and death, and "for the joy set before him endured the cross, scorning its shame" (Hebrews 12:2).

The psalm also points to His sweetness. "All your robes are fragrant with myrrh and aloes and cassia" (Psalm 45:8). Fragrance is the most exquisite and delicate of material things. It is the very soul of the flower. It expresses, better than any other earthly things, the idea of sweetness; that blending of joy and love which no other word could so well express; that quality which draws us to persons because of their loveliness, and sheds upon us such delight and comfort from their spirit. It is like the atmosphere of spices that filled the Most Holy Place—burning spices and clouds of incense.

It is that which makes the hour of prayer so sacred and sweet, and surrounds us in our closet with such a deep, delightful sense of the divine presence as nothing else on earth affords—more delightful and more sacred than the closest intimacy of human friendship, and the most perfect fellowship of kindred hearts. This is the spirit of Jesus; and if we are clothed in His garments, it will be our spirit, too, and, like His, all our robes will smell of myrrh and aloes.

These spices are significant. The myrrh was used for the dead, and the aloe is a bitter plant. The myrrh tells of the sweetness that comes from self-crucifixion, and the aloes of the bitter sweet that comes out of sanctified sorrow, while the cassia speaks of the other qualities of loveliness which fill the Savior's heart and hold us to His bosom. Such is the royal Bridegroom, "outstanding among ten thousand" (Song of Songs 5:10); "he is altogether lovely" (5:16). Well might the tongue flow as "the pen of a skillful writer" (Psalm 45:1); well might the heart glow with love and joy as he drew the picture of his glorious King and sweetest Friend. Many another heart has felt the same indwelling of the Savior's love, and oft has sung or felt:

> Jesus, the very thought of Thee
>   With sweetness fills my breast;
> But sweeter far Thy face to see,
>   And in Thy presence rest.

SECTION II—*The Bride*

We have her call. "Listen, O daughter, consider and give ear:/ Forget your people and your father's house" (45:10).

1. She is to "listen." Why is this call so expressed? It is because the voice is so soft and low that if she does not listen diligently she will not hear it. Jesus calls with a still, small voice; and if we are immersed in worldly thoughts and cares, we will miss His call. The voice which calls the Bride is not a loud voice. The lover whispers his suit, and she must listen with open ear or she will lose the whispered words of love. How often have we missed the Master's sweetest voice because we have not listened!

2. She must not only "listen" but "consider." This word literally means "to sit down together." She must sit down with Him and let Him talk to her. She must let His message sink deep into her heart. She must think. Ah, how little we meditate and let the Lord's message sink deep into our spirit! True consecration and deep spiritual life must begin in contemplation and deep communion in the secret place of the heart. "In your anger do not sin;/ when you are on your beds,/ search your hearts and be silent" (4:4), is the Psalmist's appropriate word.

But she must also "give ear." This means a willingness to hear; this means a direction of the heart to the call. Sometimes we refuse the call; we would rather not hear. We are afraid we will be called away from the world and sin, or from some choice of our own self-will; but if we will "give ear," if we will be willing to listen and catch the voice of God, we will receive His messages and be led into the closer place of His love and fellowship.

3. There must be a separation. "Forget your people and your father's house" (45:10). There is something that must be given up before she can know His love and come into the fullness of His blessing. Every high spring rises from a corresponding depth. God loves the place of sacrifice. The place on which the temple rose was the spot where Abraham had given up his child and his all to God; therefore God immortalized it forever. The place where redemption was founded was the cross of Calvary. So in each of our

lives, the everlasting memorial which God is preparing for us will spring out of some experience of separation and sacrifice.

We cannot have both the earthly and the heavenly. How much are we to give up? All, and then God will give back in Him whatever He chooses to give, no longer as it was before, but from henceforth as linked with Him. Abraham received back Isaac, but not to be the same; he was no longer his Isaac, but God's.

It is not merely giving up, but a glad giving up, a turning of the heart and affections from every other direction because of the greater attraction which draws us to Him, even as the bride no longer desires even the joys of home and the companionship of father and mother in comparison with the transcendent delight of her husband's society.

4. We have her consecration. "Honor him, for he is your lord" (45:11). She gives herself entirely to Him; she recognizes Him as divine; she worships Him. It is the dedication of all her being to One who is not only her Lover but her Lord.

5. Much is said about her wardrobe. First, her robes are all glorious within. It is her inner adorning that is emphasized. Outwardly, and in the sight of men, she may seem common and unattractive, but her inner adorning is all glorious. Her heart is pure, her love is heavenly and divine, her spirit is as beautiful as His own.

"Her gown is interwoven with gold" (45:13). Gold is the symbol of the divine. This tells of the holiness and the loveliness that are not mere human virtue, but the very nature of God Himself, and the work of the blessed Holy Spirit; the imperishable qualities that come not from human effort, but from the indwelling life of Christ Himself within the heart.

Not only is her clothing of gold, but it is "interwoven with gold." It is not ready-made clothing, but it is made expressly for her. It tells us of the grace which provides for each of us a heavenly robe exactly adapted to our own life. We are not all dressed alike, but God has given each of us a special provision of grace which He has for none besides. He adapts Himself to us with special care, and meets our every need with infinite provisions of His grace. He is ever working for us. His own loving hands provide for each emergency and meet each new situation. As the actors upon the stage have different robes for each new act, which they have simply to put on and wear, so the grace of Jesus Christ has provided for each of us "everything we need for life and godliness" (2 Peter 1:3) for every occurrence that meets us.

Again, we read of the raiment of needlework. This suggests to us the thousand little stitches which enter into our daily life, and the provisions of God's grace are as minute as the threads in your garments. There is nothing too small for God's mercy to provide, not by hours even, but by moments. We may live in Him and take Him for each new moment as it comes.

6. We have her intimacy with Him and His delight in her. "She is led to the king" (Psalm 45:14). "The king is enthralled by your beauty" (45:11). This is the best of it. What are her garments, her companions, her other joys, compared with the joy of His presence, fellowship and love? We read of the virgins, her companions. We may be virgins, or we may be the Bride. She has companions.

"The Daughter of Tyre will come with a gift" (45:12). This tells of the business of the world. Tyre was the type of earthly commerce. It means prophetically that a day is coming when the wealth of the world shall be at the feet of the Bride of the Lamb, and we who have given up all for Christ shall control and possess what others now prize so highly and risk their all to gain.

Next, we have the entering into the palace of the King. "They are led in with joy and gladness;/ they enter the palace of the king" (45:15). Oh, how the vision rises before us: The bridal procession, the joyful songs, the glorious Bride, the welcome of the Savior, the happy meeting to part no more, the joyful greetings on that eternal shore, the entering never to go out again. Oh, will you, will I be there?

There is another question: How are we answering the call now? "Listen, O daughter, consider" (45:10). "Will you go with this man?" (Genesis 24:58). God help us to answer as did Rebekah of old, "I will go" (24:58).

SECTION III—*The Offspring*

There is a glorious offspring from this marriage. "Your sons will take the place of your fathers;/ you will make them princes throughout the land" (Psalm 45:16). We do not enter upon the meaning of this glorious prophecy, the generations in the ages to come that shall be born of the Bride of the Lamb; but it is enough for the present to know that all we can be as Christians, and all that we can do to bring others to Christ, is the fruit of our own union with the Lord Jesus. "That you might belong . . . to him who was raised from the dead, in order that we might bear fruit to God" (Romans 7:4). Every soul that we bring to Christ ought to be begotten of our love, by the power of the Holy Spirit, and be the real offspring of our union with the Lord Jesus Christ. Not until we know Him in His deepest intimacy, as the Bridegroom of our heart, can we know all the fullness of His power, and can we be to others all that He would have us be.

Beloved, what place are you taking? The place of the virgins or the place of the Bride? The virgin may be pure, but the Bride is something more. She has the marriage love, the bridal robes and the nearness which no others can know. This is the high calling which we may accept and which we may miss. May the Lord Himself enable us to understand the kingdom to which we are called, and not to come short of the highest place to which mortals have ever been raised, and to which angels dare not aspire! "Listen, O daughter, consider" (Psalm 45:10), a still, small voice is whispering to you. "Forget your people and your father's house./ The king is enthralled by your beauty;/ honor him, for he is your lord" (45:10–11).

CHAPTER 9

THE MISSIONARY PSALM

Psalm 67

This beautiful psalm covers all the ages and dispensations.

SECTION I—*The Mosaic Dispensation*

It begins with the Mosaic dispensation: "May God be gracious to us and bless us/ and make his face shine upon us" (67:1).

This is almost a repetition of the blessing of the high priest under the old dispensation. These were almost the very words that Aaron was to utter when he blessed the Hebrew congregation in the name of the Lord, and said: "The LORD bless you/ and keep you;/ the LORD make his face shine upon you/ and be gracious to you;/ the LORD turn his face toward you/ and give you peace" (Numbers 6:24–26). This is the spirit of the Old Testament.

It is blessed and heavenly, but it does not reach beyond ourselves. It is our blessing rather than the blessing of others, and yet it is very precious and real; and, so far as it goes, it is our blessing still even under the new dispensation.

1. It begins with the divine mercy, the source of all our blessings, and especially of our salvation, the greatest of our mercies.

2. It speaks of our temporal blessings which form so large a part of the Old Testament promises: God's goodness to us in our natural life and our earthly needs.

3. It reaches its fullness in the third petition: "Make his face shine upon us" (Psalm 67:1). This leads up to the Lord's own personal presence with us, and the manifestation of Himself to us as He manifested Himself under the Old Testament in the Shekinah glory that shone in the Most Holy Place; and as He does in the New, through the indwelling of the Holy Spirit in our hearts and the gracious manifestation of the presence of Christ in the con-

secrated spirit. This is all the most blessed and the most real, and all this is necessary before we can be prepared to go into the deeper and broader experiences of the psalm. But this is all personal and does not reach beyond ourselves.

SECTION II—*The Christian Dispensation*

The second prayer of this beautiful psalm covers the Christian dispensation and the wider publication of the gospel to the Gentiles and to all the world: "That your ways may be known on earth,/ your salvation among all nations" (67:2).

This is just as distinct a picture of the New Testament dispensation as the first verse is of the Old. This is the wider view of the gospel for the whole human race. God's way just means His glorious way of salvation and His high and holy will respecting man. Properly speaking, Christ is Himself God's way. "I am the way and the truth and the life" (John 14:6); and so it is a prayer for the knowledge of Jesus to be spread among all the nations.

The beautiful expression, "your salvation" (Psalm 67:2), includes the idea not only of salvation, but of healing, too, or, more correctly, of that fullness of blessing which the old word *health* so perfectly expressed. The Saxon *hale* gives us the perfect meaning, and it just describes the wholeness and soundness and wholesomeness which the gospel brings into all our life, making everything right and happy and enabling us to say, "All is well." This is the gospel that men need, a gospel that brings glad tidings for every human need, and saves us utterly and perfectly in every part of our being.

The Psalmist's prayer is that this may be known. We are not to save men, but we are to make God's salvation known. All that Christ's coming is waiting for is simply the proclamation of the gospel among all nations. The world does not know this great salvation. Men will not accept it, but all should know it. This has been the business of the Church in the Christian age. For this the Holy Spirit was given. This is our calling today. This is the meaning of Christian missions—to make God's way known upon the earth, and His salvation among all nations. It is to this we are consecrating ourselves, and to this we dedicate ourselves anew this day.

After 18 centuries there are still but a few million out of earth's heathen nations who know the gospel. Perhaps one half of the population of this globe has never heard the name of Jesus, and God is sending us forth simply to tell them. A human government could reach all the tribes of earth in a very short space of time with any message of importance. But the King of kings has not found an army that could carry His commission beyond the borders of earth's unevangelized lands.

Oh, how we need to pray, "That your ways may be known on earth,/ your salvation among all nations" (67:2).

SECTION III—*The Jewish People*

God's purpose for the Jewish people is here made known. "May the peoples praise you, O God;/ may all the peoples praise you" (67:3). The "people" here mean God's chosen people Israel, as the "nations" mean the Gentiles.

This is to be the closing incident of the New Testament dispensation, the restoration and salvation of Israel. This prayer is now being fulfilled. The spirit of grace and supplication is now being poured out upon the house of David, and they that pierced Him are beginning to look upon Him (Zechariah 12:10) and to return to their rejected Messiah. Many of the ancient people of God are returning to their old land, and, better still, many of them are turning to their Messiah. God speed the day when all the people shall praise the Lord, and God, even their own God, shall bless them!

SECTION IV—*The Second Advent*

The personal coming of Christ and the blessing of the millennial earth and its redeemed nations are next referred to, in the words: "May the nations be glad and sing for joy,/ for you rule the peoples justly/ and guide the nations of the earth" (Psalm 67:4). "Then the land will yield its harvest,/ and God, our God, will bless us./ God will bless us,/ and all the ends of the earth will fear him" (67:6–7).

This is the picture of Christ's personal reign. It is He who shall judge the people righteously. It is He who shall govern the nations upon earth. It is this that is to make the nations rejoice and sing for joy. It is this that is to bring back more than Eden blessedness to the sin-cursed earth, until it shall yield its increase; and all the nations of the earth shall fear Him. God haste this glorious day for which creation is groaning and travailing in pain!

Oh, how different the picture now! Even those ancient psalms forecast the awful vision as they cry, "Have regard for your covenant,/ because haunts of violence fill the dark places of the land" (74:20).

SECTION V—*Some Practical Considerations*

1. God has revealed to us His plan for the world and the ages. This beautiful psalm contains a very clear outline of the dispensations and purposes of God. He has not called us servants, but He has called us friends; for everything that He learned from the Father He has made known to us (John 15:15). He has taken us into His confidence, and we can intelligently

cooperate with Him in carrying out His great purposes for the world which He has redeemed. This is a high honor and privilege.

Many persons are working in the dark. They do not understand God's idea for this age. They are expecting the world to be converted in the present dispensation, and they are disappointed because their hopes are not realized. This is not God's intent, but rather to gather out of all nations a people for His name, then restore His ancient people Israel, and come Himself to reign over the millennial earth, restoring it to righteousness and peace (Acts 15:14–18). Let us accept our great trust and be worthy of the high honor He has given us as coworkers with Himself.

2. God has given us a great trust for the world. This gospel is not our own, but given us for dying men. We dare not use it for ourselves without peril. Suppose some wealthy man were to bequeath a great estate to the suffering poor of New York City and leave us as trustees of the fund; and we, instead of using it according to his benevolent wishes, were to sit down and enjoy it ourselves, and squander it upon our families and our pleasures. Would we not be regarded as false to our trust, and cruel, selfish, unjust and criminal? Christ has left us the purchase of His blood, not for enjoyment merely, but for the world's salvation. Terrible indeed will be the account which they shall have to render who have used this trust for their own salvation and enjoyment, and left the world, for whom it was intended, to perish in ignorance and sin. We are trustees of the gospel. Let us never forget this.

3. We live in a very solemn time. We are on the threshold of the age to come, and at the close of the Christian dispensation. Never were times so momentous or opportunities so extraordinary. We belong to that generation for which all the ages have been waiting, and all beings might well envy; the generation whose high calling it may be to welcome their returning King and herald around the world the tidings of His coming. We have come to the kingdom for such a time as this. God help us to redeem the time and be true to His high calling!

4. God Himself has gone out before us and is working mightily in His providence and grace for the evangelization of the world. His providence has shaken every heathen nation, and opened almost all the world to the gospel. His Spirit has been marvelously poured out upon the heathen, and His hand is manifest in the remarkable history of modern missions as in nothing else since apostolic times. With such encouragements, surely, we may well go forth and expect His mighty blessing on our efforts to evangelize the world.

5. We are living in an age when God is using not the mighty and the learned, but the humblest instrumentalities to do His work. He is choosing a people out of a people. He is taking the things that are weak and foolish; "the things that are not—to nullify the things that are" (1 Corinthians 1:28). No one need, therefore, say, "I am unfit. There is nothing I can do."

All we need is the baptism of His Spirit, the power of His presence, and He can use us mightily in our weakness and nothingness as witnesses to the name of Jesus. The victory of today is to be won by Gideon's little band, the 300, and not by the 30,000.

6. Finally, the pole star of our missionary effort is the Lord's personal coming. He is near at hand. It is this that stirs our hearts. It is this that makes every sacrifice and toil seem little. He is so near, and His recompense will make amends for all. Oh, let us go forth with this all-animating hope, and bring to pass the 67th Psalm in all the fullness of the Christian dispensation and the millennial glory!

> May God be gracious to us and bless us
>   and make his face shine upon us,
> that your ways may be known on earth,
>   your salvation among all nations.
>
> May the peoples praise you, O God;
>   may all the peoples praise you.
> May the nations be glad and sing for joy,
>   for you rule the peoples justly
>   and guide the nations of the earth.
>
> May the peoples praise you, O God;
>   may all the peoples praise you.
> Then the land will yield its harvest,
>   and God, our God, will bless us.
> God will bless us,
>   and all the ends of the earth will fear him.
>   (Psalm 67:1–7)

CHAPTER 10

THE MILLENNIAL KING

Psalm 72

This psalm has primary reference to Solomon, and is called a Psalm or Song for Solomon. But it is greater than even Solomon in all his glory, and reaches its true fulfillment in the "King of kings" (Revelation 19:16) and "Prince of Peace" (Isaiah 9:6), of whom Solomon was but a type. David was the type of Christ our King, with special reference to His conflicts and conquests. Solomon typifies His peaceful throne and His millennial kingdom.

This is the picture of Christ's millennial throne.

SECTION I—*The King*

1. We behold here the picture of a wise king. "Endow the king with your justice, O God" (72:1). This word "justice" means the power to rule and judge with wisdom, such as God gave to Solomon in so preeminent a measure. This was his special request of God, and it was marvelously given.

We all remember the wonderful wisdom with which he detected the true mother of the child that was brought to him for judgment, and how his wisdom brought from the uttermost parts of the earth the wondering pilgrims, who came to sit at his feet and propound their hard questions until nothing was left unsolved of all their hearts' desires. But "one greater than Solomon is here" (Matthew 12:42), the "Wonderful Counselor" (Isaiah 9:6), the Man of whom it was said by His enemies, "No one ever spoke the way this man does" (John 7:46); the One who answered the craft and subtlety of His foes until they were glad to escape from His presence in silence and confusion— "Christ . . . the wisdom of God" (1 Corinthians 1:24).

Earth owes much to wise sovereigns, but her true King has yet to come. What a glorious day that will be when upon the throne of earth shall sit that Mighty One, whose infinite wisdom shall govern the happy nations and bring to earth its highest possibilities of blessing!

2. He is a righteous King. "He will judge your people in righteousness,/ your afflicted ones with justice" (Psalm 72:2). How much the world has suffered from injustice, oppression and wrong! All the sorrows of men spring from their sins. But the King that is coming shall be not only the Righteous One, but His people shall be all righteous. "In his days the righteous will flourish" (72:7), and sin and wrong shall disappear from the earth. This is the secret of failure in all our social and political attempts at reform. The material itself is wrong, and until that is rectified, all the best of human plans must end in failure.

A building lay in ruins, and many were discussing the cause of the wreck. The architect said that the plans were perfect; the contractors declared that the specifications had all been complied with—every brick was in its place, and every arch was rightly set. Why had it tumbled in ruins? A plain workman took up a brick and crushed it beneath his fingers. "There," he said, "is the cause; the brick is rotten, and one is not able to support the weight of another. The material is worthless, and all your best designs are useless with a lot of rotten brick." Alas! republicanism, social reform, philanthropy, humanitarianism, legislation, example, philosophy, poetry, patriotism can do nothing to elevate and save humanity so long as the human heart is corrupt and the materials are worthless.

But the day is coming when sin shall disappear, when righteousness shall prevail, and when it shall be said of earth, in the language of the ancient prophet: "The LORD bless you, O righteous dwelling, O sacred mountain" (Jeremiah 31:23). What a glorious day it will be when truth and virtue, honesty and uprightness, unselfishness and love shall bind man to man in a chain of holy benignity, and the prayer of ages shall be fulfilled: "Your will be done on earth as it is in heaven" (Matthew 6:10).

3. It is a kingdom of peace. "The mountains will bring prosperity to the people,/ the hills the fruit of righteousness" (Psalm 72:3). "In his days the righteous will flourish;/ prosperity will abound till the moon is no more" (72:7). Other kings have ruled by the sword. But He shall be called the Prince of Peace. Oh, the unspeakable horrors of war! Who can measure its frightful expense in treasure and blood, in tears and agony! Oh, the horrors of bloody strife and the mutilated forms of dying men! Oh, the wild and devilish strife of the sanguinary battlefield! Oh, the myriads of graves that have marked the track of earthly conquerors! In the last few decades there is not an important nation under the sun that has not been deluged in blood. But all this is coming to an end.

> Through the dim future, through long generations,
>   The echoing sounds grow fainter and then cease;

And, like a bell, with solemn, sweet vibrations,
I hear the voice of Christ again say "Peace."
Peace, and no longer from its brazen portals
The voice of war's loud thunder shakes the skies,
But beautiful as songs of the immortals
The holy melodies of love arise.

But that is only one side of peace. There are a thousand strifes that never end in blood. There are a thousand swords that shed only the richer blood of the spirit. Oh, the sorrows and sins that come from lack of harmony, from the discords of human hearts, from the ill adjustments of human lives, from the clash and friction of human spirits! Men are at war with themselves, at war with each other, at war with God. Oh, for the coming of the Prince of Peace! That will bring rest to every restless heart, harmony to every divided home, unity and love to all human lives, and peace with God. And it will be so perfect that like the planets around their sun, all earth's inhabitants will move in harmony with the will of God, and earth once more will become the counterpart of heaven, and its troubled sea of unrest like the sea of glass before the throne (Revelation 4:6).

4. It will be a kingdom of grace and love. "He will defend the afflicted among the people/ and save the children of the needy;/ he will crush the oppressor. . . . He will be like rain falling on a mown field,/ like showers watering the earth. . . . For he will deliver the needy who cry out,/ the afflicted who have no one to help./ He will take pity on the weak and the needy/ and save the needy from death./ He will rescue them from oppression and violence,/ for precious is their blood in his sight" (Psalm 72:4, 6, 12–14).

He will be the King of grace, of gentleness, of meekness. He will be the Protector of the poor, the Comforter of the sorrowing, the Friend of the friendless. Earth has had its Prince Arthurs and its Peters the Great, whose glory it was to live among their peasantry and to befriend the lowly and the poor. But the coming King is the ideal of gentleness and grace.

Oh, the happiness His reign will bring! "God will wipe away every tear" (Revelation 7:17) and redress all wrongs, destroy all enemies, heal all the wounds of the ages. What a world that will be where there will be no sin, no sickness, no sorrow, no selfishness, no Satan! What a Millennium that will be where we shall have our perfect bodies, our perfect spirits, our parted friends, our blessed Savior forever!

O long-expected day, begin,
Dawn on this world of pain and sin.

5. It will be a kingdom of glory, riches and splendor. "The kings of Tar-

shish and of distant shores/ will bring tribute to him;/ the kings of Sheba and Seba/ will present him gifts" (Psalm 72:10). "May gold from Sheba be given him./ May people ever pray for him/ and bless him all day long" (72:15). While all the elements of spiritual blessings will be there, there will not be lacking one thing which can constitute material happiness and glory.

The earth will be transformed. Its physical features will be materially changed, its climate adjusted, its thorns and thistles, rocks and desert waste places exchanged for beauty and fertility, "the desert and the parched land will be glad;/ the wilderness will rejoice and blossom" (Isaiah 35:1). The very animal creation will be so changed that they will perfectly minister to man as in the first creation, and violence, cruelty, and suffering will pass away from earth. The riches and the glory of earth will be laid at the feet of Jesus and shared with His redeemed. Has He not said: "But seek first his kingdom and his righteousness, and all these things will be given to you as well" (Matthew 6:33)?

It is then that the reward will come, and they who have followed Him in the sacrifice of all earthly ambitions will sit with Him on thrones and receive with Him a hundredfold of houses and lands and earthly distinctions and glories. This is not to be the chief element of their happiness. These things are nothing without Him. But having taught them to find their portion first in Him, He will give them all besides, and Himself with it and in it, and make real the old testimony of one of His saints: "First, I have everything in God, and then I have God in everything."

6. It will be a universal kingdom. "He will rule from sea to sea/ and from the River to the ends of the earth" (Psalm 72:8). "All kings will bow down to him/ and all nations will serve him" (72:11).

There will never be another universal kingdom until Jesus comes. Our boasted democracy is not going to include the world. Its next hope is a king, and the earth is waiting for His advent with groans of pain. The Church is not going to become universal, but Christ Himself, by His personal coming, shall gather all nations and tribes and tongues beneath His peaceful scepter.

7. It will be an everlasting kingdom. "He will endure as long as the sun,/ as long as the moon, through all generations" (72:5). "May his name endure forever;/ may it continue as long as the sun./ All nations will be blessed through him,/ and they will call him blessed" (72:17).

Not only for a thousand years will His kingdom last, but forever and ever. The scriptural conception of the future is very glorious. It is not a monotonous forever, but it is a succession of *aeons*, or ages, of surpassing glory. The Millennium is but one of these ages. The new heavens and the new earth will be the next, and beyond that is age after age forever. Could we be told the glory of some of these distant ages, we could not even comprehend it. But as these mighty *aeons* roll on, we shall be prepared for yet greater progressions and this mighty universe will expand until that great promise is fulfilled: "In order that in the coming ages he might show the incomparable riches of his grace, expressed in his kindness to us in Christ Jesus" (Ephesians 2:7).

Such is a feeble outline of this inspired picture of the millennial kingdom of the Lord Jesus. The other Scriptures are full of the picture of this golden age of Christian hope and promise. But what can we do to hasten it?

SECTION II—*His Subjects*

1. We can long for it. There is a great promise to those who simply and truly love His appearing. If we desire it, it will influence and transform our lives. It is the goal of our highest hopes and affections and the time when our real life shall begin. Is our treasure there? Are our hopes there? Is every fiber of our being crying: "Come, Lord Jesus" (Revelation 22:20)? Is it home forever to our homeless hearts? This is what the Master sees and loves. This is what friendship appreciates in a friend—the sense of his absence, the longing for his return.

2. We can pray for it. Do you ever pray for the things that are coming to you after Jesus comes? Have you stored up anything on the other side of the resurrection, for which you are waiting and asking? Oh, you little know the power there is in that kind of prayer! It will elevate all your being by cords that are anchored to the very throne, and attractions that will lift you above the skies.

3. We can live for it. We can be ready for His coming every moment. He can keep your garments unspotted. Let Him adorn you with the wedding robe; and when all the members of His Church are thus adorned, and the Bride is ready for her husband, He will not be long in coming.

4. We can labor for His coming. The best way to hasten it is to send the gospel to all nations and take the invitations to the wedding to all earth's inhabitants. When this shall have been done, we know the end will come. Blessed hope! Lord, hasten it! Oh, let the Spirit and the Bride say, "Come!" (22:17), and every heart respond, "Come, Lord Jesus" (22:20).

In Scotland's darkest day, the nation at last felt that its only hope lay in the return of John Knox. So he was sent for, and eagerly they awaited the first signal of the great reformer's advent. At length a messenger hastened up from Leith, entered the chamber where the delegates were secretly assembled, and carefully shutting the door, a whisper was breathed, "John Knox has come." It went from lip to lip, and men stood up with strange excitement, buckled on their armor and helmets, went from village to village, and from home to home, until, ere many hours had passed, the tidings had been whispered to every waiting heart, "John Knox has come!" Brave men gathered quickly to the secret meeting place where a mighty host stood around their glorious leader, and the enemies of Scotland trembled on their throne before the power of one mighty man. Scotland was saved, and the religious liberties of the world were settled.

Oh, this is the only hope of the world! Let us send it up to heaven as the cry of prayer, "Come, Lord Jesus!" Soon the whisper will sweep down from yonder skies, "The Lord has come!" Around Him will silently gather His faithful waiting ones; scepters will fall and thrones will crumble, and the King of kings will take the kingdom, and the saints of the Most High will reign with Him forever and ever.

Oh day of days! Oh hope of hopes! Oh King of kings and Lord of lords! We wait, we watch, we long, we hope, we pray, we work for Thee. Amen.

CHAPTER 11

JESUS OUR ABIDING HOME

Psalm 91

Like the 22nd, 23rd and 24th Psalms, more effective in their grouping than even in their individuality, the 90th and 91st Psalms are fitted into each other with singular effect.

The first was undoubtedly written by Moses, and the second, most probably, by the same author. We know it has been attributed to a much later time by many, but the internal evidences and the imagery employed point strongly to the wilderness.

The 90th Psalm was the cry of his lonely heart, as for 40 years Israel wandered in the trackless wilderness without a habitation or a home, until from that scene of desolation and death his heart turns to find rest in God, as he cries, "Lord, you have been our dwelling place/ throughout all generations" (90:1).

But even this bright and blessed comfort seems almost lost in the dirge-like strains of the closing verses of the psalm, as all his thoughts become absorbed in the scenes of depression and mortality that gather around him, so that the song becomes one long, sad wail. "You turn men back to dust" (90:3). "All our days pass away under your wrath;/ we finish our years with a moan" (90:9).

But in the 91st Psalm, his lonely heart has found its home "in the shelter of the Most High . . . in the shadow of the Almighty" (91:1), and beneath the cover of His shadowing wings. There is no doubt that all through this psalm there is a reference to the Tabernacle in the wilderness. Its holy shrine within the veil and beneath the outspread wings of the cherubim is the secret place of the Most High and the shadow where His Spirit dwells in holy fellowship and eternal security and rest.

Whoever was the author of this psalm, we know who is its great end. We know where the secret place of the Most High and the shadow of the Al-

233

mighty for us are found, even in the bosom of Jesus our abiding home. And we know also for whom it is intended, even for all who are in Him and longing to abide in Him. There are few of us who cannot claim it as our own psalm and record it as our testimony. May the Holy Spirit enlarge it to our thought once more, and make it as never before our living experience!

Let us look first at the names of God here given; secondly, His promises; and thirdly, their conditions.

SECTION I—*The Names of God*

There are four glorious names given to Him in this psalm:

1. The Most High. This tells of His supremacy as sovereign Lord, above all authority and dominion and every name that is named. High as may be our difficulties, He is higher. Our enemies may be lofty, but He is above them. The place to which He bids us rise may be beyond our reach, but He is able to raise us to the loftiest heights of faith and hope. What can be too hard or too high for the Most High?

2. The Almighty. This is the glorious name He gave to Abraham and repeated to Moses, the Hebrew *Shaddai.* It tells of the God of infinite power and resources for which nothing is too hard. It is He who formed the worlds out of nothing. It is He who holds those mighty suns in their places, and whirls those countless systems on their orbits, and keeps in motion this mighty universe without disturbance. It is He who has shown His mighty power in the miracles of the Bible, in the destruction of Pharaoh's host and Sennacherib's army, in the resurrection of Jesus Christ from the dead and in the conversion of the myriads who have passed from sin, white-robed and glorified, into the presence of His glory. It is He who is our Protector and our God.

3. Jehovah. This is the dearest of all names because it links them all with us. It means the covenant God. It means the God who is related to us, the God who is revealed in Jesus as the God of grace and mercy.

4. God. This, His absolute name, denotes His eternal deity and infinite perfection. But the best of it is, He is *my* God. He is not an abstract God, far away, but He gives Himself to me, and permits me to call Him my very own, to possess Him, to use Him, to say He is mine. Oh, have we known His mighty name? He condescends to give to us these glorious names. He might have hidden Himself away in inscrutable, inaccessible majesty, but He has deigned to come down to meet us, to tell us about Himself, to reveal Himself by names that we can understand. Let us meet Him; let us respond to His love; let us "say of the LORD, 'He is my refuge and my fortress,/ my God, in whom I trust' " (91:2).

SECTION II—*His Promises*

1. He promises protection from the wiles of temptation. "Surely he will save you from the fowler's snare" (91:3). We need first to be guarded from spiritual evil, and this is promised here even in its most subtle forms. The fowler is our great enemy, the devil, seeking to catch us like unwary little birds by his deceptive snares. But from these, the man who meets the conditions of this psalm shall be guarded.

God will not allow us to be deceived. He is able to keep us from stumbling and to present us faultless. "God is faithful; he will not let you be tempted beyond what you can bear" (1 Corinthians 10:13). Blessed promise! How much we need it! How insidious are the deceptions of the foe! How weak and foolish all our wisdom! But how secure are those whose life is hid with Christ!

2. He promises protection from physical ills. This undoubtedly denotes disease of every kind, for here the severest of all forms is mentioned—"the deadly pestilence" (Psalm 91:3). And if we are promised exemption from this, it must include all lesser forms. This must, of course, be preceded by the other promise. We must be saved first from spiritual evil. But if we are, we shall be kept from physical evil. Both these promises are preceded by the most emphatic word in the psalm, "surely." It is God's great amen. It must have a very marked meaning. God foresaw all the professors, editors and theologians who were going to write against the literal meaning of this blessed promise, and so He put this down and underscored it for all the ages, that no trembling soul need ever doubt or fear to take the Lord as a Sanctifier and Healer, and to expect to be kept in perfect peace and safety while humbly trusting in Him. Let us put our amen to God's yea, and trust Him with all our heart for all our need.

3. He promises His overshadowing presence. "He will cover you with his feathers,/ and under his wings you will find refuge" (91:4). Undoubtedly this refers in some sense to the mother bird as she broods over her little ones, covering them with her strong pinions and nestling them under her soft feathers. What a beautiful figure it is of God's tenderness! Not only the strong wings, but the soft, downy feathers. Oh, that we may claim all that the figure means; and while He stretches out His mighty wings, let us nestle close to His bosom. There is a double sense here: "He will cover," but you will trust. We are to meet His love as it comes to us. There is something in human hearts that needs caressing and comforting, and God is full of it. We need to nestle on His bosom, to be cherished and fondled. God loves to do it. "He will take great delight in you,/ he will quiet you with his love,/ he will rejoice over you with singing" (Zephaniah 3:17).

But there is another meaning in the figure. It refers undoubtedly to the cherubim in the Most Holy Place, those beautiful wings of gold that were spread out above the ark, between which shone the Shekinah glory representing the face of God, the smile of heaven. This is "the shelter of the Most High" (Psalm 91:1). These are the wings that cover us. The figure is even more complete when we include all that it contained, for still lower down beneath those wings was the covering lid of the ark, the mercy seat sprinkled with the blood which covered the sins of the people and hid them from the eye that looked down from above. So that we are covered first by the blood, and then by the wings of God, while His countenance, full of light and love, beams down upon us from between the cherub wings.

4. He promises us victorious faith. "His faithfulness will be your shield and rampart" (91:4). The shield is the uniform type of faith in the Scriptures. The shield was made very large in ancient times and covered all the person, warding off the dart that came in front. So it represents that perfect trust that covers all our person from every attack of the enemy. This is God's glorious gift. Christ is our shield; Christ is our faith.

But what about the rampart? Why, this shield might be lost; the hand that held it might let go; the blow of the enemy might strike it down; or the hand of the foe might wrest it from the bravest soldier and leave him unprotected. But the rampart could not be torn away. It was fastened on the arm, buckled to the wrist; it was part of the soldier. The rampart tells us of a faith we cannot lose. It is the faith of God, the Spirit of Christ within us, the Author and Finisher of our faith, establishing us immovably and making us "more than conquerors through him who loved us" (Romans 8:37). This is the promise. This is our privilege. Let us claim it.

5. He promises deliverance from fear. "You will not fear the terror of night,/ nor the arrow that flies by day,/ nor the pestilence that stalks in the darkness,/ nor the plague that destroys at midday" (Psalm 91:5–6). Fear is the worst of our calamities, and it brings many a calamity. But God can save us from fear and keep us from all alarm. "This poor man called, and the LORD heard him;/ he saved him out of all his troubles" (34:6). "But whoever listens to me will live in safety/ and be at ease, without fear of harm" (Proverbs 1:33). In God's hands our future is safe, and He will let no evil harm us. Knowing that, we can be calm and free from care.

Fear also includes care, worry, and anxiety of every kind. To be saved from this is indeed a haven of rest. No one is truly saved from these cares until he enters into and abides in "the shelter of the Most High" (Psalm 91:1). This is the difference between the consecrated and the ordinary Christian; the latter is oppressed with a thousand cares and fears; the former can "not be anxious about anything" (Philippians 4:6), and has the peace of God which is beyond understanding to garrison his heart and mind in Christ Jesus (4:7).

The things mentioned here are very serious and terrible evils. The calamities in whose face the saint can look in the light of the psalm without an alarm are no imaginary things: the terror, the pestilence, the arrow, the destruction. It is a time of awful pestilence and widespread desolation, but he is calm and trustful and can sing: "Therefore we will not fear, though the earth give way/ and the mountains fall into the heart of the sea" (Psalm 46:2). Beloved, are you there? Is your future horizon without a cloud because it is covered by the light of His promise and His presence?

6. He promises safety amid all danger. "A thousand may fall at your side,/ ten thousand at your right hand,/ but it will not come near you./ You will only observe with your eyes/ and see the punishment of the wicked" (91:7–8). Not only are we free from fear, but we are saved from harm. The man or woman who is in the Master's will cannot perish until His work is accomplished. How often God has carried His chosen ones through battles and oceans, tempests and wild beasts!

Look at the story of Jeremiah amid the last days of Jerusalem; of Arnot and Livingstone among the tribes of Africa; of Paton among the murderous heathen of the New Hebrides; of the Covenanters in their conventicles in Scotland; and of many another whom God has guarded amid a thousand deaths. Let us believe in our almighty God and fear not to step wherever He bids us, for we are far safer in the midst of dangers in His will than surrounded by every human precaution, but disobedient to Him.

7. He promises security from all real evil. "Then no harm will befall you,/ no disaster will come near your tent" (91:10). Literally in the Hebrew this means "any stroke." It denotes the judgment of God's displeasure; or a calamity such as often overtakes the wicked. The meaning is that nothing shall overtake the trusting and abiding child of God which has real evil in it, or any element of the divine displeasure or of actual harm. Troubles undoubtedly will come to him, but the evil will be taken out of them. The devil's sting will not reach him. "The evil one cannot harm him" (1 John 5:18), and God's displeasure will never visit him, for He has sworn "not to be angry with you,/ never to rebuke you again" (Isaiah 54:9).

Sorrow, indeed, is hard to bear when it comes with God's anger and with Satan's hate unguarded by heavenly love. But when we are conscious that the Master comes between us and everything that touches us, and that every trial that meets us is brought to us by our blessed Redeemer, and shorn of its evil by His love, then nothing can injure us or even discourage us; but up through every cloud we can look into His face and say: "Goodness and love will follow me/ all the days of my life" (Psalm 23:6), and "No good thing does he withhold/ from those whose walk is blameless" (84:11), and "Who is going to harm you if you are eager to do good?" (1 Peter 3:13).

8. He promises angelic guardianship. "For he will command his angels

concerning you/ to guard you in all your ways; they will lift you up in their hands,/ so that you will not strike your foot against a stone" (Psalm 91:11–12).

The ministry of angels is too plainly revealed in the Old and New Testaments to need any demonstration, and it has not ceased. The vision of Jacob represents the angels as ascending and descending upon the son of man, and all through the Christian age they are busy still for God's redeemed. "Are not all angels ministering spirits sent to serve those who will inherit salvation?" (Hebrews 1:14). Were we to visit heaven today, we should find it, perhaps, emptied of angels, and all their myriads busy on this earth with God's redeemed ones.

The annals of Christian biography have some very wonderful instances of angelic appearances, and we can scarcely doubt that they sometimes have become visible even since the apostolic age.

Not a single angel, but a camp of angels is represented as round about those who fear the Lord. Could we see the spiritual realm, we should behold armies of mighty beings all around us, and in the loneliest and most perilous places we should never fear. Sometimes we can almost hear the flutter of their wings and feel the touch of their interposing hands. They are never absent from us.

The devil forgot to quote this rightly when he repeated it to Christ in the wilderness. He left out this clause, "in all your ways" (Psalm 91:11). His idea was that the angels would appear on some great occasion when Christ fell from the pinnacle of the temple, but the truth was the angels were just as near in the wilderness as they could have been in Jerusalem, and their presence even at that moment was between Christ and the arch-fiend.

"Always they are with us, and upon their hands they shall bear you up." This is much more beautiful than the ordinary translation. Not "in their hands" as if they were carrying us; but "upon their hands" as if we were walking upon a pavement of angelic wings, or, rather, soaring in the heavenly places, up-borne by their mighty pinions. Oh, let us realize our heavenly escort, and go forth without fear to do our Master's work and will.

9. He promises victory over Satan. "You will tread upon the lion and the cobra;/ you will trample the great lion and the serpent" (91:13). These are figures of Satanic powers in their strength and malignity; but to the one who abides in Christ, they are all conquered foes, and it is our privilege to tread them beneath our feet and treat them as vanquished enemies.

Our Savior has given us the same promise in the New Testament. "I have given you authority to trample on snakes and scorpions and to overcome all the power of the enemy; nothing will harm you" (Luke 10:19). We shall not be exempt from temptation, but we may keep temptation beneath our feet and not allow it to come even within touch of our heart. "We know that anyone born of God does not continue to sin; the one who was born of God keeps him safe, and the evil one cannot harm him" (1 John 5:18). This is our privilege in Christ. Let us fully claim it.

There is a suggestive thought in connection with "the young lion" (Psalm 91:13, KJV). The right time to tread upon the lion is while he is young; meet the evil before it grows to importance; claim victory over the first assaults of temptation. Do not let the devil get headway even for a moment, and then shall we have no old lions to contend with. This is the secret of victory in the great conflicts, to be always on guard in the little skirmishes, and immediately triumph over the breath of temptation.

Will we take our victory over the enemy? It is our privilege. Our Lord has triumphed, and in Him we are already raised up "far above all rule and authority" (Ephesians 1:21). Let us keep them beneath our feet. Let us stand in Him triumphant, waving evermore the banner of victory as we cry, "But thanks be to God! He gives us the victory through our Lord Jesus Christ" (1 Corinthians 15:57).

10. He promises to set us on high. "I will set him on high" (Psalm 91:14, KJV). This may mean earthly honor; certainly it means spiritual exaltation. It is the same promise which Isaiah so eloquently expresses: "This is the man who will dwell on the heights,/ whose refuge will be the mountain fortress" (Isaiah 33:16). It is to dwell in heavenly places in Christ Jesus; it is to have the lofty and heavenly life. And by and by it shall reach the still higher sense of everlasting glory.

11. He promises answered prayer. "He will call upon me, and I will answer him" (Psalm 91:15). This is the privilege of those who dwell in the secret place. "If you remain in me and my words remain in you, ask whatever you wish, and it will be given you" (John 15:7). God wants us to have our prayers answered. It is as much for His glory as it is for our blessing. He tells us that He has chosen and ordained us for this, that whatsoever we ask in the name of Jesus, we may receive. We may abide so near Him that we will ask only what He wants to give, and therefore we shall never ask in vain if we catch His thought before we offer our petition.

12. He promises His presence in trouble. "I will be with him in trouble" (Psalm 91:15). The tense changes, and the Lord is with us before we have time to recognize the trouble. He comes with the trouble. There is not an instant's interval until He is there. "God is our refuge and strength,/ an ever-present help in trouble" (46:1). Never is His presence so consciously realized as when circumstances are trying, and all around is dark and sad. Then, like the stars that come out under the pall of night, His face shines with a luster that we never know in more prosperous times; and if He is with us, we are so conscious of His presence that the trouble is scarcely realized. It is possible to be so enwrapped with God that we shall not "fear when heat comes"

(Jeremiah 17:8). We shall scarcely be conscious of the dark cloud around till it is left behind us. There is nothing that more gloriously characterizes the consecrated child of God than his spirit in times of trouble. Anyone can be cheerful and happy amid prosperity. But to rejoice in the midst of suffering, to be strengthened unto all longsuffering with joyfulness (see Colossians 1:11, KJV), to meet poverty, disappointment, desertion and difficulty with patience, fortitude and cheerfulness—this is possible only to a soul that is filled with the grace and presence of Jesus.

13. He promises deliverance from trouble. God wants us first to know His presence in trouble, so sustaining us that we are enabled to triumph even before the trouble is removed. But then when He has taught us this lesson, He loves to remove the trouble and to show us His providence as well as His grace. And so, when we have learned to bear our trials with patience and victory, we usually find that they are taken away and that our path is made smooth again. The discipline has done its work, and it is not necessary that it should continue.

14. He promises to honor us. "I will . . . honor him" (Psalm 91:15). God does love to honor a soul that lives wholly for Him. He honors such men with great usefulness, with wide influence among their fellow men, by His signal blessing upon their work; by the seal of His Holy Spirit; and, by and by, by the crowns and kingdoms which He shall have to bestow, not only upon those who have served Him much, but those who have loved Him truly.

15. He promises length of days. "With long life will I satisfy him" (91:16). This does not necessarily mean that we shall live for a century, but it means that we shall be satisfied. The Lord will fulfill our hearts' desires if we abide in Him, and enable us to say before our journey is ended, "Not one of all the good promises the LORD your God gave you has failed" (Joshua 23:14). But its highest sense is to be fulfilled in the days of eternity. Oh, we are yet but babes in the great cycles of existence! But as a drop to the ocean is this life compared with the ages to come, through which we are to live in His glory and grow into higher, nobler conditions of blessing and power. For He has saved us and raised us up "that in the coming ages he might show the incomparable riches of his grace, expressed in his kindness to us in Christ Jesus" (Ephesians 2:7).

16. He promises that we will see the salvation of God. "And show him my salvation" (Psalm 91:16). Now this, of course, means the great salvation of the gospel, the unfolding of God's plan in all its beauty and glory, to know in its breadth and length and depth and height, the love of Christ which surpasses knowledge (Ephesians 3:18–19). But it is not merely to know salvation as an abstract thing, but it is to know the Savior. Standing in his trembling age in yonder temple, old Simeon holds in his arms a little

Babe; and as he drops his tears on the smiling face of Jesus, he cries, "My eyes have seen your salvation" (Luke 2:30). Ah, he must have learned the 91st Psalm by heart. And by and by we shall see Christ in all His beauty and glory and reach the climax of the 91st Psalm, and of all other psalms and songs and experiences.

> Christ to trust and Christ to know
> Constitute our bliss below;
> Christ to see and Christ to love
> Constitute our bliss above.

SECTION III—*The Conditions*

1. We must dwell "in the shelter of the Most High" and "rest in the shadow of the Almighty" (Psalm 91:1). The meaning of this is all explained in the 15th chapter of John, which is the New Testament counterpart of the 91st Psalm. It is to know Jesus in His indwelling, and to live in unbroken fellowship with Him. The Hebrew is very beautiful. The two clauses are parallel. It is not "he who dwells," etc., "will rest." It is "He who dwells and he who rests." They are coordinate clauses, both describing the same person. There is a little difference in the verb in each case: the one signifies to dwell by day; the other, to lodge by night. Together they express a continual abiding in Jesus, both day and night, that union and communion with Him that are unbroken and perpetual. This is the habit of the consecrated life. This is the secret of holiness, peace, power, victory, and every physical blessing. Let us hear Him say today, "Remain in me, and I in [you] . . . apart from me you can do nothing" (John 15:5).

2. We must confess Him as our Keeper. "I will say of the LORD" (Psalm 91:2). It is not enough to think it, to feel it, to resolve it; we must say it. "How great is your goodness,/ which you have stored up for those who fear you,/ which you bestow in the sight of men/ on those who take refuge in you" (31:19). We must not be ashamed to confess our deliverance and commit ourselves to His promises and risk our whole future upon His faithfulness. We must confess Him in order to be saved; so we must receive and keep our sanctification, our healing, and the answers to our prayers by acknowledging God, even before we see His working.

3. We must trust Him. "In whom I trust" (91:2). We must claim His promise and lean upon it, and steadily rest without doubt or fear, meeting every temptation and questioning with the victorious answer, "I will trust."

4. We must give ourselves utterly to Him, and be His, and His alone. " 'Because he loves me,' says the LORD, 'I will rescue him' " (91:14). God seems to be so deeply stirred by the devotion of the heart to Him, that there is nothing

that He will not do. He seems to rise up in holy gladness and say, " 'Because he loves me,' says the LORD, 'I will rescue him;/ I will protect him, for he acknowledges my name' " (91:14).

God loves a single and devoted heart. Oh beloved, He is calling you to choose Him. To every one of you the test will come; but as it comes, it will show in the depths of your being whether you love Him with all your heart, or know whether you have so set your love upon Him that all else shall go, before you let go His love or disobey His will. Christ's heart is longing for devotion, and to the man or woman who will give it, there is nothing which He will withhold.

5. We must take our victory by putting our foot upon the lion and the adder and trampling our foes in victorious faith. God has the victory for us, but we must take it by putting our feet upon the necks of our foes, and claim His power to make good our bold, aggressive stand. He is not going to annihilate the devil and stop our temptations, but He is going to give us victory if we will take it.

Oh, may He enable us thus to abide in Him, thus to trust Him, thus to confess Him, thus to set our heart upon Him, and thus to triumph in Him over all our foes. And may we know in all its meaning this glorious psalm, which the Master Himself so grandly fulfilled, and then left as the heritage of His children until the wilderness of trial shall be past and the closing echoes shall be fulfilled in the song we shall sing before the throne, "Salvation belongs to our God,/ who sits on the throne,/ and to the Lamb" (Revelation 7:10).

CHAPTER 12

THE PIVOT PSALM

Psalm 103

This is a strange term to give this psalm, but it is an appropriate and impressive one. The first verse of this psalm is said to be the very center of the Old Testament. In their jealousy for the integrity of the sacred Scriptures, the Jews counted the chapters and verses so that they could tell how many chapters and verses there were in the whole Bible, and know at once if there had been any addition to, or subtraction from, the original Scriptures.

In the very center of these chapters and verses we find this sublime note of praise. Surely, this is not an accident. Surely, it fittingly expresses the great truth that praise is the true center of Christianity and the Christian life, the true pivot on which to hang our faith and hope and happiness and holiness. Surely, we will not have looked at this psalm in vain if we learn from it nothing more than this, the high and fixed purpose that from this moment we shall make praise the very heart and center of our whole life.

What is faith but just such confidence in God that we can praise Him for what we desire? What is prayer but an ineffectual cry, until it reaches the spirit of praise and claims the answer which God cannot refuse to thanksgiving? It was when Paul and Silas ceased their praying and sang praises to God that the answer came from the rending earth and the responding heavens. This will turn every sorrow into joy, every cloud into sunshine, every hour into gladness, to say, no matter what meets us in the circumstances of life, "I will extol the LORD at all times;/ his praise will always be on my lips" (Psalm 34:1). This is the praise psalm of the Bible. Let it be the pivot of our life and the keynote of our songs. Many reasons are given here why we should praise the Lord.

SECTION I—*The Lord Himself*

The first reason is found in the Lord Himself. Before any of His benefits are mentioned, or any causes for our thanksgiving are found in the circumstances of our life, he cries, "Praise the LORD, O my soul;/ all my inmost being, praise his holy name" (103:1).

It is the Lord and His holy name that constitute our first and last and highest cause for praise. I sometimes have tried to realize the thought: What if there had been no God, no universe, no creature, no man, no time, no eternity, no being to call anything into being, forever and forever, forever and forever—nothing, nothing, and no possibility of anything. It is too terrible, and the brain sinks, crushed beneath its awful weight. We are so glad to arouse ourselves from the hideous dream and realize that God is, as we cry, "Praise the LORD, O my soul;/ all my inmost being, praise his holy name" (103:1).

But, again, how different God might have been! He might have been a God of stern justice, of awful majesty, without mercy, grace or love. Suppose He had been such a being as some of earth's cruel conquerors—a Nebuchadnezzar or a Nero—the embodiment of selfishness and power. We could not have resisted His will. But He could only have been to us a terror and an adversary. How we thank Him for what He is; that His nature and His name are love; that He delights in mercy; that He is slow to anger; that He is all that is lovely as well as all that is mighty. Again we cry, "Praise the LORD, O my soul;/ all my inmost being, praise his holy name" (103:1).

Again, He might have been all this and yet we never might have known Him. The millions of China know Him not. The animists of Africa know Him not. The devotees of Islam know Him not. Millions among us in Christian lands have never known Him. Why is it that we know Him? Only by His infinite grace that He has given us the light.

Oh, how much cause we have to praise Him! That He has revealed Himself to us; that He has given us the Bible; that He has given to us His Son; that He has given to us His Spirit; that He has cast our lot in Christian lands; that He has called us by His grace; that He has opened our eyes; that He is our God; that we know He loves us, cares for us. Again we lift our hearts in the joyful song, "Praise the LORD, O my soul;/ all my inmost being, praise his holy name" (103:1).

SECTION II—*His Benefits*

The next cause for praise is His benefits: His kind acts toward us, His gracious dealings with us even before our spiritual mercies are mentioned and our salvation is referred to. The goodness of God, even apart from salvation, is wonderful. How much God has done for us in our natural life and in His works of creation and providence! How kind the hand that formed us! How differently He might have made us!

Oh, the manifold wisdom and love displayed even in the human body and mind, and the constitution of our social and domestic life! How easy it would have been for God to have made us without these exquisite senses, tastes and capacities! Suppose He had made the heavens yellow and the earth red. Our eyes would have been strained with agony and bewildered with the harsh, strong colors. Instead, He has made the curtain above us a delicate blue, and the carpet beneath us a soft green, resting our organs of vision, and affording the most exquisite delight by their beauty.

Suppose He had made us without the sense of taste. We might have been nourished by our food, but we would not have enjoyed it. But He has given us these sensitive palates that recognize the delicious flavor of things, and then He has provided the objects that gratify them. He might have made all the food alike, but He has spread our table with a hundred bounties, each contributing some new pleasure to our physical senses, and He has made the sense of smell, with all the delicious odors of the garden and the air. And so He has adjusted us to the world around us and adjusted the world to us.

More exquisite still are the affections that He has placed within our breasts, and the objects of love, the ties of nature, the home bonds that meet them with such blessed objects of regard and link us one to another by the cords of love! Oh, as we think of all the thousand ways in which He has studied the happiness of His creatures, our hearts respond with the glad song, "Praise the LORD, O my soul,/ and forget not all his benefits" (103:2).

SECTION III—*Salvation*

The third ground for praising God is salvation. "Who forgives all your sins" (103:3). This is the greatest blessing of all. Deeply as we realize it now, we never shall fully know what it means till that hour when we stand with Him amid the dissolving universe; and as we see the past from which we have been rescued, we shall send forth one shout of praise that shall reecho around the universe, "To him who sits on the throne and to the Lamb" (Revelation 5:13).

"Who forgives all your sins" (Psalm 103:3). It is in the present tense, and the most universal sense. It is not some of our iniquities, but all. It is not merely once that He forgave, but He still forgives, and He will forever. He is forgiving now, and He is waiting today to be gracious. Jesus' blood keeps cleansing us from all sin. "Therefore he is able to save completely those who come to God through him, because he always lives to intercede for them" (Hebrews 7:25). We never get beyond that blood. Even as of old they carried the blood of the sacrifice into the Most Holy Place and touched every article in the Tabernacle with it, so, still, the blood of Jesus Christ goes with us all the way, and in our deepest and highest experiences it is more and more precious to our souls. We never get beyond the cross.

It is not necessary that we should sin willfully, but the holiest saint has 10,000 shortcomings of which he is ever conscious, and needs and loves to bathe afresh in the precious blood, and wash his feet in the basin which the blessed Master still holds for the feet of all His travel-stained disciples. Never need we remain a moment under the power or dominion of sin. Ever may we freely come to the precious fountain and sing the glad refrain,

> They're all taken away, away,
> My sins are all taken away.

Later in the psalm, a very beautiful figure is added to express the completeness of our salvation. "As far as the east is from the west,/ so far has he removed our transgressions from us" (Psalm 103:12). This is a more beautiful figure than even David understood.

We know in the light of modern science that the east is infinitely distant from the west. We may go north a while, but we shall soon come to the end of north; or if we begin to go south, we soon reach the end of the southern limit and begin to go north. But go eastward, and there is no transition line that you can cross and begin to move westward. It is east forever, and though you encircle the world a thousand times, you still are going east. And so it is with your journey westward, so that there is no place where east and west can meet. "So far has he removed our transgressions from us" (103:12). They are traveling eternally apart from us, and the longer we live, the farther apart will they go. So perfect, so eternal is His forgiveness.

SECTION IV—*Physical Blessing and Healing*

The next ground of his thanksgiving is God's physical blessing and healing of our diseases through His mercy and love. "Praise the LORD, O my soul/ . . . who . . ./ heals all your diseases" (103:2–3). This is expressed in the very same terms as salvation. It is as absolute. It is as present. It is as universal and complete. It is as divine. He heals. They who try to contradict it are foolishly taking the bread of life from their own lips, and making of none effect the grace and mercy of God which they might enjoy.

In the next clause the source of this healing is represented. It is through Christ's redemption. "Who redeems your life from the pit" (103:4). It is through the blood of Calvary and the redeeming purchase of Christ's atoning blood that this also comes to us. On the cross He bore our physical liabilities, and those who trust in Him are thus set free from the physical penalties of disease on account of sin.

There is still a higher phase of this precious truth brought out in this passage: "Your youth is renewed like the eagle's" (103:5). This is the quickening life of Christ in our mortal flesh, giving vitality and spring to the body, taking away the effects of age and infirmity, keeping us in youthful vigor when nature has become exhausted and imparting to our frame the life and energy of our risen Lord as the source of our health and strength.

This is more than being healed of disease and redeemed from death. It is being quickened in the higher life and filled with the vigor and energy of our Lord. Oh, how we should bless the Lord for it! Those of us who have experienced it can never tell how much it means. Oh, the weariness and pains it has taken away, the dreadful nights and wearing days that it has changed to times of sweet repose and hours of joyful service! Oh, the spring and gladness that it has put into our existence! Oh, the power it has given us for service! Oh, how much it has added to the years of time, multiplying each hour and making it manifoldly more by the enriching of His strength and love! How precious it has made Him! How real He has become, so that every nerve cord understands Him, every organ enjoys Him and every fiber of our flesh seems to sing: "Praise the LORD, O my soul/ . . . who . . ./ heals all your diseases;/ who redeems your life from the pit/ and crowns you with love and compassion,/ . . ./ so that your youth is renewed like the eagle's" (103:2–5).

SECTION V—*Deeper Spiritual Blessings*

The next ground of gratitude to God is our deeper spiritual blessings and joys. "Who . . ./ crowns you with love and compassion,/ who satisfies your desires (thy mouth, KJV) with good things/ so that your youth is renewed like the eagle's" (103:4–5). This latter clause is unhappily translated. It is not "thy mouth," but "thy being." It means the inmost being. It is not "good things" but, literally, "the good." "Who satisfies your being with the good." It is not possible to satisfy our deeper being with earthly things, with anything.

It was a fool who said in his heart to his soul, "You have plenty of good things laid up for many years. Take life easy; eat, drink, and be merry" (Luke 12:19). He tried to feed his soul on corn and wine and barns, farms and grain. But he was a fool. God told him so. The only thing that can meet the hunger of the heart is God Himself. It is He who is the good and who meets the need of the inmost being, satisfies it to the core. They that touch Him are conscious that they touch the center of our life; that He fills the inmost core of their being.

There is something in Christ that does meet our spirit's utmost need. Put that flower away in the cellar, and it will get white and withered; bring it into the sun, and its whole organism will open up and absorb the light and life of that which is its god. So our being is made for Him, and He alone can fill it. There is not an instinct in your spirit, there is not a feeling in your heart, there is not a capacity in your mind, there is nothing in the little child, the maiden, the youth, the man, the woman, the sage, the poet, the artist, the loftiest or the lowliest intellect, but Christ can utterly satisfy. There is not a moment of our existence but may be spent in perfect rest and utter delight in His communion and blessing, and every fiber of our nature throb with the song of gladness: "Praise the LORD, O my soul . . ./ who satisfies your desires with good things" (Psalm 103:1, 5) and who "crowns you with love and compassion" (103:4).

SECTION VI—*Covenant Relations to Israel*

Next the Psalmist praises God for His covenant relations to Israel and His people. Amid all their changes, frailties, and failures, He has been their faithful God, and, like a father, has carried them, remembering their frailty, forgiving their sin, and keeping covenant with them that serve Him.

SECTION VII—*His Coming*

He finally praises God because of His kingdom and His coming. "The LORD has established his throne in heaven,/ and his kingdom rules over all" (103:19). Oh, how much cause we have to praise God for this! How glad I am that I am not king, but that Jesus is on the throne, and that He is coming soon to reign over this revolted, disordered world. Things may look very strange and confused at times; someone else may seem to hold the reins, but bless the Lord, "The LORD is enthroned as King forever" (29:10). "The LORD reigns, let the earth be glad" (97:1).

And soon He will come again. Not forever shall wrong be triumphant and right be trampled upon. Not forever shall we weep and wait. He is coming soon with His kingdom and righteousness and peace, and with our robes and crowns. Let us rejoice because "The LORD has established his throne in heaven,/ and his kingdom rules over all" (103:19) and "We know that in all things God works for the good of those who love him, who have been called according to his purpose" (Romans 8:28).

Then the psalm closes with the majestic peroration in which he calls upon the heavenly hosts, the universe, creation and all the works of God to praise and magnify His glorious name.

What does this mean? Why, beloved, that you and I, His ransomed ones, are to lead the chorus of earth and heaven, and to sing a louder, sweeter song than angels in glory can ever know or warbling bird or sweet songster of earth can ever sing. Could you and I enter heaven today, we would be astonished at its music. But, oh beloved, there is something higher and nobler for you and me than even the songs of angels. God calls upon us here, not to listen to them, but to lead them, to rise above them and to awake their harps to melodies they never knew before. The day is coming when, higher and nearer the throne than they, we shall give the keynote to the choruses of heaven, and they shall be glad to follow in the loud refrain.

Think! We can have a song they never can sing, of that redemption they have not needed and they have never shared.

And then it means still further, that as we go out among the works of God, which are full of praise and gladness, we shall be gladder than they. As we look in the sunshine, we are to shine with a radiance that the sun can never know. As we gaze upon the beauty and bloom of nature, we are to glorify God with a loveliness and with a radiance that earth can never wear. As we hear the hum of 10,000 insects, and the songs that warble from the branches of the summer woods, from the bursting throats of the little birds and the thrilling melodies of nature, we are to praise Him whom they can never know as we know Him. He is our Father and our Friend.

Oh, is it ever so? Is it not often sadly, shamefully different? Have you gone out in this bright, glad world many a time with a shadowed face and a mournful spirit, with a dirge in every tone and a groan in every breath? Why, the little birds upon the trees and the insects at your feet were reproving you to your face, and seeming to say, Praise the Lord. God forbid that they should have to wake our songs! Rather does this glorious psalm mean that we are to lead them in a chorus of praise; and, taking our place in the center of this universe, to strike the keynote of every strain, until, through heaven and earth, His redemption song shall ring, and roll away to the boundaries of immensity, a "Hallelujah Chorus" to Him that sits upon the throne and to the Lamb.

This is the glorious picture that inspiration has given us in the Apocalypse of John. In the closing verses of the fifth chapter of Revelation, we find the redeemed in the very center of the throne. Around them, farther and farther out, are the circles of creation. First, the angels, and then the whole creation of God, to the utmost confines of the universe; and, as they strike the song that angels cannot sing: "Because you were slain,/ and with your blood you purchased men for God/ . . . you have made them to be a kingdom and priests" (Revelation 5:9–10), angels take up the chorus, the only chorus they can sing, and repeat the fourfold doxology: "To him who sits on the throne and to the Lamb/ be praise and honor and glory and power, for ever and ever!" (5:13).

And then, further, our song is caught up by the whole creation, out and out, and on and on, from world to world and then away:

Where worlds beyond the farthest star
   That ever met the human eye
Catch the loud anthem from afar,
   That rolls along immensity.

Until at last the outermost boundary of creation is reached, and then the tide rolls back to the throne. The waves of melody, like the reflux billows of the ocean, return. And as they reach the center once again, lo! the elders fall upon their faces before the throne, and the song is lost in silence. Then the deepest, highest of all praise, and all worship, and all speech, and all thought, and all feeling, completes the great doxology—the silence that falls upon its face, and in the wordless praise of the spirit's deepest joy, worships God.

Beloved, this is to be our eternal employ, to lead the songs of heaven. Oh, let us learn it now.

CHAPTER 13

THE PRIEST-KING

Psalm 110

This has been called by Luther the most beautiful of the Psalms. It is the picture of Christ upon His mediatorial throne. We have seen Him as the suffering Savior in the 22nd Psalm, as the Shepherd in the 23rd, as the risen and ascended Lord in the 24th and 68th Psalms. Now we see Him seated upon His throne in the 110th Psalm, reigning over His mediatorial kingdom and exercising His holy priesthood as our Advocate with God.

SECTION I—*The Priest-King*

1. He is a divine King. "The LORD says to my Lord" (Psalm 110:1). He Himself is called Lord, not only by David, but by the eternal Father. We see two divine personalities here: "the LORD" and "my Lord." This is not uncommon in the Old Testament, and a very dull eye can find in many places the evidence of the divine Trinity, even in the Hebrew Scriptures. How glad we are to know that our King is the Lord of heaven and earth, and nothing can be too hard for Him (Jeremiah 32:17)!

2. Back of Him there is another person as mighty and divine—the Father. There is a power behind the throne, even all the Godhead.

We read in Daniel of these two personalities: "The Ancient of Days" (Daniel 7:13) who came in the clouds of heaven, and "The son of man" (7:13) who came with Him, and to whom He gave the kingdom and a dominion which should never pass away. He can say, "All that belongs to the Father is mine" (John 16:15); "All authority in heaven and on earth has been given to me" (Matthew 28:18); and above all the rage of the heathen and the wrath of His enemies, "the One enthroned in heaven" (Psalm 2:4) said, "I have installed my King/ on Zion, my holy hill" (2:6). "Kiss the Son, lest he be angry/ and you be destroyed in your way" (2:12).

251

3. He is ruling over a rebellious empire. He is not acknowledged. He is not as yet a millennial King as we see Him in other psalms, seated upon a peaceful throne, but He is in the midst of a conflict and waging the holy war of gospel dispensation against sin and Satan. But amid all opposition and conflict, He is calmly seated upon His throne, not dismayed or distracted by the violence of His foes, but "he waits for his enemies to be made his footstool" (Hebrews 10:13). He is confident of victory. He sees ever before Him the issue; and while amid the smoke of the battle we may be oft perplexed and discouraged, yet He is smiling calmly at our fears and waiting for the consummation of all His plans and all our hopes.

4. He is the King of Righteousness. The name of His glorious type, Melchizedek, suggests this. The two roots of the word signify "king" and "righteousness." This does not mean merely that He is the righteous King, but it means especially that He is a King who dispenses righteousness to His followers and subjects. Other kings require righteousness from them, but His business is to give them righteousness, to make them holy and just and good. He takes them as a race of sinners, justifies them freely through His grace, and then imparts to them His own spirit and nature and makes them partakers of His righteousness. It is His royal gift to us. Let us take it freely. He came "to rescue us from the hand of our enemies,/ and to enable us to serve him without fear/ in holiness and righteousness before him all our days" (Luke 1:74–75).

5. He is the King of Peace. For Melchizedek was the King of Salem, which means peace. This is His next royal gift—peace. It is His great legacy. "Peace I leave with you; my peace I give you" (John 14:27).

It is His royal blessing to all His subjects. He is the Prince of Peace. They that follow Him find rest unto their souls and know the peace of God that passes all understanding. Has He given us His righteousness and His peace? Do we dwell with Him in the land of rest where "the fruit of righteousness will be peace;/ the effect of righteousness will be quietness and confidence forever" (Isaiah 32:17)?

6. He is our Great High Priest. Not only does He rule over us, and for us, but stands between us and all our sins and their present and eternal consequences. He settles for us every question that can rise between us and God. He represents us in heaven in all our interests. He keeps our relations with God ever right. He secures for us the grace we need from moment to moment and day to day. He presents our petitions to the Father, taking out of them their faults and imperfections, correcting and directing them, and adding to them His own intercessions, mingling with them the incense of His perfect offering, and claiming acceptance for them through the merits of His own all-prevailing name.

Like the priests of old, He bears our names upon His shoulders in the place of strength, carrying all our burdens and bearing all our sorrows. Like Aaron, He bears our names upon His breast as well as on His shoulders, carrying us in the place of sympathy and love. "Therefore, since we have a great high priest" (Hebrews 4:14) who is able "to sympathize with our weaknesses" (4:15), "able to deal gently with those who are ignorant and are going astray" (5:2), "let us then approach the throne of grace with confidence, so that we may receive mercy and find grace to help us in our time of need" (4:16). Such is the picture of our great Priest-King.

His ancient type of Melchizedek stands in the record of the past like the great sphinx of the desert, a strange enigma. The apostle speaks of him almost as if he had no origin and no descent, but this may simply mean that we have no record of these, and that he is the same as though he came out of the darkness and went into the dimness of obscurity. Some have supposed that he was a divine person, the Son of God anticipating His incarnation, but we see no reason for this or proof of it. He was, doubtless, simply a human type of the divine Son of God.

He was the only one in the Old Testament who held both the office of a priest and a king. The Judges in some measure anticipated this: Eli ministering at the altar and also judging Israel; and Samuel, for a time, exercising both functions. But none of them could be called a king. Jesus holds both offices. He, who rules us with His mighty scepter and holds our destinies in His hand, is the same One who died for our sins, who intercedes for us at the Father's side, and who ever lives to save us to the uttermost. Blessed King, faithful Priest, precious Savior—blessed be His glorious name forever!

SECTION II—*His Followers*

"Your troops will be willing [a free-will offering]/ on your day of battle./ Arrayed in holy majesty,/ from the womb of the dawn/ you will receive the dew of your youth" (Psalm 110:3). This is the beautiful picture of the subjects of the glorious King.

1. They are free-will offerings. They are a consecrated people; they are not bound to Him by fetters of iron or forces of compulsion, but by a free, glad surrender of their hearts and sacrifice of their lives. They love Him, they delight to do His will, they have been conquered by His love. Their watchword is "whose I am and whom I serve" (Acts 27:23). They are not their own, but are bought with a price. They have presented their bodies a living sacrifice, holy, acceptable unto God, their reasonable service. This is the condition of all full blessing in the kingdom of Christ. God gives all, and we give all.

Only as we freely give do we freely receive. A heart half-consecrated can never be fully saved, or perfectly victorious and happy; but he who yields himself fully to God finds God as fully yielded to him. This is the true condition of all effective service. God does not ask our work first, but ourselves first, and then our service follows. He does not use hired servants or borrowed vessels. He owns His servants and puts His coat-of-arms on all the vessels of His house, and will use nothing fully until it becomes His and His alone.

I know a wealthy friend who desired at one time to adopt a child. The mother was unwilling to part with it permanently, but very glad to have it taken to the rich man's home and educated and befriended. When it came to the point of surrendering it utterly, her heart naturally shrank and almost refused; but she was told that in no other way would he accept the child. The reason was that he wished to make it his heir and bestow upon it his great wealth. Then she saw the advantage of complete surrender, and in the highest love to the little one, she gave up her personal claims that it might receive a greater blessing than she in her poverty could ever give it. So God asks us to give ourselves utterly to Him, only because He wants to give us His all in return and make us the heirs of all His riches and joint-heirs with His own dear Son.

2. They are clothed in holy majesty (beauty of holiness, KJV). They are not only a consecrated people but a holy people. Here we see the true spiritual order of our higher experiences and blessings. Consecration must come first and then sanctification. We can consecrate ourselves as free-will offerings. Then God sanctifies us and clothes us with the beauties of His holiness. The consecration is ours; the sanctification is His. It is with Christ's robes that He covers us; with Christ's virtues that He adorns us. Our holiness is as much His gift as our pardon. " 'Fine linen, bright and clean,/ was given her to wear.' (Fine linen stands for the righteous acts of the saints.)" (Revelation 19:8). The bride receives her robe as the free gift of her Lord. She does not weave it and stitch it with her own weak hands, but she receives the seamless robe of her Lord in all its completeness, and puts on the Lord Jesus Himself as her sanctification and glory.

But here we read not only of holiness, but of the beauties of holiness. It is not merely a right character and life, but a lovely bearing, adorning the doctrine of God our Savior, and shedding luster upon our Christian profession and the name of our Lord.

We read not only of the garments that were clean, but of the garments that were bright and lustrous. Every housewife knows the difference between her clothes as she takes them from her clothesline and as she takes them from the laundry. They are clean when they leave the clothesline, but they are bright when they leave the laundry.

There is a stern and blameless righteousness which a man may live before the world and before the Lord, in which no fault can be found, and yet it may be as cold as the granite cliffs of some lone mountain peak. There is a sweet, soft, mellow and beautiful holiness which is as different from the other as the lovely mountainside all covered with moss and flowers and fountains is different from the mountain peak. The life of Jesus was not stern virtue but sweet love. It was full of the beauty of holiness. How gentle, how tender, how thoughtful, how courteous, how unselfish, how refined, how delicate in its sensitiveness, how lofty, majestic, devoted, how transparent and sincere, how sweet and affectionate; how it attracted the little child, how it drew the poor sinner, how it fascinated the loftiest minds, how it satisfied the warmest hearts! Who can ever paint the beauties of Christ's character, the little touches of loveliness that filled up His life, the thousand trifles that others neglect, and that constitute the fullness of His perfection?

Look at Him as a little Child. What a perfect Child, and yet how far beyond other children. Look at Him as He bows His head to receive the baptism of John that He may fulfill all righteousness. Look at Him as He takes the little child in His arms. Look at Him as He refuses to meet the gaze of the poor woman whom they brought to Him in her sin, lest He should hurt her sensitive feelings by looking into her eyes in the presence of those pitiless men. Look at Him as He anticipates Peter's perplexity about the taxes at Capernaum, and sends him to find the coin in the mouth of the fish, even before he has time to speak of it. Look at Him as, with the towel around His waist, He bows at the disciples' feet, the lowliest, yet the loftiest of them all.

Listen to Him as, with heart already anticipating the burden of the cross, he forgets His sorrow and tenderly says: "Do not let your hearts be troubled" (John 14:1). Listen as He speaks of His peace and joy even in that dark hour. See how perfectly human He is in His tears at Lazarus' tomb, and in His sorrow in Gethsemane, and yet how perfectly yielded to the will of God. Look at Him in the bright morning of the resurrection with His glad "Greetings" (Matthew 28:9) and His shining joy. Look at that exquisite scene in the garden as He calls Mary by name. Look at Him as He gently suggests her sin to the woman of Samaria without telling it; and again, by one look breaks Peter's heart without an upbraiding word, and then by that wonderful threefold question by the Sea of Tiberias restores him again and suggests many things which He did not utter, but which the disciple could perfectly understand.

See the affection that took Mary to His heart and John to His bosom, and on the cross of Calvary remembered the mother who bore Him and consigned her to the care of the one whom He loved best. Oh, incomparable Christ! How the faintest touches of the picture put our coarseness and incompleteness to shame, and make us long to hide beneath the folds of His vesture, and be covered with His perfect righteousness! And so He would have us, like Himself, clothed with all the beauties of a holy life and character.

How minute are the little directions of the Holy Spirit about our spirit and conduct! How many little things are described in the Christian's investiture! Not only the things that are honest and just and pure, but the things that are lovely and of good report. Here are some of them: courtesy, considerateness of others, sensitiveness to the feelings of one another, thinking no evil, rejoicing with them that rejoice, weeping with them that weep, condescending to men of low estate, in honor preferring one another, believing all things, hoping all things of the worst of men, rejoicing evermore, submitting one to another, and many more which the Holy Spirit has interwoven with almost every fiber of the Holy Scriptures, in little threads which make up the warp of holy living.

A great sculptor was once asked by his friend how he could linger so long over the marble statue which months before seemed complete to him, as he looked upon it. "Why," said the sculptor, "I have touched every part of this figure in these months and changed the whole expression by a thousand little touches. Here an eye has received a deeper fullness, a lip a more sensitive expression, a nostril is more dilated, an eyebrow is more expressive. These may be trifles, but trifles make perfection, and perfection is no trifle."

Oh, that the old story might be translated into the holier art of Christian living, and that we might go forth robed in the beauties of holiness, not only wearing the linen of the saint but the wedding garment of the bride.

3. They are bright with the light of the morning, born "from the womb of the dawn" (Psalm 110:3). The truly consecrated and sanctified Christian is bright, joyous, radiant and hopeful. Our light should shine before men. Our countenance should be radiant with the glory of God, and our whole bearing tell that we are the children of the light. The morning is the type of gladness, brightness, hopefulness. How different we feel after a night of rest and with the opening dawn! We lay down weary, jaded, perhaps exhausted, but we awake with such new strength and hopefulness that the tasks which yesterday depressed us today seem lighter than a feather, and we go out into life with zest and spring.

The Christian's life may be an everlasting morning. We may ever have the privilege of beginning afresh and, "forgetting what is behind" (Philippians 3:13) stepping out each moment into a new and eternal future of sunshine and blessing. Let our lives be more joyous, our spirits more like the morning. "Arise, shine, for your light has come,/ and the glory of the LORD rises upon you" (Isaiah 60:1). "Your sun will never set again,/ and your moon will wane no more;/ the LORD will be your everlasting light,/ and your days of sorrow will end" (60:20).

4. They are fresh with the dew of His youth. The consecrated Christian

knows what this means. It is a spirit of perpetual youth. It is a continual zest. It is a delightful freshness that keeps us watered and spontaneous in our spirit every moment. How soon the world ages, but the heart that is filled with Jesus is ever young. Holiness is the best preservative of youthfulness, freshness, sweetness and joy.

It is possible to go through everything we touch with this spirit of springing freshness. It is not only for the hour of prayer and praise and the mountain tops of holy ecstasy; we can carry it through the drudgery of life, through the humdrum, monotonous steps of toil, through the commonplace occupations of long days and hours, in the kitchen, the nursery, the crowded street, the noisy factory, at the office desk. We can keep the sweet fragrance of this heavenly blossom, not only amid the smoke and grime of earthly toil, but even amid the fumes of the pit itself. When the dragon breathes upon us with his fiery breath, and 10,000 shafts of temptation whirl around us, this sweet atmosphere will purify the air and fortify us against even the touch of the foe, and the very smell of the pit will be dispelled by the heavenly fragrance that we carry in our breast.

Not only will this exhilarate our hearts and freshen our spirits, but even our bodies will be kept in health and buoyancy and our physical strength renewed at the fountain of His immortal youth.

We must not forget the source of this. It is not in ourselves but in Him. It is not our youth, but His youth that refreshes and bedews us. It is only as we have the heart of Christ within us that we have the fountain of perpetual freshness. Christ is ever young. How beautiful the thought that Jesus ever remains the young man of 33! He never grew old, and He never will. That glorious face that beamed upon Mary and Peter and John on the morning of the resurrection with His glad "Greetings" (Matthew 28:9) remains forever the same, and He is willing to touch us with His freshness, and fill us with His immortal youth.

One of Wellington's generals, it is said, came back to him for a moment just before setting out on a very difficult commission to which his commander had appointed him. Reaching out his hand, he said: "General, let me grasp your hand before I go." He took the hand of the chief. His face brightened; and as he dashed away, he said: "Now I feel able for my work, since I have touched that conquering hand." So each moment we can touch that conquering Hand that never lost a battle, that never relinquished a trust, that never grows weak or weary; and, strong in the strength of Christ, we can do all things hand in hand with Him.

Fresh with the dew of His youth. The figure of the dew is very suggestive. It comes at night. So out of our nights of darkness, sorrow and waiting, come our mornings of refreshing and our days of victory. Again, it comes on quiet nights, never on stormy nights. And so, as we get before the Lord and hush our frettings and tumults, our thoughts and cares, and fears and plans, He fills us with His fullness and waters us with His refreshings. Again, the dew is always in the air; and we may always absorb it if we have the right temperature and spiritual condition to create it. The dew does not fall from heaven, but it gathers from the air around us. The old familiar illustration will stand repeating. The ice pitcher, on the warmest and sultriest day, in a moment is covered with crystal dew-drops. And so our Lord is ever around us in the very air we breathe. His freshness is ever within our reach if we will adjust ourselves to that presence. If we will grow cool and quiet, and open our being to receive His life, He is ever ready to bedew us with His blessing, to fill us with His joy and peace and love, to send us forth the children of the morning, fresh with the dew of His youth.

The palm tree is the most glorious of all trees, with its waving branches and the precious clusters of fruit hanging from its laden boughs. But where does the palm tree grow? In the burning desert where the ground beneath is like consuming fire, and the air above as a heated oven. Whence does it draw its life? Just because of its situation, the palm tree is provided with immense leaves, through all of whose pores the vapor of the air is absorbed, while its sensitive roots reach down to the hidden fountains and absorb from beneath the sand every particle of moisture that it can find. And so from the depths and heights it draws the life that sustains its glorious verdure and rich fruitfulness and makes it the queen of the vegetable creation. It is like unto him of whom the Oriental prophet has said with such truth and beauty: "He will be like a tree planted by the water/ that sends out its roots by the stream./ It does not fear when heat comes;/ its leaves are always green./ It has no worries in a year of drought/ and never fails to bear fruit" (Jeremiah 17:8).

Such is the blessed heritage of the children of the heavenly King. Such is the glorious recompense of entire consecration. Such is the reversion that comes to those who are willing to be a free-will offering in His day of battle. Oh, let that day begin with some of us! Oh, let us make the full surrender now, and begin to follow Him to the glorious procession of the children of the morning, who, robed in the beauties of holiness and the bridal garments of the advent glory, already throbbing with the pulse-beats of immortal youth, are waiting for that glad day that shall bring us in fullness to that of which we are now permitted to enjoy the blessed foretaste and anticipation.

CHAPTER 14

THE HALLEL

Psalm 118

This was Luther's favorite psalm. He says respecting it: "This is my psalm which I love. Although the whole of the Psalms and the Scripture, which is my only consolation in life, are also dear to me, I have chosen this psalm particularly to be called and to be mine; for it has often deserved my love, and helped me out of many deep distresses, when neither emperors, nor kings, nor the wise and prudent, nor the saints could have helped me." Indeed, no better panorama of the great Reformer's conflicts and victories can be found than these graphic verses. They "surrounded me on every side,/ but in the name of the LORD I cut them off./ They swarmed around me like bees . . ./ in the name of the LORD I cut them off" (Psalm 118:11–12). "It is better to take refuge in the LORD/ than to trust in man./ It is better to take refuge in the LORD/ than to trust in princes" (118:8–9).

But the psalm has higher claims than those that associate it with the great Reformer.

It was the last psalm of the Hebrew Hallel, the closing refrain of that great sacred oratorio which the Hebrews chanted at their great festivals, and it is most probable that it was the very hymn which Jesus sang as He went from the upper chamber to the Mount of Olives. It contains a summary of the whole work of redemption and the conflict and victory of Christ. Its Messianic character is established by the frequent references to it in the New Testament by Christ Himself and His apostles, and it is indeed a picture of His own inner life in the sufferings and conflicts of Calvary. Let us briefly glance at some of these expressions.

A PRELUDE OF PRAISE

The whole house of Israel is summoned to praise the Lord; then the house of Aaron; then the whole company of them that fear the Lord. They are

259

called to praise Him because He is good and because He is merciful and His mercy endures forever. His goodness is the outflow of His love, and His mercy is the special direction of that love to the unworthy and sinful. But for His mercy His goodness never could reach us, an unworthy and fallen race. But His mercy endures forever, and even sinful men may rejoice in its fullness and claim its richest blessings.

A CONFESSION OF FAITH

It is the utterance of a trust that looks from man to God, from the highest princes and the mightiest human names to the Almighty Himself. God usually calls His people to the spirit of praise and of faith first, and then He lets the pressure of conflict fall upon us to prove the sincerity of our confession and the reality of our trust. And so, after these bold claims of faith and notes of praise, we have the picture of a conflict.

THE PICTURE OF CONFLICT

It is a desperate conflict. It is the conflict of a soul with innumerable spiritual forces and malignant foes that seem like clouds of bees filling the air, and fiery thorns scorching him with their consuming breath. It is the conflict of Christ in the dark hour of His sorrow and suffering. It is the conflict of the great suffering hearts of brave, true men in all ages, during which the soldiers of faith have followed the great Captain of their salvation, and, like Him, been made perfect through suffering.

THE SHOUT OF VICTORY

It is also the shout of victory. "Shouts of joy and victory/ resound in the tents of the righteous" (118:15). "I will not die but live,/ and will proclaim what the LORD has done" (118:17). It is the triumph of Jesus over death and the grave. It is the victorious shout of His Church militant as she follows in His triumph.

THE OPEN GATES

Next, we have the open gates of righteousness and salvation. "Open for me the gates of righteousness;/ I will enter and give thanks to the LORD./ This is the gate of the LORD/ through which the righteous may enter" (118:19–20). This is a picture of an opened salvation through the Savior's cross. This is the shout of accomplished redemption and full salvation. This is the cry of Stephen amid the pains of martyrdom: "Look . . . I see heaven open and the Son of Man standing at the right hand of God" (Acts 7:56). This is the far-off echo of the sacred litany: "When Thou by the sharpness of death hadst born our sins, Thou didst open the kingdom of heaven to all believers."

THE RESURRECTION DAY

It speaks of the glorious resurrection day and the day of grace. "This is the day the LORD has made;/ let us rejoice and be glad in it" (Psalm 118:24). This may well describe any day of glorious victory, but it especially refers to the resurrection day; to the day when Jesus burst the fetters of the tomb, and made for us the Lord's Day forever the day of days, because it commemorates the greatest of all the facts of Christianity, the resurrection of the Lord. This is the cornerstone of our precious hopes. This is the foundation of the Church. This is the greatest principle of Christianity. The Lord is risen, and we are risen with Him.

THE PENITENT'S PRAYER

"O LORD, save us;/ O LORD, grant us success" (118:25). Literally this means Hosannah! This was the cry which became so familiar in the streets of Jerusalem, that the very children took it up and rang it out on the air as their little prayer to Jesus, in defiance of the hate of scribes and Pharisees.

In its place in the psalm it describes the salvation of the gospel as it follows in its natural order the death and resurrection of the Lord Jesus. Oh, how often has this cry gone up during the Christian ages, and how often has it been answered by the love and mercy of God until "Hosannah" has been changed to "Hallelujah"!

THE FOUNDING OF THE CHURCH

"The stone the builders rejected/ has become the capstone" (118:22). This is a proverbial expression, but Christ Himself has applied it to His own rejection by man and His election by God as the Cornerstone of the Church.

It is just as true of Christ's people. "God chose the foolish things of the world . . . and things that are not" (1 Corinthians 1:27–28). The most beautiful window in Europe was made by a little apprentice boy with the thrown-away fragments of his master's workshop. One day that master saw the wonderful mosaic of light and color which the little hands had wrought together; and when he learned who had made it, he took him in his arms and said, "You have surpassed your master and made for yourself an imperishable monument of genius out of worthless fragments." So God is taking the world's rejected ones; and, by and by, the universe will gaze upon the New Jerusalem with rapturous wonder as it shall shine above the glory of the sapphire and the ruby, the tints of the rainbow and the light of a thousand suns.

THE COMING OF THE LORD

The climax of all will be the coming of the Lord. "Blessed is he who comes in the name of the LORD" (Psalm 118:26). Our Savior has given us the true application of this verse in His own solemn parting words to Jerusalem, after His sorrowful appeal to them for whom He so often had longed and labored. He said as He left the temple: "Look, your house is left to you desolate. For I tell you, you will not see me again until you say, 'Blessed is he who comes in the name of the Lord' " (Matthew 23:38–39).

We know when that day shall be, the day of His personal coming, and the return of His ancient people to their true Messiah. And so the verse is the promise of His advent. This is our blessed hope. This is the pole star of redemption. This is the future of Christian hope and aspiration. And this is the imminent, overshadowing reality for which hushed hearts are waiting today in all the Church of God.

THE ABIDING PLACE AND CONSECRATED SERVICE

The psalm does not close without a picture of the deeper inner life of the saint. "From the house of the LORD we bless you./ The LORD is God,/ and he has made his light shine upon us./ With boughs in hand, join in the festal procession/ up to the horns of the altar" (Psalm 118:26–27). Surely, this is the picture of consecration and union with God. This is the life into which redemption leads us. The language here is borrowed from the tabernacle. The house of the Lord is the inner abiding place. The light which God has shone us is the Shekinah glory that shines above the mercy seat. The sacrifice is that living consecration which we make as we enter in, and which, as we enter more closely in, we make more perfectly. Have we come into this sacred place? Do we know this abiding life? Are we dwelling under the shining of the Shekinah? Are we bound to the horns of the altar by the cords of love and self-surrender? Can we sing

> I have come with my guilt to the altar of God;
>   In the laver of cleansing I'm washed from my sin,
> And now, to the innermost presence of God,
>   To the holy of holies I am entering in.
>
> In my blood-sprinkled robes I can stand without dread
>   Where the lamps of the Lord o'er the cherubim shine.
> I am feasting my soul on the heavenly bread;
>   I am breathing the odors of incense divine.
>
> I have passed through the veil to that sacred abode
>   Where His glory the Savior reveals to His own,
> And now, in the innermost presence of God,
>   I am dwelling forever with Jesus alone.

Oh, it is not until we enter in that we know the fullness and blessedness of salvation. Looking at yonder tabernacle from the outside, it appeared a very common thing—an old tent covered with badger skins. But looking at it from within, it was resplendent with the dazzling glory of light and gold and gems of rarest beauty.

You cannot know Christ until you come into the bosom of His love. You cannot truly serve Him or bless others until you reach the center and can say, "From the house of the LORD we bless you" (118:26). Then no sacrifice seems hard. Then you can say, "With boughs in hand, join in the festal procession/ up to the horns of the altar" (118:27). Then the life becomes a chorus of joy and praise, a glad, eternal Hallel, echoing evermore: "You are my God, and I will give you thanks;/ you are my God, and I will exalt you./ Give thanks to the LORD, for he is good;/ his love endures forever" (118:28–29).

CHAPTER 15

THE PEARL PSALM

Psalm 133

We have called this the Pearl Psalm because it is the picture of the Church of Christ in unity, and this picture Christ has given to us in the New Testament in one of His most beautiful parables, under the image of the Pearl of Great Price (Matthew 13:45–46).

At first sight this may not seem to be a Messianic psalm, for it tells of the Church rather than Christ. But what is the Church but the Body of Christ? He is only a Head without her; she constitutes His completeness; nor can we ever think of her unity apart from her living Head.

SECTION I—*The Excellency of Christian Unity*

"How good . . . it is/ when brothers live together in unity!" (Psalm 133:1). It is good. It is God's great plan, not only for His Church, but for the universe. It is the end for which He has been working from the beginning. Far back in the past eternity He dwelt alone, the inaccessible and infinite Jehovah. Then from His hand there came this wondrous universe, these worlds of space that roll afar and cover yonder vast immensity.

But there was a void impassable between the Creator and the creature. The highest angel could not look across that mighty abyss. The distance was infinite.

But there was One who from the beginning was designed to be the Reconciler. It was the Son of God, and into this created universe He descended to gather together into one all things in Himself.

The Creator became the creature; the Invisible became incarnate. He took upon Himself the form of man, and then He came still nearer to dwell in the very hearts of men Himself. And now there is one Being who is the link that binds this mighty universe to its Creator, and upon yonder throne shall forever sit a Man who in His own person combines the infinite and transcendent glory of God with the form and face and spirit of one of Adam's race. He and His glorious Church are the uniting links of the whole universe, and in Him all things are already being made one.

He has designed His glorious Church, therefore, to be the special expression of all the diversity in this universe combined in perfect unity. She is the microcosm of the universe and the reflection of God Himself. It is, therefore, His purpose for her that she might be made perfect in oneness, both with Him her glorious Head, and in all her parts and members.

This was His last command respecting her as he went away, that her members should love one another as He had loved them. This was the burden of His parting prayer as He stood at the entrance of the Garden of Gethsemane on the night of His agony, and prayed: "That all of them may be one, Father, just as you are in me and I am in you. May they also be in us so that the world may believe that you have sent me" (John 17:21).

SECTION II—*The Pleasantness of Christian Unity*

It is not only "good," but it is "pleasant." Nothing is more sweet than the joy of love; nothing is more bitter than the sting of hate; nothing is more keen than the anguish of separation. God's own nature is love, and therefore it is blessedness. If we would know His joy, we must rise to His love and live out of ourselves and for others. How happy the heart where love reigns supreme! How delightful the church where all the members love one another! How blessed the people that dwell in peace! How miserable the hearts that are ever indulging their bitterness, strife, jealousy, envy and malignity! You may hurt others by the stings of passion, but you hurt yourselves much more. "How . . . pleasant it is/ when brothers live together in unity!" (Psalm 133:1).

SECTION III—*The Blessing That Follows*

The blessing that follows Christian unity is described in the words, "For there the LORD bestows his blessing,/ even life forevermore" (133:3).

God's special blessing attends His people when they dwell in love and walk in unity. He has promised to be with them as they walk in love.

1. He promises a blessing upon the soul that walks in love. You will be blessed yourself if you walk in unity.

2. It will promote the blessing of others. It will create an atmosphere that will create spiritual growth. It is when the members are fitly framed together that they grow into an holy temple in the Lord. It is like the warm sunshine of May which brings out the fruits and flowers of the earth. The church

which is bathed in the atmosphere of love will always be fragrant with the blossoms of Christian loveliness and usefulness.

3. It brings answers to our prayers. The prayer of unity has a peculiar promise. "If two of you on earth agree about anything you ask for, it will be done for you by my Father in heaven" (Matthew 18:19).

4. It will impress the unbelieving world. It is given by an infidel historian as the chief ground for the rapid progress of Christianity in the early centuries, that the Christians loved one another so tenderly and faithfully.

5. It will bring down the special gifts of the Holy Spirit. The heavenly Dove will only dwell in an atmosphere of love and peace. If the Church would only return to her primitive unity, she would soon be restored to her ancient power, and all the gifts of the Holy Spirit would crown the grace of love and bring the world to the feet of Jesus.

6. It will bring the blessing of salvation to sinners. The world is drawn to such an atmosphere, and lost men find it an attractive and congenial home. We must love them to Christ by the love we bear to one another and which overflows to them. Show me a church full of love, and I will show you a church which enjoys a perpetual revival.

SECTION IV—*The Source of Christian Unity*

"It is like precious oil poured on the head,/ running down on the beard,/ running down on Aaron's beard,/ down upon the collar of his robes./ It is as if the dew of Hermon/ were falling on Mount Zion" (Psalm 133:2–3).

These two beautiful figures represent very distinctly: 1. The person of Jesus Christ, our Great High Priest, under the image of Aaron; and, 2. The Holy Spirit under the double image of the ointment and the dew. The oil falls on Aaron's head and descends to the collar of his robes. And so, the spirit of unity and love comes to us from Jesus Christ. He is the Head and the High Priest, and we, lying at His feet, receive the anointing and the Spirit that fell on Him. It is only as we are united to Christ and drink in His very own spirit that we can be filled with love. Our love is a poor, worthless thing. We must have His, and He is willing to give us the same anointing that fell on Him, and which reaches and rests on us.

We may have the very love that He had and the very Holy Spirit that baptized and filled Him. It is our relation to Christ that fixes our relation to each other. It is when we are in Him that we can be one with others. It is a vain attempt to try to get into unity with men by touching them directly, and trying to arrange our creeds, plans, and human mechanisms. The true spirit is to be right with Him and near to Him, and then we shall touch all that are in Him as they touch Him.

But the figure also tells us of the Holy Spirit Himself. The sacred anointing that fell on Aaron's head reached to the fringes of his robe. He is the Spirit of unity and love. The same Spirit that dwelt in Christ makes us all one in Him. Oh, if we were all baptized with the Holy Spirit, we should all be one. It is easy to get on with men and women who are filled with the Spirit. People half-filled with the Holy Spirit are very difficult to get on with. They have just enough to make them spiritually conceited, willful, sensitive and critical; but the heart filled with the Holy Spirit is always simple, adjustable, free from self-will and angularities of every kind. You cannot hurt such a man because he is not there to hurt. The cloud has come in, and Moses has moved out. We may have this blessed Holy Spirit in all His fullness, as fully as He fell on the head of Jesus. All that is necessary is that we get down to the skirts of His garment; keep low enough, empty enough, open enough, and we shall be filled.

The figure of the dew is still more beautiful. The same dew that fell on lofty Hermon descended also on the little mountains of Zion. It tells us that the lowliest child of God can have the same grace that was given to the loftiest; that the humblest Christian may have the same spirit that made John the beloved and enabled Mary to pour the fragrant anointing on the Master's head. This love is not our virtue, or the result of our struggles and endeavors, but it is the grace of Jesus and the very Spirit of our Lord Himself shed abroad in us and enabling us to live in this world even as He.

SECTION V—*Some Considerations to Enable Us to Walk in Unity*

1. Let us determine and endeavor to walk in unity. Every victory must be won and every grace attained and established through a fixed purpose and a definite committal of ourselves to this. You can have from Christ whatever you will determine to have. The very strongest terms are used in the New Testament to express the importance of this purpose. We are to "follow the way of love" (1 Corinthians 14:1). We are to endeavor "to keep the unity of the Spirit through the bond of peace" (Ephesians 4:3). As much as lies in us we are to "live at peace with everyone" (Romans 12:18). These terms express the most intense determination and the most eager pursuit of an object. The same eagerness with which the hunter pursues his prey, and the worldling his fortune, we are to show in the pursuit of love.

Some earnest Christians have found it most helpful to pledge that they will stand in the spirit of love, and let nothing offend them or break their unity. It would be a good thing if all who read these lines would, on their knees before God and in His strength, solemnly determine and pledge their word that they will never again willingly allow themselves to sin against love, or to break their unity of spirit toward any of God's children.

2. It will help us to remember that we are always responsible for any breach of unity. Do not think of your brother's fault, or say what he has done, but think of your place, and remember that if you keep right, it is impossible for others to strive with you. There are some men with whom you cannot quarrel. They are so gentle and loving they will not take offense. The next time someone tries you or wrongs you, do not begin to think of what he has done, but rather what you are going to do. Keep your eyes off of their fault, and think only of your duty and responsibility to keep in sweetness and victory.

3. Remember that God permits every test to come into your life, and that He is watching to see what you will do. He is glorified and pleased if you triumph with all longsuffering, gentleness and love; grieved and shamed if you lose your victory and give way to passion and temptation. Your heavenly Father is using all these situations in life which come to you to educate you for something higher; and the way in which you meet them is determining your own future position in His glorious kingdom. He wants a race of men and women who can walk in perfect love and triumph under all circumstances.

After all, the test of everything is love. The characters that will stand prominent in the ages to come are those who have overcome in this arena. Those who are offended with every trifling trouble now are not going to stand in the places of high honor and service in the ages of glory.

Oh beloved, remember the next time some little trial meets you that your heavenly Father is waiting to see what you will do, and whether you will be worthy of the crown and the place of glorious trust when Jesus comes to reign with His saints. The Scottish housekeepers in the old times used to leave a broomstick across the hall when a new girl came to apply for a place in the family. They wished to see if she would pick it up or stumble over it, and her fate was decided by the way she met it. Beloved, do not be so foolish as to fall over a broomstick and miss a kingdom.

4. Remember also that the devil is waiting to see you slip and fall. These spaces above us are not empty. Myriads of eyes are gazing down; myriads are thronging yonder galleries, and many of them laugh with a fiendish joy when you are provoked to some thought or act of unkindness or bitterness. And if you could see the faces of yonder heavenly beings, you might behold a blush of shame as they hang their heads; and the Master turns away that He may not see the dishonor of His child. Yes, we are made a gazing stock to angels and principalities. Let us not please our foes by yielding to their wiles, but let us keep our victory and triumph in our love.

5. Think of others, not in the light of their faults and failures, but in the light of God's promises for them, and as they will be some day when the grace of Christ has completed their sanctification, and they shine in all the glory of the ransomed. Anticipate their future as you do your own. Think of them with a love that "always trusts, always hopes" (1 Corinthians 13:7),

and that clothes them with the qualities which they shall some day possess even if they do not now. To God this is everything. Time is nothing in His eye, which sweeps eternity and sees you each moment as you will be when you shine like the sun in the kingdom of your Father. See your brother in the same light, and you will be able to walk in love.

6. Look at people as Christ looks at them; see them in the light of His love. They are dear to Him. He does not condemn them for every failure and reject them even for their most glaring faults; and if you have His heart toward them, you will be patient and gentle. Think how He looked on Peter; forgave the woman taken in her sin; spoke to Judas even in tenderness and love; and for His enemies prayed, "Father, forgive them, for they do not know what they are doing" (Luke 23:34).

Think how long He overlooked your faults before you were even saved; always loving you for what you should be. Treat your brother with the heart of Christ and look upon him with the eyes of Jesus.

7. Ask God to sanctify your natural affections. Most of them are full of selfishness and constant provocations of envy, jealously and strife. You have inordinate and passionate loves that are purely earthly even if not immoral; and if you walk in heavenly love, you must have them crucified and purified, and exchanged for holy affections which are raised above all bitterness and strife, and characterized by peace, unselfishness, gentleness, forbearance and all the fruits of the Spirit.

8. Above all else, if you would walk in unity, ask Christ to crucify you. The greatest enemy to love is self. Learn to "look not only to your own interests, but also to the interests of others" (Philippians 2:4), and consider every moment not how this is going to affect you, but how it is going to affect your brother, and you will be kept in love and sweetness.

9. Keep the joy and sweetness of the Lord. A happy heart, full of Christ's gladness, wants to make everybody else happy. It is when you are morose and gloomy that you feel like scowling at others and getting offended at everybody you meet. Ask God to give you His joy and to keep it full, and you will find it easy to love.

10. Take Christ's love. He will put His own heart in you; He will enable you to love even as He loves. He who commanded it will make the command possible and enable you to realize it.

The torch of Christian love must be lighted at the flame of Christ's own love. They tell us that on Easter morning, in the Church of the Holy Sepulchre at Jerusalem, it is very beautiful, in the deep gloom, to see, suddenly, one flash of light appear in the tomb of Jesus. Instantly the song rings through the aisles and galleries, "The Lord has risen" (Luke 24:34). And then that flash of light touches the torches in the hands of the priests, and, suddenly, all along the line of hundreds of white-robed men, the light shines in a great circle of glory, while the song echoes again and again, "The Lord has risen" (24:34).

That single light from the open grave of Jesus lights all the torches. So from His heart must come the flame that will kindle our hearts to love Him. And so the oil that fell on His blessed head shall flow down to us as we lie at His feet covered by the skirts of His garments.

> Spirit of Love, upon us shed
> The oil that fell on Aaron's head
>   And bathed his holy feet.
> Oh, let our hearts like censers glow!
> Oh, let our love like incense flow
>   In fragrant odors sweet!

ISAIAH

CHAPTER 1

ISAIAH'S CALL AND CONSECRATION

In the year that King Uzziah died, I saw the Lord seated on a throne, high and exalted. (Isaiah 6:1)

The eighth century before Christ gave birth to the most momentous epochs of ancient history. We find in it the eras both of Babylon and Rome, the two mightiest monarchies of the past. It also saw the fall of Israel and Assyria and the decline of Judah until the kingdom at last fell under Gentile sway. Great events are the mold in which great men are developed and the momentous events of this age developed the greatest of the Hebrew prophets, Isaiah.

Before entering upon his writings in detail, we shall look at the frontispiece which appears in the beginning of the volume, a picture of the prophet himself. It is given in the sixth chapter of his prophecies although chronologically it belongs to an earlier date. The story was deferred until for some years he had actually proved in his experience and work the truth of the great commission which had been given to him at the beginning.

The story of Isaiah's call and consecration is a living picture which speaks to living men today as personally and practically as when it first became true of the great prophet himself. While history changes from age to age, the nature of God and the needs and experiences of human souls are still the same. May it prove to some who read this chapter a similar call and consecration.

THE TIME

1. "In the year that King Uzziah died." This is not a mere note of time or item of chronology. It suggests a dark background for the picture of divine grace and human consecration which shines out in the story.

The time that King Uzziah died was a very dark one for Judah and doubtless for Isaiah, too. Uzziah had been the most illustrious of the nation's rulers since the days of David and Solomon. He had carried the banners of his country before mighty and victorious armies until every enemy had been subdued and Judah had almost reached the ancient boundaries of the Abrahamic promise and the days of Solomon. And it is, perhaps, not too much to say that the throne had reached a height of power and influence unequaled by any earthly dynasty at the time. At the same time the trade of the country had kept pace with its military advance and wealth, and prosperity filled all the land with patriotic hope and confidence.

Suddenly all this was interrupted by the death of Uzziah. It was not an ordinary death, but it was overshadowed by the most tragic and dreadful accompaniments. It had come as a stroke of divine judgment because of a fearful and presumptuous sin. Swollen with pride and self-sufficiency, Uzziah had presumptuously ventured, in defiance of the warnings of the priesthood, to arrogate to himself the functions of the high priest and had dared to enter the Holy of holies (Most Holy Place, NIV) to offer incense with his own hands. Instantly the stroke of heaven fell upon his daring head and he came out a leper as white as snow, and sank to his grave with the fearful badge of heaven's most tremendous judgment resting upon him. The effect of such a catastrophe upon the nation must have been overwhelming, and all the excellence of the brief succeeding reign of Jotham was unable to counteract it.

Isaiah had doubtless shared with others the hopes and dreams which Uzziah's glorious reign had inspired. An intense patriot, and, like all great souls, an enthusiast, Isaiah had entered into the hopes and triumphs of his country with deepest ardor. Doubtless, like most young dreamers, he had built a castle of earthly ambition until its towers had reached to heaven, and had dreamed of the grandeur of his country until it seemed to him that the glowing vision that was already burning in his soul of the latter day glory was to be fulfilled before his eyes and in his own lifetime. But the fearful death of Uzziah shattered his idol and rudely dispelled his early dream, and for a time there seemed nothing before him but desolation and despair.

But at last, out of the wreck of his earthly hopes, there burst upon his soul the vision of God and the unseen world where he was henceforth to look for the realization of his shattered earthly dreams. While the throne of Judah was tottering, the everlasting throne was forever unmoved. While earthly heroes might pass away, and earthly ideals be shattered in the dust, God remained forever true, and faith only needed to take the highest flight and look for its realization above. "In the year that King Uzziah died, I saw the Lord seated on a throne, high and exalted." Such an experience as this has to come to every great soul before he or she is prepared to live both for time and eternity and to be a true prophet for God in the midst of all human vicissitudes.

Such a rude awakening had to come to the disciples of the Master as they too dreamed of an earthly kingdom and wondered that their Master would not allow the enthusiastic multitudes to "take Him by force and make Him a king." Even after His resurrection they still continued to ask: "Lord, are you at this time going to restore the kingdom to Israel?" (Acts 1:6). Their dreams also were shattered and they saw the Master to whom they looked as the successor of David and Solomon hanging upon a shameful cross and consigned to a dark and dreary tomb. But out of that rose the vision of the resurrection and that greater coming and better kingdom which He is yet to bring.

So, too, most of us begin our work for God with enthusiastic expectations of earthly success and God has to let us down, as He did Isaiah, until we are prepared to follow the Master outside the camp, to be crucified to earthly honors and triumphs and to look for the realization of our faith and hope in the ages to come.

How often, too, the individual Christian has to be awakened to the vision of God by some such painful shock. You had built your nest securely amid the bowers of love; you had fastened the tendrils of your heart to some sweet face or loved friend; you had dreamed that your security could never be shaken and you had pictured a bright and beautiful earthly future; and lo, instead there came consuming sickness, days and nights of weary pain and moldering grave. For a while your heart was crushed and your spirit was broken and even life itself had no longer anything in it worth living for. But at last the vision of God began to rise upon your view and the face of Jesus grew real as you looked up through your brimming tears and learned at last that it is only through the wreck of our earthly hope that we begin to seek the things that cannot pass away. And today, with a chastened peace and a hope that cannot fail, you are thanking God for the day that someone died that you might learn to live.

Or perhaps you had a severe shock, for there is something worse than death. You attached yourself to some human cause; you yielded your confidence and your devotion to some earthly leader. You surrounded him with a halo of your ideals and dreams and you almost worshiped him as God. And then came the rude awakening, the failure of your ideal, the discovery of human weakness, perhaps of sin and shame, and your idol was shattered in the dust and with it all the hopes, ambitions and purposes of your life. Never again would you be deceived into any enterprise of usefulness or service. You had found that "all men are liars," and you were in danger of becoming cynical and sour and losing faith not only in human nature but in all possible virtue and goodness.

It was then that you found God and learned that there was but one true Leader worth worshiping, but one cause worth embracing, but one life worth living. And today you are patiently, hopefully, victoriously pressing on, gathering out of the wreckage of time all that you can, looking for no perfection here, but laying up the fruits of your service in heaven and some day expecting the Master to show the finished product and to give to you the glad "well done" and the great reward. We are not fitted for any earthly ministry until we have seen the failure of life and learned to live for the things that cannot pass away.

Dear friend, look up through your tears and your shattered ideals and idols and see God. Begin to live for Him and the things that are above.

THE VISION

2. The Apostle John tells us that it was Jesus Christ that Isaiah saw in this vision of heavenly glory. "Isaiah said this because he saw Jesus' glory and spoke about him" (John 12:41). This was his first view of that glorious Christ, whom he, above all other ancient seers, beheld afar off and proclaimed as the Hope of the ages. He saw Him "sitting on a throne high and exalted" (Isaiah 6:1). It was the vision of the heavenly temple with the seraphim or "the burning ones," His minister and courtiers.

The expression "high and exalted" is intended to convey the idea that the God of Isaiah was a very much higher Being than the conceptions and ideals of the people. The God they wanted was a kind of fetish who could help them in their temporal needs and deliver them from their troubles somewhat as the idol of the pagan was expected to answer to his call and deliver him in his difficulties or be soundly abused for not doing so. That is the idea of God that many people have. This little planet is at the present time the center of His greatest activities and the object of His loftiest plans. He is preparing for the advent of His Son upon this earth and here He is to work out through Him the greatest problem of the universe. His supreme purpose is to fill the earth with His glory and for this consummation, everything in earth and heaven is combining.

This was Isaiah's sublime lesson as he listened to the heavenly song and then went forth to be a worker with God in the great plan of bringing back this revolted planet to its orbit around His throne.

Such a vision must come to us before we are truly prepared for the work of God. Then we, too, will spring to our places in this mighty plan and, instead of dreaming about some far off heaven, will begin to work to make this green old earth a heaven below.

The heavenly vision had one lesson more for Isaiah: the pattern of true service. He was to go forth into the work of heaven and God permitted him to see the way His servants yonder ministered at His command. The first thing he would be struck with as he gazed upon them was their deep humility. Of their six wings, two were used to cover their faces, two to cover their feet and only two left for flight. They were veiled workers. Even their own transcendent beauty covered them from the sight of others and themselves; and their work, suggested by their feet, was hidden as soon as it was done and they swept on to new commissions without stopping to reflect on what they had done. What pattern of true service here! God give us the veiled face and the veiled feet.

But again their wings suggested celerity, swiftness and service. They were ready to fly at God's command and fulfill His messages of love without a moment's delay. True service still will be ever ready, for the "King's business requires haste."

The next thought suggested by the vision of the seraphim was worship and praise. Our highest service is to glorify Him. Have we given Him the fire-touched lips and is He using them like aeolian harps to respond to His touch and show forth His praise?

THE SHADOW OF THE VISION

3. The first effect of this vision was another vision that rose like a dark shadow in the background—the vision of himself. In the light of God's glory and heaven's pure service, he could only see his own utter vileness and cry out, "Woe to me! . . . I am ruined! For I am a man of unclean lips, and I live among a people of unclean lips, and my eyes have seen the King, the LORD Almighty" (6:5).

The story is told of a little child from the slums that stumbled into a mission hall where a kindergarten teacher was giving an object lesson to the little grimy children of the streets, in the form of a beautiful white lily. Not a word was spoken, but the children were permitted to gaze upon and even touch that spotless flower. Immediately the wondering eyes of one of the little girls fell upon herself, and with a shadow of shame upon her face she swiftly turned and fled from the building, and never stopped till she got to her miserable garret home. There soap and washbasin and every little trinket she could find in the way of cleanliness and ornamentation was brought into requisition, and when she returned half an hour later, she was transformed. That beautiful lily had shown her herself and had awakened in her a longing for at least external purity. So God reveals us to ourselves.

Has He shown to you the vision, and has it cured you forevermore of ever expecting anything good in that old self, and led you to say, "I no longer live, but Christ lives in me" (Galatians 2:20)?

It is not a good or wholesome thing to be always sitting in judgment upon ourselves in mortification and condemnation. The chagrin and disappointment which we feel, because we expected to find something good in ourselves and have not, is oftentimes but the result of pride. True humility, however, has given up self forever, and never again expects to see anything worth approving, but leaving it forever in the bottomless grave of Christ, turns to Him and takes Him and His righteousness as our beauty and our glorious rest. God keep us there.

THE CLEANSING

4. "Then one of the seraphs flew to me with a live coal in his hand, which he had taken with tongs from the altar. With it he touched my mouth and said, 'See, this has touched your lips; your guilt is taken away and your sin atoned for' " (Isaiah 6:6–7).

Thus Isaiah anticipated by eight centuries the glorious promise of John the Baptist and its fulfillment in the story of Pentecost.

If we find no reference here to the atoning blood in the picture of our cleansing, let us remember it is results rather than processes that God is teaching. Behind the fire and the oil we always find the blood in the Old Testament ritual, and the altar here from which the coal was taken suggests that sacrifice which had already been consumed by that altar fire. But the result of Calvary is the Holy Spirit, the baptism of fire that burns *up* and burns *out* the life of self and sin and then burns *in* the blessed image of the Master through the Holy Spirit.

Beloved, have we received that cleansing fire? Thus and thus alone can we be prepared either for holy living or efficient service.

THE CALL

5. Now comes the call to service; but it was not a call so much as a permission. It was not a command so much as the acceptance of a volunteer. With newly cleansed and quickened ears he was able now to hear what had been unheard before, the voice of the heavens. He seemed to have been brought so very near to the council chamber of Jehovah that he was listening to the counsels of the Godhead as they sadly exclaimed, "Whom shall I send? And who will go for us?" (6:8). Why did not God say at once, "We want you to go." Ah, this is the very secret of true service. The Old Testament servant was a slave, who went because he was told. The New Testament servant is a son and partner, who goes because his heart prompts him. Isaiah rose to the regal height of New Testament sonship, and without compulsion or command, he asked the privilege of being a worker together with God. The moment he understood that thought of God, the plan of heaven and the desire of those glorious beings who were filling the earth with His glory, his heart responded, his life was offered and the glad and willing cry came forth, "Here am I. Send me!" (6:8).

In the beautiful story of David we have the picture of a time when he longed that someone would "give [him] a drink of the water from the well near the gate of Bethlehem." (2 Samuel 23:15). He did not send any soldier on such a fearful enterprise, but unconsciously the cry came from his heart for a draught of the waters from the well of his childhood. But that was enough for the three brave men that heard his longing, and, dashing through the ranks of the Philistines, they came back with their helmets filled with the waters of Bethlehem's well. That was service so sacred that even David could not bear to drink of such a costly draught. That is true service for our heavenly Master. We are kings and priests unto God. It is royal service He wants. The men who go into the ministry because somebody bids them, or because it offers a professional channel for support, are the ecclesiastical flotsam and jetsam of society and are useless to God and their fellowmen. The missionary call is the cry of the heart that has heard the heavenly message and "cannot but" go forth to tell the world of His love.

THE COMMISSION

6. His service is accepted, and God says, "Go." But, oh, what a commission! Go, not to triumph, but more frequently to fail. Go, not to be admired and loved, but to be rejected, and at last "sawed in two" (Hebrews 11:37). Go, to say, "Lord, who has believed our message?" (Romans 10:16; referring to Isaiah 53:1). "All day long I have held out my hands/ to a disobedient and obstinate people" (Romans 10:21; referring to Isaiah 65:2).

Go, not only to a crucified life but to a crucified ministry. Go, to see that nation go down until at last there is nothing left but the very root of the tree, from which the future growth is yet to spring. Go, not to save the nation, but to gather the remnant out from the nation, the one out of 10 who will be willing to hear your voice. And he went, and witnessed and suffered and died. But, oh, the resurrection that has come from the seed Isaiah planted in tears and seeming failure!

Beloved, so He is sending us. Let us not look for an earthly future even in our Christian work. Let us be willing to gather "the remnant," to have "the 10th," to save men one by one for that glorious time and that heavenly temple when He shall manifest our work, and we shall find that our "labor in the Lord is not in vain" (1 Corinthians 15:58).

I am indebted to a gifted friend for the fine suggestion of the three epigrammatic words that sum up the teaching of this chapter and story of a true life.

The first word is *woe.* "Woe is me," is a vision of self and its eternal renunciation.

The second word is *lo* (KJV). "Lo, this hath touched thy lips," is a revelation of God and the cleansing baptism of the Holy Spirit that prepares us for life and service.

And the third word, *go,* is a call to service.

Have we gone through these three chapters of Christian life and service and met the *woe,* the *lo,* and the *go,* like the ancient prophet of Jerusalem?

CHAPTER 2

SIN AND SALVATION

"Come now, let us reason together,"
says the LORD.
"Though your sins are like scarlet,
they shall be as white as snow;
though they are red as crimson,
they shall be like wool."
(Isaiah 1:18)

The method of the ancient prophet was very different from a modern literary writer. He did not sit down in his library and calmly dictate his message in flowing periods of paragraphs. Rather, he suddenly appeared in some public concourse or in the temple court, and with dramatic pose and gesture, poured forth a torrent of vehement eloquence, sometimes of stern denunciation, sometimes of solemn warning, sometimes of tender appeal and expostulation. These were afterwards gathered up and published, not as a series of logical addresses, but with all the dramatic irregularity of their first utterance. They resembled not so much the current of some flowing river pursuing its tranquil course to the sea, but rather they were like some volcanic stream rolling down the mountain side and gathering up in its course the rocks and trees of the mountain, or turning aside in its fiery course by the obstructions that it meets on its way and then sweeping on again in some new channel with its mingled current of lava and earth. While the critical would fail to find much logical connection, the eye of faith can discern through every prophetic message an unbroken thread of spiritual connection and one uniform message of divine reproof and mercy.

The first chapter of Isaiah was probably the first of the prophet's public messages, and it is a good sample of many others. It may be described generally as a message concerning sin and salvation. Its form is most dramatic. Suddenly appearing in the temple court or the public square, with impressive gestures he calls the attention of the multitude by repeating the very words with which Moses had begun his last message to Israel. "Hear, O heavens!" he cries, "Listen, O earth!/ For the LORD has spoken" (1:2).

Then he arraigns the nation before the bar of heaven and calls as his witnesses the heavens and the earth and the very dumb brutes of the lower order of creation, whose fidelity to their masters is a silent reproof to the disobedience of God's people. Then follows the arraignment of the sinful nation as he proceeds to characterize the unnaturalness, ingratitude and fearful wickedness of the people, declaring at last that their wickedness has almost brought them to the condition of Sodom and Gomorrah.

Then there seems to have come some voice of protest or defense from someone in the multitude, calling attention to their costly worship and offerings as a proof of their loyalty to God. But this only calls forth a more vehement denunciation for their wickedness. And the prophet proceeds to tell them that the very worst thing about them is their religion, inasmuch as it is a cloak of hypocrisy to cover their sins, and that their prayers and sacrifices are not only rejected, but are an abomination to God so long as their hearts are corrupt and their "hands are full of blood."

At last the voice of denunciation is changed to one of mercy. The loving heart of God seems to grow weary of reproof and longs to pour itself out in mercy and compassion. One is reminded of the time when the Lord Jesus Himself while on earth had upbraided the cities of Galilee for rejecting His message and had begun to say to them, "But I tell you, it will be more bearable for Tyre and Sidon on the day of judgment than for you. And you, Capernaum, will you be lifted up to the skies? No, you will go down to the depths. If the miracles that were performed in you had been performed in Sodom, it would have remained to this day" (Matthew 11:22–23).

But at that moment the Master's heart seemed unable longer to endure the pain of His own reproof, and suddenly He breaks out into an appeal of unspeakable tenderness as perhaps He sees in the multitude before Him some weeping face or penitent heart. "Come to me," He cries, "all you who are weary and burdened, and I will give you rest" (11:28).

There is a similar revulsion of feeling a little later in His ministry, when after He had pronounced upon the Pharisees the fearful woes of the 23rd chapter of Matthew, He suddenly pauses again and breaks out with an appeal of divine compassion, "Oh, Jerusalem, Jerusalem, you who kill the prophets and stone those sent to you, how often I have longed to gather your children together, as a hen gathers her chicks under her wings, but you were not willing" (23:37).

Such a change comes over the prophet's message here. Suddenly his denunciations close, and turning to the people with tones of tenderness he cries,

"Come now, let us reason together,"
  says the LORD.
"Though your sins are like scarlet,
  they shall be as white as snow;
though they are red as crimson,
  they shall be like wool.
If you are willing and obedient,
  you will eat the best from the land;
but if you resist and rebel,
  you will be devoured by the sword."
    For the mouth of the LORD has spoken.
    (Isaiah 1:18–20)

SECTION I—*Sin*

The prophet gives us a graphic picture of sin and its aggravations,

CONTRARY TO NATURE

1. It is contrary to nature. The very heavens and the earth are appealed to against it. The stars in their courses follow the laws of nature. The earth pursues her orbit in obedience to the great principle of gravitation. There is harmony everywhere in the material universe and the slightest breach of law brings collision, confusion and destruction. Man alone defies the laws of his being and the will of his Creator and involves himself in catastrophe and destruction. The mute creatures of the lower orders of animal life are appealed to against us. "The ox knows his master" (1:3), and patiently and obediently follows the furrow and goes to the altar of sacrifice without a murmur. The ass, usually accounted foolish and obstinate, knows at least where its fodder is found and finds its way to its master's crib, rather than to the weeds and thistles of the wilderness.

Man alone turns away from the true source of all his supplies and blessings and "[digs his] own cisterns,/ broken cisterns that cannot hold water" (Jeremiah 2:13). The stupendous folly and unnaturalness of human sin is vividly brought out by this appeal to the very lowest order of the natural creation.

The instincts of human nature are opposed to man's sin. "I reared children and brought them up" (Isaiah 1:2) is the complaint of the divine Father, "but they have rebelled against me" (1:2).

The heathen Chinese understand the rights and claims of parents to the respect and obedience of their children, and without the knowledge of God's Word to guide them, they present a beautiful example of devotion to filial duty. But Israel, although treated with more than paternal kindness by the divine Parent, has made no return, but even lifted his puny arm in rebellion against the loving heart that nourished and brought him up as a child.

CONTRARY TO REASON

2. Sin is contrary to reason. "My people do not understand" (1:3) is God's next complaint. Sin results from inconsiderateness. It is contrary to all right reason. God does not require our obedience and service for His glory and greatness, but for your good. His commandments are founded upon inherent righteousness, and disobedience must bring suffering and loss just as certainly as the transgression of any law of nature must be followed by a corresponding retribution. Just as surely as a straight line is the shortest road to a given point, so righteousness and obedience bring to us happiness and reward. As certainly as the fire will burn us if we touch it and the precipice will destroy us if we plunge over its verge, so our going contrary to the will of God must bring to us calamity and misery. Common reason should teach us this.

Therefore "The fear of the LORD is the beginning of wisdom,/ and knowledge of the Holy One is understanding" (Proverbs 9:10). While, on the other hand, the sinner is a "fool" and disobedience is not only wickedness, but it is bad judgment and reckless folly. It was when the prodigal "came to his senses" (Luke 15:17a) that he began to go back to his father, and so salvation is a coming to our right mind and a turning back from the path of foolishness as well as sin.

A WEIGHT

3. Sin is a weight that drags us down. "Ah, sinful nation,/ a people loaded with guilt [iniquity, KJV]" (Isaiah 1:4). Iniquity is spoken of as a burden, a handicap, a weight that drags us down. The Lord appeals to sinners as "burdened" (Matthew 11:28). Truly, "the way of the unfaithful is hard" (Proverbs 13:15). Oh, the load of anxious care, remorseful fear and mourning shame that the sinner carries! Oh, the expedients to which he has to resort to hide his tracks and bury the consequence of his sins! Oh, the darkness and despair of the afterview of the sinful pleasure that looked so alluring when seen from the front! Oh, the lives that are being dragged down to untimely graves, to hopeless despair, to suicide and even to madness by the fearful load of sin! Bunyan represents it under the figure of the pilgrim with the burden upon his back; and our blessed Lord is represented as bearing the sinner's load and finding it so heavy that it crushed out His life on Calvary.

Oh, Christ! what burdens bowed Thy head,
  Our load was laid on Thee.

Such is the millstone bound to the neck of every sinner that is surely dragging him down. "Loaded with guilt."

A SEED OF EVIL

4. Sin is represented as a seed of evil, self-propagating and full of malign power to reproduce itself. "A seed of evildoers" (Isaiah 1:4, KJV). It is not only the first generation of sin that we have to fear, but its countless brood of evil reproduction. It is like those malign germs of disease that are all around us in the air, in the elements of nature, bacilli which propagate themselves by millions every hour and take possession of our vital organs and prey upon our very life.

One sin multiplies itself a thousandfold. Cain's first act of unbelief soon grew into a bloody murder and then into an everlasting separation from God. Adam's single disobedience multiplied itself in the ruin of all the race, and your sin is to perpetuate its career of evil in generations yet unborn. You cannot sin alone and you cannot bury your wickedness with your bones.

AN INFECTION

5. Sin is an infection. "Children given to corruption" (1:4). Literally, this means "children that corrupt others." The language suggests some contagious disease which spreads itself to all that come in contact with it. You would not, for any consideration, lie down in the bed in which a smallpox patient had died last night, and yet you are exposing yourselves to the germs of moral infection in the people you meet, in the friends you cherish, in the books you read, in the plays you attend, in the music you hear and in the objects upon which you allow your eyes to gaze. There is pollution in these things. They poison your spiritual health and inject into your souls the germs of mortal disease. Sin is a plague spot in society, a blight to the family, the church, the holiest friendship and every precious thing.

A PROVOCATION OF THE LORD

6. Sin is a provocation of the Lord. "They have provoked the Holy One of Israel unto anger" (1:4, KJV). God cannot endure sin. There is something in His holiness which instinctively consumes it. Just as the mother bird drives the serpent from her nest, so God, even as the God of love, is bound by His very goodness to protect His universe from the poison of sin.

You would scarcely dare to go out beneath the naked lightning of the skies and defy your Creator. And yet every sin, the most secret, is an open defiance of the Almighty, and most offensive often because you try to excuse it by some deceitful plea that you did not really mean it. Remember every time you sin you are flying in the face of an angry God.

SIN IS INCORRIGIBLE

7. Sin is incorrigible. "Why should you be beaten anymore?/ Why do you persist in rebellion?" (1:5). When God's chastenings fail to move us, but lead us on to more reckless disobedience, we are in fearful danger. When we can come back from the gates of death or the graveside of some loved friend and quickly forget all the solemn vows we made and all the good resolutions we pledged if God would only try us once more, we are slowly hardening our hearts and preparing ourselves for the sin against the Holy Spirit.

There is a story told of one who, feeling badly after an act of sin, was told by Satan, "Do it again and you won't feel so badly," and, as he obeyed, the sensitiveness passed away and he was soon able to commit sin without the reproof of his conscience. This is indeed true, but it is a fearful truth, and such callousness of heart soon leads to the judgment of God, for "A man who remains stiff-necked after many rebukes/ will suddenly be destroyed—without remedy" (Proverbs 29:1). It is mentioned as the most fearful aggravation of the sin of Ahaz that "in his time of trouble King Ahaz became even more unfaithful to the LORD" (2 Chronicles 28:22). It is as if a great note of exclamation had been drawn across the sacred page and a finger pointing to this monster of wickedness whose very warnings seemed only to harden his heart the more.

A DISEASE

8. Sin is a vile, loathsome and incurable disease. What a fearful picture! "From the sole of your foot to the top of your head/ there is no soundness—/ only wounds and welts/ and open sores,/ not cleansed or bandaged/ or soothed with oil" (Isaiah 1:6). Sin is soul sickness—desperate, incurable and revolting. Not always does it develop its most loathsome features at first, but the malignity of the disease is there and sooner or later it will break out into shameless sin and disgusting depravity.

A NATIONAL CURSE

9. Sin is a national curse. "Your country is desolate,/ your cities burned with fire,/ your fields are being stripped by foreigners/ right before you,/ laid waste as when overthrown by strangers" (1:7). Has not this always been true? The empires and monarchies of the past crumbled to decay through the weight of their own corruptions. Nebuchadnezzar fell through his pride; Medo-Persia through its luxury; Alexander the Great through the success that ruined him; Rome through the moral corruptions which undermined society. And among the kingdoms of Europe, Spain and France are striking examples of the loss of national greatness through the spirit of national corruption. Prosperity leads to luxury, luxury leads to license and self-indul-

gence, and the mightiest nations of today are drifting to the common lot.

The trouble with human society is not that it needs better principles, better government, better politics, but better materials. It is like the arch which tumbled in ruins. And while the experts were discussing the wreck and trying to explain the scientific causes through some defect in the lines of the arch, a common workman picked up a bit of the crumbling brick and, squeezing it between his finger and thumb, it crumbled into dust, as pointing to it he cried, "That is what's the matter with your arch; the brick is rotten." The only remedy for national calamity and degeneration is the transformation of human nature through the grace of the Lord Jesus Christ.

RUIN AND DESOLATION

10. Sin brings ruin and desolation to the individual. The picture of Isaiah applies not only to nations and communities, but to families and individuals. Oh, the wrecked homes and lives that have come about through sin, the great destroyer! Dr. Thomas Guthrie has eloquently said:

> Name me the evil that springs not from this root—the crime that I may not lay at its door. Who is the hoary sexton that digs man's grave? Who is the painted temptress that steals his virtue? Who is the murderess that destroys his life? Who is this sorceress that first deceives and then damns his soul?—Sin. Who with icy breath blights the fair blossom of youth? Who breaks the hearts of parents? Who brings old men's gray hairs with sorrows to the grave?—Sin. Who by a more hideous metamorphosis than Ovid even fancied, changes gentle children into vipers, tender mothers into monsters, and their fathers into worse than Herods, the murderers of their own innocents?—Sin. Who casts the apple of discord on the housetops? Who lights the torch of war and bears it blazing over trembling lands? Who by divisions in the church rends Christ's seamless robe?—Sin. Who is the Delilah that sings the Nazarite to sleep, and delivers up the strength of God into the hands of the uncircumcised? Who, winning smiles on her face, honeyed flattery on her tongue, stands in the door to offer the sacred rites of hospitality, and when suspicion sleeps treacherously pierces our temples with a nail? What fair Siren is this, who is seated on a rock by the deadly pool, smiles to deceive, sings to lure, kisses to betray, and flings her arm around our neck to leap with us into perdition?—Sin. Who turns the soft and gentlest heart to stone? Who hurls reason from her lofty throne and impels sinners, mad as Gadarenes' swine, down the precipice, into a lake of fire?—Sin.

THE CLOAK OF RELIGION

11. Sin seeks to veil its vileness by the cloak of religion. They pleaded their costly and splendid worship, the multitude of their sacrifices and offerings as some excuse for their faults. But the prophet tells them that this is the very worst thing about their sin; that it culminates in hypocrisy and tries to make religion a substitute for righteousness. The world has plenty of religion but the devil uses it as a channel for the very worst forms of sensuality, licentiousness and sin. God will not accept the worship of insincere hearts and impure hands. Sin prevents His answering our prayers, for if we hide sin in our hearts then God will not hear us (Psalm 66:18). Sin defiles our most sacred offerings. Sin makes our religion the very worst of all our crimes.

> Stop bringing meaningless offerings!
> 　Your incense is detestable to me.
> New Moons, Sabbaths and convocations—
> 　I cannot bear your evil assemblies. . . .
> When you spread out your hands in prayer,
> 　I will hide my eyes from you;
> even if you offer many prayers,
> 　I will not listen.
> Your hands are full of blood.
> 　　　(Isaiah 1:13, 15)

The two words which express the character of Judah as given by Isaiah are wickedness and worship. They had plenty of worship—costly worship, splendid worship—but it was stained with sin, and more offensive than even their grossest crimes.

Is your very religion cursed by unrighteousness? Are your prayers neutralized by your unhallowed lives, and are you shutting the very gates of mercy against your poor soul by your presumptuous sins? Oh, stop and consider before the day shall come of which He has spoken, "Then they will call to me but I will not answer;/ they will look for me but will not find me" (Proverbs 1:28).

INDELIBLE, INCURABLE AND INVETERATE

12. Their sin was indelible, incurable and inveterate. The strong adjectives used in our text, "scarlet" and "crimson," describe not merely the deepest tint possible but a kind of dye that was absolutely indelible. It was made from the eggs of a certain insect, and the stain could never be effaced. The word literally means "double-dyed." There is no earthly power that can take away the stain of human depravity. Culture will not do it. Educate and

refine a monster, but at heart he is a monster still.

A quaint story is told of an Oriental despot, who among his queer pets had a little educated pig, which he dressed up in costly raiment, with jeweled rings and chains of gold. Whenever he let it free to gambol in the garden, it invariably plunged into the ditch, and came back defiled with mire and filth. At last he threatened it with death if it ever transgressed again. As it lay that night in terror of the morrow, knowing that the old habit would come back again and plunge it in the ditch once more, a nymph came to its side and offered to cure its swinish heart; and then, the juvenile legend tells us, the nymph took a little lamb and by a surgical operation took out its heart, and after a similar operation on the pig, exchanged the two hearts, and transferred the heart of the lamb to the heart of the trembling little culprit. Next day it was all right, and with the nature of the lamb it loved to gambol in the green fields and keep itself pure. The king was delighted and the pet was saved.

The foolish parable tells the story of the helplessness of the human heart apart from the grace of God. Let us find it out as quickly as we can, for true hope can only begin when we come to self-despair.

SECTION II—*Salvation*

REPENTANCE

1. The first step in our deliverance from sin is one that *we* must take. There is something *we* can do. "Wash and make yourselves clean./ Take your evil deeds/ out of my sight!/ Stop doing wrong,/ learn to do right!" (Isaiah 1:16). This is the preliminary step to every transformed life. You must refuse the evil. You must say no to sin. You must give God the right to make you holy. You cannot make yourself holy, but you can consent that He shall. Are you sick enough of sin to do this? Are you ready to take the first step which the old soldier so well described as "right about face"? That is what the word repentance really means. It is to look the other way, to think the other way and to change your attitude towards sin and God.

MERCY

2. " 'Come now, let us reason together,' says the LORD./ 'Though your sins are like scarlet,/ they shall be as white as snow;/ though they are red as crimson,/ they shall be like wool' " (1:18).

There is a double process here. The first is expressed by the figure of the snow. It does not cleanse, but it covers our sin. After the first fall of the virgin snow, your backyard has still the old refuse there, but the snowy mantle covers it immediately. This is what God does for every sinner when He justifies him through the blood and righteousness of Jesus Christ. This is the imputed righteousness of Christ, and the vilest sinner may accept it, and in a moment be covered by the spotless robe of the Redeemer and be as white as snow. The other process is deeper and more intrinsic. The cleansing of the wool suggests the finer fibers of our nature and represents the sanctifying work which the Holy Spirit accomplishes in the soul that yields to Him. That begins with the work of regeneration and reaches on to all the fullness of the Spirit, until we are completely transformed into the image of the Lord Jesus Christ, and every fiber of our being is spotless as His holy nature.

AN ACT OF THE WILL

3. The act by which we become partakers of all this grace is an act of the will. "If you are willing and obedient,/ you will eat the best from the land" (1:19). It is not an emotional feeling merely that brings us into contact with the grace of God, but it is a choice, a decision, a fixed purpose. "Whoever wishes, let him take the free gift of the water of life" (Revelation 22:17). Shall we meet this simple, practical condition, and with the whole strength of our will say "no" to sin and "yes" to God forevermore?

AN OBEDIENT LIFE

4. The sequel of all this is an obedient life. "If you are willing and obedient" (Isaiah 1:19). The essence of sin is disobedience, and the remedy for sin is a life of willing love and obedience to Him who asks us only to obey Him because it is best for us.

THE RECOMPENSE

5. And finally, the blessed recompense. "You will eat the best from the land" (1:19). Oh, how good the land of obedience is to its happy children here, and how glorious the inheritance to which it leads forevermore!

God help us to see our sin, to accept His salvation and to walk with Him in holy obedience and happy fellowship.

CHAPTER 3

ISAIAH'S VISION

In the last days
the mountain of the LORD'S temple will be established
  as chief among the mountains;
it will be raised above the hills,
  and all nations will stream to it.

Many peoples will come and say,

"Come, let us go to the mountain of the LORD,
  to the house of the God of Jacob.
He will teach us his ways,
  so that we may walk in his paths."
The law will go out from Zion,
  the word of the LORD from Jerusalem.
He will judge between the nations
  and will settle disputes for many peoples.
They will beat their swords into plowshares
  and their spears into pruning hooks.
Nation will not take up sword against nation,
  nor will they train for war anymore.

Come, O house of Jacob,
  let us walk in the light of the LORD."
  (Isaiah 2:2–5)

The second address of the prophet is contained in chapters two to four inclusive. It begins with a sublime vision of the future glory of Israel and Jerusalem. This is immediately followed by the dark picture of the present condition of things which was anything but ideal. But after the dark eclipse and the long interval of sin and judgment, the vision returns and the closing paragraphs of the fourth chapter are radiant with the promise of a holy people and the presence of their covenant God in the fullness of blessing and the fulfillment of the opening vision.

SECTION I—*The Ideal*

Isaiah's vision was not original. His words are quoted from an older prophet—the stern and eccentric figure that suddenly appeared in Jerusalem in the early days of Hezekiah's reign and, with wild gestures and tones of agony and terror, summoned the king and the people to repentance and became the instrument of Hezekiah's conversion. It was the prophet Micah who first uttered this sublime picture of the future glory of the house of the Lord, and Isaiah prefixes it to his second address somewhat as a modern minister would put a text at the commencement of his sermon.

CENTER STAGE

1. In the vision of Micah and Isaiah, the Lord's house occupies the center of the stage and the foreground of the picture. It is the old conception of the theocracy, a state founded upon the throne of Jehovah and placing His authority and worship above all other obligations.

A MOUNTAIN

2. The house of the Lord is represented as a mountain. The figure suggests vastness, loftiness and glory and the conception in the prophet's mind is that God's house, which simply stands for His cause, is the grandest of all causes and the noblest of all institutions. Mountains are used in prophetic imagery to represent great kingdoms. But all earthly organizations dwindle into insignificance in comparison: "His kingdom is an eternal kingdom;/ his dominion endures from generation to generation" (Daniel 4:3).

A distinguished statesman, having been appointed as an elder in a humble village church and permitted to pass to the congregation the emblems of the Lord's supper, remarked that he felt more highly honored in having the humblest place in the service of God than when he had held the highest offices from his sovereign and his country. The day is coming when the lowliest servant of the King of kings will be a prince compared with the proud rulers of time.

ABOVE ALL MOUNTAINS

3. It is above all other mountains. It is to be "established/ as chief among the mountains;/ it will be raised above the hills" (Isaiah 2:2).

The Chinese place their sacred pagodas on the loftiest hills and will not suffer a commercial building or a missionary edifice to overtop their sacred temples. They literally carry out the idea that the houses of their gods must be exalted above all hills.

The spiritual conception is fine. The claims of Christ should overtop all other claims. The authority of God should be supreme above all other influences. Have we thus exalted His throne in our hearts and crowned Him "Lord of all"?

CENTER OF WORLD'S ATTRACTION

4. The Lord's house is to be the center of attraction for the world. "All nations will stream to it" (2:2). The name of Jesus already is the mightiest name on earth and the day is coming when every knee will bow and every tongue confess that He is Lord, and when all men shall come to Him as the source of life and every blessing. "But I, when I am lifted up from the earth, will draw all men to myself" (John 12:32).

Zechariah has given us a sublime vision of a day that is coming when Jesus shall hold an annual reception in Jerusalem and all nations shall go up once a year to Jerusalem to keep the Feast of Tabernacles and to worship at the feet of our glorified Lord.

The vision of Isaiah shall then be fulfilled and Christ will indeed be the center of all hearts and all nations.

THE LIGHT OF THE WORLD

5. The house of the Lord is to be the light of the world for "He will teach us his ways,/ so that we may walk in his paths" (Isaiah 2:3). Jerusalem was the light of the ancient world. All true knowledge of God and righteousness came from the divine oracles committed to the chosen people. And from the same Jerusalem came the light of the gospel in the apostolic age. Once more in the millennial age is Jerusalem again to be the center of light for all men, and the Word of God will go forth to all earth's millions, so that the "earth will be full of the knowledge of the LORD/ as the waters cover the sea" (11:9). That day has not yet come. At present we are simply giving the gospel as a witness to all nations and gathering out from among the Gentiles a people for His name (Acts 15:13), but a brighter light is yet to shine from shore to shore and all nations shall walk in the light of the Lord.

A SEAT OF GOVERNMENT

6. The house of the Lord is to be the seat of government for the world. "The law will go out from Zion" (Isaiah 2:3). One of the curses of the nations today is bad government. It has been somewhat improved through the influence of Christianity among the nations, but we have no Christian na-

tions as yet and never will have a truly Christian nation until the Lord Jesus comes. Then "a king will reign in righteousness/ and rulers will rule with justice" (32:1). Then "He will defend the afflicted among the people/ and save the children of the needy;/ he will crush the oppressor./ He will endure as long as the sun,/ as long as the moon, through all generations" (Psalm 72:4–5).

THE GOLDEN AGE OF THE WORLD

7. This will bring the golden age of the world. "They will beat their swords into plowshares/ and their spears into pruning hooks./ Nation will not take up sword against nation,/ nor will they train for war anymore" (Isaiah 2:4). Man is trying to bring this about through human governments and arbitration treaties. We thank God for what has been accomplished, but the facts of current history are almost a caricature of man's pretensions. The very heavens must laugh as they behold the kings who at one time were most active in establishing the tribunals of peace a little later provoking by their tyranny the horrors of the world's most terrible wars.

But the sentiment for peace is born from above and the echoes that float along the centuries in human sentiment and poetry speak forth a deep undercurrent of divine intuition. Not vainly has the poet dreamed of that golden age:

> Through the dark future, down long generations
> The echoing sounds grow fainter and then cease,
> And like a bell with solemn, sweet vibration
> I hear the voice of God again say Peace;
> Peace, and no longer from its brazen portals
> The voice of war's loud thunder shakes the skies,
> But beautiful as songs of the immortals
> The holy melodies of Love arise.

SECTION II—*The Failure*

But not yet is the vision. It is as true as it is sublime and beautiful; but, like Isaiah's, it must wait till He comes, the Prince of Peace, the Lord of lords. How very stirring to find the young prophet of Jerusalem starting out in his splendid career with this glorious vision. How true to the loftiest natures and the history of every great movement. All great lives begin with such vision. It is this that stirs the breast of patriotism and makes the heroes whose lives have illuminated the pages of history. It is this that moved the Crusader and still inspires the philanthropist, the social reformer, the Christian worker and the worldwide missionary. No life will ever be illustrious until it has had its visions.

> Gideons must Isaiahs be,
> Visions first, then victory.

But alas, the brightest vision must seem to fade and imagination and hope must learn to join hands with patience and faith and wait till God's full time has come. It is all true. It is less than the glorious truth, for "No eye has seen,/ no ear has heard,/ no mind has conceived/ what God has prepared for those who love him" (1 Corinthians 2:9).

But there is another vision and that is the actual reality of life and humanity. In looking at that vision we will find, as Isaiah did when he turned his eyes from heaven to earth, that the "gold has lost its luster,/ the fine gold become dull!" (Lamentations 4:1). What a picture of corruption met his gaze!

CORRUPT RULERS

1. First we see the corruption of the rulers.

> See how the faithful city
>   has become a harlot!
> She once was full of justice;
>   righteousness used to dwell in her—
>   but now murderers!
> Your silver has become dross,
>   your choice wine is diluted with water.
> Your rulers are rebels,
>   companions of thieves;
> they all love bribes
>   and chase after gifts.
> They do not defend the cause of the fatherless;
>   the widow's case does not come before them.
>   (Isaiah 1:21–23)

And here is another picture.

> Youths oppress my people,
>   women rule over them.
> O my people, your guides lead you astray;
>   they turn you from the path.

> The LORD takes his place in court;
>   he rises to judge the people.
> The LORD enters into judgment
>   against the elders and leaders of his people:
> "It is you who have ruined my vineyard;
>   the plunder from the poor is in your houses.
> What do you mean by crushing my people
>   and grinding the faces of the poor?"
>   declares the Lord,
>   the LORD Almighty.
>   (3:12–15)

We have become accustomed even in our modern democracy to such exposures of official corruption. Even the best forms of government do not change the selfishness and unscrupulousness of fallen nature. The righteous Judge looks down with indignation upon the reeking and ever-recurring spectacle of oppression, selfishness and misrule and longs for the day when the scepter of righteousness shall be the scepter of His kingdom and earth shall cease to groan beneath the heels of her oppressors.

LUXURY

2. Next we see luxury. "Their land is full of silver and gold;/ there is no end to their treasures./ Their land is full of horses;/ there is no end to their chariots" (2:7). Prosperity and wealth had debauched the nation. The leading families were given up to self-indulgence and luxurious pleasure which is always a demoralizing influence in the life of nations and which today is threatening the very foundations of society.

IDOLATRY AND SUPERSTITION

3. Idolatry and superstition are portrayed in this vision. "You have abandoned your people, the house of Jacob./ They are full of superstitions from the East;/ they practice divination like the Philistines/ and clasp hands with pagans./ . . ./ Their land is full of idols;/ they bow down to the work of their hands,/ to what their fingers have made" (2:6, 8).

Their intercourse with heathen nations had introduced their abominations in the form of idolatry, sorcery and devil worship. Our own times, not withstanding our boasted civilization, have not escaped the same peril. While we do not bow down to idols of wood and stone, we are running after the identical things that had this outcome of their coarser idolatries, and idolatry is but devil worship. In modern Spiritualism, clairvoyance, Buddhism, Theosophy and Christian Science, we have simply later forms of the same devil worship which the great father of lies is seeking to substitute for the worship of the true God in every age, and which he is refining to suit the tastes of the times and succeeding in palming off upon our boasted culture with unprecedented success.

PRIDE

4. Next we see pride.

> The eyes of the arrogant man will be humbled
>   and the pride of men brought low;
> the LORD alone will be exalted in that day.
>
> The LORD Almighty has a day in store
>   for all the proud and lofty,
>   for all that is exalted
>   (and they will be humbled),
> for all the cedars of Lebanon, tall and lofty,
>   and all the oaks of Bashan,
> for all the towering mountains
>   and all the high hills,
> for every lofty tower
>   and every fortified wall,
> for every trading ship
>   and every stately vessel.
> The arrogance of man will be brought low
>   and the pride of men humbled;
> the LORD alone will be exalted in that day,
>   and the idols will totally disappear.
>   (2:11–18)

The spirit of pride is particularly offensive to God. It grows with prosperity and human progress until man becomes his own god. The prophet's severest denunciations are hurled against the high looks and the haughty pride of Jerusalem. And the modern prophet might as fittingly denounce the swollen vanity, the self-sufficiency, the assumption, the national vainglory and the intellectual boastfulness of our own age. A recent writer stated that it was the glory of the 19th century that it has given us humanity. Man's confidence in himself and his own sufficiency is a practical atheism that dominates much of human thought today.

VANITY AND CORRUPTION OF WOMEN

5. Last we see the vanity and corruption of woman. Finally the prophet's piercing glance turns to the loud and showy women who form perhaps a

large part of his audience and who with haughty eyes are beginning to frown down the awful message of the young enthusiast to whom they had listened for awhile with such admiration and pride. But now their faces blanch while he cries:

> The LORD says,
>   "The women of Zion are haughty,
> walking along with outstretched necks,
>   flirting with their eyes,
> tripping along with mincing steps,
>   with ornaments jingling on their ankles.
> Therefore the Lord will bring sores on the heads of the women of
>   Zion;
>   the LORD will make their scalps bald."

> In that day the Lord will snatch away their finery: the bangles and headbands and crescent necklaces, the earrings and bracelets and veils, the headdresses and ankle chains and sashes, the perfume bottles and charms, the signet rings and nose rings, the fine robes and the capes and cloaks, the purses and mirrors, and the linen garments and tiaras and shawls.

> Instead of fragrance there will be a stench;
>   instead of a sash, a rope;
> instead of well-dressed hair, baldness;
>   instead of fine clothing, sackcloth;
>   instead of beauty, branding.
>   (3:16–24)

This fearful picture might be adjusted without much strain to one of the fashionable parades of today. It is not wrong for women to dress with modest taste, for God has made the world beautiful and given to woman the instinct of good taste. But when a woman dresses for display, for adornment, for personal vanity and to become a center of attraction for the eyes of men, she degrades herself and dishonors her womanhood and her God. It is very significant that the one thing he says about women here is about their dress. It would seem as if a woman's character was expressed in her apparel. You can tell the pure and modest woman by her dress. You can tell the loud, vain and immodest woman by her walk, her look and her array.

God help you, dear sisters, to dress as women becoming godliness, and above all other charms to wear the "unfading beauty of a gentle and quiet spirit, which is of great worth in God's sight" (1 Peter 3:4).

The condition of woman in Isaiah's time was one of the very evidences of the degeneration of the nation and the awful precursor of the shame, the outrage and the ruin in which they were so soon to be involved in the ruthless grasp of their pitiless enemies.

SECTION III—*The Later Vision*

But the dark eclipse is to pass away and when judgment shall have done its fearful work, the day at last will come of which the prophet says,

> In that day the Branch of the LORD will be beautiful and glorious, and the fruit of the land will be the pride and glory of the survivors in Israel. Those who are left in Zion, who remain in Jerusalem, will be called holy, all who are recorded among the living in Jerusalem. The Lord will wash away the filth of the women of Zion; he will cleanse the bloodstains from Jerusalem by a spirit of judgment and a spirit of fire. (Isaiah 4:2–4)

The change is to come about partly by divine judgment, bringing the conviction of sin, but more fully through the work of the Holy Spirit whom the Messiah is to bring and who is to cleanse them "by a spirit of judgment and a spirit of fire" (4:4). This was the message later of John the Baptist, as he announced the coming Savior, "He will baptize you with the Holy Spirit and with fire" (Matthew 3:11).

This is the only remedy for all wrong social conditions and for all the evils of our hearts and lives. The coal that touched Isaiah's lips and consumed his sins must burn out from us the taint of depravity and burn in the holy image of our God.

But it was only the remnant that was to be delivered. "For out of Jerusalem will come a remnant,/ and out of Mount Zion a band of survivors./ The zeal of the LORD Almighty/ will accomplish this" (Isaiah 37:32). The whole nation was not to be saved, but "a remnant chosen by grace" (Romans 11:5b).

This is the principle on which God is working now for both Jew and Gentile. He is not saving all the world, but "all the Gentiles who bear my name" (Acts 15:17). He is not saving all Israel, but a remnant from among them are finding the light, accepting the Messiah and getting ready for the glory of the latter days. The work of God is not a wholesale work today, but a little flock, a humble minority.

Are you in this remnant? Have you turned from the great broad road of time and are you in the narrow way and with the little flock?

And when this remnant shall have been saved, sanctified and prepared, then will come in all its fullness, the vision of the glory. How sublimely the prophet describes it: "Then the LORD will create over all of Mount Zion and over those who assemble there a cloud of smoke by day and a glow of flaming fire by night; over all the glory will be a canopy. It will be a shelter and shade from the heat of the day, and a refuge and hiding place from the storm and rain" (Isaiah 4:5–6).

It is the old symbolism of the pillar of cloud and fire that led them through the wilderness and the tabernacle round which they gathered before their covenant God; only all this ancient symbolism is to reach a splendor in the coming age such as only the later visions of the New Testament fully unfolded.

The Apostle John describes the vision of this tabernacle in the language of the Apocalypse,

> Now the dwelling of God is with men, and he will live with them. They will be his people, and God himself will be with them and be their God. He will wipe every tear from their eyes. There will be no more death or mourning or crying or pain, for the old order of things has passed away. (Revelation 21:3–4)

> And he who sits on the throne will spread his tent over them.
> Never again will they hunger;
>   never again will they thirst.
> The sun will not beat upon them,
>   nor any scorching heat.
> For the Lamb at the center of the throne will be their shepherd;
>   he will lead them to springs of living water.
> And God will wipe away every tear from their eyes.
>   (7:15b–17)

God bring us to that glorious time and that happy company. Isaiah began his visions of sin and sorrow, of darkness and judgment, with this glorious picture. He could not have stood the darkness if he had not first seen the light. Let us go forth into our mission in this world of sin and sorrow with a vision as bright and clear as the ancient prophet. And when our hearts grow sick with sin and all seems dark and wrong, let us remember the vision and keep saying, "For in just a very little while, He who is coming will come and not delay" (Hebrew 10:37), and the light of that blessed hope will lift us above the shadows of the present evil world and enable us to live under "the powers of the coming age" (6:5).

CHAPTER 4

ISAIAH AND JERUSALEM

W hile the great prophet surveys the whole worldwide horizon and has a message for all nations, yet his special message is to Judah and Jerusalem, and he looks at every other question from the standpoint of the chosen people.

A VISION OF SIN AND JUDGMENT

1. His first message to his own people is a vision of sin and judgment. This occupies the first chapter and is a fearful indictment to the sinful nation, closing with the solemn announcement of judgment which is surely coming.

I will turn my hand against you;
    I will thoroughly purge away your dross
and remove your impurities.
    (Isaiah 1:25)

Zion will be redeemed with justice,
    her penitent ones with righteousness.
But rebels and sinners will both be broken,
    and those who forsake the LORD will perish.
    (1:27–28)

A VISION OF THE LAST DAYS

2. This is followed in the second chapter by a glorious vision of Judah and Jerusalem in the last days.

In the last days

the mountain of the LORD's temple will be established
    as chief among the mountains;

it will be raised above the hills,
    and all nations will stream to it.

Many peoples will come and say,

"Come, let us go up to the mountain of the LORD,
    to the house of the God of Jacob.
He will teach us his ways,
    so that we may walk in His paths."
The law will go out from Zion,
    the word of the LORD from Jerusalem.
He will judge between the nations
    and will settle disputes for many peoples.
They will beat their swords into plowshares
    and their spears into pruning hooks.
Nations will not take up sword against nation,
    nor will they train for war anymore.
      (2:2–4)

The vision of faith does not rest long upon the dark shadows of sin and judgment, but looks onward to the glory of the latter days, "for God's gifts and his call are irrevocable" (Romans 11:29), and Jehovah will not suffer even Judah's sins to frustrate His purpose of blessing.

THE APPROACHING JUDGMENT

3. The prophet's vision next turns to the approaching judgment which is about to fall upon Jerusalem on account of her rebellion and disobedience. This is described in chapter 22:1–12. This message is called "The Burden of the Valley of Vision" and is a vivid picture of the siege of the city by the Assyrians.

What troubles you now,
    that you have gone up on the roofs,
O town full of commotion,
    O city of tumult and revelry?
Your slain were not killed by the sword,
    nor did they die in battle.

Therefore I said, "Turn away from me;
    let me weep bitterly.
Do not try to console me
    over the destruction of my people."

> The Lord, the LORD Almighty, has a day
>> of tumult and trampling and terror
>> in the Valley of Vision,
> a day of battering down walls
>> and of crying out to the mountains.
>> (22:2, 4–5)

The vision is repeated in chapter 29:1–8, where Jerusalem is represented under the name of Ariel; that is, the Lion of God. "Then the hordes of all the nations that fight against Ariel,/ that attack her and her fortress and besiege her,/ will be as it is with a dream,/ with a vision in the night" (29:7).

WARNING ABOUT THE EGYPTIAN ALLIANCE

4. Next we have the warning of Isaiah against the Egyptian alliance in chapter 31:1–3. The prophet foretells the humiliation of Egypt and the confession of the foolish politicians that had leaned on this broken reed, instead of trusting in the Lord. "But Pharaoh's protection will be to your shame,/ Egypt's shade will bring you disgrace./ . . ./ to Egypt whose help is utterly useless./ Therefore I call her/ Rahab the Do-Nothing" (30:3, 7).

> Woe to those who go down to Egypt for help,
>> who rely on horses,
> who trust in the multitude of their chariots
>> and in the great strength of their horsemen,
> but do not look to the Holy One of Israel,
>> or seek help from the LORD.
> Yet he too is wise and can bring disaster;
>> he does not take back his words.
> He will rise up against the house of the wicked,
>> against those who help evildoers.
> But the Egyptians are men and not God;
>> their horses are flesh and not spirit.
> When the LORD stretches out his hand,
>> he who helps will stumble,
>> he who is helped will fall;
>> both will perish together.
>> (31:1–3)

A VISION OF HOPE AND DELIVERANCE

5. But now the vision changes from warning and judgment to hope and deliverance. God sees His people in the distress which they have brought

upon themselves and He flies to their relief.

This is what the LORD says to me:

"As a lion growls,
   a great lion over his prey—
and though a whole band of shepherds
   is called together against him,
he is not frightened by their shouts
   or disturbed by their clamor—
so the LORD Almighty will come down
   to do battle on Mount Zion and on its heights.
Like birds hovering overhead,
   the LORD Almighty will shield Jerusalem;
he will shield it and deliver it,
   he will 'pass over' it and will rescue it."
    (31:4–5)

This, no doubt, refers to the sudden and glorious deliverance of Jerusalem from the army of Sennacherib (37:36). This promise is repeated when the hour of danger comes; and like the answering echo, the word is answered by the deed and the record of promise and deliverance follow each other.

Therefore this is what the LORD says concerning the king of Assyria:

"He will not enter this city
   or shoot an arrow here.
He will not come before it with shield
   or build a siege ramp against it.
By the way that he came he will return;
   he will not enter this city,"
     declares the LORD.
"I will defend this city and save it,
   for my sake and for the sake of David my servant!"

Then the angel of the LORD went out and put to death a hundred and eighty-five thousand men in the Assyrian camp. When the people got up the next morning—there were all the dead bodies! (37:33–36)

THE RETURN FROM CAPTIVITY

6. The prediction of Judah's captivity was left for a later prophet, Jeremiah; but to Isaiah was given the distinguished honor of looking beyond the captivity and foretelling the glorious return of the captive bands from Babylon. Chapter 35:1–10 is the exquisite panorama of this joyful procession. As they passed homeward "the wilderness will rejoice and blossom./ Like the crocus, it will burst into bloom" (35:1).

This beautiful picture has become the panorama of the pilgrim's progress along the heavenly highway to the home above. What a beautiful return it was to the captives of Zion, we learn from the story of Ezra, as he tells us how the fathers that remembered the time when they had left Jerusalem led in chains, wept for joy when they looked once more upon the heights of Zion after the 70 years at Babylon.

In the vision of 44:28 through 45:4, we have a more exact account of the principal circumstances connected with their return at last, with the most important of these circumstances; namely, the fact that it was to come about through Cyrus, king of Persia. That Isaiah should be able to tell us the name of the very man that would be sitting upon the throne of Persia at that time, and that would send back the captives of Jerusalem, is one of the miracles of prophecy. When we realize that this was nearly 200 years before the event occurred, it is not wonderful that the critics, who cannot understand anything supernatural, should feel compelled to conclude that there must have been two Isaiahs, one in the days of Hezekiah and one in the days of Cyrus, who knew what he was talking about, because he was describing the history of his own times. How sublime the picture given of this mighty conqueror, like a pawn in the hands of Jehovah. "For the sake of Jacob my servant, of Israel my chosen, I summon you by name and bestow on you a title of honor, though you do not acknowledge me" (45:4).

Many of the later visions of Isaiah are but echoes of this glad story of Israel's return from Babylon. To the prophet's imagination the vision came with no exact logical or chronological order, but with mingled lights and shades in which events overlapped, and often overleaped each other in sublime confusion, so that the same verse often describes the return of the captives from Babylon, and the restoration of Israel in the last days. As when we gaze at two mountains perspectively, they seem to blend as one mountain, although they may be miles apart; so the vision of the prophet often combines two events far removed in time and yet having common features of resemblance.

THE COMING OF THE MESSIAH

7. The next chapter in the history of Judah was the coming of Messiah

and His rejection by the nation. The light which falls upon this vision in Isaiah is somewhat dim, and yet it is clear enough for us to recognize "the man of sorrows." "He was despised and rejected by men,/ a man of sorrows, and familiar with suffering./ Like one from whom men hide their faces/ he was despised, and we esteemed him not" (53:3). Still later we see Him treading "the winepress alone;/ from the nations no one was with [him]" (63:3). The Apostle Paul quotes from Isaiah with reference to the rejection of Christ by Israel and says, "all day long I have held out my hands/ to a disobedient and obstinate people" (Romans 10:21). The very chapter which most vividly describes the coming of the Messiah, Isaiah 53, begins with a wail of disappointment over the unbelief of the nation, "Who has believed our message/ and to whom has the arm of the LORD been revealed?" (53:1).

THE RESTORATION OF THE PEOPLE

8. But there is a brighter vision in Isaiah—the restoration of the people at the last, through the coming of their Messiah once more and their repentance and return to Him. The Apostle Paul quotes again, from Isaiah 59:20 in his triumphant conclusion in Romans 11:26: "The deliverer will come from Zion; he will turn godlessness away from Jacob./ And this is my covenant with them/ when I take away their sins."

The last five chapters of Isaiah are bright with the promise of the glory of Jerusalem in the latter days. "Arise, shine, for your light has come" (60:1) is the call that summons Zion to her restoration and glorious destiny. Her blessing is to overflow to all the nations.

> The nations will see your righteousness,
>   and all kings your glory. (62:2)

> Behold, I will create
>   new heavens and a new earth.
> The former things will not be remembered,
>   nor will they come to mind.
> But be glad and rejoice forever
>   in what I will create,
> for I will create Jerusalem to be a delight
>   and its people a joy.
>   (65:17–18)

As the apostle expresses it in his profound discussion of the whole question of Israel in Romans 9–11: "For if their rejection is the reconciliation of the world, what will their acceptance be but life from the dead?" (11:15).

CHAPTER 5

ISAIAH AND THE NATIONS

W e cannot properly understand the visions of Isaiah without having a clear conception of the neighboring nations which filled so large a place in contemporary history, and so frequently form the subject of the prophets' messages.

Palestine was situated midway between the two great empires of the world. On the west was Egypt with her tributary states in Africa, generally described under the name of Ethiopia. On the east was Assyria, which was superseded and succeeded later by Babylon. These two mighty empires lived in constant jealousy and conflict, and in the marching and counter-marching of their mighty armies, the intervening states of Western Asia became the constant battleground of the world. These states clustered close to the Mediterranean coast. Chief among them were Judah and Israel. The one with its capital at Jerusalem, shut away to a considerable extent by its inaccessible situation among the hills, was more likely to escape the notice of these passing armies. The other, Israel, with its beautiful capital Samaria in the most fertile part of the valley of Northern Palestine, lay in the very path of these contending armies. Further north were the three powerful kingdoms of Syria, Hamath and Tyre, the great maritime kingdom of antiquity. Around the southern frontier of Judah were Edom, Moab and Arabia. These midway states, exposed as they were to one or the other of the great contending parties, were under the constant temptation of joining forces either with Egypt or Assyria for their own protection. Sometimes their joint action took the form of a mutual alliance between each other against the common foe. The politics of Judah and Israel, therefore, circulated around the question of these alliances. The shrewd politicians of Hezekiah's court were always plotting for some convention, either with Egypt, Assyria or the smaller states. In opposition to this we constantly find Isaiah protesting against all entangling alliances and appealing to the people to remember that God is their national King and able to protect them Himself, without their leaning upon the broken reed of earthly powers. All these states, he tells them, are themselves to be involved ere long in national ruin and their fate will only drag God's people down with them.

We find the early portion of Isaiah's prophecies occupied, therefore, with a series of visions relating to these surrounding nations.

SYRIA

1. In Isaiah 7:1, an alliance between Israel and Syria was made against Jerusalem, and King Ahaz was greatly alarmed. This was the occasion for Isaiah's first vision and message regarding Syria in chapter 8:4. In this message the prophet declares that before the child, which had just been born to him, "Before the boy knows how to say 'My father' or 'My mother,' the wealth of Damascus and the plunder of Samaria will be carried off by the king of Assyria." The vision is renewed in Isaiah 17:1–11, and a fuller description is given of the fall of Damascus and the extinction of Syria. "See, Damascus will no longer be a city/ but will become a heap of ruins./ . . ./ The fortified city will disappear from Ephraim,/ and royal power from Damascus" (17:1b–3). All this came to pass under Shalmaneser in the same invasion in which the 10 tribes were carried away captive and the kingdom of Israel destroyed.

ASSYRIA

Isaiah 10:5–16

2. This is a sublime passage in which Assyria is represented as a proud, vainglorious power which imagines that its victories are through its own strength and through the favor of its idol gods; while it is merely a rod and an axe in the hand of God, used to chasten His people and then broken and thrown away. So Assyria was to be broken too. Again in Isaiah 14:25 the vision is continued, "I will crush the Assyrian in my land;/ on my mountains I will trample him down./ His yoke will be taken from my people,/ and his burden removed from their shoulders."

BABYLON

3. Babylon is the next of these world powers to come in for judgment.

The remarkable feature about the prophet's vision of Babylon is that as yet the mighty Babylonian monarchy had not risen, Babylon being only a province of Assyria. Nearly two centuries were yet to elapse before the destruction of this mighty city, and yet the prophet describes in the minutest details the ruin which came through Cyrus. The ages which followed have only proved how exact was the prophetic picture of Isaiah.

> Therefore I will make the heavens tremble;
>   and the earth will shake from its place

at the wrath of the LORD Almighty,
　　in the day of his burning anger.
Like a hunted gazelle,
　　like sheep without a shepherd,
each will return to his own people,
　　each will flee to his native land.
Whoever is captured will be thrust through;
　　all who are caught will fall by the sword.
Their infants will be dashed to pieces before their eyes;
　　their houses will be looted and their wives ravished.

See, I will stir up against them the Medes,
　　who do not care for silver
　　and have no delight in gold.
Their bows will strike down the young men;
　　they will have no mercy on infants
　　nor will they look with compassion on children.
Babylon, the jewel of kingdoms,
　　the glory of the Babylonians' pride,
will be overthrown by God
　　like Sodom and Gomorrah.
She will never be inhabited
　　or lived in through all generations;
no Arab will pitch his tent there,
　　no shepherd will rest his flocks there.
But desert creatures will lie there,
　　jackals will fill her houses;
there the owls will dwell,
　　and there the wild goats will leap about.
Hyenas will howl in her strongholds,
　　jackals in her luxurious palaces.
Her time is at hand,
　　and her days will not be prolonged.
　　　　(13:13–22)

You will take up this taunt against the king of Babylon:

How the oppressor has come to an end!
　　How his fury has ended!
The LORD has broken the rod of the wicked,
　　the scepter of the rulers,
which in anger struck down peoples

with unceasing blows,
and in fury subdued nations
with relentless aggression.
    (14:4–6)

Edom's streams will be turned into pitch,
    her dust into burning sulfur;
    her land will become blazing pitch!
It will not be quenched night and day;
    its smoke will rise forever.
From generation to generation it will lie desolate;
    no one will ever pass through it again.
The desert owl and screech owl will possess it;
    the great owl and the raven will nest there.
God will stretch out over Edom
    the measuring line of chaos
    and the plumb line of desolation.
Her nobles will have nothing there to be called a kingdom,
    all her princes will vanish away.
Thorns will overrun her citadels,
    nettles and brambles her strongholds.
She will become a haunt for jackals,
    a home for owls.
Desert creatures will meet with hyenas,
    and wild goats will bleat to each other;
there the night creatures will also repose
    and find for themselves places of rest.
The owl will nest there and lay eggs,
    she will hatch them, and care for her young under the shadow
        of her wings;
there also the falcons will gather,
    each with its mate.
    (34:9–15)

MOAB

4. Moab was really a kindred race to Judah and Israel, being descended from Lot through his wicked daughters. Moab was always jealous of Israel and richly deserved the judgment which at last came upon her. Balak, the king of Moab, tried his best to destroy Israel as they passed through the wilderness, and afterwards succeeded through Balaam in bringing them into unholy relations with the daughters of Moab and thus falling under the divine judgment. In the later history of Judah, Moab proved herself a

treacherous foe by standing guard at the fords of the river and refusing to let the fugitives from the destruction of Jerusalem escape. The two chapters, Isaiah 15 and 16, contain "the burden of Moab" and pronounce punishment and ruin upon the people and their cities.

ETHIOPIA

5. The 18th chapter of Isaiah contains the burden of Ethiopia—"the land of whirring wings/ along the rivers of Cush" (18:1). How perfectly this describes that great Eastern Sudan, whose bird-life is fluttering ever upon the air, and whose people have indeed been "tall and smooth-skinned,/ . . . feared far and wide" (18:2). "They will all be left to the mountain birds of prey/ and to the wild animals;/ the birds will feed on them all summer,/ the wild animals all winter" (18:6). But even from this people "gifts will be brought to Mount Zion, the place of the Name of the LORD Almighty" (18:7b).

EGYPT
Isaiah 19:1–25

6. Generally speaking, this prediction is intended to show to the people of Isaiah's time the utter vanity of trusting in the Egyptian alliance, because Egypt herself is to be led away captive by the king of Assyria.

> Then the LORD said, "Just as my servant Isaiah has gone stripped and barefoot for three years, as a sign and portent against Egypt and Cush, so the king of Assyria will lead away stripped and barefoot the Egyptian captives and Cushite exiles, young and old with buttocks bared—to Egypt's shame." (20:3–4)

Thus the confidence of those who had looked for safety in an Egyptian alliance is to be confounded and put to shame. There are some mysterious and remarkable references in the 19th chapter which have been variously interpreted. The 19th verse has been supposed by many to refer to the extraordinary galleries in the great pyramid of Egypt, which are considered by some to be a symbolical picture of the ages and of the plan of redemption. The 22nd verse, "he will strike them and heal them," has been wondrously fulfilled, and the closing verse is, no doubt, prophetic of millennial times when Israel's blessings, as the queen of nations, shall also reach and overflow to Egypt and Assyria.

EDOM
Isaiah 21:11–13

7. Edom was a sort of cousin to Israel, but, like many other secondhand

relations, was more unfriendly than even Israel's enemies. "Someone calls to me from Seir,/ 'Watchman, what is left of the night?/ Watchman, what is left of the night?'/ The watchman replies,/ 'Morning is coming, but also the night./ If you would ask, then ask;/ and come back yet again' " (21:11–12). Edom's watchmen are represented as crying unto the prophetic watchman, "What of the night?" and the answer comes, "Morning is coming, but also the night." For Israel it was to be morning, but for Edom night. How dark the night of Edom history tells us. Travelers today can only find the ruins of that greatness which has forever passed away.

ARABIA
Isaiah 21:13–17

8. The vision of Edom is followed by that of Arabia. Even the scattered tribes of the desert were to share in the awful tide of carnage and war, which the Assyrian was to bring over the whole of western Asia. The glory of Kedar should fail and the traveling companies of Dedanim be scattered abroad.

TYRE
Isaiah 23:1–18

9. The mighty city of commerce and worldwide riches was to be smitten too.

> An oracle concerning Tyre:
>
> Wail, O ships of Tarshish!
>   For Tyre is destroyed
>   and left without house or harbor.
> From the land of Cyprus
>   word has come to them.
>
> Be silent, you people of the island
>   and you merchants of Sidon,
>   whom the seafarers have enriched.
> On the great waters
>   came the grain of the Shihor;
> the harvest of the Nile was the revenue of Tyre,
>   and she became the market place of the nations.
>
> Be ashamed, O Sidon, and you, O fortress of the sea,
>   for the sea has spoken:
> "I have neither been in labor nor given birth;
>   I have neither reared sons nor brought up daughters."

The LORD has stretched out his hand over the sea
 and made its kingdoms tremble.
He has given an order concerning Phoenicia
 that her fortresses be destroyed.
He said, "No more of your reveling,
 O Virgin Daughter of Sidon, now crushed!

"Up, cross over to Cyprus;
 even there you will find no rest."
Look at the land of the Babylonians,
 this people that is now of no account!

At that time Tyre will be forgotten for seventy years, the span
of a king's life. But at the end of these seventy years, it will happen to Tyre as in the song of the prostitute.

At the end of seventy years, the LORD will deal with Tyre. She
will return to her hire as a prostitute and will ply her trade with
all the kingdoms on the face of the earth. Yet her profit and her
earnings will be set apart for the LORD; they will not be stored
up or hoarded. Her profits will go to those who live before the
LORD, for abundant food and fine clothes." (23:1–4, 11–13a,
15, 17–18)

For 70 years Tyre was to be broken and then restored and the day was to
come when even her selfish and godless trade should be consecrated to the
service of the Lord. This represents, no doubt, the general idea of the consecration of wealth and becomes a type for our own times. Oh, that it might
be true today, in this age of commercial selfishness and corruption, that our
"profit" and our "earnings will be set apart for the LORD" (23:18a).

ISRAEL
10. The Northern Kingdom of the 10 tribes also comes in for its message
of judgment.

Woe to that wreath, the pride of Ephraim's drunkards,
 to the fading flower, his glorious beauty,
set on the head of a fertile valley—
 to that city, the pride of those laid low by wine!
See, the Lord has one who is powerful and strong.
 Like a hailstorm and a destructive wind,
like a driving rain and a flooding downpour,

    he will throw it forcefully to the ground.
That wreath, the pride of Ephraim's drunkards,
    will be trampled underfoot.
That fading flower, his glorious beauty,
    set on the head of a fertile valley,
will be like a fig ripe before harvest—
    as soon as someone sees it and takes it in his hand,
    he swallows it."
    (28:1–4)

What a picture of earthliness, drunkenness and prostitution of natural beauty and blessing to selfishness and sin! What a message to this age of luxury and culture! How fearfully all this was at length fulfilled in the fall of Samaria and the ruin of the kingdom of Israel! And how surely the same moral conditions are to bring the same judgment to every godless and sinful people.

CHAPTER 6

THE INCARNATION SIGN

Again the LORD spoke to Ahaz, "Ask the LORD your God for a sign, whether in the deepest depths or in the highest heights."
But Ahaz said, "I will not ask; I will not put the LORD to the test."
Then Isaiah said, "Hear now, you house of David! Is it not enough to try the patience of men? Will you try the patience of my God also? Therefore the Lord himself will give you a sign: The virgin will be with child and will give birth to a son, and will call him Immanuel." (Isaiah 7:10–14)

King Ahaz was in great perplexity and despair. The allied armies of Syria and Israel were invading his land, and he had determined to apply to the great king of Assyria to come to his assistance. While this would undoubtedly bring temporary relief, yet to the farseeing faith of Isaiah it was plain that it would inevitably lead to greater danger in the future, and that as soon as the conqueror had found his way to the Mediterranean coast he would speedily come back to lay his greedy hand upon Judah and Jerusalem too. This was exactly what came to pass. The Assyrian king did go against Damascus and Samaria, and eventually blotted out both kingdoms; but he came back also against Jerusalem before long, and the most terrible dangers and sufferings of the dynasty of David came through the very alliance which Ahaz was now about to make.

The prophet Isaiah therefore threw all the weight of his influence against this proposed alliance with Assyria. Going out to meet the king in one of the public avenues of the suburbs, as he was driving in his chariot with his retinue, he earnestly appealed to him not to be afraid of the two firebrands of Syria and Israel, because God had said, "It will not take place,/ it will not happen" (7:7). As the king hesitated, the prophet appealed to him to ask a sign of God for the encouragement of his weak faith; but the king, persisting in his willful purpose, with mock humility declined, and said, "I will not ask;

I will not put the LORD to the test" (7:12). Then the prophet turned from Ahaz to his attendants, and cried out, "Hear now, you house of David! Is it not enough to try the patience of men? Will you try the patience of my God also? Therefore the Lord himself will give you a sign: The virgin will be with child and will give birth to a son, and will call him Immanuel" (7:13–14).

The local meaning and application of this message has been much discussed by Bible expositors. Many believe that the primary reference was to some woman unmarried at the time, who was afterwards to be married and give birth to a child, in connection, perhaps with the royal family, and that this was to be the immediate sign intended by the prophet, while ultimately the type looked forward to the greater event of the Messiah's birth. It seems unworthy of so great a theme to make any temporary and local application. To apply this prophecy at all to the birth of a child through the ordinary course of nature would throw discredit upon the stupendous miracle of the Savior's supernatural birth at Bethlehem. There seems no reason at all to attempt any other fulfillment than that which actually did occur when Christ was born of the virgin in the fullness of time.

The only objection seems to be that the prophet appeared to expect this event immediately. But in the perspective of prophecy it has always been the case that such events loomed so large that they appeared nearer than they actually were. The prophecies of our Lord's second coming in the New Testament read as though the writers expected the Lord to come during their own lifetime, and yet nearly 2,000 years have rolled away and the actual event is not yet. Like some vast mountain, which looms so high as you approach that it seems just before you, although it is scores of miles away, so the coming of the Messiah, more than seven centuries distant, appeared to Isaiah's vision to be just at hand.

We do not hesitate, therefore, in applying this verse directly to the birth of Jesus Christ in Bethlehem. The prophetic announcement of this event in itself is almost as great a miracle as the Incarnation itself. So supernatural was the conception of one born of a virgin that it is said the translators of the Hebrew Scriptures into the Septuagint tried to find some other word than "virgin," and to substitute the word "woman." They felt that the Greek scholars of Alexandria and the common sense of the world would laugh at the idea of the Virgin Born.

This bold and naked prophecy, standing out like a mountain crag 750 years before the event in the writings of the greatest of the Hebrew prophets, is in itself a sublime witness to Jesus Christ, which to the present time the Jew is unable to explain away. A French scholar has said that the story of Jesus Christ as a human invention would have been more wonderful than the actual events of His history. If it was an invention, who is the stupendous genius that created this transcendent work of literature? We know the author of the *Iliad*, of Milton's *Paradise Lost* and of other great works of literature, but who is the great Unknown that gave to the ages the book of Jesus of Nazareth? Nay, the story is as marvelous as the Christ. And so this prophecy of Isaiah stands out as a finger pointing to Bethlehem, and as the prophet here expressed it God's great "sign."

In what sense is Jesus, and especially the Incarnation of Jesus, God's sign to Israel and the world?

THE PROPHETIC ANNOUNCEMENT

1. As already indicated, the prophetic announcement, coupled with its extraordinary fulfillment as recorded in the Gospels, is a convincing sign and demonstration that Jesus Christ is indeed the Messiah, and that Christianity must be divine. It is not merely the gospel story which establishes this, but the extraordinary fact that more than seven centuries before the greatest of the Hebrew prophets had declared to an unbelieving age that this very thing should occur. The prophecy was not understood at the time, and was an inexplicable riddle to the Jewish rabbis. The very strangeness of the announcement makes it all the more impossible for it to have been a collusion or a merely human utterance. And the exact correspondence, later, of the fact with the prediction gives to the miraculous birth of our Lord an emphasis which, to a candid inquirer, is simply beyond criticism.

HIS INTEREST IN THE HUMAN RACE

2. The Incarnation is God's sign to Israel and the world of His interest in the human race and in the chosen people. The translation of the prophetic name "Immanuel" expresses all this in a single sentence—"God with us." What stronger assurance can we ask of the divine love and care? It was the dying message of John Wesley, "The best of all is, 'God with us.'" So great did this manifestation of the divine love seem to Zacharias that it unsealed his dumb lips and called forth the joyful cry, "Praise be to the Lord, the God of Israel,/ because he has come and has redeemed his people" (Luke 1:68).

The dream of ancient mythology was the coming down of the gods into human form and human life. But the Incarnation has brought us the everlasting union of the Deity with our fallen race. God has committed Himself to humanity and has taken up humanity into Deity, and through endless ages a Man shall sit upon the throne of the universe and share with the infinite God all His attributes and glories.

One of the rulers of Egypt, it is said, was rearing a valuable obelisk upon its base. At the last moment, in order to impress the engineer with the importance of his responsibility, he fastened his only son to the summit of the obelisk, and then pointing to it said, "Be careful, the life of the heir hangs upon the fate of the obelisk."

In an infinitely higher sense, God has attached the very life of His own dear Son to the fortunes of this world. Jesus Christ is so identified with man that our failure would be His failure, and He cannot afford to let us fail. Just as your child is part of your very life and cannot cease to be your child, so we belong to God, and God is bound by His own very nature to guard our interests and guarantee our glorious destiny.

Speaking of this in the epistle to the Hebrews, the inspired apostle says:

> Both the one who makes men holy and those who are made holy are of the same family. So Jesus is not ashamed to call them brothers. . . .
>
> Since the children have flesh and blood, he too shared in their humanity so that by his death he might destroy him who holds the power of death—that is, the devil—and free those who all their lives were held in slavery by their fear of death. For surely it is not angels he helps, but Abraham's descendants. For this reason he had to be made like his brothers in every way, in order that he might become a merciful and faithful high priest in service to God, and that he might make atonement for the sins of the people. (2:11, 14–17)

THE SUPERNATURAL CHARACTER OF CHRISTIANITY

3. The Incarnation is the sign of the supernatural character of Christianity. Two schools of thought divide the minds of men, the one is evolution, the other is the supernatural. The tendency of unbelief today is to explain everything on the principles of rationalism. The whole character of the gospel is opposed to this. It is not a development; it is not the improvement of moral and social conditions through culture. It is a revolution rather than an evolution and the apostle's words are true of the whole process of redemption. "Therefore, if anyone is in Christ, he is a new creation; the old has gone, the new has come. All this is from God" (2 Corinthians 5:17–18a).

Even Isaac, the type of the great Messiah, could not come in the ordinary course of nature, but the promise had to wait until Abraham and Sarah had outlived their natural strength and the birth of the seed of promise was through a physical miracle in their own bodies. Still more manifestly was the Messiah Himself born, not through natural generation, but through the miraculous power of the Holy Spirit.

But the supernatural did not cease there. Christianity is divine from first to last. The resurrection and ascension of Jesus Christ were the fitting climaxes of His miraculous birth and the conversion of every follower of the Savior is a miracle just as divine. "I tell you the truth, no one can enter the kingdom of God unless he is born of water and the Spirit" (John 3:5). Sanctification, too, is not a mere process of self-denial and spiritual endeavor, but it is a miracle of the indwelling Christ incarnate again in every believer.

Prayer is just an open door through which the Deity still interposes in the affairs of human life. And the great consummation is to come, not in the gradual uplift of human society through the forces of civilization, but in "the new Jerusalem coming down out of heaven from God" (Revelation 21:2), and an age of righteousness and glory that will only come with the coming of the King Himself. The Virgin Birth in Bethlehem was God's great sign of all of this.

A REVERSAL OF ALL MAN'S IDEAS

4. The Incarnation was a reversal of all man's ideas of character, goodness and greatness. Other kings are born amid the acclamations of the multitude and crowned with earthly state and splendid pageantry. Other systems of thought tell us about self-exaltation, self-reliance and self-assertion. Christianity begins with self-renunciation. The first step is downward. The only pathway to ascension and glory is the way of humiliation. "Whoever humbles himself will be exalted" (Matthew 23:12b). "Just as the Son of Man did not come to be served, but to serve, and to give his life a ransom for many" (20:28).

The apostle has given us the great pattern in the second chapter of Philippians,

> Your attitude should be the same as that of Christ Jesus: Who, being in very nature God, did not consider equality with God something to be grasped, but made himself nothing, taking the very nature of a servant, being made in human likeness. And being found in appearance as a man, he humbled himself and became obedient to death—even death on a cross! Therefore God exalted him to the highest place and gave him the name that is above every name, that at the name of Jesus every knee should bow, in heaven and on earth and under the earth, and every tongue confess that Jesus Christ is Lord, to the glory of God the Father. (2:5–11)

HIS OWN CHARACTER AND WILL

5. The Incarnation is God's sign and revelation of His own character and will concerning men.

Therefore in connection with His incarnation our Lord is called "The

Word." "The Word became flesh and made his dwelling among us. We have seen his glory, the glory of the One and Only, who came from the Father, full of grace and truth" (John 1:14). Christ as the Word is the expression of God's character and will toward men. Christ is the Answer to all our questions and the personal Messenger of God to men. "In the past God spoke to our forefathers through the prophets at many times and in various ways, but in these last days he has spoken to us by his Son" (Hebrews 1:1–2). The blessed Babe of Bethlehem, the loving Friend of sinners, the Teacher who unfolded such wondrous words of grace, He was but the voice of the mysterious Being whom human hearts so long have dreaded. "Anyone who has seen me has seen the Father. . . . The words I say to you are not just my own. Rather, it is the Father, living in me, who is doing his work" (John 14:9b–10). Would you know how God feels toward sinners, sufferers and helpless mortals? Jesus is the Answer speaking more loudly than words, for He is "the way and the truth and the life" (14:6).

REVEALING THE HEARTS OF MEN

6. The Incarnate Christ is God's sign in another sense, namely: as revealing the hearts of men. This was what Simeon prophesied to Mary when he blessed her Baby in the temple, "This Child is destined to cause the falling and rising of many in Israel, and to be a sign that will be spoken against, so that the thoughts of many hearts will be revealed" (Luke 2:34b–35a).

Human character and destiny are revealed by contact with Jesus Christ. Men are not saved or lost merely by moral character, but by their attitude toward the Son of God. As of old He hung on Calvary between two men that represented at once both heaven and hell, so still it is true that the cross of Jesus is the dividing line between lost and saved men. "On either side one and Jesus in the midst." On which side are you? Your present character and eternal destiny are to be decided by your attitude toward Him.

THE CONDITION AND GUARANTEE

7. Jesus Christ is a sign in the sense that He is the condition and guarantee of all God's promises and covenants. "For no matter how many promises God has made, they are 'Yes' in Christ. And so through him the 'Amen' " (2 Corinthians 1:20). He is the Surety and Guarantor of every claim we have upon God. Just as the endorsement of the bank official passes your draft, so every petition we present in the high court of heaven must bear the sign of His name. We are chosen in Him. We are made accepted in Him. We are complete in Him. The Father sees us only in Him. In His name we pray and receive the answer to our prayers. People often want to ask a sign from God that their prayers are heard and some important petition granted. We need no other sign than Christ Himself. His smile, His manifested Presence, His

loving acceptance, guarantee every other blessing. Having Him, we may well add, "He who did not spare his own Son, but gave him up for us all—how will he not also, along with him, graciously give us all things" (Romans 8:32).

A man of wealth had died intestate and no trace could be found of any will. At last his house was being sold at auction and all its contents. Among the various articles was a picture of his only son, for which nobody seemed to care but a poor old woman who had nursed him when a baby. Eagerly she bought it for a pittance and when she took it home and began to clean the dusty frame she found inside of it the old man's will, bequeathing all his fortune to the person who loved his son well enough to buy his picture. And so the old lady got the fortune because she loved the son.

Our highest claim upon God is that we are dear to the heart of Jesus Christ, and He is dear to us.

THE DEEPEST MYSTERY

8. The Incarnation of Jesus Christ signifies above all else the deepest mystery of Christian life, namely, the incarnation of Christ in the consecrated heart. True indeed it is, as the old monk sings:

> Though Christ a thousand times in Bethlehem be born,
> If He's not born in thee, thy heart is still forlorn;
> The Christ on Golgotha can never save thy soul,
> The Christ in thine own heart alone can make thee whole.

We cannot better express this than in the following eloquent words from an article by Dr. Henry Wilson:

> A piece of tin may reflect the light near which it is placed. The glass surrounding the light radiates the light within.
>
> Just so we many become reflectors of Jesus Christ by coming to Him, following Him closely, imitating His life by the grace of His Holy Spirit, "enabling" us so to do; and further we may in a beautiful and true sense be changed by thus constantly "looking unto" and into the face of Jesus.
>
> "We all with unveiled face reflecting as a mirror the glory of the Lord are transformed (transfigured) into the same image from glory to glory, even as from the Lord the Spirit" (II. Cor. iii. 18, R.V.).
>
> But surely the deeper thought and the deeper life is radiating as a lamp the light and life of an indwelling Christ. Paul himself, who, in the passage just quoted, gives us the reflector side of the

truth, gives us in Galatians ii. 20, and many another passage, such as II. Corinthians vi. 16: "I will dwell in them and walk in them," the radiating side of the deepest variety of the Christian life—the power of an indwelling Lord, Jesus Christ.

Moses, from whom the last text is quoted, was himself the best example of a soul reflecting the glory, when he came down from the mount with the skin of his face shining with the light in which he had been living during those wonderful forty days in communion with God.

But a greater than Moses is the highest example of His own indwelling when He came down from another mount, and "His face did shine as the sun" (Matt. xvii. 2, and cf. Rev. i. 16), not reflecting, but radiating the light of the knowledge of the glory of God (II. Cor. iv. 6).

A locomotive is standing on the track, just completed; painted, polished, perfect in every part, and the sun at midday shining upon it and making every bit of brass and steel a burnished blaze of glory. But no motion, except that which comes from without as the workmen painfully "pinch" it forward inch by inch with crowbars.

Another engine is within the shed, grimy and stained with the wear and tear of many a journey. But the fire is lighted in the furnace; the water in the boiler reaches 212 degrees; steam begins to pass into the cylinders; the piston moves; the wheels turn; the engine goes forward. Not by external pressure, but by the force of an energizing power within.

These two illustrations, the lamp radiating and not reflecting light; and the engine moved from within and not from without, may serve to make the difference between the two great schools of teaching on this subject.

Three words similar in sound may also serve to accent the difference in degree, if not in kind, between these modes of presenting "the truth as it is in Jesus"—*imitation, inspiration, incarnation* of Christ.

For each view abundance of Scripture might be quoted, but our purpose is to emphasize the last as the highest and deepest of all.

Incarnations and reincarnations are words much used these days and in various senses. To us as Bible Christians the only incarnation worthy of the name is that which took place in Bethlehem of Judea nearly two thousand years ago, and the only reincarnation in which we believe is that which takes place in the heart first and then in the life of all who are "born from above" in the sense in which Jesus used the words to Nicodemus in the third chapter of St. John; Christmas Day repeated daily in human lives; Christ reborn, reincarnated in lowly hearts and yielded bodies; the whole Christ in the whole man,

"A living, bright reality."

A TYPE AND PLEDGE OF THE ADVENT

9. Finally, the Incarnation is a type and pledge of the Advent. The Christ of Bethlehem will soon be the Christ of glory. He who came in humble stall and manger bed is coming in a little while in power and glory, but it will still be the same human form and the same loving Christ. And it is only as we know Him in His fullness that we will be welcomed by Him then to a place upon His throne. Blessed Christ, so near, so one. God grant that He may be all this, dear reader, to you and me.

No distant Lord have I,
   Loving afar to be,
Made flesh for me, He cannot rest
   Until He rests in me.

Brother in joy or pain,
   Bone of my bone is He,
More than my nearest, closest friend,
   He dwells Himself in me.

Oh, glorious Son of God,
   Incarnate Deity,
I shall forever dwell with Thee
   Because Thou art in me.

CHAPTER 7

THE WONDERFUL NAME

For to us a child is born,
*   to us a son is given,*
*   and the government will be on his shoulders.*
And he will be called
*   Wonderful Counselor, Mighty God,*
*   Everlasting Father, Prince of Peace.*
Of the increase of his government and peace
*   there will be no end.*
He will reign on David's throne
*   and over his kingdom,*
establishing and upholding it
*   with justice and righteousness*
*   from that time on and forever.*
The zeal of the LORD Almighty
*   will accomplish this.*
*   (Isaiah 9:6–7)*

W e have in this chapter a picture of darkness and dawn, and out of the dawn the rising of the Sun of righteousness.

SECTION I—*The Darkness*

The fifth and eighth chapters both close with a vision of gloom. The ninth chapter takes it up with special reference to "the land of Zebulon and Naphtali," Galilee of the Gentiles, and refers especially to the afflictions of this region in contrast with the great light that afterwards rose upon it. The translation in the first verse of the ninth chapter is quite unsatisfactory. The Revised Version is much better: "But there shall be no gloom to her that was in anguish. In the former time He brought into contempt the land of

Zebulon and the land of Naphtali, but in the latter time hath He made it glorious by the way of the sea beyond Jordan, Galilee of the nations. The people that walked in darkness have seen a great light; they that dwelt in the land of the shadow of death upon them hath the light shined" (9:1–2).

The Gospel of Matthew refers especially to this prediction (4:13–16) in explanation of the fact that the Lord Jesus began His ministry in this region which had formerly been the most blighted section of all the land. The reason why this region was so severely afflicted was because of its nearness to the Syrian and Assyrian conquerors who swept over the land in their periodical invasions. They always struck this section first, and then, when returning, carried with them its captured population in their cruel and victorious train.

After the fall of Samaria and the subjugation of the northern kingdom, this whole country was settled with immigrants from Assyria, and these colonists gradually became mixed with the former inhabitants, so that the moral and spiritual condition of the land sank lower than its external state.

But the darkness of Galilee was but a sample of the deep gloom that rests upon every section of the world where the light of Christ's Gospel has not come. That pall of darkness rests today on every heathen nation. How dark are their conceptions of our God and Father! How false are their ideals for righteousness and holiness! How hopeless and comfortless is their sorrow and how black the despair that rests upon the vision of the future! The old Saxon sage expressed it well. One night as they sat in the banqueting hall, a little bird came fluttering in from the darkness and flew for a little through the lighted chamber, passing out at the other end into the darkness again. The old sage turned to the company, that was even then discussing whether to receive the Christian missionaries into their land or not, and said, "Our life is like this picture that we have just seen. We come out of the darkness into existence and flutter a little in the light of life, and then we pass out of the light into the same darkness again. We know not whence we come or whither we go; surely we need some one to bring us the light." So dark, so desolate is this sad world without the knowledge of Jesus Christ.

Just as the night lamp seems to make the midnight darker beyond its radiance, so the gladness of our Christmas days and our gospel privileges only seem to bring into more vivid relief the fearful gloom of a Christless world. How sad to think that still two-thirds of its vast population are sunk in just such darkness, while we are rejoicing in the light of Bethlehem, Calvary and the blessed hope of His coming again.

SECTION II—*The Dawn*

The people walking in darkness
have seen a great light;

on those living in the land of the shadow of death
   a light has dawned.
You have enlarged the nation
   and increased their joy;
they rejoice before you
   as people rejoice at the harvest,
as men rejoice
   when dividing the plunder.
      (9:2–3)

The coming of Jesus Christ has indeed brought a great light into this dark world. When He taught us to say "Our Father in heaven" (Matthew 6:9), the whole heaven became illumined with the vision of a God of Love; and all the mummeries of idolatry, like the shadows of the night, shrank away before the rising dawn. The world's best wisdom has no such conception of God. In all the writings of the sages, in all the libraries of the world, there is nothing to compare with the parable of the prodigal son and the good shepherd, or with these three promises from the lips of Jesus:

Come to me, all you who are weary and burdened, and I will give you rest. (11:28)

Whoever hears my word and believes him who sent me has eternal life and will not be condemned; he has crossed over from death to life. (John 5:24)

In My Father's house are many rooms; if it were not so, I would have told you. I am going there to prepare a place for you. And if I go and prepare a place for you, I will come back and take you to be with me that you also may be where I am. (14:2–3)

The best light that Jesus gives, however, is what He calls the "light of life," the light that shows us how to walk and gives us strength so to walk. "I am the light of the world. Whoever follows me will never walk in darkness, but will have the light of life" (8:12).

And, oh, the glorious light that He has shed beyond the grave, for "Christ Jesus, who has destroyed death and has brought life and immortality to light through the gospel" (2 Timothy 1:10).

Ancient superstition hung up little lamps in the tombs of the dead, but their faint glimmer only deepened the gloom of Christless despair. The resurrection of Christ has dispelled the darkness of the grave and made the future of every child of God as bright as heaven. In that blessed light we have learned to dry our tears of mourning and to go forth ourselves into the seeming gloom with a shout of victory. " 'Where, O death, is your victory?/ Where, O death, is your sting?'/ . . . But thanks be to God! He gives us the victory through our Lord Jesus Christ" (1 Corinthians 15:55, 57).

What follows in Isaiah 9:4–7 is a fine picture of the new order of things which the Savior is to introduce. Reading again from the Revised Version we quote, "For the yoke of his burden and the staff his shoulder, the rod of his oppressor Thou hast broken as in the day of Midian; for all the armor of the armed man in the tumult and the garments rolled in blood shall forever be for burning, for fuel of fire. For unto us a child is born, unto us a Son is given, and the government shall be upon His shoulder . . . " The idea is that the coming of this King is to change the old order of the world. The weapons of war will be burned to ashes, the din of strife will pass away in the sweet music of the gospel, and the Prince of Peace will begin His everlasting reign. Instead of the battle with confused noise and garments rolled in blood is to be the birth of the heavenly Babe and the kingdom of the Prince of Peace. A new order of forces is to be established upon the earth, and a King of meekness shall supersede the tyrants of bloody oppression and brutal war.

The very center of the light, He is to dawn upon this dark world as the Sun of Righteousness Himself, the blessed Christ who forms the center of the prophet's vision and whose birth ushers in a new day in the annals of time.

SECTION III—*The Sun of Righteousness*

THE CHILD

1. The birth of a child was a very significant thing for every Jewish mother and every Hebrew household. From that early hour when Eve forgot her maternal anguish in the joy of her firstborn's smile, and cried out, "With the help of the LORD I have brought forth a man" (Genesis 4:1), the highest hope of every Hebrew woman was to be the mother of the Messiah. This deep national instinct could well understand the exulting cry of the prophet, "For to us a child is born,/ to us a son is given" (Isaiah 9:6). It was true to nature as well as redemption, and it carried in its bosom a deeper and larger truth than even their Messianic hopes could comprehend, for that Holy Child has lifted every other child into new dignity and importance, and forever has made the child-spirit the true type of the heavenly character.

The childhood of Jesus Christ was one of the charming and attractive features in all His humiliation. Adam, the first of men, stepped upon the threshold a full-grown man, but Adam fell, and dragged the race down with him to ruin and sorrow. Jesus Christ came along the feeble steps of infancy and traversed every stage of the pilgrimage of man from the cradle to the grave; and Jesus has not failed. So dear to Him and to the thought of God is this feature of His character that even amid the exaltation of His heavenly throne, He is still worshiped as "thy Holy Child Jesus" (Acts 4:30, KJV). There is something in Him which is as simple as childhood, and He Himself has said, "And whoever welcomes a little child like this in my name welcomes me" (Matthew 18:5). In some mysterious sense a little child is the truest image both of the Father and the Son.

THE KING

2. This Child was born to be a king. "The government will be on his shoulders" (Isaiah 9:6). This means not only the government of the universe but the government of our lives. He is the true Sovereign, and the only One that can ever rule this world so as to realize for it its true ideal of blessing. Man has tried the government of monarchies and they have all failed. He is again trying the government of democracies, and they will also fail. The last vision in the Apocalypse is a lot of commonwealths without crowns, and they are all arrayed against the Lord. No, republicanism is not going to do it any more than despotism. The true King is God's Holy Child Jesus, of whom the older prophet had already sung,

> He will judge your people in righteousness,
> your afflicted ones with justice.
> (Psalm 72:2)

> In his days the righteous will flourish;
> prosperity will abound till the moon is no more.
> (72:7)

> His rule will extend from sea to sea
> and from the River to the ends of the earth.
> (Zechariah 9:10b)

> All kings will bow down to him
> and all nations will serve him.
> (Psalm 72:11)

Is He your King? Have you committed the government of your life to His hands and crowned Him "Lord of all"?

THE WONDERFUL

3. "He will be called Wonderful" (Isaiah 9:6). The Hebrew word literally means "a miracle." The idea underlying the verse is the supernatural. His birth was supernatural, but all His works and ways are to be supernatural,

too. He has projected into human history a higher plane, and under His administration we are to expect not the ordinary laws of cause and effect, but the transcendent working of an Almighty hand, superior to all methods and means and prepared to interpose the supernatural wherever it is needed for the accomplishment of the great purposes of His redemption. What an inspiring thought this is! We so easily fall into the old ruts and get accustomed to the trend of things that we forget that the very idea of Christianity is something above the common, beyond the natural order of things, and involving the wonderful working of our God.

Is this Wonderful One in your life? Have you anything supernatural in your religion? Is your salvation a new creation and a miracle of grace? Is your spiritual life superhuman and divine? Has He touched your body with His miraculous power? Have you looked to Him to answer your prayers, to overcome your difficulties and to use your ministries by His wonderful providence and His almighty Spirit, so that your life will be a supernatural witness to that supernatural Book which the devil is trying today to reduce to a mere collection of human documents and ancient literature? The very point of the conflict that is going on today touches this question. Satan, with the help of modern scholarship, is trying to eliminate the supernatural from the Bible, from the story of Jesus of Nazareth and from the church of God. Our young people are being educated in the schools today to apply the doctrine of evolution to everything and to discard the miraculous story of creation and all that is accessory to it. Oh, that we might rise to the issue, and by a supernatural faith and a supernatural life might prove to the world that this Book is indeed supernatural and divine, and that His name is truly Wonderful!

THE COUNSELOR

4. The greatest of Israel's kings, was greatest in his wisdom, but "a greater than Solomon" is here. The royal Babe of Bethlehem is the wisdom of God. Nothing is more wonderful in the life of our Lord than the quiet, instinctive wisdom with which He met every situation and every difficulty. No victory was more impressive than that last day in the temple court, when the Pharisees, Sadducees, Herodians and others came to Him in succession, determined to confuse Him with their fractious questioning. But with calm, imperturbable wisdom He silenced them one by one, until they were glad to slink away from His majestic presence, and "from then on no one dared ask him any more questions" (Mark 12:34).

The blessed Counselor is not only wise for Himself, but He is able to give us wisdom. How often a single step in life is the turning point of blessing for all the future. To know just what to do is so important. All night long the disciples toiled at their nets and got nothing, but when the morning came all they needed was just one word of guidance, "Throw your net on the right side of the boat and you will find some" (John 21:6) and lo! the fishes came crowding to their nets.

Jesus Christ is our Counselor, and if we surrender our fancied wisdom and trust His guidance, we will not be allowed to err but will be guided in judgment and kept from stumbling.

THE MIGHTY GOD

5. This King is no mere human potentate, but the omnipotent One. All His power is at the service of His people, but His power must be claimed by faith and prayer. Do we know Him in His almightiness, and have we allowed Him to clothe us with His mighty power and make our lives efficient through His strength?

THE FATHER OF ETERNITY

6. This is the correct translation of the phrase. It does not mean that He takes the place of the Father among the persons of the Deity, because He is not the Father, but He is the Father of eternity; that is to say, all His plans and purposes are everlasting, and when we take Him in our lives all our ways take hold on eternity. Earthly kings must pass away. The very benignity of the reign of a Josiah only made his death the more distressing. But the King is everlasting, and when we receive Him, He makes our lives eternal, too. How sad to think of friendships formed only to be severed, plans conceived and executed only to be buried in the tomb, and results that are as ephemeral as our mortal lives! How sublime the Psalmist's prayer, "Lead me in the way everlasting" (139:24)! This is what the Father of eternity will do for us:

> Take from us the things that wither and decay,
> Give to us the things that cannot pass away,
> And lead us in the way everlasting.

THE PRINCE OF PEACE

7. This is His sweetest gift, "Peace I leave with you; my peace I give you" (John 14:27). This is His bequest to us, and the prophet tells "of the increase of His government and peace there will be no end" (Isaiah 9:7).

Shall we take Him for the increase of His peace, and in order that we may have it, shall we also give Him the increase of the government? So shall we find as we surrender to Him all our life that He will make real to us His gracious promise, "Take my yoke upon you and learn from me, for I am gentle and humble in heart, and you will find rest for your souls" (Matthew 11:29).

CHAPTER 8

THE PARABLE OF THE VINEYARD

I will sing for the one I love
a song about his vineyard.
(Isaiah 5:1)

The fifth chapter of Isaiah is a sort of parable in poetry and song very similar to one of the parables of our Lord, as recorded in the 21st chapter of Matthew. This parable was followed by a series of woes addressed by Christ to the Scribes and Pharisees (Matthew 23:13–29), just as Isaiah's parable of the vineyard is followed by a similar series of woes (Isaiah 5:8–22).

SECTION I—*The Vineyard*

He describes the selection of the site on a very fruitful hill. Later, in the seventh verse, he tells us that the vineyard of the Lord of hosts is the house of Israel. The fruitful hill, where He planted this vineyard, was Mount Zion. "He fenced it" (5:2, KJV). This, no doubt refers to His separation of Israel from the nations, the restrictions and safeguards He placed around them through the law and ordinances which He gave to them and the peculiar isolation of the land and the people from all other peoples.

He "planted it with the choicest vines" (5:2). This refers to the oracles of God, the Word of revelation which He gave to them and all the covenant privileges and blessings which He committed to them. The tower and the winepress which follow are part of the picture of the vineyard and still further refer to God's provision for the spiritual culture of the chosen people and the blessed fruit which He expected to come from the love and grace invested among them. This is no new figure, but a very familiar one in the Old Testament. "You brought a vine out of Egypt" (Psalm 80:8), says the Psalmist,

you drove out the nations and planted it.
You cleared the ground for it,
   and it took root and filled the land.
The mountains were covered with its shade,
   the mighty cedars with its branches.
It sent out its boughs to the Sea,
   its shoots as far as the River.

Why have you broken down its walls
   so that all who pass by pick its grapes?
Boars from the forest ravage it
   and the creatures of the field feed on it.
      (80:8–13)

So Jesus uses the same figure of His own people, "I am the vine, you are the branches" (John 15:5). The richest and most valuable of all the products of nature is used to represent the richest of God's graces to His people. But just as the devil has perverted the vine of the earth to the basest and most destructive purposes, so the vine of the Lord's planting has been assailed by the adversary and turned aside from its divine purposes through the unfaithfulness of men.

SECTION II—*The Wild Grapes*

And so the prophet quickly turns from the beautiful vision of the divine Husbandman and His care for His vineyard, to the failure of the vineyard. "Then he looked for a crop of good grapes,/ but it yielded only bad fruit" (Isaiah 5:2b). The peculiarity of the wild grape is that it is purely natural, an ungrafted fruit. Therefore it represents most fittingly the quality of all mere natural and human goodness. Human nature can only produce wild grapes; luxuriant and beautiful the vine may seem, but the fruit is worthless. So are all the fruits and graces that grow upon the stalk of humanity. It is only when it is cut back and Christ is grafted into the stalk of our old human nature that there is any good in us. All the failures of the Old Testament were intended to demonstrate this fact. Yet, still men are looking for the development of goodness through education and Christian endeavor, instead of through fellowship with the cross of Jesus Christ and entering into His death and resurrection life.

The prophet then proceeds to describe these wild grapes by a series of woes which differentiate and distinguish the various forms of sin in a picture which is as true today as it was in the days of Isaiah.

THE SIN OF GREED

1. The first of these is greed. Each of these specifications begins with a woe. "Woe to you who add house to house/ and join field to field/ till no space is left/ and you live alone in the land" (5:8). The spirit of monopoly had begun in Isaiah's time, and the men of great wealth were buying up the whole land and laying it out in vast estates, so that the common people were crowded out of house and home, and the soil that the Creator gave for the support of the people was being used for the luxury of the proud.

Isaiah was not a socialist, but the whole spirit of divine legislation is against selfishness, greed and monopoly. It is no sin to be wealthy, but it is a fearful sin to absorb wealth in the spirit of greed and spend it in selfish luxury. A true citizen will always regard his wealth as a trust for society and his fellowmen. There is nothing more alarming in the spirit of our times than the colossal fortunes that are built up and the selfish and godless use that is being made of them by so many.

The Apostle James tells us that these are the signs of the last days. "You have hoarded wealth in the last days" (James 5:3c).

THE SINS OF SENSUALITY

2. Next there is selfish and sensual pleasure and unreasonable and unseasonable indulgence in appetite and sensual enjoyment. "Woe to those who rise early in the morning/ to run after their drinks,/ who stay up late at night/ till they are inflamed with wine./ They have harps and lyres at their banquets,/ tambourines and flutes and wine,/ but they have no regard for the deeds of the LORD,/ no respect for the work of his hands" (Isaiah 5:11–12).

It is not so much the sin of drunkenness that is here condemned as the sin of pleasure seeking, of which drinking is a part. These devotees of self-indulgence give up the whole day as well as the whole night to feasting. The effect of this voluptuous life is the deadening of conscience and all spiritual life. "They have no regard for the deeds of the LORD,/ no respect for the work of his hands." It was the same condition of brutal sensuality which the prophet Amos denounced in the Northern Kingdom,

> You lie on beds inlaid with ivory
> and lounge on your couches.
> You dine on choice lambs
> and fattened calves.
> You strum away on your harps like David
> and improvise on musical instruments.
> You drink wine by the bowlful
> and use the finest lotions,

but you do not grieve over the ruin of Joseph.
(Amos 6:4–6)

A life of self-indulgence deadens every high and holy feeling of the heart and makes men selfish and indifferent to God and the claims of their fellow-men. They rest in their delicious dream of security, until suddenly the sky darkens, the crash comes and the fearful picture of Isaiah is fulfilled. "Therefore the grave enlarges its appetite/ and opens its mouth without limit;/ into it will descend their nobles and masses/ with all their brawlers and revelers" (Isaiah 5:14).

THE SIN OF PRESUMPTION

3. Then there is the sin of presumption. "Woe to those who draw sin along with cords of deceit,/ and wickedness as with cart ropes,/ to those who say, 'Let God hurry,/ let him hasten his work/ so we may see it./ Let it approach,/ the plan of the Holy One of Israel come,/ so we may know it' " (5:18–19). These are the scoffers who the Apostle Peter says shall come in the last days saying, "where is this 'coming' he promised?" (2 Peter 3:4).

They were abroad in Isaiah's time. They made light of the prophet's message and the prophet's word. They put aside all finer fears and feelings and drew iniquity with cords of vanity and sin with cart rope. They hardened their hearts in brutal atheism and laughed at the idea of God, righteousness and judgment to come. They saw no sign of the coming tempest, and in their fool's paradise they went on in reckless defiance of God and man. So still, men sometimes harden their necks against the warnings of heaven. God sits in the heavens and laughs, for He sees that their day is coming. It does not often happen that these reckless men are permitted to repent. Like Korah, Dathan and Abiram in the days of Moses, they are permitted to work out to the full judgment of heaven.

FALSE TEACHING AND PERVERTED MORAL IDEAS

4. Next we see false teaching and perverted moral ideas. "Woe to those who call evil good/ and good evil,/ who put darkness for light/ and light for darkness,/ who put bitter for sweet/ and sweet for bitter" (Isaiah 5:20). This is another class of moral evils. It is a very subtle form of sin and a very serious one. It is the false philosophy, poetry and religion that come as angels of light and aim at the perversion of the human conscience and the obliteration of all true convictions of right and wrong. It insidiously seeks to undermine virtue by painting in the poetry of passion the charms of license and the delights of sin. It makes the beautiful, rather than the true, the aim of life and subverts the stern authority of God's Holy Word and makes it all a myth and allegory.

It is abroad today in the poetry of passion, in the popular novel, in the meretricious theater, in the suggestiveness of fashion, in the easy manners of society, in the mixed conditions of the church itself, in the false teachings of Romanism cloaking over sin through ecclesiastical indulgence, in the gauzy sophistries of Christian Science, which do away with all real moral principles; and still more, it is present in the unholy mysteries of Theosophy, Spiritualism and occult science that are pouring over us from the Orient with its filthy tide. Our modern literature, our modern plays, our modern society are full of it. The word sin is being eliminated from the popular ethics of our day, and compromise, expediency and sentimentalism are taking the place of God's eternal law and the claims of conscience and righteousness. God says to all these things, "Woe to them that call evil good, . . ./ who put darkness for light . . ./ who put bitter for sweet."

SELF-CONCEIT AND PRIDE OF INTELLECT

5. There are the sins of self-conceit and pride of intellect. "Woe to those who are wise in their own eyes/ and clever in their own sight" (5:21). These are the men that had no need of the counsel of Isaiah or the Word of God. They were a law to themselves. The generation is not yet extinct. Pride of intellect, self-sufficiency, all human culture: these form the greatest obstacle to the reception of the Word of God, and it is forever true that "If any one of you thinks he is wise by the standards of this age, he should become a 'fool' so that he may become wise. For the wisdom of this world is foolishness in God's sight. As it is written: 'He catches the wise in their craftiness.' " (1 Corinthians 3:18–19). How very sad that very much of the culture of even the present age is arrayed against Christianity. It is because man hates to acknowledge his own ignorance and nothingness and take his place at the feet of Jesus and learn of Him. Therefore the mysterious words of Jesus Christ are always true of the followers of the kingdom of heaven, "I praise you, Father, Lord of heaven and earth, because you have hidden these things from the wise and learned, and revealed them to little children. Yes, Father, for this was your good pleasure" (Matthew 11:25–26).

THE SIN OF DRUNKENNESS

6. The sin of drunkenness is discussed. "Woe to those who are heroes at drinking wine/ and champions at mixing drinks" (Isaiah 5:22). It is not so much the vice of becoming drunk that is here denounced as the power to drink like a beast and not get drunk. It is the sensual animalism that can load itself with liquor and lead others into stupid, beastly insensibility, and yet glory in its own self-control and ability to drink without limitation. This is downright beastliness, and yet the picture is not hard to find in our Christian lands, which, above all other lands, are blighted and disgraced with the

curse of drunkenness. The woe that Isaiah here pronounces is one that reverberates through all the centuries of the corridors of time, all the vaults of hell. It is the saddest wail ever extorted from human sin and sorrow. It is indeed the devil's most dreadful curse upon lost humanity, and fearful indeed will be the punishment of every man and woman that has any part in spreading it among his fellowmen.

THE SIN OF UNRIGHTEOUS JUDGMENT

7. Finally, there is the sin of unrighteous judgment. There is one more class here described, although they are included in the last woe. "Who acquit the guilty for a bribe,/ but deny justice to the innocent" (5:23).

Perverted judgment for the sake of gain, to wrong the innocent and to whitewash the vile: these were the characteristics of men in high places in Isaiah's time; and God denounces their wickedness in the most severe and unmeasured terms. When the fountains of justice are corrupted and the very courts of law become market places for bribery, violence and oppression, then the very life of a nation is in peril.

SECTION III—*The Harvest*

Therefore, the prophet can no longer keep back the vials of God's wrath, and the most vivid metaphors are used to describe the coming judgment. It will be like the devouring fire as it sweeps over the prairie stubble. "Therefore, as tongues of fire lick up straw/ and as dry grass sinks down in the flames,/ so their roots will decay/ and their flowers blow away like dust;/ for they have rejected the law of the LORD Almighty/ and spurned the word of the Holy One of Israel" (5:24).

It will be like the terrific earthquake as it rends the mountains. "Therefore the LORD's anger burns against his people;/ his hand is raised and he strikes them down./ The mountains shake,/ and the dead bodies are like refuse in the streets./ Yet for all this, his anger is not turned away,/ his hand is still upraised" (5:25).

It will be like the invasion of a desolating army as it sweeps like a whirlwind over the plains.

> He lifts up a banner for the distant nations,
>   he whistles for those at the ends of the earth.
> Here they come,
>   swiftly and speedily!
> Not one of them grows tired or stumbles,
>   not one slumbers or sleeps;
> not a belt is loosened at the waist,

> not a sandal thong is broken.
> Their arrows are sharp,
>   all their bows are strung;
>   their horses' hoofs seem like flint,
>   their chariot wheels like a whirlwind.
>   (5:26–28)

It will be like the roaring of a pack of lions as they leap upon their prey. "Their roar is like that of the lion,/ they roar like young lions;/ they growl as they seize their prey/ and carry it off with no one to rescue" (5:29).

It will be like the raging tide as it sweeps away the barriers and breaks over the land in desolation, "In that day they will roar over it/ like the roaring of the sea" (5:30).

And it will be like a land over which the darkness of Egypt has fallen. The heavens are black with anger and sorrow and terror hangs like a pall of impenetrable gloom, "And if one looks at the land,/ he will see darkness and distress;/ even the light will be darkened by the clouds" (5:30b).

All this came to Judah in a little while. All this has been coming from age to age to nations and races that have brought upon themselves these woes by their corresponding sins and crimes.

All this came upon Assyria and Babylon in their turn when they at length went down under the storm of judgment. All this came to Jerusalem when she perished under the cruel talons of the Roman eagle, and all this is coming to the civilized nations of today when their sin shall have grown ripe for the winepress of the wrath of God. And just as certainly will it come into the life of the individual, for "Whoever watches the wind will not plant;/ whoever looks at the clouds will not reap" (Ecclesiastes 11:4). Even in the present age to a great extent it is literally true. "There will be trouble and distress for every human being who does evil: first for the Jew, then for the Gentile" (Romans 2:9).

The evil grapes must find their place in the winepress of God. "Do not be deceived: God cannot be mocked. A man reaps what he sows. The one who sows to please his sinful nature, from that nature will reap destruction; the one who sows to please the Spirit, from the Spirit will reap eternal life" (Galatians 6:7–8).

CHAPTER 9

THE KING OF RIGHTEOUSNESS AND PEACE

The Spirit of the LORD will rest on him—
the Spirit of wisdom and of understanding,
the Spirit of counsel and of power,
the Spirit of knowledge and of the fear of the LORD—
and he will delight in the fear of the LORD.

He will not judge by what he sees with his eyes,
or decide by what he hears with his ears;
but with righteousness he will judge the needy,
with justice he will give decisions for the poor of the earth.
He will strike the earth with the rod of his mouth;
with the breath of his lips he will slay the wicked.
Righteousness will be his belt
and faithfulness the sash around his waist.

The wolf will live with the lamb,
the leopard will lie down with the goat,
the calf and the lion and the yearling together;
and a little child will lead them.
(Isaiah 11:2–6)

This is the third picture of Christ in the book of Isaiah. The first is the prophecy of Immanuel in the seventh chapter, the next the Wonderful Counselor in the ninth chapter. Now comes the great antitype to Melchizedek, the King of righteousness and peace.

SECTION I—*The Lineage of Christ*

He is a Shoot from the stem of Jesse and a Branch from his roots. The idea is that the family of David was to pass into decay like an old rotting stem, and out of the ruin was to spring a shoot who should become the heir of David's house and throne. That the Jewish rabbis understood this as a prophecy of the Messiah is evidenced from the Chaldean paraphrase of the Old Testament in which this is translated as a *son* and *heir* and the name Messiah is used.

There is a fine contrast in the whole paragraph including the previous context in which the king of Assyria is described under the image of a great cedar forest which is to be cut down and utterly fall, while the house of David, although seeming to pass into decay, is to be revived by this Branch that is to spring from its ruin.

A great principle is here expressed, the principle which underlies the whole Christian system, namely, life out of death. The Lord Jesus Christ came as the outgrowth of a ruined race. He was born of our sinful humanity. He took not on Him the nature of angels, but "He took on him the seed of Abraham" (Hebrews 2:16, KJV). Humanity had fallen into ruins, when out of its decaying roots sprang this new and heavenly Branch which was to "bud and blossom/ and fill all the world with fruit" (Isaiah 27:6). Christ Himself was true to this principle all through His life and work. In accordance with it, He went down into death itself and out of the grave He arose in resurrection, life and power, to be the Tree of Life for earth's dying millions.

In like manner, our life must come out of death. Every saved soul is a shoot from the decaying root of a lost past. Every sanctified soul is as one resurrected from the dead, and the glory of the new age is to come through the death of the old and the resurrection not only of men, but of nature, too.

The Hebrew word *nazar* signifies a little scrubby shoot. The name is applied again to the Lord Jesus in the 53rd chapter of Isaiah. "A root out of dry ground" (53:2). This is forever true not only of the Master, but of all His followers. "The Nazarene" was a name of contempt and humiliation. It signified the last degree of human merit and earthly promise, but from this root has sprung all the hope of earth and all the glory of heaven.

SECTION II—*The Supernatural Character of Christ*

He is endowed with supernatural character. The qualities of wisdom and righteousness here ascribed to this scion of the house of David are not merely remarkable in themselves, but still more remarkable in their source. They are not the inherent qualities of the Messiah, but they are communicated to Him directly and supernaturally by the Holy Spirit Himself. Here is the radical distinction between human ethics and divine righteousness. Man's morality is the result of natural virtue and ethical culture. God's righteousness comes down from heaven and is directly communicated by the indwelling of the Holy Spirit. Therefore Jesus Christ Himself set the example of this new divine righteousness by delaying and suspending all His official ministry until after He received the baptism of the Holy Spirit. Although the Son of God, possessing the attributes of deity, He did not exercise them in His own person. Rather, He humbled Himself and took the place of dependence upon His Father like any other man, and at length He received all the gifts and graces required for His public ministry by receiving the Holy Spirit as we are to receive Him, and living ever after a life of constant dependence by faith and prayer upon God for the supply of wisdom, strength and righteousness for His whole life and ministry. Such stupendous condescension surpasses all other acts of humiliation on the part of our Lord. He consented to be nothing and to receive everything as given Him from above. "By myself I can do nothing" (John 5:30a), He testified. "These words you hear are not my own; they belong to the Father who sent me" (14:24). "But if I drive out demons by the Spirit of God" (Matthew 12:28a). "Just as the living Father sent me and I live because of the Father, so the one who feeds on me will live because of me" (John 6:57). The Master received all His gifts and graces just as we receive them—through the Holy Spirit.

The Apostle John speaks of "the seven spirits before his throne" (Revelation 1:4), that is, the sevenfold ministry and equipment of the divine Spirit. This passage in Isaiah presents to us seven operations of the Holy Spirit in connection with the character and ministry of Christ.

THE SPIRIT OF WISDOM

1. Wisdom is that quality which enables us to use the right means for the end in view. It is the ability to accomplish results, to bring things to pass, to do the right thing. It is the quality which gives success and efficiency in practical life.

THE SPIRIT OF UNDERSTANDING

2. This has reference to knowledge in general. One may possess wisdom and yet have a very limited knowledge. On the other hand, one may possess stores of knowledge and yet have no practical sense or sound judgment. It is said of one of England's kings:

> He never said a foolish thing
> And never did a wise one.

The Lord Jesus was eminently wise and yet had boundless knowledge. How marvelously He met the snares His subtle foes set for Him and always did the right thing and so answered their ensnaring questions, so that at last no man dared ask Him anything. At the same time, how marvelous His knowledge of the Word of God. Even at the age of 12, His familiarity with the Scriptures amazed the Jewish scholars in the temple, and the testimony of all that listened to Him through His public ministry might be expressed in the one admiring reply of the men that tried to arrest Him, "No one ever spoke the way this man does" (John 7:46).

THE SPIRIT OF COUNSEL

3. This is the ability to impart wisdom to others and to guide safely and rightly the steps of those that look to Him for direction. What a "Wonderful Counselor" He is! "When He has brought out all his own, he goes on ahead of them, and his sheep follow him because they know his voice" (John 10:4). He leads His people "on a level path where they will not stumble" (Jeremiah 31:9). They that follow Him will not stumble, and "the wayfaring men, though fools, shall not err therein" (Isaiah 35:8, KJV).

THE SPIRIT OF MIGHT

4. The Holy Spirit endowed Christ with miraculous power over all the power of Satan, over the forces and laws of nature and over disease and men. The promise of the Comforter still involves the same power for the followers of Christ. Christianity is not a mere set of harmless opinions but the presence of a living potency that brings things to pass.

THE SPIRIT OF THE KNOWLEDGE OF GOD

5. The Holy Spirit was the medium of fellowship between the Father and the Son. In His light and presence, we come to know God and hold intimate converse with Him. Divine things and the Divine Being become intensely real.

THE SPIRIT OF THE FEAR OF GOD

6. This means devotedness, godliness, piety, sensitive regard for God's authority and will, and that absolute obedience and faithfulness of which the Lord Jesus could say, "The one who sent me is with me; he has not left me alone, for I always do what pleases him" (John 8:29).

THE SENSE OF SMELL

7. The final quality in this sevenfold equipment of the Holy Spirit is expressed by an extremely significant figure, whose beauty and force are brought out by the marginal reading, "and shall make him of quick scent (or smell) in the fear of the LORD" (Isaiah 11:3).

The sense of smell is the finest exercise of all our physical qualities. It approaches more nearly to the spiritual and ethereal than any other. The fragrance of the flower has been compared to the sound of nature breathing out in sweet perfume. The scent in animals is the instinct which detects things as no operation of the human intellect possibly can. The dog recognizes his master and his enemy. The wild bird knows where the warm breezes of the Southland blow and the difference between the poisoned berry and the wholesome fruit of the wilderness.

And so the Holy Spirit gives to us an instinctive life that is higher than the operation of our reasoning powers. We know God, and we know right and wrong. Yes, and we know His messages, His directions, His intimations to us by those finer touches, those more delicate instincts which do not appeal to our reasoning powers or our coarser senses, but which speak to our consciousness with the authority of intuitions, and which bring to us the certainty that we cannot explain to others and yet could not for a moment question.

How marvelously the Lord perceived the thoughts and characters of those around Him. How often He answered men without their having spoken. How He sensed conditions, characters and things by something within Himself which was as unerring as it was incomprehensible to men. The Holy Spirit will be to us such an instinct and will give to us intuitions of God, of truth, of right, of approaching evil and of the will of God for us which will make us "of quick understanding in the fear of the LORD" (11:3, KJV), and which will lead us likewise to judge. "He will not judge by what he sees with his eyes,/ or decide by what he hears with his ears" (11:3).

SECTION III—*The Spirit of Righteousness and Holiness*

"Righteousness will be his belt/ and faithfulness the sash around his waist" (11:5). The mightiest thing about the Lord Jesus was not His miraculous power but His unimpeachable righteousness. It was this that saved us from the curse which our unrighteousness had brought upon the race. Had He for one moment failed to meet the tests of Satan, our race would have been wrecked forever and the plan of redemption been an irretrievable failure. Just once Moses, the great lawgiver, failed, and that one failure shut him out of the Land of Promise. With what subtle art the great enemy sought to overthrow the righteousness of Jesus! Could Satan have but ensnared Him for an instant and lured Him aside from the pathway of obedience upon which He had staked His life and our redemption, what despair must have filled the heavens, and what hopeless anguish must have been the endless portion of our race! But Jesus overcame because righteousness was His belt and faithfulness the sash around His waist. Not for a moment did He even think of or desire aught but His Father's will, and so "also through the obedience of the one man the many will be made righteous" (Romans 5:19b). It was through the Holy Spirit that He stood victorious in this awful test, and that same Holy Spirit is the Sanctifier who still comes to lead us through the same conflict and to the same victory.

SECTION IV—*The Spirit of Judgment*

The righteousness of Jesus Christ, however, was not only personal, it also became a consuming fire to destroy the wicked. Only once or twice in His earthly life did that flame flash forth in the words that withered the barren fig tree, and the woes that scathed the hypocritical Pharisees, who knew the right but chose the wrong. He did not come to judge the world, but to save the world. Therefore, when He read from the book of Isaiah in His inaugural sermon at Nazareth the words of His great commission, "The Spirit of the Sovereign LORD is on me,/ because the LORD has anointed me/ to preach good news to the poor./ He has sent me to bind up the brokenhearted,/ to proclaim freedom for the captives/ and release from darkness for the prisoners,/ to proclaim the year of the LORD's favor" (Isaiah 61:1–2a), He closed the book at that point, and left unuttered the last sentence of the prophecy—"and the day of vengeance of our God" (61:2b). The time for that had not yet come, but none the less surely is coming. The fire that melts the gold and makes it pure, burns up the chaff to ashes. The holiness of Christ must either save or destroy. The announcement of the forerunner was, "He will baptize you with the Holy Spirit and with fire" (Matthew 3:11). The Lord Jesus Christ must inevitably judge all evil which refuses to be cleansed by His grace and brought into subjection to His Father's will.

Therefore, He is here revealed as the reprover and avenger of the wickedness of the wicked. "With righteousness he will judge the needy,/ with justice he will give decisions for the poor of the earth./ He will strike the earth with the rod of his mouth;/ with the breath of his lips he will slay the wicked" (Isaiah 11:4).

This last clause has been quoted by the Apostle Paul in a remarkable passage in his description of the coming of the Lord, and especially the judgment that is to fall upon the man of sin, the great antichrist of the last days. After speaking of the mystery of iniquity which already works and which is to culminate in that wicked one who is coming "in accordance with the work of Satan displayed in all kinds of counterfeit miracles, signs and wonders, and in every sort of evil that deceives those who are perishing" (2 Thessalonians 2:9–10), he adds, "whom the Lord Jesus will overthrow with the breath of his mouth and destroy by the splendor of his coming" (2:8).

This is a literal quotation from our text, and it brings into view the second coming of the Lord Jesus Christ in His sublime character as the leader of the last great conflict and the destroyer of antichrist and Satan.

Let us not, therefore, dream that the mercy of our Savior is a soft and weak emotion, without character or principle behind it. It is a love that can smite as well as save. Of all the fearful pictures of a lost eternity, there is none so terrible and none from which the men that have rejected Christ will so wish to hide themselves behind rocks and mountains as "the wrath of the Lamb" (Revelation 6:16).

God save you from that wrath which is but the righteousness of wounded love, of rejected mercy—the wrath of the Lamb.

SECTION V—*The Vision of Millennial Peace and Blessedness*

The picture that follows describes the golden age of faith and hope and prophecy. Human poetry has dreamed of it, but only inspiration has been able to portray it. It is to bring the redemption of the lower orders of creation and the restoration of this sin-cursed earth, as well as the harmony of man with man and man with God. Oh, how warbling birds will acclaim it! Oh, how the abused beasts of burden, that have groaned under man's oppression, will almost speak their words of thankfulness! Oh, how heaven will smile as it looks down again upon this paradise restored!

> The wolf will live with the lamb,
>   the leopard will lie down with the goat,
> the calf and the lion and the yearling together;
>   and a little child will lead them. . . .
> The infant will play near the hole of the cobra,
>   and the young child put his hand into the viper's nest.
> They will neither harm nor destroy
>   on all my holy mountain,
> for the earth will be full of the knowledge of the LORD
>   as the waters cover the sea.
>   (Isaiah 11:6, 8–9)

> Come, then, oh, Christ, earth's Monarch and Redeemer,
>   Thy glorious Eden bring;
> Where peace at length, no more a timid stranger,
>   Shall fold her weary wing.

SECTION VI—*The Restoration of Israel*

Along with this comes the restoration of God's chosen people, the seed of Abraham.

In that day the Lord will reach out his hand a second time to reclaim the remnant that is left of his people from Assyria, from Lower Egypt, from Upper Egypt, from Cush, from Elam, from Babylonia, from Hamath and from the islands of the sea.

He will raise a banner for the nations
    and gather the exiles of Israel;
he will assemble the scattered people of Judah
    from the four quarters of the earth.
Ephraim's jealousy will vanish,
    and Judah's enemies will be cut off;
Ephraim will not be jealous of Judah,
    nor Judah hostile toward Ephraim.
    (11:11–13)

There can be no doubt about the literal application of this prophecy. This is not the first restoration under Ezra and Nehemiah, for we are distinctly told that the Lord shall set His hand again a second time to recover the remnant of His people. This also includes the 10 tribes represented by Ephraim, as well as the captives of Judah. All are to be united in an everlasting homecoming, such as the sons of Jacob have never seen since the days of Solomon. The envy of Ephraim is to depart, and the vision of Ezekiel (chapter 37) is to be fulfilled, and the children of Joseph and the children of Judah are to be one forever. The physical barriers are to be removed, "The LORD will dry up/ the gulf of the Egyptian sea" (Isaiah 11:15). The political obstacles are to be set aside, for "He will break it up into seven streams" (11:15). This is the river Euphrates, described by the Apostle John in Revelation 16:12, representing the Turkish power, which is to be dried up "so that men can cross over in sandals" (Isaiah 11:15). These kings of the East are the returning children of Israel, who are to go back as the rulers of the Orient when the filthy rover of Mohammedan persecution and corruption shall have been put aside. Then will come the glad millennial song of Isaiah 12 when the universe shall be summoned to celebrate the great deliverance and the advent of the new creation and the millennial age.

In conclusion, what personal application can we make of this sublime vision to our individual lives?

1. As Christ came out of the ruined stump of Israel, so still our Christian life is born out of death, and at every stage we still must trace the principle of death and resurrection.

2. As the Lord Jesus Christ derived His holiness and righteousness from the Holy Spirit, so still the Christian character is not culture but a supernatural gift of the Spirit of God, which must be received by faith and main-

tained by union with the Lord Jesus through the spirit of holiness.

3. Like Him, we too may be baptized with the spirit of wisdom and understanding, the spirit of counsel and might, the spirit of the knowledge and the fear of the Lord, and above all, with that intuitive life which will make us of quick scent in the fear of the Lord, and give us the instinct of holiness and divine communion.

4. There is a sense in which the vision of Isaiah 6:6 is still fulfilled in our hearts and homes. The lion and the bear, the asp and the adder are not always found in the jungle or menagerie. There are human hearts and lives so like these wild beasts of earth that one cannot altogether wonder that men have thought of the doctrine of evolution and have fancied that our progenitors were monkeys and brutes. But when Jesus comes into human lives, the lion will become a lamb, the poison of the asp will cease to be found behind our lips, the subtlety of the serpent will be taken from our hearts, and our strifes and alienations will be healed, and we will walk in love even as Christ loves us. We have not the right to be looking for the millennium unless we have the millennium in our own hearts. We have no business to expect an eternity of peace if we are living in strife and envy now. Let us begin the millennial life here if we expect to enjoy it by and by.

5. The Restorer of Israel will also be our Restorer. How much there is waiting for "until the time comes for God to restore everything, as promised long ago through his holy prophets" (Acts 3:21). How much God gives back to us here of that which sin and Satan have robbed us, and, oh, how much is waiting for that glad day when the lost shall be found and "the years the locusts have eaten" (Joel 2:25) will be given back untarnished forever.

How can we have this blessed King of righteousness and peace and hail and help on His glorious advent which shall make

> This blighted earth of ours
> His own fair world again.

CHAPTER 10

A NAIL IN A SURE PLACE

I will place on his shoulder the key to the house of David; what he opens no one can shut, and what he shuts no one can open. I will drive him like a peg into a firm place; he will be a seat of honor for the house of his father. All the glory of his family will hang on him: its offspring and offshoots—all its lesser vessels, from the bowls to all the jars. (Isaiah 22:22–24)

This is the fourth picture of the Messiah in the book of Isaiah. He is presented here under the name Eliakim, the son of Hilkiah, to whom is to be given the key of the house of David, and he is "fastened as a nail in a sure place" (KJV).

SECTION I—*Shebna: The Contrasting Figure*

The old painters used to heighten the effect of their visions of beauty by putting in the foreground some hideous picture of a reptile or a toad so that by the effect of contrast the picture itself might be made more striking through the effect of antithesis.

In front of this picture of our Lord the prophet puts in contrast another figure. It is that of Shebna, the treasurer of the king's house, a prominent official in the service of Hezekiah, who seems to have been puffed up with such egregious vanity that he had actually prepared for himself a splendid sepulchre in some prominent place, perhaps among the tombs of kings, that he might be buried with great honor. Isaiah is sent to him with a terrific message of rebuke and judgment.

> What are you doing here and who gave you permission
> to cut out a grave for yourself here,
> hewing your grave on the height

and chiseling your resting place in the rock?

Beware, the LORD is about to take firm hold of you
and hurl you away, O you mighty man.
He will roll you up tightly like a ball
and throw you into a large country.
There you will die
and there your splendid chariots will remain—
you disgrace to your master's house!
I will depose you from your office,
and you will be ousted from your position.
(22:16–19)

It is in the place of this corrupt and selfish official that Eliakim, the faithful one, is to be appointed. He is to exhibit in his character and public administration qualities so different and so lofty that the picture of Eliakim soon passes into the higher vision of the Son of God Himself, of whom he becomes the honored type.

Shebna is a fearful example of official corruption, of personal vanity, and of that sordid earthliness that would even make the grave itself the means of exploiting its ambition and its pride. The judgment of God is revealed from heaven against the spirit of worldliness and selfishness in every form.

Some of our Lord's most solemn parables were intended to show the fearful doom of the man that lives only to amass money and win success in this world. One of these parables is the story of the rich man who added to his barns and storehouses and kept saying to his soul: "You have plenty of good things laid up for many years. Take life easy; eat, drink and be merry" (Luke 12:19). But God said to him, "You fool! This very night your life will be demanded from you. Then who will get what you have prepared for yourself?" Then the Master points out the heart searching moral: "This is how it will be with anyone who stores up things for himself but is not rich toward God" (12:20–21).

Another of these solemn parables portrays the doom of the selfish worldling on the other side of death. It is the picture of Dives and Lazarus. There is nothing said against the character of this rich man. He was not a bad man, so far as we know, but he simply lived for himself, and this is what we are told of him: "The rich man also died and was buried." He had a funeral, as Shebna planned to have, and doubtless it was a splendid one. But oh! the sequel: "In hell, where he was in torment." He begged that Lazarus, the wretched beggar that had often lain at his door, might be sent with a drop of water to cool his burning tongue. The only fault uttered against him by Father Abraham was: "Son, remember that in your lifetime you received your good things, while Lazarus received bad things, but now he is comforted here and you are in agony" (see Luke 16:19–31).

Are you meeting the great responsibility which increased wealth brings to every man? Are you recognizing your means as a sacred trust? Are you "laying up in store . . . against the time to come" (1 Timothy 6:19, KJV) and investing your wealth "where moth and rust do not destroy, and where thieves do not break in and steal?" (Matthew 6:20).

SECTION II—*Eliakim: The Lofty Figure*

Over against this hideous character of vainglory and selfishness arises the lofty figure of Eliakim.

HIS NAME

1. His name is very suggestive. It means "whom God raised up." Just as Shebna stood for death and the grave, Eliakim stands for the resurrection, for a life that seeks its portion not in the natural world, but in the new creation which Christ has ushered in. In keeping with this is his father's name, Hilkiah, which means, "God is his portion." This also leads our minds to that higher world of which Shebna knew nothing, and to which Jesus Christ is ever opening our faith and hope.

HIS ADMINISTRATION

2. His administration is described in beautiful terms: "He will be a father to those who live in Jerusalem and to the house of Judah" (Isaiah 22:21). Just as we are accustomed to call Washington "the father of his country," so this good man was a paternal governor over the people, and finely represents our blessed coming King,

> He rules the world with truth and grace,
> And makes the nations prove
> The glories of His righteousness
> And wonders of His love.

HIS SASH AND ROBE

3. The sash and robe with which he was to be clothed represent our blessed Lord in His life service. The sash always stands for service, in contrast with the loose robes that express self-indulgence and ease. While Shebna was living for pleasure, Eliakim was girded for work. Our blessed Master is always represented, even in heaven, as a girded priest, busy in His high offices of intercession and dominion. No sinecure of luxury or selfish glory has

He set yonder, but a place of unceasing and faithful ministry as He bears our iniquities, sympathizes with our sorrows and there represents us before the Father, while at the same time He directs all the wheels of Providence from His mediatorial throne in the interests of His people and His kingdom.

Like Him, Christian life is strenuous toil and holy activity.

> No time for trifling in this life of mine;
> Not thus the path the blessed Master trod,
> But strenuous toil each hour and power employ,
> Always and all for God.

THE KEY OF DAVID

4. The key of David was given to him. Our Lord applies this to Himself in the third chapter of Revelation, in His message from the throne to the church in Philadelphia: "What he opens no one can shut, and what he shuts no one can open" (3:7). There can be no doubt, therefore, about the application of the figure to the Lord Jesus Christ. He carries this key upon His shoulder, which is quite customary in oriental countries for officials entrusted with the care of some great household. The reference to His shoulder reminds us of the former picture of Jesus Christ in this book: "The government will be on his shoulders" (Isaiah 9:6b). Jesus Christ holds the keys of heaven and earth and hell. How many things He opens for us!—the gates of heaven, the gates of prayer, the closed pathway of difficulty, the doors of service, the hearts of men. And how many things He shuts for us: the blessed hand of God which holds us so that none can pluck us out of His hand; the blessed ark of safety, like Noah, of whom it is said, "Then the LORD shut him in" (Genesis 7:16); the mouths of lions and the tongues of wicked men and women, which He alone can shut and keep shut.

Blessed Prince of the house of David! Let us give Him all the keys of all the chambers of our being, of all the treasure houses of our life, and we will find that He is able to keep that which we have committed to His trust against that day (2 Timothy 1:12).

A NAIL

5. Much is represented by the figure of a nail in a sure place. This is a very striking figure, and may refer either to the pegs by which the Arab secures his tent or the iron spikes which they were accustomed to fasten in the masonry of their buildings, at once securing the walls of the building and at the same time becoming a hook on which they hung their valuables inside the house.

A Sure Place

A. This is a nail in a sure place. The Lord Jesus Christ is not a guess, a possibility, a theory. He is a mighty certainty. All the assaults of skepticism have only succeeded in establishing Him more firmly in the sure place which He holds in the Word of God, in the hearts of His people and in the plan of redemption. When we trust Him we know that we are resting on a solid rock, and that all else "is sinking sand." His kingdom is the only certainty of the future. Our best systems of government, our highest forms of civilization, will all pass away, but "[God's] kingdom is an everlasting kingdom,/ and [his] dominion endures through all generations" (Psalm 145:13). The only stable investment for our lives is there.

The Glory of His Family

B. On this nail the prophet said, should be hung "all the glory of his family" (Isaiah 22:24). This does not merely refer to His inheritance in the throne of David, but rather to His heirship to all the glory of His heavenly Father. Truly He could say, "All things have been committed to me by my Father" (Matthew 11:27) and again, "The Father judges no one, but has entrusted all judgment to the Son" (John 5:22). All the glory, all the power, all the authority of the Father has been handed over to the Lord Jesus, so that in receiving Him as our portion we are joint heirs with Him of all the glory of His Father's house.

The Head of a New Race

C. He is the Head of a new race. The "offspring and the offshoots" (Isaiah 22:24) referred to here signify what our Lord Jesus Himself has expressed in one of His last messages in the Apocalypse: "I am the root and offspring of David" (Revelation 22:16). He is the real head of David's house, and at the same time the heir of David's throne. David sprang from Him quite as truly as He sprang from David. Still more the truth is implied which the apostle expresses so forcibly in First Corinthians, where he speaks of the Adam race and the Christ race: "For as in Adam all die, so in Christ all will be made alive" (15:22). There are two races of men in this world: one is the race of humanity born from Adam and inheriting his curse and his doom; the other is the Christ race born from the loins of the Lord Jesus, the second Adam, and inheriting His righteousness and His glory. It is only this new race that can ever enter the kingdom of heaven. The old race is doomed and must pass away under the penalty of sin, but the Christ race shall dwell forevermore and inherit all the glories of Christ, its Head.

To which of these do you and I belong, dear friend? Has your life been reborn from the heart of Jesus Christ, and through Him are you the heir of God and the joint heir of Jesus Christ?

The Vessels

D. Still further we are told that they shall hang upon Him all vessels, both large and small, the cups and the flagons, the vessels of the kitchen and the vessels of the feast, the vessels of commonplace need and service and the vessels of high and holy joy and ministry.

A very deep and practical truth is here expressed. Jesus Christ is the source and the supply of all our needs. These vessels represent the needs of our lives, the temporal and spiritual supplies for which we must go continually to Him. The idea is that we do not have the blessing within ourselves. We are not self-contained depositories of grace, but we come to Him moment by moment and hang upon Him our every need—the little vessels of commonplace life and testing, the flagons of higher and holier joy that stand for the hours of rapture and the moments of blessing. The whole weight of our need hangs upon Him, and all our future hopes are dependent likewise upon our Lord and Head.

How blessed to know that there is nothing which we cannot bring to Him!

> There's no time too busy for His leisure,
> There's no task too hard for Him to share,
> There's no soul too lowly for His notice,
> There's no need too trifling for His care,
> There's no place too humble for His presence,
> There's no pain His bosom cannot feel,
> There's no sorrow that He cannot comfort,
> There's no sickness that He cannot heal.

CHAPTER 11

THE KING AND THE MAN

See, a king will reign in righteousness
and rulers will rule with justice.
Each man will be like a shelter from the wind
and a refuge from the storm,
like streams of water in the desert
and the shadow of a great rock in a thirsty land.
(Isaiah 32:1–2)

We have here Isaiah's fifth picture of the Lord Jesus.

SECTION I—*The King*

"See, a king will reign in righteousness/ and rulers will rule with justice."

In this land of freedom it is hard for us to realize the cruel horrors of ancient despotism. The traveler who gazes with admiration on the splendid architecture of the cities of the past, can scarcely believe that these magnificent ruins were cemented by the blood and the tears of millions of toiling slaves, who spent their lives in unrequited drudgery to adorn the palaces and tombs of cruel tyrants. But an object lesson has just been presented to the world, even in this enlightened age, which gives a touch of realism to these nightmares of history. In the public squares of St. Petersburg we see a multitude of men, women and children assembled to plead at the footstool of their king for liberty and protection, in words so pathetic as to move a heart of stone, and met by squadrons of cavalry, batteries of artillery and a rain of murderous bullets drenching the snows beneath their feet with streams of innocent blood.

Such a king was the cruel Ahaz of Judah. After years of wickedness and oppression, he at last sold his country to Assyria for an alliance that would protect him from his northern neighbors. He finally crowned the wickedness of his life by setting up a heathen altar in the temple of Jerusalem, and making his own children pass through the fire as living sacrifices to the hideous idol of Moloch. The epitaph he left on the page of history is like a great black note of exclamation, "In his time of trouble King Ahaz became even more unfaithful to the LORD" (2 Chronicles 28:22).

Out of the darkness and sorrow of such times, rose Isaiah's vision of the King of righteousness and peace. Like a burst of sunlight or a rainbow arch, after a dark, stormy cloud had passed, our text shines with celestial benignity, "See, a king will reign in righteousness/ and rulers will rule with justice." While, doubtless, the immediate reference of the prophecy was to the good King Hezekiah, who succeeded Ahaz; yet, remotely and supremely, it points to the coming Messiah. He is the only One that can completely fulfill the prophetic ideal. Solomon could draw the picture better than he could live it. The 72nd Psalm, which probably he wrote, is God's portrait of earth's true King, coming, we rejoice to believe, before very long, when it will at last be true:

> He will judge your people in righteousness,
>   your afflicted ones with justice.
>
> He will defend the afflicted among the people
>   and save the children of the needy;
>   he will crush the oppressor.
>
> In his days the righteous will flourish;
>   prosperity will abound till the moon is no more.
>
> All kings will bow down to him
>   and all nations will serve him.
>
> For he will deliver the needy who cry out,
>   the afflicted who have no one to help.
>
> He will rescue them from oppression and violence,
>   for precious is their blood in his sight.
>   (Psalm 72:2, 4, 7, 11, 12, 14)

Let us notice some particulars concerning this glorious King.

A RIGHTEOUS RULER

1. He will be a righteous ruler. Righteousness is the only true foundation for any throne. Selfishness, injustice, political corruption, the prostituting of

political influence and high position for ambition or gain can bring only demoralization and ruin to any people. The declension of the world's decaying nations, as they have been well called, can all be traced to the corrupt fountains where the processes of demoralization began; and all history is but a commentary on the sacred words, "Righteousness exalts a nation,/ but sin is a disgrace to any people," (Proverbs 14:34) or, Isaiah's own significant words, "The fruit of righteousness will be peace;/ the effect of righteousness will be quietness and confidence forever" (32:17).

A RIGHTEOUS COURT

2. He will have a righteous court. "Rulers will rule with justice." The officers of His kingdom will be as upright as their King. He is choosing and training these officers today from all the ranks of His redeemed ones. The princes who are to share with Him that coming kingdom are being saved and sanctified, and educated in the church now.

David gathered about him, in the years of his exile, the refugees who flocked to his standard from all the land. These men had but one merit amid all their sins and crimes, namely, that they were true to David. Because of this fact David welcomed, trained and afterward appointed them as the princes and rulers of his kingdom. Likewise, Christ, today, our King in disguise, and almost exiled, is gathering around His standard the sinful men who accept Him as their Captain and Lord, and who are fighting the battles of His militant kingdom. But these shall, by and by, sit down with Him upon His throne and be the princes and rulers of the millennium, and He shall say to one and another, "You have been faithful with a few things; I will put you in charge of many things. Come and share your master's happiness!" (Matthew 25:21).

A REIGN OF LOVE

3. His will be a reign of love. "You have been a refuge for the poor,/ a refuge for the needy in his distress,/ a shelter from the storm/ and a shade from the heat" (Isaiah 25:4).

PROPER STANDARDS

4. He will establish proper standards of character and conduct. Isaiah 32:3–8 describes a condition of things in which the masks of our present social system shall be torn away, and men and women shall stand out in their true character. "No longer will the fool be called noble/ nor the scoundrel be highly respected" (32:5). All disguises will be removed, all counterfeits will be detected and truth as well as righteousness shall evermore prevail. Today almost everything is false and the world is waiting for its true King to turn society upside down and put things in their true places.

THE FRUITS OF THE SPIRIT

5. The fruits of the Spirit will fill this blessed age with beauty and blessing.

> Till the Spirit is poured upon us from on high,
>   and the desert becomes a fertile field,
>   and the fertile field seems like a forest.
> Justice will dwell in the desert
>   and righteousness live in the fertile field.
> The fruit of righteousness will be peace;
>   the effect of righteousness will be quietness and confidence
>   forever.
>   (32:15–17)

SECTION II—*The Man*

Human life is not all politics. We need more than a king and a good government. We need sympathy, love, help and a human heart to which we can go and on which we can lean with our sorrows and our needs. Back of this throne there is a Man, and His heart is as human as His nature is divine. How real and perfect that humanity appears in the gospel story of the Christ! Look at Him in the gradual development of His infancy, childhood and youth—a real child! Look at Him in His boyhood, as His mind begins to open to the light of truth and the knowledge of His Father's word and will like any other growing intelligence. See Him in the workshop at Nazareth, a working man like His toiling brothers! See Him as He sits upon the stone at Jacob's well, or sleeps in the "stern on a cushion" (Mark 4:38) worn out with weariness! Behold the Man as He weeps at Bethany, as He struggles in Gethsemane, as He dies on Calvary! Watch Him as He comes forth from the tomb, in His interview with Mary, in His walk to Emmaus, in His tender treatment of Peter and Thomas, and it will help you to realize how much we owe to the humanity of Jesus Christ. We have indeed in Him "someone to arbitrate between us,/ to lay his hand upon us both" (Job 9:33). He is bone of our bone, flesh of our flesh, heart of our heart, brother of our race.

But the prophetic picture is even stronger than this. In the original it is "*the* man." There is but one Man who fully represents the race; one Man who has made it acceptable to God, and forever will sit on the throne of the universe in our likeness and our nature. He is the Son of Man, the Man above all other men who has met our obligations, paid our debts, settled our liabilities, worked out the problem of our salvation and redeemed and restored and glorified the human race.

Three things are predicated of this wondrous Man in the prophet's vision.

A REFUGE

1. He is a "refuge for the poor,/ a refuge for the needy in his distress,/ a shelter from the storm/ and a shade from the heat" (Isaiah 25:4). He is a refuge from our guilt and sin. He saves us from the wrath of God and the penalty of our guilt. As a man He bore for all men the punishment of sin and by accepting His atonement we are free. This is the old gospel of substitution. But there is no other way to escape the tempest which is surely gathering against all unforgiven sin, "The wrath of God is being revealed from heaven against all the godlessness and wickedness of men who suppress the truth by their wickedness" (Romans 1:18), and the sentence is "trouble and distress for every human being who does evil" (2:9). But this Man has come between us and our sins. For every soul that will receive Him He offers a shelter, not only from the judgments of God but from the accusations of Satan, and the very memory of our own heart and the condemnation of our own conscience.

He is a "shelter" from temptation, "a way to escape" (1 Corinthians 10:13, KJV) into which we may run and hide while He meets the devil for us as our conquered foe. He is a "shelter" from our sorrows, a refuge from the storms of life and a comforter and deliverer in every hour of trial and of need. Is there any one who reads these lines in a place of difficulty, perplexity or extremity, where all other help has failed? Where you have lost confidence in yourself and no human hand can save and no human heart may care? There is One who loves, who understands, who pities, who can take us at our worst, and turn the curse into a blessing, and change the shadow of death into the morning of hope and victory.

Indeed, Christ cannot do much with us until we reach the end of ourselves. The greatest victories of His grace come to us when we reach the end of self.

A writer tells of the origin of the chrysanthemum; that the first chrysanthemum sprang from an abortion in the vegetable world. A little plant, that bore only leaves, failed through some blight to bring a leaf to perfection, and instead it grew into a tinted form half way between a leaf and a flower. A gardener caught the freak of nature and developed it until it became the glorious autumn flower which almost rivals the rose itself in variety and splendor. It was out of its failure that the new life was born. And so it is when we come to the place of despair we often emerge on the higher plane of resurrection life and victory. The same writer tells of a beautiful trailing plant that also owes its beauty to a similar cause. In its former life it was a stout and self-contained shrub, but under the stress of a storm its roots were almost washed away, and it was left trailing and perishing on the ground. Then it began to lean upon a supporting trunk, and gradually crept up its side until it developed into a trailing plant, slender and unable to support its own weight, but trained into forms of rich beauty and delicacy.

Even so, when we lose our strength and are unable to stand alone, we grow into new strength by learning to lean on Him. Let us bring to Him our weakness, our sin, the things that no one else will take, and we shall find a friend who will do for us what no other friend could do, and turn life's failures into heaven's triumphs.

THE FOUNTAIN OF REFRESHING

2. "Like streams of water in the desert" (Isaiah 32:2), Christ is the fountain of refreshing. These rivers of water represent the blessed influences of the Holy Spirit which all spring from Him. We know something, perhaps, of that heavenly Comforter. Perhaps He led you to the Savior and brought you the sense of His forgiveness and acceptance. But there is much more for you. Perhaps He has come to abide in your heart as a personal indwelling presence. But there is still much more for you. There are rivers of living water. It is one thing to receive the Spirit. It is another thing to be filled with the Spirit in every avenue of our being and with every attribute of His being. It is still another thing to have these rivers of water in a dry place. We expect the Holy Spirit to come to us in the high places of life, in the closet, in the sanctuary, in the hour of holy ecstasy. But life is largely made up of very different places, hard places, places of toil, failure, conflict, desertion, discouragement. These are the dry places where the rivers of water are promised to flow. Do we need them? Have we received that blessed Comforter, who gives zest to drudgery, joy in sorrow, and enables us to glory even in tribulation? Have we, with Achsah learned to claim not only the upper springs of heavenly communion and high achievement, but the nether springs that run through the streets of toil, the marts of trade, the monotony of the kitchen and the pain and agony of sickness, bereavement and wrong? All this is for us in the friendship of the Man of sorrows, the Man that not only knew what sorrow was Himself, but still comes to be with us in our sorrows, too.

QUIETNESS AND REST

3. The "shadow of a great rock in a thirsty land" (32:2) speaks to us of quietness and rest. Life is not all in the open. It needs its quiet hours, the place of retreat, silence and shade. Have we found and proved this promise? "The LORD is your shade at your right hand;/ the sun will not harm you by day,/ nor the moon by night" (Psalm 121:5–6).

The figure of a great rock is beautiful and expressive. A little rock becomes heated in the burning sunshine and only heats you the more. But the great rock absorbs the heat on one side, and has on the other the cool shade where you can sit down and be refreshed and rested. So human friends are like the little rock, filled with their own troubles, and with little leisure or sympathy for us. But He is always at leisure to hear our complaint and bear our burden. In that night when the shadow of the cross was hanging heavily over His heart, not one word escaped His lips about His troubles. Instead, His own message was, "Do not let *your* hearts be troubled" (John 14:1). It is not until we reach the dry place and the weary land that we ever know the preciousness of Christ and the sympathy of this blessed Man.

In conclusion, let us not forget that if Jesus has been all this to us, He expects us to be all this to others. Are we places of refuge to whom poor sinners come? Are we rivers of water refreshing the sad lives that are all around us? Are we as a shadow of a great rock in a weary land to the fainting pilgrims who need our sympathy and help? Lord, help us to know this blessed Man and to minister Him to a broken-hearted world.

CHAPTER 12

QUIETNESS AND TRUST

In quietness and trust is your strength,
but you would have none of it.
  (Isaiah 30:15)

SECTION I—*The Historical Setting*

The historical setting of this chapter furnishes the key to its spiritual meaning. In the days of Isaiah, two great empires were contending for the control of the world, Assyria on the east and Egypt on the west. When they met in conflict, the battleground was frequently the Mediterranean coast, and the small states in that region were the chief sufferers in the clash of arms, and were often ground to powder between the two millstones as they came together. The result of all this was a constant diplomacy on the part of these small states, aiming to combine against their formidable oppressors and to join forces with one or the other as it might seem most politic.

The kingdom of Judah had suffered much from these alliances. God does not love human politics and His prophets ever protested against these compromises with the arm of flesh.

At this time the Jewish politicians were advocating an Egyptian alliance against the increasing power of Assyria, whose invading armies loomed large in the vision and the fears of the people. Isaiah used all the energy and force of his glowing tongue to prevent this move which was both bad politics and bad religion.

So far he had failed and already the ambassadors of the court had gone down to Egypt to arrange for an alliance with Pharaoh. The prophet was commanded to hold this up to ridicule and say that Egypt should help in vain. To give more emphasis to his warnings, he had a great sign made and wrote it in the public view as a sort of epigrammatic caricature of Egypt, "Rahab [a mythical sea monster, whose name means 'storm'] the Do-Noth-

367

ing" (Isaiah 30:7). He told them that the Egyptians would fail them and that the compromise would only bring them into deeper trouble. All this really came to pass. Pharaoh had more than he could do to take care of himself. An Ethiopian invasion came down from the upper Nile, defeated the armies and burned the king alive, and the ambassadors of Judah returned humiliated and disappointed. Meanwhile, the Assyrians, provoked by all this temporizing, as soon as they got through with their eastern troubles, swept down upon the Mediterranean coast and were soon encamped about Jerusalem. All that Isaiah had prophesied had come to pass.

How vividly these texts stand out in the light of history.

This is what the Sovereign LORD, the Holy One of Israel, says:

"In repentance and rest is your salvation,
     in quietness and trust is your strength,
but you would have none of it.
You said, 'No, we will flee on horses.' "
          (30:15–16a)

They refused to take counsel of God and quietly rest and trust in Him, and they said that they would turn to the cavalry of Egypt. With bitter sarcasm the prophet answers,

"We will ride off on swift horses."
     Therefore your pursuers will be swift!
A thousand will flee
     at the threat of one;
at the threat of five
     you will all flee away,
till you are left
     like a flagstaff on a mountaintop,
     like a banner on a hill.
          (30:16–17)

The help of Egypt was to fail them and the Assyrians were to pursue them until they had learned no longer to lean upon the arm of flesh.

But in their distress, God would not forsake them. Beleaguered and besieged by a cruel enemy, His presence would still be with them, comforting, teaching, guiding, cleansing, and at last delivering them. "Yet the LORD longs to be gracious to you;/ he rises to show you compassion./ For the LORD is a God of justice./ Blessed are all who wait for him!" (30:18).

How tenderly will He comfort them in the hour of their distress! "How gracious he will be when you cry for help! As soon as he hears, he will answer you" (30:19). And so near will He come to them that they shall learn to know His voice and follow His direction now, instead of their own fleshly counsel and self-sufficient wisdom. "Whether you turn to the right or to the left, your ears will hear a voice behind you, saying, 'This is the way; walk in it' " (30:21). Better still, their trials shall bring cleansing and righteousness. They will throw away their idols and dishonor their images of silver and gold and their sorrows will be a purifying fire as God intended. Then when all this shall have been accomplished, will come their deliverance.

The picture that follows is one of a beleaguered city set free and a land oppressed with invading armies once more bearing its harvests and covered with its waving orchards and feeding flocks in large pastures and undisturbed tranquility. Instead of scant supplies of water, rivers and streams of waters shall flow from hill and valley. Instead of darkness and gloom, "the moon will shine like the sun, and the sunlight will be seven times brighter, like the light of seven full days, when the LORD binds up the bruises of his people and heals the wounds he inflicted" (30:26).

Then follows the sublime description of the tempest of wrath and judgment with which God shall come down against their enemies. Like the lightning flash and the devouring fire, like the overflowing flood, like the lion defending its young from the foe, like the mother bird fluttering over her nest and guarding her young, and out of the terror of the scene rises at length the joyful sound of praise from a happy and redeemed people.

> And you will sing
>   as on the night you celebrate a holy festival;
> your hearts will rejoice
>   as when people go up with flutes
> to the mountain of the LORD,
>   to the Rock of Israel.
> The LORD will cause men to hear his majestic voice
>   and will make them see his arm coming down
> with raging anger and consuming fire,
>   with cloudburst, thunderstorm and hail.
> The voice of the LORD will shatter Assyria;
>   with his scepter he will strike them down.
>   (30:29–31)

Isaiah has told us in a later chapter how all this came to pass. In the very height of his pride, as the Assyrian with scorn and blasphemy demanded the surrender of the city, the angel of the Lord came forth and in a single night, by one touch of his awful wing, smote down to death a whole army of

185,000 men. And in the book of Psalms we have the record of the songs they sang. The 46th Psalm no doubt celebrates this great deliverance.

> Come and see the works of the LORD,
>   the desolations he has brought on the earth.
> He makes wars cease to the ends of the earth;
>   he breaks the bow and shatters the spear,
>   he burns the shields with fire.
> "Be still, and know that I am God;
>   I will be exalted among the nations,
>   I will be exalted in the earth."
>
> The LORD Almighty is with us;
>   the God of Jacob is our fortress.
>   (46:8–11)

SECTION II—*The Personal Meaning*

All this has a personal meaning for our individual lives. The story of ancient Israel is reenacted in Christian experience still and the lessons of this precious chapter are among the richest and most practical that many of us have ever learned.

OUR TRIALS

1. We too are placed in circumstances of difficulty and danger, even as they. But these are not accidents, but divine ordeals intended to test our spiritual character and bring God into our lives. There are no accidents for the children of God; but all things come through a divine plan and a divine permission, and if rightly met "all things God works for the good of those who love him" (Romans 8:28).

How are we using our trials? Do we become vessels for Him to fill with His larger blessing, or do we let them come in vain and shed the bitter tears of sorrow and find no fruit in compensation?

THE ARM OF THE FLESH

2. Next, there is the danger of trusting in the arm of the flesh. For us, as well as for them, there is still the danger of going down to Egypt and looking to men instead of God for help. Egypt for us represents the world with its resources, its compromises, its empty promises of aid. God is very jealous of His people's confidence. He may use second causes as His means and instruments, but He always wants us to look to Him as the great first Cause

and commit our way to His hands and then leave Him to deliver with or without the help of man.

QUIETNESS AND TRUST

3. This is the attitude in which we should meet every trouble. "In quietness and trust is your strength" (Isaiah 30:15). This is true even in the plane of human reason. It is the man that keeps a cool head and holds himself in tranquil self-command that carries his vessel through the stream and his army through the forlorn hope. It is true in spiritual emergencies. "The one who trusts will never be dismayed" (28:16).

The first thing to do when trouble comes is to be calm and look to God before we think a thought or take a step in our own wisdom. Confidence will bring quietness. It is unbelief that makes us restless and leads us to rush to the first expedient that comes to our mind instead of waiting upon the Lord to show us the way and interpose with His help.

THE RESTLESSNESS AND RECKLESSNESS OF UNBELIEF

4. "But you would have none of it./ You said, 'We will ride off on swift horses' " (30:15d–16a). And so God sometimes lets us have our way. We refuse to leave ourselves in His hand. We rush hither and thither in our great excitement and like them we find that they that pursue are swift. Our expedients fail. Our resources prove unsatisfactory. Our friends are powerless and at last our condition is worse than at the first.

GOD IS WAITING

5. Meanwhile God withdraws and waits till we get through our restlessness and are ready for His help. He does not leave us in our emergency, but He lets us alone to learn our lesson and come to the place where He can really help us and we will let Him. There is nothing more touching than God's waiting love. When Israel refused to follow Him into the Land of Promise and went back for 40 years to their wretched wandering, God did not leave them to wander alone, but "In all their distress he too was distressed,/ and the angel of his presence saved them./ In his love and mercy he redeemed them;/ he lifted them up and carried them all the days of old" (63:9).

The way was hard, but it was not the way He chose for them. They had gone, in spite of Him, back to the wilderness; but lovingly He went with them and cheered them and sustained them through all the trials of the way, until another generation had been born that could understand Him better and follow Him in the path of safety and obedience. So still He comes with us through the weary, wasted years that we have brought upon ourselves. It might have been all so different. He had a better way for us, but we chose our own and He went with us through it. Even in our folly and our wandering His promise is still true, "He will never leave you nor forsake you" (Deuteronomy 31:6).

Beloved, is He waiting thus for you? Have you refused to take the better things He meant for you? Have you kept Him waiting until you have learned by experience your folly and your sin and are ready at last to let Him give you what He meant for you at first?

And while He waits, He comforts, teaches, guides and sanctifies. He uses our very blunders to show us our folly and bring us to wisdom and righteousness. He turns the curse into a blessing. He teaches us through our troubles and at last he becomes so real to us that we too will know "Whether you turn to the right or to the left, your ears will hear a voice behind you, saying, 'This is the way; walk in it' " (Isaiah 30:21).

"Thine eyes shall see thy teachers" (30:20, KJV). By our teachers God means the trials, the experiences, the providences that have come to us through our failure and disobedience. We are so apt to think when things cross our inclination that what we need is that somebody else or something else be made right, when the truth is that it is ourselves who need to be made right. Until we are right God cannot readjust the things of which we complain. Indeed, they are His file designed to polish and smooth our roughness.

A lady went to Mr. Andrew Murray requesting him to speak to her husband about some matters that were greatly grieving her in his conduct toward her and his family. After listening to her complaint, Mr. Murray declined to speak to her husband, but said he would like to talk to her about her own life. She was much surprised when he insisted that the trouble was with her rather than with her husband, and that her first duty was to get her lesson, her blessing, her quietness and peace of mind with the victory over all these things, and when that was accomplished all the rest would easily come about. At first she was offended, but after reflection and prayer, she found he was right and she went to God in humiliation and prayer for her own soul and obtained the quietness and confidence which she needed. A few weeks later she came back to tell her counselor how God had changed all these things in her life and made them so different that everything was harmonious and happy.

The question is not what is the matter with somebody else, but what is the matter with me? The promise to the tried one is, "I will be with him in trouble" (Psalm 91:15), and then comes the next promise, "I will deliver him" (91:15), but we must first have Him with us in victory and then we shall have His deliverance. "God is within her, she will not fall" (46:5), is the first stage. "God will help her at break of day" (46:5), is the consummation. Let us learn the first lesson, and when we are able to stand unmoved, then we shall soon find God's providence working for our deliverance and relief.

It is possible to go through the most trying conditions unmoved. It is possible to find amid the storms of sorrow, a quietness and stillness which we never knew when all was calm without, and it is this which glorifies God as no mere outward condition of circumstances could ever do.

> There is a peace that cometh after sorrow,
> Of hope surrendered, not of hope fulfilled,
> That looks not out upon a bright tomorrow,
> But on a tempest which His hand hath stilled.

CHAPTER 13

THE RIGHTEOUS MAN AND HIS BLESSING

The sinners in Zion are terrified;
  trembling grips the godless:
"Who of us can dwell with the consuming fire?
  Who of us can dwell with everlasting burning?"
He who walks righteously
  and speaks what is right,
who rejects gain from extortion
  and keeps his hand from accepting bribes,
who stops his ears against plots of murder
  and shuts his eyes against contemplating evil—
this is the man who will dwell on the heights,
  whose refuge will be the mountain fortress.
His bread will be supplied,
  and water will not fail him.
    (Isaiah 33:14–16)

The outlook of this prophecy is from the standpoint of Sennacherib's invasion. The prophet represents the land as desolate, the city beleaguered, the ambassadors returning with bitter tears and the hope of the nation crushed as the Assyrian breaks his covenant and turns back to renew the siege of Jerusalem. But suddenly a voice from heaven breaks upon the scene. " 'Now will I arise,' says the LORD" (33:10). God appears upon the stage and in a single night the Assyrian army is destroyed. So tremendous is the impression of this mighty miracle of saving power that the people are appalled. "The sinners in Zion are terrified," and they begin to ask, "Who of us can dwell with the consuming fire?/ Who of us can dwell with everlasting burning?" (33:14). God has appeared as a consuming fire, and although it is their enemies that have perished, yet they tremble at the thought of such a God in their midst and feel as did Peter afterwards when he shrank from the

Master's presence after the miracle of His power, crying, "Go away from me, Lord; I am a sinful man!" (Luke 5:8)

Dr. Adam Smith, in his notes on this passage, introduces a fine figure representing a man looking at a great city fire through a colored glass which neutralizes the flame so that nothing appears but the crumbling pillars and tumbling walls and buildings, and the power that is working the destruction is invisible. But let him drop the glass and look with open face at the scene and instantly he perceives the tremendous element that is working the havoc.

So the people had been looking at the events around them as through a glass that colored their vision. All they could see was the Assyrian coming and going—the mere facts of God's working. But suddenly God had come so near that the scales had fallen from their eyes, the distorting medium through which they looked at things had dropped; and lo, they beheld the presence of Jehovah like the fires and flame, and they shrank from its terrible power, conscious of their utter sinfulness and unfitness for such holy fellowship.

The prophet answers the question. Yes, he says, it is possible to dwell with One who is a consuming fire and not be afraid of the searchlight of His presence. It is possible to get so close to Him that our "eyes will see the king in his beauty/ and view a land that stretches afar" (Isaiah 33:17). But there are moral and spiritual conditions which must precede the vision. It is the man that "walks righteously," that "speaks what is right," that "rejects gain from extortion," "that keeps his hand from accepting bribes," "who stops his ears against plots of murder/ and shuts his eyes against contemplating evil" (33:15). He "will dwell on the heights" (33:16a), and he will enter into the beatific vision of the glory of Jehovah.

SECTION I—*The Righteous Man*

Five things are predicated of the righteous man. They refer to his feet, his tongue, his hands, his ears and his eyes. It is a very realistic picture of practical righteousness.

HIS FEET

1. "He . . . walks righteously" (33:15). His feet are in the right path. The figure of our walk is a common one in the Bible. It describes our whole outward conduct and deportment. It would not be difficult to fill a volume with the divine picture of the path of the saint. Like Enoch he walks with God, keeping step with his heavenly Father and enjoying His intimate companionship and communion. "Whoever claims to live in him must walk as Jesus did" (1 John 2:6). We are to "walk by faith" (2 Corinthians 5:7, KJV).

We are to "walk in love" (Ephesians 5:2, KJV). We are to "walk worthy of the vocation wherewith we are called" (4:1, KJV). We are to "walk circumspectly, not as fools, but as wise" (5:15, KJV). How are we walking? What paths are we treading? What footprints are we leaving? Do we go anywhere where He does not go before us and would not accompany us? Are we walking in the narrow path or in the broad road that leads to destruction?

HIS TONGUE

2. He "speaks what is right" (Isaiah 33:15). His tongue is the next object of the prophet's attention. The condition of our tongue is one of the medical tests of health. This man's tongue is right. "He speaks what is right," that is, as in the sight of God and the hearing of heaven. It is a very solemn thought that just as the phonograph records and keeps the sounds of the human voice and can reproduce our very words in after years, so perhaps yonder God has an automatic mechanism which will reproduce every utterance of our lips and furnish the records of the judgment by and by when, "men will have to give account on the day of judgment for every careless word they have spoken" (Matthew 12:36). The Word of God has much to, say about the tongue. It is not merely what we think and feel, but what we say that defiles and sets on fire our whole being. The spoken word reacts upon us with fatal and corroding poison.

Let us bring our words to the divine standard. Is our tongue pure, reverent, truthful, kind, wise and touched with the fire of Pentecost? Does it belong to God? Does it speak for God? Is it anointed of God and consecrated to His service and His praise? Can we meet the test? He who "speaks what is right." Christians little realize how much they lose by idle, vain and foolish talking. If we had conserved the strength that is wasted on empty talk, it would add years to our lives. "Let your conversation be always full of grace seasoned with salt, so that you may know how to answer everyone" (Colossians 4:6).

HIS HANDS

3. The righteous man has clean hands. He "keeps his hand from accepting bribes" (Isaiah 33:15). The political, social and business world are reeking with corruption of every kind. The true Christian scorns all such things, refuses dishonest gain and avoids the popular methods of reckless speculation and unfair if not unlawful business finances. It is easy to be caught in the whirl of promising ventures and brilliant commercial speculations, the alluring promise of a speedy fortune and enormous profits on trifling investments. These are temptations that beset us on every side. The true servant of Christ will always weigh every transaction not only in the light of conscience

and even of human law, but in the light and the spirit of God's Word. Will our business bear the searchlight of the Scriptures and permit us to dwell with the devouring fire and the everlasting burnings? And will our books stand the inquisition of that day when the fire shall burn the wood, the stubble and the hay?

HIS EARS

4. The righteous man has sanctified ears. He "stops his ears against plots of murder" (33:15). We have no more business to listen to evil than to speak it. A righteous man or woman will refuse to hear scandal, gossip and evil speaking. It is perfectly proper when some malodorous story is brought to you by a gossiping friend to refuse to listen, unless the accuser is willing to have his victim in your presence. You will always find this a sure preventive and you will never be troubled a second time. The injury that is done to character and reputation in this sinful way is not half so great as the injury done to the people that listen to it and that perpetuate it with their scorpion tongues. It is a blessed exemption to have one's mind and memory free from these defiling streams of uncharitableness and sin.

HIS EYES

5. The righteous man has sanctified eyes. "And shuts his eyes against contemplating evil" (33:15). There are many things to which the servant of the Lord should be blind. One of them is his own virtues. Another is the evils of his brethren, and a third is the vanities and the follies of the world. There are evil things that hypnotize. It was by a look that David was led into his great crime. "Turn my eyes away from worthless things" (Psalm 119:37), was the wise petition of the Psalmist. "Let your eyes look straight ahead,/ fix your gaze directly before you./ Make level paths for your feet/ and take only ways that are firm" (Proverbs 4:25–26), was the equally wise direction of the sage of Jerusalem.

Beloved reader, how does your life stand this fivefold test? How can you abide the devouring fire and everlasting burnings when all your ways shall pass under the searchlight of heaven?

SECTION II—*His Blessing*

This righteous man has great and mighty promises.

EXALTATION

1. He "will dwell on the heights" (Isaiah 33:16). We need the New Testament to interpret this promise. It is more than moral sublimity, more than lofty aspiration, more than a high and a noble purpose. It is what the apostle

describes in Ephesians 2:6, "And God raised us up with Christ and seated us with him in the heavenly realms in Christ Jesus."

It is a great spiritual transformation that links our life with Christ upon the throne and makes us citizens of heaven. There is our homeland. There we belong more truly than to any place on earth. There are our affections. There our friends are going fast. There is our future and everlasting home.

Are we claiming this high place? Are we walking with our feet on earth but our heads and hearts above? Are we keeping in close touch with the loved ones that have gone, not through the sinful attempts of spiritualism, but by loving fellowship with Jesus Christ with whom we can ever have communion and know that those we love are with Him there? Are we looking at our trials as we shall one day look upon them from on high and truly dwelling above?

SECURITY

2. "Whose refuge will be the mountain fortress" (Isaiah 33:16). The righteous man who dwells on high in union and fellowship with Jesus Christ is impregnable. "If God is for us, who can be against us?" (Romans 8:31). "Who is going to harm you if you are eager to do good?" (1 Peter 3:13).

There is nothing that we need fear while we abide in Him. We do not have to fight our battles, but take refuge in our Savior and see Him conquer. Oh how safe they are who have found their dwelling "in the shelter of the Most High," and "rest in the shadow of the Almighty" (Psalm 91:1). Of such it is true, "The LORD will watch over your coming and going/ both now and forevermore" (121:8).

SUFFICIENCY

3. "His bread will be supplied,/ and water will not fail him" (Isaiah 33:16). God's blessing includes all temporal things. He does not promise us the bread of idleness nor the bread of luxury, but sufficiency. The records of faith have no richer story than the providence of God in common things in answer to His people's believing prayers.

A LARGER VISION

4. "Your eyes will see the king in his beauty/ and view a land that stretches afar" (33:17). The spiritual vision is characterized by a life of holiness and obedience. "I have more insight than all my teachers," David could say, "for I meditate on your statutes" (Psalm 119:99). There is such a vision of Jesus possible to the soul as will make Him more real than all persons and things and give to the heart such utter satisfaction and rest that we never again can want anything else. The historical Christ apprehended by the intellect is one thing; the living Christ known, realized and loved by the heart is another.

The vision does not add to His beauty, but it makes Him real to us. And from that hour all other attractions fade and all other delights pale before the vision of His love.

> I have seen Jesus and I'm weaned from all beside,
> I have seen Jesus and my wants are all supplied,
> I have seen Jesus and my heart is satisfied,
> Satisfied with Jesus.

But the vision takes in the whole horizon. They will "view a land that stretches afar" (Isaiah 33:17). He will reveal to us not only His beauty, but all that inheritance of blessing which He has for us. "The riches of his glorious inheritance in the saints, and his incomparably great power for us who believe" (Ephesians 1:18b–19a). There is a Land of Promise for every saint just as real as the hills and valleys of ancient Canaan and just as large as our faith is able to take from Him.

Most people have such a limited range of vision. But God promises to give us wider horizons when we see all the fullness of His purpose for us, and all the glory of our destiny as the redeemed children of God, and the years of His kingdom and glory that lift us above the lesser attractions of the world and sin, and we press on to apprehend all for which we have been apprehended of Christ Jesus. Will we ask Him to open our eyes and show us the vision of the "land that stretches afar"?

And then the prophet adds, "your eyes will see Jerusalem,/ a peaceful abode, a tent that will not be moved" (Isaiah 33:20). God will give us the vision of His work and its blessing and prosperity, and then send us forth to make it real.

THE GLORIOUS LIBERTY OF GOD'S FULLNESS

5. "There the LORD will be our Mighty One./ It will be like a place of broad rivers and streams./ No galley with oars will ride them,/ no mighty ship will sail them" (33:21).

This is a very fine figure of the fullness and the freedom into which the Holy Spirit brings the surrendered heart and life. God becomes to us a glorious Lord, and life becomes not a hard struggle like the fight of the toiling rower making his way with strenuous effort through the opposing waves, but like a vessel born on by the mighty current, making our life spontaneous, victorious and sublime.

Beloved, do we know Him as the glorious Lord? Have we found our place in the mid-current of this mighty river of His love and power, and is our life not a desperate endeavor, but a glorious liberty of love and power? Let us grasp the vision and let us rise to meet it.

CHAPTER 14

PENTECOSTAL OUTPOURINGS
OF THE HOLY SPIRIT

Till the Spirit is poured upon us from on high,
and the desert becomes a fertile field,
and the fertile field seems like a forest.
(Isaiah 32:15)

The prophet Isaiah is not only a witness to the Messiah but also to the Holy Spirit. It was the touch of the heavenly fire upon his lips that called and consecrated him to his high vocation as we read in chapter six. And it was by His anointing that the Messiah Himself was to be prepared for His greater ministry as we read in chapter 11. Here we have the picture of a great outpouring of the Holy Spirit upon Israel and the world, and the glorious results of this—transforming the wilderness into a fruitful field and making the fruitful field seem to be a forest in contrast with the new scene of fertility and beauty which this great revival would bring.

The air is full of the tokens of revival. The hearts of God's people are going out in earnest prayer for a great outpouring of the Holy Spirit. We turn with intense interest to this picture of the necessity and the effects of such an awakening.

SECTION I—*The Need*

"For the land of my people,/ a land overgrown with thorns and briers—/ . . . till the Spirit is poured upon us from on high" (Isaiah 32:13, 15). These thorns and briers may well describe the character of every product of the soil of nature. All man's philosophies and religions are but weeds. Only the Holy Spirit can transform the wilderness into a garden of the Lord. Man's culture and husbandry have failed. Social reform and ethical teaching will not regenerate society. Let us not waste our strength in second-class things, but work with God on His higher plane through the gospel of Jesus Christ and the power of the Holy Spirit.

But the thorns and briers are not all found in the wilderness of the world, but often in the hearts of Christians and in the enclosures of the church itself. Without the Holy Spirit our life and our work are filled with weeds and our best things turn to waste. Our Lord has taught us in the parable of the sower what these thorns are. "Other seed fell among thorns, which grew up and choked the plants" (Matthew 13:7). "The one who received the seed that fell among the thorns is the man who hears the word, but the worries of this life and the deceitfulness of wealth choke it, making it unfruitful" (13:22). Or as expressed by Luke in chapter 8:14, "The seed that fell among thorns stands for those who hear, but as they go on their way they are choked by life's worries, riches and pleasures, and they do not mature."

"But the worries of this life, the deceitfulness of wealth and the desires for other things come in and choke the word, making it unfruitful" (Mark 4:19). What a picture of many of our hearts and lives! The strength of our nature absorbed in seeking pleasure, pursuing ambition or amassing wealth, little time for God, the business of the week day encroaching even on God's Sabbath, the family altar pushed aside and both mind and body so worn with care and pleasure that there is little energy or leisure for private prayer, for the study of God's Word or for the work of winning souls.

I recently met a young fellow one Sabbath morning who lately used to be an earnest Christian worker. He was on his way to business. "How are you getting on?" was asked. "Oh, very well." "Are you busy?" "Yes, very busy." And looking into his face earnestly the question was added, "Are you too busy?" A look of earnestness lighted up his countenance and with an expression of pain he answered, "Yes, too busy; for I am now on my way to business, and it seems as if I cannot help it without giving up my position altogether."

Ah, Christian brother, take care lest you get too busy. The lives of most Christians today, it is to be feared, are like the old garden grown up with weeds and thorns. Some day you will have to take time to meet the Master. Alas for you if you will have nothing to bring but thorns!

SECTION II—*The Pentecostal Blessing*

"Till the Spirit is poured upon us from on high" (Isaiah 32:15). This is more than the coming of the Holy Spirit in our individual lives. This is a public outpouring of the Holy Spirit upon the church and a special visitation to the individual heart. This is one of the promises of the New Testament: there will be days of refreshing from the presence of the Lord (Acts

3:19). Such an outpouring came on the day of Pentecost, and such seasons of revival were occasional features of the Apostolic church and have been among the richest blessings of the church of Christ in all ages. God is pouring out His Spirit at this time in very wonderful ways in the valleys of Wales and upon the great cities of England. Some of these seasons of blessing are quite phenomenal, having little human leadership or machinery about them and showing the mighty hand of God alone.

Such an outpouring of the Holy Spirit is the best remedy for all the evils of our individual and church life. It will lead sinners to repentance. It will bring men to realize the presence and power of God. It will awaken Christians from their sleep of death. It will honor the Word of God and revive the work of the gospel in all the world and it will bring about a mighty uplift in the work of the world's evangelization. God is waiting to send us such a blessing. Let us earnestly desire it. Let us prayerfully seek it and let us put ourselves in line with it before it comes.

SECTION III—*The Great Transformation*

"The desert becomes a fertile field" (Isaiah 32:15). It is very beautiful to travel through the western prairies, and after hours of sweeping over the arid desert with nothing but the drifting sand and the scrubby sage brush, to suddenly come upon a little town lying like an island of beauty in a sea of desolation, the fields and gardens exquisitely green, streams flowing through every garden and along every highway, and the whole place literally blossoming like a rose. Ask someone for an explanation and he will tell you it is the very same desolate soil that you have been passing through all day, but in this case the only explanation is the single word, "irrigation." The waters have been brought down from the mountains and the wilderness has become a fruitful field.

Such a transformation takes place in the most wretched and sinful lives when God comes into them with His grace. How we have seen them in these years come from the street, from the saloon, from the depths of sin, haggard, unkempt, with hollow eyes and hopeless hearts, and at the feet of Jesus receive His cleansing touch, bathe in the living water and begin to drink of the fountain of life! How marvelously they have changed! In a few days you behold them clothed and in their right mind; happy-faced girls, manly men, transformed lives literally resurrected from the grave, and entering upon a career of happiness, usefulness and blessing to the world. Hundreds of such men and women today are leading our rescue missions at home and working on our fields abroad and passing on the blessing that has come to them to thousands more. When we think that the coming of the Holy Spirit will bring just such transformations to thousands of wretched hearts and homes around us, oh, surely we should give ourselves no rest until we seek and gain these promised showers of blessings.

SECTION IV—*Righteousness and Peace*

Justice will dwell in the desert
  and righteousness live in the fertile field.
The fruit of righteousness will be peace;
  the effect of righteousness will be quietness and confidence
    forever.
My people will live in peaceful dwelling places,
  in secure homes,
  in undisturbed places of rest.
    (32:16–18)

The outpouring of the Holy Spirit will bring righteousness to the wilderness. Even in the social and secular world, conditions will be revolutionized, wickedness will be checked, intemperance, vice and misery will be restrained and the face of society will be transformed. So much is this the case in the recent revival in Wales that the very saloons have lost their business and the courts of justice are without occupation. We are not going to see this come to pass everywhere in the present age. These, however, are samples of what the Holy Spirit can do and what the coming of our Lord in a little while will do throughout the entire world. Oh let us realize it and seek it to the utmost possible extent even in this present mingled condition of human society. "Righteousness lives in the fertile field" (32:16) refers to the sanctification of believers and the higher standard of holiness in the church which the outpouring of the Holy Spirit will bring.

The final result of this blessing will be the reign of peace and joy in every heart and home. "The fruit of righteousness will be peace" (32:17). It is not designed that our life shall be occupied in the constant excitement of religious meetings, but in our hearts and homes and the normal current of duty, this beautiful picture will be realized and "the peace of God, which transcends all understanding, will guard your hearts and your minds in Christ Jesus" (Philippians 4:7).

Through such awakenings thousands of God's happy children today, at one time entered into the rest of faith and the deeper life which has not only satisfied their spiritual needs but multiplied a hundredfold their power to bless others. Such blessings are waiting the present generation through the coming of the Holy Spirit. Oh that we may seek and find that blessing in all its fullness!

SECTION V—*The Uplifting of Our Christian Life to Higher Ideals*

"The fertile field seems like a forest" (Isaiah 32:15). This is a very remarkable expression and the obvious meaning is that so great shall be the transformation of the church, hearts and Christian life of the individual, that the vision we have hitherto known shall seem as nothing in comparison with the blessing that is to come. Even the fruitful valley will be so improved that it will seem as if it had only been a forest before.

One of the worst features of the private and public life, even of the people of God, is the tendency to sink into ruts and to grow rigid and frigid in the formal, conventional routine of life. The old proverb, "Good enough is never good," is in place here. No doubt the reason so little progress is made by very many persons is because they are measuring themselves by old standards and really never getting any further on. When the Holy Spirit comes, He lifts our minds to new ideals and gives us conceptions of things so much in advance of our present experiences that we long for higher ground; the saved become sanctified and the sanctified rise to a life of sacrifice and unselfish service. We see our own shortcomings, our sins of omission of duty, self life, our worries, anxieties and cares, our narrow sympathies, our low conceptions of God, our little faith and our unworthy standards and aims so that we cry out for all the fullness of God, "forgetting what is behind and straining toward what is ahead" (Philippians 3:13). The promises of God rise before us with new vividness, the possibilities of a victorious Christian life allure us, and the voice of God is heard crying, "Whom shall I send? And who will go for us?" (Isaiah 6:8). Sometimes God permits us to see in some other life the glorious possibilities we are missing and we rise up to new planes, new ambitions, new visions and new commissions of service of God and man. It was the apostle's prayer for the Ephesians that they might know "his incomparably great power for us who believe" (Ephesians 1:19), and this was to come about through "the eyes of your heart [being] enlightened" (1:18). Again he declares in the second chapter of First Corinthians, "No eye has seen, no ear has heard, no mind has conceived what God has prepared for those who love him" (2:9).

When this vision comes there rises before us the alluring prospect of that better country which Christ is waiting to bring us into:

> Rejoicing now in earnest hope,
> We stand, and from the mountain top
> We see all the land below.
> Rivers of milk and honey rise
> And all the fruits of paradise
> In endless plenty grow.

To dull eyes which can appreciate only earthly things, the things of God are clothed with enchanting beauty. The sinner grows sick of his sin, the worldling turns from his elusive dreams, the discouraged and defeated saint takes heart again and our dull, cold Christian life becomes a romance of beauty and blessing.

There is a thrilling story told of a man of great wealth and brilliant genius who had become a leader in the industrial life of the land and the master of an enormous fortune, but who had no taste for art or music or high things. One day he was called upon by an old schoolmate from the distant land where both were born and who in turn had become illustrious in his profession as a musician. He invited the merchant prince to come to one of his concerts and hear him play on his famous violin, but the millionaire laughed at him and said he had no time for such trifles; he was engaged in more practical things. At last the musician caught his friend by strategy. He took his violin one day to the factory of the rich man and asked him to make some trifling repairs upon it, as he was a machinist while the other was only a musician. After the trifling work had been done, the musician began to play to see if it was all right, but before half a dozen bars of music had been rolled off, the millionaire was standing with the tears streaming down his face with undisguised admiration and delight. The music had broken his heart and the musician had conquered him by his wiles. Not only so, the whole factory became demoralized; and as he played on, the entrancing strains gathered clerks, foremen, porters, everybody, in crowds around the door, and at last the musician apologized for disturbing their business. But the great man, wiping tears from his eyes, said, "Don't stop for the world. Play on; I never knew till this moment how much I had missed out of my life." Poor man, he found that day a new world of sweetness to which he had been a stranger, and his heart longed for more.

In a far higher sense, that is what happens when the light of heaven falls upon the heart and we see the King in His beauty and view a land that is very far off. Then earthly things pale before the vision of that better country and our hearts long for God and heaven. Oh, if we should go on in our blindness until it is too late! Oh, if some day we should wake to hear "harpists playing their harps" (Revelation 14:2), and the new song they sing above, and discover at last that we have no part in it, but have thrown our lives away upon the barren, empty wilderness of life, ours would be the eternal sorrow and an irretrievable loss!

Let us ask God to open our vision, to waken our hearts, to show us the things that are true and good and beautiful and everlasting, the things which "no eye has seen,/ no ear has heard,/ no mind has conceived/ [but] what God has prepared for those who love him" and which "God has revealed . . . to us by his Spirit" (1 Corinthians 2:9–10).

Oh, that the great Revealer might come to us and show us the vision! Oh, that the great Inspirer might come to us and lift our hearts to meet it! Oh, that the great Enabler might come and transform our lives and make the vision real even here as well as in the life everlasting!

CHAPTER 15

SHOWERS OF BLESSING

For I will pour water on the thirsty land,
and streams on the dry ground.
(Isaiah 44:3)

The Holy Spirit is falling upon His people. An organized religious movement of great power is sweeping over Great Britain and centering at the present time in its metropolis. A still more remarkable spontaneous revival is rolling over the valleys of Wales. Already it has brought tens of thousands to God and changed the face of society in scores of communities. In our own land, the Holy Spirit is working with great power in many places. Such tokens give blessed emphasis to the promise of our text and encourage us to expect yet greater things through the outpouring of the Spirit from on high. This gives us a threefold picture.

SECTION I—*The Field*

The prophet repeats himself in the familiar form of a Hebrew parallelism, and yet the verses are not exactly parallel when he speaks of "him who is thirsty" (KJV) and the "dry ground."

THE DRY GROUND

1. This means that the Holy Spirit is waiting to come, in answer to the prayers of God's people, upon the hardest, the deadest and the most discouraging fields. It reminds one of the soil of some tropical country after months of drought, when the ground is baked like stone and clouds of dust sweep over the land with every passing breeze, while the very air seems like liquid fire and no green or living thing remains in forest or field, until the monsoons pour down and "the wilderness will rejoice and blossom" (35:1).

Such is the transformation that the Holy Spirit brings to a wretched heathen community, to the besotted drunkard's home, to the heart that has been steeped in sin and hardened with years of daring wickedness and to the church which has become like a cemetery in its cold formalism while God has been saying to it, "you have a reputation of being alive, but you are dead" (Revelation 3:1). It is upon just such people and communities that the power of a great revival falls, and God is waiting to work these wonders of His grace and power in answer to our believing prayers.

HIM THAT IS THIRSTY

2. This is the promise for the individual Christian. It describes that on which the coming of the Holy Spirit to the individual heart depends. In the natural world a vacuum always brings a current of air to fill, and in the spiritual realm it is just as true that a condition of conscious need never fails to bring supply of God's presence and Holy Spirit. I never can forget my visit to the Telegu mission in India and the extraordinary way in which this promise was fulfilled in the experience of one of the native teachers at Rampatam.

Our little party had just come late on Saturday night and on Sabbath morning we went to the native church with the good pastor. After his sermon, he announced that in the evening two strangers would give an address on the Holy Spirit. It seems that at the time a great spiritual awakening was coming over this wonderful mission. A few years before tens of thousands had been converted, but now they were seeking the deeper blessing, the baptism of the Holy Spirit; the announcement of a meeting for that purpose evidently awakened the deepest interest, and a look of expectancy brightened their countenances.

On returning from the service to the pastor's house, one of the native teachers, a physician, was waiting. Approaching the pastor he said with great earnestness that he had come to hear about this blessing, for he greatly needed it and could not be satisfied to wait till evening. As we looked at that earnest face, we felt that the Spirit had already fallen upon him and he was indeed thirsty. We all knelt down and began to repeat special promises. This was the first that came to our mind, "I will pour water upon him that is thirsty, and floods upon the dry ground." It seemed to take hold of him and after a few other promises had been successively repeated, he began to pray in his native Telegu. It was one of the most touching prayers we have ever heard. We could not follow the words and yet we could follow the spirit of it every moment. With cries of heart agony, he called upon God, told Him how he longed for this blessing. After a while his tone changed and a look of trust began to overspread his countenance. As he still prayed on, the tone of hope and joy increased and in a little while his face was shining with holy gladness and he was pouring out his thanksgivings for the blessing that had come to him. When at length he was able to stop this torrent of prayer, he turned to us and began to embrace us one by one, and such a look of unutterable joy I have seldom seen upon a human countenance.

The Holy Spirit is just as ready to meet our cry and satisfy our thirst. It would seem as if a condition of intense desire were necessary as a preparation for the blessing. Just as hunger prepares us to assimilate food, so the deep desires of the heart for the divine blessing prepares it to receive that blessing according to a great spiritual law of the fitness of things. Are we thirsting for this priceless blessing? Have we found the fountains of earthly pleasure disappointing? Have the waters of time turned to bitterness? Do we long to rise to the highest things and be used of God in blessing to others? Let us send up our cry:

> While on others Thou art calling
> Let some blessing fall on me.

SECTION II—*The Flood*

The Holy Spirit is compared to water frequently in the Scriptures. The stream that flowed from the smitten rock in Horeb was God's peculiar type of the coming of the Spirit through the atoning death of Jesus Christ. The subsequent history of that stream, that flowed through the desert and could be tapped and opened at any time and made to give forth from its subterranean depths the fullness of supply for themselves, their children and their cattle, is a still more complete type of the deeper fullness of the Holy Spirit in the hearts and lives of the children of God. Like water, the Holy Spirit satisfies, cleanses and fertilizes. Nothing else can fill the void of the human heart. Nothing else can take away the power of sin. Nothing else can make the desert to bloom as the rose.

Two forms of the Spirit's operations are here set forth, the ordinary and the extraordinary. Even the ordinary work of the Spirit is expressed by the strong figure, "I will pour water," but His extraordinary ministry is described by a more emphatic figure, "I will pour . . . streams [floods, KJV] on the dry ground" (Isaiah 44:3). These floods represent the occasional outpouring of the Spirit of God in seasons of great revival which the church is witnessing now in many places and which earnest Christian hearts are longing to see everywhere.

Such seasons of mighty blessing are powerful witnesses for God, awakening the attention of a careless world and compelling even the most skeptical and indifferent to recognize the reality and power of the gospel of Jesus Christ. Such seasons, for a time at least, lift up a standard against the enemy and check the prevalence and power of evil as no mere human words or authorities ever can. God becomes His own witness and the scoffer and the sinner are awed and humbled before the majesty of the Lord. Let us pray for such a mighty outpouring of the Holy Spirit in our day. We are warranted to expect such manifestations of divine power especially as the coming of our Lord draws nigh. These are to be the very signs that will herald His return, "I will pour out my Spirit on all people" (Joel 2:28), He says, "I will show wonders in the heavens and on the earth . . . before the coming of the great and dreadful day of the LORD" (2:30–31).

SECTION III—*The Fruit*

"They will spring up like grass in a meadow,/ like willows [KJV] by flowing streams" (Isaiah 44:4). One thing about the grass is the multitudinousness of it. Even the little lawn that fronts your cottage has myriads of blades of grass in it, and each one is different from its fellow. When the Holy Spirit comes in power, He will touch myriads of hearts and multitudes will respond to His call and thousands and tens of thousands of souls will flock to the Savior.

Another thing about the grass is its commonness. It represents those things of the Holy Spirit that touch our ordinary life and make its most secular and simple duties to shine with the grace and glory of the Lord.

Then there is nothing more beautiful than the grass, so fresh, so green and so unfading in its verdure. The flowers may come and go, but the grass is perennial. And so the Holy Spirit brings the blessing that is abiding and covers the life of a Christian, the home, the church, with a beauty and glory that can never fade.

Another fine illustration of the fruit of the Spirit is the willow by the water courses. The most remarkable thing about the willow is that it cannot live apart from the water courses, and so the Christian cannot live without the Holy Spirit. Indeed, it is absolutely true that the more fully we are surrendered to God, the more utterly are we dependent upon Him, so that we cannot take one step or breathe a single breath apart from Him. The willow follows that water, and when the fountains are abundant, its leaves are green and its beauty unfading. I have heard of a gardener who tried for a year to change the shape of a willow which insisted upon growing all to one side. In vain he pruned and slashed at the lopsided branches; they still persisted in growing that way. One day he took a spade and dug down below the roots of the tree and then he found that a subterranean stream was running on the side to which the willow leaned. It simply followed the fountain that fed its life. He put away his pruning knife and then dug a little channel for the river around the other side of the tree, and lo, next year it grew toward the river and became symmetrical and beautiful without a touch of violence.

That is what we need to change the deformities of our lives; not more trying, not more suffering, not more scolding, not more condemning of ourselves, but more life, more help, more love, more of the precious grace of Jesus Christ and the power of the Holy Spirit. Then our lives will grow to Him by whom they are sustained, and it will be true of us, "For from him and through him and to him are all things./ To him be the glory forever! Amen" (Romans 11:36).

SECTION IV—*Individual Blessings*

The prophet next describes the individual blessing that will follow these gracious outpourings.

CONVERSION

1. "One will say, 'I belong to the LORD' " (Isaiah 44:5). The Holy Spirit will lead souls, one by one, to Christ. How beautiful it is to read in the account of the Welsh revival of people springing up all over the meeting spontaneously and confessing the Savior they had just found. It was not through preaching, but through personal dealing with the Holy Spirit who was present pleading with souls all over the place, and they yielded and confessed Him one by one just as they settled the great transaction. Anyone can be saved the moment he is ready to confess Christ as his Savior: "If you confess with your mouth, 'Jesus is Lord,' and believe in your heart that God raised him from the dead, you will be saved" (Romans 10:9). This is a personal confession directly to God and He accepts it and records the name of the confessor in the Lamb's book of life.

UNITING WITH THE PEOPLE OF GOD

2. "Another will call himself by the name of Jacob" (Isaiah 44:5b). This undoubtedly represents the identifying of the individual with the Lord's people. When the Holy Spirit truly leads souls to Christ, they always want to belong to His people. How quickly all censorious criticism about churches and church members disappears and the true and humble spirit turns to the children of God for fellowship, sympathy and help. It is the duty of the young convert to attach himself to the fold of Christ. Although there may be many imperfections in the visible church, yet it is far safer to be inside than outside, and all who truly love the Master will want to be identified with some branch of His cause.

THE COVENANTED LIFE

3. "Still another will write on his hand, 'The LORD'S' " (44:5c). This

represents that closer covenant into which it is the privilege of the individual soul to enter with the Lord Jesus. Dr. Phillip Dodrige recommends to young Christians to write down their covenant and formally sign it and ratify it, and then preserve it, and he suggests a very solemn form in which the soul may give itself to the Lord and claim His covenant blessing.

There is no doubt that such personal covenants have brought great blessing to those that have faithfully kept them. And as we look back upon the records of our own lives we will find that even where we have failed "He will remain faithful" (2 Timothy 2:13).

HIGHER SPIRITUAL BLESSING

4. The next clause, "and will take the name Israel" (Isaiah 44:5c), seems to express the highest spiritual experiences. Israel stands for much more than Jacob. It marks the second stage of the patriarch's spiritual life when the Supplanter became the Prince of God. When the Holy Spirit comes, He leads the willing heart in the deeper and higher things of God. He shows the young convert that it is his privilege to be baptized with the Holy Spirit, to receive the Lord Jesus as an indwelling presence, to be delivered from the power of self and sin and to enter into a life of abiding victory, rest and power.

Indeed, these are among the richest fruits of every true revival, and no wise Christian worker will be satisfied until the souls committed to his care have been led into all the fullness of Christ. This is presented here as a voluntary act and as the privilege of all who are willing to rise to it. God does not force His best things upon us, but offers them to our holy ambition.

Will we, as we realize this mighty promise, rise to it for ourselves and claim, even as we read these lines, these showers of blessing, these floods of power and these glorious fruits for our own individual Christian life and the cause and kingdom of our Lord and Savior, Jesus Christ?

CHAPTER 16

THE HOLY SPIRIT AND THE GOSPEL

The Spirit of the Sovereign LORD is on me,
because the LORD has anointed me
to preach good news to the poor.
He has sent me to bind up the brokenhearted,
to proclaim freedom for the captives
and release from darkness for the prisoners,
to proclaim the year of the LORD'S favor
and the day of vengeance of our God,
to comfort all who mourn.
(Isaiah 61:1–2)

T he New Testament quotation of this verse leaves no doubt of its Messianic meaning. To say that it was only the prophet's vision of his own inspiration is beneath its obvious meaning and the grandeur of its true application. In this verse the Lord Jesus is personified in anticipation of His future ministry and applies to Himself the language which He afterwards uttered with His own lips in the synagogue at Nazareth.

There came a day when the Master went forth from Nazareth after 30 years of quiet, patient toil, to the banks of the Jordan and, offering up His life to the Father and the world in the beautiful, symbolical rite of baptism, received from the open heavens the visible baptism of the Holy Spirit and the distinct testimony of His Father's voice to His divine Sonship and Messiahship.

Then came 40 days of testing and conflict in the wilderness and this led up to a deeper baptism of the Spirit and the commencement of His public ministry. Speaking of it in the context before us, Luke says, "Jesus returned to Galilee in the power of the Spirit, and news about him spread through the whole countryside. He taught in their synagogues, and everyone praised him" (Luke 4:14–15).

It was eminently proper that the first public announcement of the objects of His ministry should be made at Nazareth, His former home. Therefore, with deliberate purpose, He entered the synagogue on the Sabbath day, and being recognized already as a Rabbi and public teacher, the leader of the services courteously offered to Him the scroll of the sacred Scriptures and invited Him to give some message in connection with the services of the day. Turning at once to this passage in Isaiah, He read the text. Then, stopping abruptly before reading the last clause about the "day of vengeance of our God," He closed the book or scroll, and sitting down began to offer, as was customary, a few words of exposition and application. His very first sentence awakened the astonished interest of all His audience as, applying the prophecy directly to Himself, He declared, "Today this scripture is fulfilled in your hearing" (Luke 4:21). There can therefore be no doubt about the meaning of the prophecy and its application to our Lord Himself.

SECTION I—*The Relation of the Holy Spirit to Christ*

The first lesson suggested by the text in its historical fulfillment is the relation of the Holy Spirit to Christ.

This is a subject that is well worthy of the closest study, for it teaches us much practical truth not only in connection with the Master, but also with our own spiritual life. For if He was our forerunner, and if it is true that "because in this world we are like him" (1 John 4:17), then the definite steps of our Lord's experience should be repeated and fulfilled in the lives of His followers. There is no doubt that in some sense the Lord Jesus had the Presence of the Holy Spirit in connection with His birth and His early life. The announcement of His birth stated explicitly, "The Holy Spirit will come upon you, and the power of the Most High will overshadow you. So the holy one to be born will be called the Son of God" (Luke 1:35). Christ, therefore, was born in His divine and human person through the Holy Spirit. Nor can we question that the wonderful grace and wisdom which marked His childhood and youth were the result of the Holy Spirit's influence. And yet there came a day when in some entirely new and higher sense the Holy Spirit, like a dove, descended and abode upon Him. From that time there were two personalities connected with the life and work of our Lord. Jesus, the Son of God, was in direct union with the Spirit of God, and all His words and all His works were inspired by the Holy Spirit. He could truly say, "The Spirit of the Lord is on me, because he has anointed me to preach good news to the poor" (4:18). Indeed, from this time He attributed all His works to the power of the Holy Spirit who dwelt in Him, and one of the very reasons why the sin of rejecting Him was so aggravated was just because it was a sin not only against Him, but against the Holy Spirit who dwelt in Him and spoke and wrought through Him.

Now, if this be true of the Master, it should also be true of His followers. If our Lord did not venture to begin His public ministry until He had been baptized with power from on high, and if He attributed all His work to the power and anointing of the Holy Spirit, what folly and presumption it must be for us to try to serve Him by our own resources, gifts and wisdom. Is it applying the parallel too rigidly to say that just as He was born of the Spirit and yet afterwards baptized of the Spirit in the sense of a direct personal union and indwelling of the Holy Spirit, so likewise His people should not only experience a new birth through the grace and power of the Holy Spirit, but should yield themselves, as he did in His baptism, for the indwelling and abiding of the Comforter in the very same sense in which the Spirit came to Him? There is no stronger argument for the scripturalness of this deeper experience which God is giving to so many of His children in these days than the example of the Master Himself.

Beloved reader, have you received the Holy Spirit since you believed, and have you been endowed with power from on high for your life and work even as He?

But this truth has another side, not only affecting our individual privileges as believers, but the whole gospel dispensation. In one very remarkable passage, the Lord Jesus explained to His disciples the reason why He wrought His miracles by the power of the Holy Spirit. "But if I drive out demons by the Spirit of God," He said, "then the kingdom of God has come upon you" (Matthew 12:28). It was as if He had said, "If I perform my miracles and accomplish my work by virtue of my own inherent power and deity, and then withdraw from the world after my resurrection and ascension, it might be said that I had taken the power with me; but if, on the other hand, these ministries and miracles are accomplished not by my own inherent power, but by the Spirit that dwells in me, and is afterwards to dwell in you and perpetuate my ministry, then indeed the kingdom of God has come nigh to you. The gifts and powers of the kingdom are not withdrawn by my return to heaven, but they continue permanently through all the future generations of the Christian age, and the Holy Spirit still carries on my work just as truly as I have begun to carry it on during my earthly ministry."

This gives perpetuity to all the supernatural features of Christ's life and work and to the apostolic age. And, as someone has said with great beauty and power, it makes the Lord Jesus our contemporary to the end of time. Then we should cease to talk about the apostolic age as though it were a privileged period, for there is but one age, the age of the Holy Spirit, and we are living in it just as truly as the apostles and immediate followers of the Lord Jesus were.

What a blessed reality all this gives to our Christian faith and hope! The kingdom of God has indeed come upon us. It is in our midst, and the promise of the departing Master is just as true as we will allow Him to make it. "Surely I am with you always, to the very end of the age" (28:20b). "I tell you the truth, anyone who has faith in me will do what I have been doing. He will do even greater things than these, because I am going to the Father" (John 14:12). When this fully dawns upon the conception of the church of God, she will arise to her heavenly birthright, and the promise of Joel will be fulfilled in a more glorious way than has been witnessed even in the past. "I will show wonders in the heavens/ and on the earth,/ . . ./ before the coming of the great and dreadful day of the LORD" (Joel 2:30–31).

SECTION II—*The Holy Spirit and the Gospel*

Not only does this glorious text give us the revelation of the Spirit in His relation to Christ, but an equally blessed revelation of the Spirit in His relation to the gospel. For the Holy Spirit came upon Christ to anoint Him for the publication of the gospel, and the same Holy Spirit still comes upon the church and ministry for the same purpose and with the same gospel.

What a glorious gospel it is, and what a glorious thing to think about it, not merely as the gospel of Jesus Christ, but as the gospel of the Holy Spirit; for it is not only a proclamation once made by lips that are dead, but it is a proclamation repeated afresh to every soul that will receive it by the very One who first breathed it from the lips of Christ, the Holy Comforter. Someone has well called it the gospel of the Jubilee, for the whole setting of this proclamation is just a figure and the frame of Israel's ancient year of Jubilee.

There was nothing more splendid in all the glorious ceremonial ritual of ancient Israel than the event of the 50th year, or the year of Jubilee. It was a great national festival a whole year long, and its one keynote was rejoicing and gladness. With the early dawn of the 10th day of the seventh month, the glad trumpets of the Jubilee were heard resounding from every mountain top throughout the land, and immediately the whole nation set itself to keep the glad holiday for an entire year. Even the fields rested from their accustomed harvest, the workman laid aside the implements of his toil and the very cattle entered into the national rest and rejoicing. Then you could have seen the little family circles all over the land winding their way back to the little cottage, which years before they had been obliged to leave because it was mortgaged and sold over their heads; but on the year of Jubilee all debts were canceled, all mortgages were worthless, all lost estates were restored, and again with tears and songs of gladness they embraced each other on the threshold of their home and felt that they were back to their own again. And as they sat rejoicing under their vine and fig tree, here and there you might behold a son or a daughter welcomed home. They had been slaves in some distant town, or to some wealthy family, and had to serve for weary years in payment of some debt or obligations, but now they were free. The year of Jubilee emancipated every slave, and fathers and mothers, and brothers and sisters, welcomed back the lost one to the family circle. There too, you could have seen the prisoner stepping out from his dungeon and hastening to his home and beginning life again with the assurance that all his liabilities, disabilities and reproaches were blotted out by this glad year of emancipation. It was just a little bit of heaven let down on earth and might well afford a splendid figure of that glorious age of happiness, hope and holy liberty which the Lord Jesus and the glorious gospel have brought to men and which His second coming in a little while will bring to grander consummation.

It is to this our text refers when it says, "To proclaim the year of the LORD'S favor" (Isaiah 61:2a). But indeed, every clause and every phrase has a note of the Jubilee in it. Good tidings to the poor, liberty to the captive, joy to the brokenhearted, all these are just fulfillment of the ancient type. Four points will sufficiently sum up this gospel of the Jubilee.

THE PAYMENT OF ALL DEBTS

1. The Jubilee canceled every debt, and so the coming of the Lord has provided for our debt of sin and blotted out our condemnation, and given to us God's decree of righteousness and making us "accepted in the beloved" "even as He."

LIBERTY TO THE CAPTIVES

2. Christ has brought us deliverance from the slavery of sin and Satan, and power to overcome our old hearts, our evil habits and all our temptations and spiritual foes. Not only is this the Gospel of Christ, but it is the Gospel of the Holy Spirit. Not only was it proclaimed once, but it is made real 10,000 times as men receive Him and let Him work it out in their surrendered lives.

THE RESTORATION OF OUR LOST HERITAGE

3. The Jubilee gave back the home that had been forfeited and the inheritance that had been lost; and so Christ comes to us proclaiming:

> Ye that have sold for naught
>   Your heritage above,
> Receive it back unbought,
>   The price of Jesus' love;
> The year of Jubilee has come,
>   Return, ye ransomed sinners, home.

Not only has Christ proclaimed it, but the Holy Spirit is constantly making it true. He comes to the discouraged life dragged down by its hopeless past and He says, "I will repay you for the years the locusts have eaten" (Joel 2:25). Oh this blessed Friend, that gives back the things that we have lost. No life is too blighted, no past is too discouraging, no case is too hard for His grace and power.

> Nothing is too hard for Jesus;
> No man can work like Him.

But all this is as nothing compared with what awaits us in the days of restitution in which His coming again is to bring back our moldering body, our departed friends, our lost paradise, and it shall be true:

> Our more than Egypt's shame
> Exchanged for Canaan's glory,
> And our lost heaven won.

A GOSPEL OF GLADNESS

4. Above all else the year of Jubilee was a year of joy and the gospel of the Holy Spirit is a gospel of gladness. The Holy Spirit is the messenger and the source of peace and lasting joy. We do not need to go to heaven to know its joys. "For the kingdom of God is not a matter of eating and drinking, but of righteousness, peace and joy in the Holy Spirit" (Romans 14:17).

Now all this is not an old gospel merely, but a gospel ever new. The blessed Spirit is with us not only to whisper it to the troubled heart, but to make it real in our deepest life. Let us not attempt to preach that gospel without "the Holy Spirit sent from heaven" (1 Peter 1:12). Salvation is not a creed; it is a life, and the world is yet to realize all that is meant by the dispensation of the Holy Spirit.

Oh, that we might have in our hearts the joy that He brings to commend this gospel, and that we might so believe in Him that He will also work in the hearts of all who hear and make our gospel to be not in word only, but in power.

But there is one impressive fact in connection with this text that we must not pass by without a further reference. It was not without deep significance that the Lord Jesus paused and "closed the book" at the passage in the prophecy which He did. The book which He closed was the record of judgment, "the day of vengeance of our God" (Isaiah 61:2b). The time for that had not yet come. This is the day of grace, the day of mercy, the day of probation, but we read in the sacred volume of a day when the "books shall be opened." The Lord will take up the scroll again and turn to the place where He left off, and the heavens will echo with that last clause, "the day of vengeance of our God." The parenthesis of grace is almost over, the climax will come with His appearing. Dear reader, make haste to know Him as your Friend and Savior before you meet Him as your Judge. Make haste to take refuge in the gospel of the Jubilee before you shall be awakened by the trumpet of the judgment.

There is a story told of a lady who had a case at law that caused her much concern. She went to an attorney and asked him to take it up, and he was disposed to do so. Although the case was a bad one, he said, "If you will commit it to my hands, I can carry you through." Day after day she dallied and delayed, until at last the summons came to her that the case was coming on for hearing and she must at once decide upon her course of defense. She hastened to the attorney and said, "I am ready now to give you the case." His answer filled her with confusion and despair. "Madam," he said, "it is too late. I would have taken your case if you had come to me sooner, and I could have carried you through. I was willing to act as your attorney, but within the last days I have been appointed to be your judge, and when the case comes up for hearing, I must sit upon it not as your friend, but as an impartial arbiter of your fate. You should have come to me before."

The illustration needs no application. This is the day of grace. Tomorrow will be the day of judgment. Oh, take the Savior as your Advocate before you have to meet Him as your Judge.

CHAPTER 17

PREPARING THE WAY OF THE LORD

A voice of one calling:
"In the desert prepare
the way for the LORD;
make straight in the wilderness
a highway for our God."
(Isaiah 40:3)

T his chapter opens the third section in the book of Isaiah of the prophecies relating to the return, consisting chiefly of longer captives from the exile and the coming of the Messiah.

Many modern critics hold that it was written by a second Isaiah in the time of the captivity, and 150 years after the earlier portion of the book. Conservative expositors will hold to the old view that the prophet anticipated the future and wrote in inspired vision of things to come as if they were taking place at the time.

The text is written from the standpoint of the exile. The captives are waiting in sorrow and bondage for the coming of the Lord to set them free. The one bright hope of their bondage is, "See, the Sovereign LORD comes with power,/ and his arm rules for him. . . . He tends his flock like a shepherd" (40:10a, 11a). But this coming of the Lord for Israel's deliverance was but a type of all those other comings which were to follow at the great epochs of the ages. A few centuries later He was to come again in the flesh as the incarnate Son of God. The promise also may well include the coming of the Holy Spirit in times of special blessing to the church of God; a coming such as God's people are waiting and praying for today in every land. The climax of all these comings will be the glorious return of our Lord and King "on the day he comes to be glorified in his holy people and to be marveled at among all those who have believed" (2 Thessalonians 1:10).

The prophet calls upon the people to prepare for the coming of their king, and this is also a summons to us bidding us to meet the conditions which will bring His presence in our midst and in our day.

There are five voices in this dramatic passage that speak in the wilderness, each with a distinct message. The first is the voice of divine love and pardon, assuring the people of God's forgiveness and grace. The second is the voice of preparation that bids them get ready for His presence, for He is to come Himself to dwell among them. The third is the voice of the Spirit as He breathes upon all fleshly and forbidden things, and leads them down into that deeper death which is to bring the spiritual realization of the promise. The fourth is the voice of faith as it proclaims from the mountain tops the glad tidings to Jerusalem and Zion, "The Sovereign LORD comes." And the last is the voice of God Himself responding to their faith and declaring, "See, the Sovereign LORD comes with power,/ and his arm rules for him./ See, his reward is with him,/ and his recompense accompanies him./ He tends his flock like a shepherd:/ He gathers the lambs in his arms/ and carries them close to his heart;/ he gently leads those that have young" (Isaiah 40:10–11).

THE VOICE OF PARDON

1. The Hebrew construction here is dramatic and beautiful. Softly breathing upon the air like the faint notes of rising music comes the whisper, "Comfort, comfort my people,/ says your God./ Speak tenderly to Jerusalem" (40:1). It is like a love note wooing a maiden's heart. Then the notes rise to bolder tones and ring out like a trumpet call, "proclaim to her/ that her hard service has been completed," or, as the margin reads, "that her appointed time has come; that her iniquity is pardoned, for she has received of the LORD'S hand double for all her sins" (40:2).

The very first thing that is necessary in our preparing to meet the Lord is that we should accept His grace, dismiss our doubts and fears and be reconciled at our Father's feet. We can have no fellowship with God while guilt and fear interpose their heavy clouds between us and His love. God meets us with the frank and full proclamation of His grace and love and bids us accept His pardon without conditions and without reserve. The very first thing for the sinner to do is to receive God's mercy. You may not be able to understand how He can offer you such grace, but that is His business, not yours; it is yours to take it in thankful confidence and enter into the relations of a forgiven and accepted child. Then He can lead you on into all the fullness of His manifested presence and deeper blessing.

"She has received from the LORD'S hand/ double for all her sins" (40:2b). This is a strange and striking announcement. Does it mean that God's mercy is given on the principle that where sin abounded, grace should much more abound? Does He, in His marvelous generosity, treat us so much better than we deserve, that the most unworthy receive most richly of His grace?

Or does this double portion mean that the sufferings of Israel were a type of the sufferings of their great Messiah; that Israel, the servant of the Lord, was fulfilling in some measure now the vicarious work of the greater Servant of the Lord that was soon to come, and that their calamities as a nation had been a foreshadowing of that great atonement which was to be made for them by the Son of Man, and which was, as it were, discounted and anticipated now in the mercy of God and deemed a double satisfaction for all their sins? This, at least, we know that great sacrifice is the ground of our forgiveness and salvation, and that it is for every believing soul

> Of sin the double cure,
> Cleansing from its guilt and power.

Would we prepare for the deeper blessing which the Lord is waiting to give, let us begin at the foot of the cross; let us take the riches of His grace in Jesus Christ and God's double for all our sins.

THE VOICE OF PREPARATION

> A voice of one calling:
> "In the desert prepare
>   the way for the LORD;
> make straight in the wilderness
>   a highway for our God.
> Every valley shall be raised up,
>   every mountain and hill made low;
> the rough ground shall become level,
>   the rugged places a plain.
> And the glory of the LORD will be revealed,
>   and all mankind together will see it.
>   For the mouth of the LORD has spoken."
>   (40:3–5)

2. After God meets us in His pardon and love, there is a deeper experience into which He would bring us. He wants to come Himself and dwell within us. This is the climax of the believer's experience, the highest possibility of blessing here. But for this we must prepare the way. The promise also includes His coming in blessing to His church and people. There are special seasons of spiritual blessing promised to the church and the people of God. The Holy Spirit does come in a very glorious way and give power to His word and salvation to His people; but for this also there must

be special preparation. The crooked must be made straight and the rough places plain. The stumbling blocks must be removed and the way of the Lord prepared. To each conscience and heart the light will come directly and individually. If we want to know, God will show us what hinders the fullness of blessing; and He will make us both willing and able to put it aside and then He will come into our own hearts and through us into the hearts of others in the fullness of His power and blessing.

Is He speaking this word to the conscience of any reader of these lines? Are there low places in our life that should be raised to a higher level of fellowship and obedience? Are there crooked places that need to be made straight? Are there rough places that need to be made smooth? Is there sin unconfessed and uncleansed? Is there strife or strain with any fellow Christian? Is there any forbidden thing in our relations with man or woman? Is there a neglect of the family altar, the Word of God, the house of God and the habit of secret prayer? Is there something which stands out before the searchlight of the Holy Spirit as we read these lines, and which we know is a stumbling block and a hindrance in our life? God help us to meet it without reserve, and so to open the way that the glory of the Lord shall be revealed in our hearts and lives and divine things shall shine with a beauty and reality so heavenly that it will almost seem as if we had never known the Lord before. God is waiting to show His glory and to lift us to a plane where all that we have known of His grace and blessing shall seem but as the light of the moon to the sunshine of His face. Shall we prepare the way of the Lord?

THE VOICE OF THE SPIRIT

> A voice says, "Cry out."
>   And I said, "What shall I cry?"
>
> "All men are like grass,
>   and all their glory is like the flowers of the field.
> The grass withers and the flowers fall,
>   because the breath of the LORD blows on them.
>   Surely the people are grass.
> The grass withers and the flowers fall,
>   but the word of our God stands forever."
>   (40:6–8)

3. There is a still more searching, penetrating voice. It is the very breath of the Spirit, withering our fleshly life and bringing to death all that is of the old natural life, that we may rise to the supernatural and resurrection life with our risen Lord, and His Word may have free course through all our

being. Life must always begin with death, both in the individual soul and in the church work of the Master. God cannot purify or improve the flesh. It must be condemned and crucified, and God cannot use the worldly and unscriptural methods by which the church too often is seeking, through fleshly means, to bring people to its fold. All this must die, and through the simplicity and power of His Word and Spirit alone, the work must be accomplished. Oh, how much rubbish in the form of religious machinery and man-made revivals must be got out of the way before the Holy Spirit can come in the fullness of His power, and how much of mere sentimentalism and worthless formalism must be burned out of our individual experience before we can go down to death with our Lord and come forth in the fullness of His resurrection life!

THE VOICE OF FAITH

4. The next voice rings out in trumpet notes of confidence from the mountain height. It is the voice of faith proclaiming that the blessing has begun and the Lord Himself is coming to His people. The Greek translation is, "Oh, thou that bringest good tidings unto Zion, get thee up into the high mountain; Oh, thou that bringest good tidings unto Jerusalem, lift up thy voice with strength, say unto the cities of Judah: Behold, thy God" (40:9). The herald of faith must precede the coming of the Lord. We must believe before we can receive, whether for ourselves or for the work of the Master, and we must believe so utterly and unreservedly that we shall not fear to commit ourselves to our confidence and go forth to confess our blessing.

THE VOICE OF GOD

5. Finally, the voice of God Himself responds, "See, the Sovereign LORD comes with power,/ and his arm rules for him" (40:10).

He will come in power. He will come to bring things to pass. He will come to answer prayer. He will come to silence the adversary and deliver His people. He will come to convict the indifferent and unbelieving world of sin. He will come to break down hardened hearts. He will come to lead ungodly men to the feet of Jesus and save the worst of sinners, and separate His people from the world and sin and reenact once more the victories of Pentecost. He will come to do the things we cannot do. He will come to consecrate the wealth of His selfish people and enable them to go forth with the message of salvation to the uttermost parts of the earth. He will come to silence the voice of unbelief and answer the unbeliever and the agnostic, not with words, but with mighty demonstrations of His power and presence.

And He will come in providence as well as grace to judge among the nations and prepare the way for His more glorious coming as earth's millennial King. Already we see some signs of His mighty working as the Ancient of

Days and the Judge of sinful nations, but we are to behold more wondrous things as the latter days hasten to their consummation.

But these things must come to pass first through the revelation of His power in the hearts of His people. It is true His body, the church, with the Head, is to work in the victories of His providence in the world; and so it is from a great awakening that there must come the prayer, the faith and the cooperation that are to bring the mightier victories of His hand in the world at large. He is able to "do immeasurably more than all we ask or imagine," but it is "according to his power that is at work within us" that His mighty working in the world is to be revealed (Ephesians 3:20). He works through His people, and according to their faith and spiritual preparation.

If, therefore, we would see the coming of our King in glory and the preparation of the world to meet Him, let us first receive Him in our own hearts, and work and pray for the opening of the hearts of His people everywhere for His incoming and indwelling, until the standard of Christian life shall rise to such a level that God can accomplish through His people all the highest possibilities of His promise and His grace.

The expression "His reward is with him" (Isaiah 40:10b) literally means His recompense. This has reference, no doubt, to His judicial working in connection with the wicked and sinful nations of men. Already we see Him dealing with them in judgment and giving to us some pledges of that far-reaching and impartial retribution which He is yet to mete out to those that have oppressed His people and abused their sacred trust as the selfish and sinful rulers of this godless age. We are to expect more and more the manifestations of His judgments as his people rise to that plane of holy fellowship which will enable them to stand with Him in the conflicts and victories of these last days.

But it is not all judgment. It is not all power. He is coming also in the gentleness of His grace. "He tends his flock like a shepherd" (40:11a). His coming will bring His people into all that is meant by the "green pastures" and the "still waters" of His grace. And His coming is to include the children, too. "He gathers the lambs in his arms/ and carries them close to his heart" (40:11). But what is meant by that last clause, "He gently leads those that have young" (40:11d)? Perhaps it is the picture of the tenderness with which the Shepherd will guard them in the helplessness of motherhood. Not hurrying or driving them as the cruel conqueror when he carried them across the land in that fearful captivity which we find depicted on the Babylonian monuments showing the brutal soldiers driving helpless women and children before them, and tossing aside the weak and fainting ones to perish by the wayside. Not so will this gentle Shepherd lead His flock, but with tender care will He conduct them in the noontide heat and rest them by the still waters, and carry the feeble ones in His loving arms.

But the phrase has perhaps a different meaning. "Those that have young" would suggest the mother and the young as they travel together. And when the mother is unwilling to follow the shepherd he sometimes carries the lamb across the river, and then she follows because her lamb has gone before. So sometimes He has led us by taking our loved ones from us and calling them on before, that we might follow them when we would not follow Him.

So He is waiting to come—to come to our hearts in personal blessing; to come to our work in the power of the Holy Spirit; and to come again in the fullness of His glory and make all things new. Do we long for His coming? Then let us arise and "prepare the way for the LORD."

CHAPTER 18

THE PASSION OF GOD

For a long time I have kept silent,
I have been quiet and held myself back.
But now, like a woman in childbirth,
I cry out, I gasp and pant.
(Isaiah 42:14)

This impassioned text has been appropriately and not irreverently described as the passion of God. But it is not the only passage in this intense prophetic volume which expresses the majestic appearing of Jehovah as He arises for the vindication of His glory and the deliverance of His people. Again and again we find the prophet's soul enkindled to the most sublime enthusiasm as he describes the march of God's glorious purpose toward its end. The picture becomes a sort of heavenly drama in which the heart of God upon the throne and the Holy Spirit in the church below move in sympathy in mighty conflict.

Our text is really associated with a number of similar texts which together afford a striking picture of the intense conflict in the heavenly places which is ever going forward with intense force as the crisis of the age draws nigh.

SECTION I—*The Cry*

The first passage in this sublime drama is Isaiah 64:1–4,

> Oh, that you would rend the heavens and come down,
>   that the mountains would tremble before you!
> As when fire sets twigs ablaze
>   and causes water to boil,
> come down to make your name known to your enemies
>   and cause the nations to quake before you!

For when you did awesome things that we did not expect,
    you came down, and the mountains trembled before you.
Since ancient times no one has heard,
    no ear has perceived,
no eye has seen any God besides you,
    who acts on behalf of those who wait for him.

This is the cry of the waiting soul for God to reveal Himself in the majesty of His glory and His power. There are times when the hearts of men seem to have become so stupidly indifferent, when the church herself is so fast asleep, and when even earnest hearts seem to have settled down to such a dead life of self-content, that the praying souls who look out upon the religious conditions of our time are compelled to send up this passionate cry as they feel that nothing less than the very dynamite of God can clear the air and wake the dead.

It is like one of those days which sometimes come in summer when the atmosphere is so sultry and the air so dead that we breathe by gasps, and after a while we instinctively look out upon the horizon and long for the electric storm, the cleaving lightning and the crashing thunder to break the awful spell, to clear the air and restore our vital breath.

Such a condition is upon us today in the religious history of our time. The public conscience is so corrupted that vice has ceased to stir us. The horrors of war grow insipid through the hardening influence of habit. The moral and social standards of mankind and the tone of public opinion grow looser and lower. The chief interest of the study of even God's Holy Word is centered upon the excitement of higher criticism. Intellectual doubt has pushed aside the simple faith of other days. The world has swept away the barriers for separation and the church is sleeping on the enchanted ground of self-complacency. Even those who know and love the Master best feel paralyzed by the presence of depressing conditions in the air, and Zion's watchmen are crying out in desperate earnestness, "Oh, that you would rend the heavens and come down,/ that the mountains would tremble before you!" (64:1).

This is not a figure of speech referring to God's historical manifestation at Mt. Sinai and in the wilderness or as He came in Isaiah's time to destroy the armies of Sennacherib and deliver Jerusalem; for as we read the passage through, we find that verse four forms part of one of the most important quotations in one of Paul's epistles to the Corinthians (1 Corinthians 2:9–10). There he applies all this directly to the Holy Spirit, " 'No eye has seen,/ no ear has heard,/ no mind has conceived/ what God has prepared for those who love him'—/ but God has revealed it to us by his Spirit."

The mighty revelation of God for which the prophet cries is not a mere miraculous display of His glory and His power before the nations, but a spiritual coming of the Holy Spirit to the hearts of His people as they seek Him in earnestness and faith; for he adds, "You come to the help of those who gladly do right,/ who remember your ways" (Isaiah 64:5). God is waiting therefore to reveal to earnest souls the glory of His grace and power in a measure such as "no eye has seen [or] ear heard," nor our highest spiritual conceptions have ever dreamed. Will we meet His challenge? Will we send up the cry until the heavens open and God comes down in the revelation of His presence and His power, and the mountains of opposition and iniquity melt away at His presence, and the melting fire of apostolic love kindles the heart of the church of God, and the waters boil in the engines of our spiritual machinery, and the power of God goes forth into every agency of Christian work and worldwide evangelization?

That is what the prayer may mean according as our faith will dare to claim it. God give us the prayer and the answer until the church of God shall wake from her debasing slumber and once more stand forth "fair as the moon, bright as the sun,/ majestic as the stars in procession" (Song of Songs 6:10).

SECTION II—*The Answer*

Our text proper is the answer to this cry. "For a long time I have kept silent,/ I have been quiet and held myself back./ But now, like a woman in childbirth" (Isaiah 42:14). "The LORD will march out like a mighty man,/ like a warrior he will stir up his zeal;/ with a shout he will raise the battle cry/ and will triumph over his enemies" (42:13).

Yes, God waits and suffers long. The cry of the needy seems unheeded, the triumph of the proud appears unchallenged, the prayer of the saint finds no answer, but God is not asleep or dead. Prayer is accumulating before the throne. God is waiting till the cup of sin is full and the moment strikes when all the forces of His omnipotence are let loose in a cyclone of glorious power and victorious majesty.

What a blending of splendid figures we have here! There is the shout of the warrior. There is the cry of the travailing woman. There is the convulsion of a great cyclone. There is the gasp and the panting of a mighty wrestle, and there is the final overthrow of every obstacle and opposition. What does all this mean?

THE HEART OF GOD

1. It is a picture of the heart of God. Our heavenly Father is not a selfish embodiment of isolation and power like the Buddhist's dream of Nirvana, but a great, loving, living heart in constant touch with the needs of His people and the conditions of the world over which He reigns. He that made

the heart of the soldier has in Him all the heroic qualities which have il-luminated the battlefields of earth. He who made the tempest and the lightning has in Him all the force of which they are but heart throbs. He who gave the mother her passionate love has in Him all the depths of mater-nal tenderness for His suffering children. He who created the father's heart is the great Father Himself. Look at Him as He seeks for His lost Adam amid the shades of Eden crying, "Where are you?" (Genesis 3:9). Listen to Him as He cries out over a sin-cursed world, "I will wipe mankind, whom I have created, from the face of the earth" (6:7). Listen again as He cries over the sufferings of Israel in the brick-fields of Egypt, "I have indeed seen the misery of my people in Egypt. I have heard them crying out because of their slave drivers, and I am concerned about their suffering" (Exodus 3:7). Hear Him as He wails over Ephraim, His prodigal child, "How can I give you up, Ephraim?/ How can I hand you over, Israel?/ My heart is changed within me;/ all my compassion is aroused" (Hosea 11:8).

Listen as He pleads through Jeremiah with His wandering bride, Israel. "I remember the devotion of your youth,/ how as a bride you loved me/ and followed me through the desert" (Jeremiah 2:2). Hark again as there falls from heaven the sweet cadence of His love. "As the father has compassion on his children,/ so the LORD has compassion on those who fear him;/ for he knows how we are formed,/ he remembers that we are dust" (Psalm 103:13–14). And yet once more a softer cadence falls and the words breathe out the tenderest depths of maternal love. "As a mother comforts her child,/ so will I comfort you;/ and you will be comforted over Jerusalem" (Isaiah 66:13).

Yes, that is the great Heart whose pulse beats move the mighty universe and throb responsively to His children's need and His people's cry. He will not always be silent. He will respond.

> Oh, watchers on the mountain height,
>   Stand firm and steadfast there;
> Oh, wrestlers in the vale beneath,
>   Cease not your seven-fold prayer;
> God will not always wait;
>   He will accept your sacrifice;
> Oh, loving hearts and praying hands,
>   God will in love arise.

THE PASSION OF CHRIST

2. It means not only the heart of God, but the passion of Christ, His beloved Son. Isaiah has given us a picture of this passion (63:1–5). He be-

holds a mighty Conqueror marching from Edom, glorious in His apparel and yet with garments stained with blood; and as he listens the Conqueror proclaims His mighty name, "It is I, speaking in righteousness,/ mighty to save" (63:1). But the prophet asks, "Why are your garments red,/ like those of one treading the winepress?" (63:2). Once more comes the answer, "I have trodden the winepress alone;/ from the nations no one was with me./ . . ./ I looked, but there was no one to help,/ I was appalled that no one gave support;/ so my own arm worked salvation for me,/ and my own wrath sustained me" (63:3–5).

This is a picture of the Son of God in the mighty conflict of redemption. The passion of His Father's heart was passed on to Him, and with obedience and willing love He has hastened down to meet the awful emergency and lead the mightiest battle of the ages. The hate of Satan, the opposition of men, the power of earth and hell were all arrayed against Him. And as He pressed through to the cross, He cried in the intensity of His agony, "But I have a baptism to undergo, and how distressed I am until it is completed!" (Luke 12:50). The curtain rises for a moment on that agony in Gethsemane and His sweat is as great drops of blood falling down to the ground. Once more He seems to sink in dying anguish on the cross, but again we hear the shout of victory, "It is finished" (John 19:30), and we see the rending gates of death as He comes forth a conqueror in His resurrection. He passes through the heavenly gates in His ascension glory, but even there the conflict does not end. Still He is regarded as the great High Priest and mediatorial King. Still He is leading the hosts of God as the Captain of our salvation, and still we hear the shout of the Conqueror, and we feel the falling tear of the Sufferer as "He is able to be touched with the feeling of our infirmities" (Hebrews 4:15, KJV). Bending from the throne, He whispers to persecuting Saul, "Why do you persecute me?" (Acts 9:4). Pleading at the closed heart of the sinner, He cries, "I stand at the door and knock" (Revelation 3:20).

Yes, it is the passion of God still in the heart of Jesus, and the conflict must still go on until the last enemy is subdued and the last saint is gathered home.

THE PASSION OF THE HOLY SPIRIT

3. The Father passes on the burden to His beloved Son, and the Son in turn has transferred it to the Holy Spirit. It is His high vocation to finish the work which Jesus began on earth. Unlike the Lord Jesus, the Holy Spirit has no body of His own, and therefore His conflict is carried on in the body of Christ, which is the church. It is our hearts that must feel His agony. It is our lips that must breathe His prayer. It is our hands that must be responsive to His touch. And in all this we are but representing our Living Head, the

Lord Jesus in heaven as well as our Living Heart, the Holy Spirit on earth.

Now, the Spirit is constantly represented in the New Testament as a suffering, sympathizing Being. We can "grieve" Him, thus implying that His heart is sensitive to slight and to sorrow. The Apostle James tells us that "The spirit he caused to live in us envies intensely" (4:5). Therefore we can wound His jealous love by failing to meet His expectations and give to God our whole devotion. In a very remarkable passage in the eighth chapter of Romans, He is said to intercede "for us with groans that words cannot express" (8:26b). These groanings represent the agony of prayer by which He works out in the hearts of His people the victories of grace.

In yet another passage (Ephesians 6:10–18) we find Him leading the great conflict in the heavenly realms where the weapon is "the sword of the Spirit, which is the Word of God," and the agency of victory is "[praying] in the Spirit on all occasions with all kind of prayers and requests." So we find the Holy Spirit sharing the passion of God and all through the Christian age representing the suffering of heaven in the long agony of the redemption's conflict.

THE COOPERATION OF THE PEOPLE OF GOD

4. But it is through the hearts of His people that the Holy Spirit must work; and if we are not responsive to His touch, how can He work? If you had a paralyzed tongue and arms and limbs enfeebled by disease, your brain might think ever so wisely, your will might purpose ever so forcibly, but all would be futile if your tongue refused to speak a word, your feet to move to the message and your hands to fulfill the plan.

So the Holy Spirit is hindered by the unresponsiveness of His people. And the agony is often caused chiefly by His struggle to awake our slumbering souls to understand His thought and to enter into His prayer. As we look back through the history of earnest lives, we find that the servants of God were sufferers. Jeremiah was like a sensitive harp echoing every sorrow of his suffering people. "Oh, that my head were a spring of water/ and my eyes a fountain of tears!" was his cry, "I would weep day and night/ for the slain of my people (Jeremiah 9:1). Again he cries, "But if I say, 'I will not mention him/ or speak any more in his name,'/ his word is in my heart like a fire,/ a fire shut up in my bones./ I am weary of holding it in;/ indeed I cannot" (20:9).

We find the great Isaiah crying out as he watches the burden of Dumah, "At this my body is racked with pain,/ pangs seize me, like those of a woman in labor" (Isaiah 21:3). " 'Watchman, what is left of the night?'/ The watchman replies,/ 'Morning is coming, but also the night' " (21:11b–12a). Habakkuk, the poet prophet, pleaded with God, "Renew them in our day,/ in our time make them known;/ in wrath remember mercy" (3:2), and God answers his prayer by a hurricane of power. "His glory covered the heavens/ and his praise filled the earth" (3:3). "The mountains saw you and writhed./ Torrents of water swept by;/ the deep roared/ and lifted its waves on high" (3:10). "You came out to deliver your people" (3:13).

We find Deborah raised up in Israel as the counselor of Barak; and while he leads the battle in the front, she waits in her tent in a greater conflict of prayer. As she prays, the whole panorama passes before her until the enemy is scattered and the shout of triumph rises over the land and Deborah is in it all. And as the cyclone in her soul subsides in peace, she breathes out her glad relief in the cry, "march on my soul; be strong" (Judges 5:21).

It was thus that Elijah prayed on Carmel when his body was bowed together in soul travail until an answer came.

It was thus that Paul described his spiritual sufferings for his flock. "I want you to know how much I am struggling for you" (Colossians 2:1). He explains it all in that profound passage, "I rejoice in what was suffered for you, and I fill up in my flesh what is still lacking in regard to Christ's afflictions, for the sake of his body, which is the church" (1:24). And a little later, "I labor, struggling with all his energy, which so powerfully works in me" (1:29).

Writing to the Galatians he says, "My dear children, for whom I am again in the pains of childbirth, until Christ is formed in you" (4:19). And to the Philippians he says, "God can testify how I long for all of you with the affection of Christ Jesus" (1:8). It is with reference to them he writes, "For it has been granted to you on behalf of Christ not only to believe on him, but also to suffer for him, since you are going through the same struggle you saw I had, and now hear that I still have" (1:29–30).

This is the very mystery of fellowship with Jesus. This is the deepest secret of power. This is the highest service that we can render to Christ and His church. Sometimes the prayer becomes a groan until we think our prayer is lost, but that is the very moment when it has overcome. Sometimes God lays upon a praying one the burden of a worker. While the one is active, the other is silent, and yet the silent force is the real power.

Anna Shipton tells of having had upon her heart for some weeks a minister of Christ in a ceaseless agony of prayer. During that time, ignorant altogether of her prayer for him, he was led into the fullness of Christ and became the instrument in the salvation of scores of souls, and never knew till afterwards that the secret of it all was a silent, suffering life which was not even in outward contact with him.

This was the secret of that wonderful revival that swept through the valleys of Wales. This was the secret of the power of David Brainerd, Jonathan Edwards and William Burns. It is this that is to set the church on fire with consecration and holiness. It is this that is to awaken a zeal which will give to her languid work something of the energy of the great enterprise of modern commerce. It is this that is to bring the great evangelistic and missionary campaign which will give the gospel as a witness to the world and prepare the way of our coming Lord. And it is this which is to set in motion the mighty forces of providence among the nations which will bring about "A ruin! A ruin! I will make it a ruin! It will not be restored until he comes to whom it rightfully belongs; to him I will give it" (Ezekiel 21:27).

There was a man in ancient Babylon to whom God gave the name, "Oh, man of desires." The secret of Daniel's character was a great capacity for holy desire. He had insatiable longings for the kingdom of God, and he prayed them out for weeks together in an agony of love. What followed?

The mightiest conqueror on earth was sitting upon the throne of the empire. Cyrus, sated with conquests, had nothing more to ask of earthly success. Suddenly there came to him a strange purpose and he issued a decree telling the world that the Lord God of heaven had commanded him to build Him a house in Jerusalem and to send back the captive Jews. But behind that decree and that band of returning captives and that restored city and temple, see that "man of desires" silently praying in Babylon.

Or shall we look at a still grander vision? There is silence in heaven. The voice of God has hushed every angelic song, for the prayers of the saints are being brought in. They have been long accumulating; they have been treasured up in golden bowls. God sends for them to be presented at His throne, and as He breathes in their sweetness, mingled with the incense of the great High Priest Himself, no sound is permitted to disturb the sacred hour. But this is not all. The command is next given to take these prayers and pour them out upon the earth again; and as they are emptied back upon the world from which they came, lo, there are voices and thunderings and a great earthquake, and the mighty angels of the coming advent begin to sound the trumpets that proclaim that the consummation of the age has come.

And come through prayer; come through the passion of holy desire, in loving, longing Christian hearts. Oh, that we might understand our high calling! Oh, that we might enter into the Holiest by His precious blood! Oh, that we might know the power of His resurrection and the fellowship of His sufferings! Oh, that we might be saved from the curse of lukewarmness and "kindled with the passion fire of love divine"!

CHAPTER 19

THE SERVANT OF THE LORD

(Part 1)

Here is my servant, whom I uphold,
my chosen one in whom I delight;
I will put my Spirit on him
and he will bring justice to the nations.
He will not shout or cry out,
or raise his voice in the streets.
A bruised reed he will not break,
and a smoldering wick he will not snuff out.
In faithfulness he will bring forth justice;
he will not falter or be discouraged
till he establishes justice on earth.
In his law the islands will put their hope.
(Isaiah 42:1–4)

This expression, "the servant of the LORD," is a sort of keynote to a large portion of the prophecies of Isaiah. The phrase is used in three senses. First, it is applied to Israel, the servant of the Lord. We find it so used in Isaiah 41:8, and other passages, "you, O Israel, my servant,/ Jacob, whom I have chosen,/ you descendants of Abraham my friend."

But Israel failed to fulfill his great trust as the servant of the Lord and was put aside and the Lord Jesus Christ now becomes the Servant of the Lord. So the expression is used in the present text. So again in Isaiah 49:3, 52:13, 53:11, etc. Then the plural form is used and in several passages toward the end of the prophecy we find, "The servants of the LORD" spoken of. The reference here is the people of God individually who, as members of Christ and fellow servants of the great Minister of the covenant follow in His steps of service. So we find it in Isaiah 54:17, 65:13, etc. It is to the second application of this term that our attention is now called.

SECTION I—*The Great Servant*

God wanted someone to represent Him in the world. He had given to mankind a revelation of His will and it was necessary that someone should fulfill it. God's law could not be left a broken and dishonored memorial of man's disobedience like some splendid architectural plan which no one could be found to transform into an actual edifice. His honor and glory demanded that someone should fulfill it and render unto heaven a devotion and service which man had failed to give.

It was for this purpose that Israel had her high calling, and yet Israel utterly failed to keep her own law. At last one Man was found who could render unto heaven the obedience due to the authority of God. "Here I am, I have come," was his cry, "I desire to do your will, O my God;/ your law is within my heart" (Psalm 40:7–8). At every step of His earthly life, the supreme business of Jesus was to do His Father's will, and He was able to say, "I always do what pleases him" (John 8:29). The one supreme purpose of His life was to glorify the Father and finish the work He had given Him to do. And at last He could say, as He handed over His accomplished task, "I have brought you glory on earth by completing the work you gave me to do" (17:4).

Among the types of Moses, there was a beautiful ceremony by which a Hebrew slave, when his term of service had expired and he had the option to go free, was permitted, if he preferred, to resume the yoke of bondage and continue a slave by his own choice. Perhaps his wife and children were slaves and he did not want to leave them in bondage. Perhaps he loved his master better than his liberty and did not want to go free, and so he was permitted to say, "I love my master, I love my wife and children, I will not go out free." And then this ceremony was performed. His ear was pierced and he was nailed to the doorpost of his master's house by his ear in token of voluntary subjection and servitude.

This beautiful type has been applied to Christ in one of the prophetic Psalms where the Messiah is represented as saying,

> Sacrifice and offering you did not desire,
>   but my ears you have pierced;
> burnt offerings and sin offerings
>   you did not require.
> Then I said, "Here I am, I have come—
>   it is written about me in the scroll.
> I desire to do your will, O my God;

your law is within my heart."
    (40:6–8)

This is a picture of Christ as the Servant. He might have retained His liberty and remained in heaven. But He loved His Father, He loved His Bride, the Church, He loved His lost children here, and He gave up His liberty. As the apostle expresses in Galatians, "When the time had fully come, God sent his Son, born of a woman, born under law, to redeem those under law, that we might receive the full rights of sons" (4:4). He fulfilled our tasks. He paid our debts. He offered to God the righteousness which we had failed to give and of His finished work the Father could say, "It pleased the LORD/ for the sake of his righteousness/ to make his law great and glorious" (Isaiah 42:21).

But there was another purpose which Israel failed to serve as the Lord's servant, and that was to be God's messenger to the world, the light of the Gentiles and the revealer of God's holiness and grace to the children of men. Instead of this, Israel sank, through their sins, to a condition that the prophets describe as even worse than the heathen. God had to humble them before their enemies and send them into shameful captivity under the Gentile nations. This glorious ministry has been committed unto the divine Servant and so we read in this passage,

> I, the LORD, have called you in righteousness;
>   I will take hold of your hand.
> I will keep you and will make you
>   to be a covenant for the people
>   and a light for the Gentiles,
> to open eyes that are blind,
>   to free captives from prison
>   and to release from the dungeon those who sit in darkness.
>
> I am the LORD; that is my name!
>   I will not give my glory to another
>   or my praise to idols.
>   (42:6–8)

In these respects, we are called likewise to be servants of the Lord, to represent Him by our lives and by our testimony as the messengers of His Word to all mankind. The apostles loved to call themselves the servants of the Lord. Christ taught His disciples that the highest honor was in the lowliest service. "Whoever wants to become great among you must be your servant, and whosoever wants to be first must be your slave" (Matthew 20:26–27).

Oh, that we might be able to say, of our High Priest, "Whose I am and Whom I serve" (Acts 27:23).

SECTION II—*The Servant's Acceptance*

"Here is my servant, whom I uphold,/ my chosen one in whom I delight" (Isaiah 42:1a). God's heart had been disappointed in the race. There had come up to Him from this sinful world the stench of human vileness, and age after age He had sought for some one that could bring the sacrifices of a sweet smelling savor. At last on Jordan's banks, there stood a man to whom He could say, "This is my Son, whom I love; with him I am well pleased" (Matthew 3:17). God's face shone with a light so bright that it broke through the opening heavens, and for a moment shed its glory upon the earth beneath.

It is because of that acceptance that we are justified and accepted now. "He has made us accepted in the beloved" (Ephesians 1:6, KJV), is the measure of our standing as justified believers in the sight of God. Literally, the verse means "accepted in the Son of His love," and it conveys the force that we are accepted just as He and loved the same as He. Not only so, our sanctification comes through Him. In His sublime prayer in John 17, He thus prays concerning the Father's love "that the love you have for me may be in them and that I myself may be in them" (17:26). He asks His Father to love us just as He loves the Son. The reason: He is so in us Himself that our personality disappears from view and it is only the Christ in us that the Father sees and loves. So we can pass out of our own self-consciousness and into this blessed Christ-consciousness, and although feeling utterly unworthy in our own name we can ever by the righteousness of Jesus Christ our perfect sacrifice, know that this is true:

So dear, so very dear to God,
   More dear I cannot be;
The love wherewith He loves His Son,
   That love He has for me.

SECTION III—*The Servant's Anointing*

"I will put my Spirit on him" (Isaiah 42:1). The Father endued Him for His work by the anointing of the Holy Spirit. That Spirit He shares with us, and in Him we claim the same anointing for the same service. We are not asked to render unto Him our service at our own charges, but it is said of our ministry that we are "created in Christ Jesus to do good works, which

God prepared in advance for us to do" (Ephesians 2:10). The gifts of power, wisdom, faith and supernatural efficiency prescribed for the church in the 12th chapter of First Corinthians are called *charismata,* that is, abilities "bestowed" upon us, not talents original with us.

Even love itself, the greatest of all the graces, is a gift and not a virtue. It is Christ's love shed abroad in our hearts and flowing out to others from Him.

Beloved, are we anointed for service? Are we faithful servants and are we walking in the light of the blessed "Well done, good and faithful servant! You have been faithful with a few things; I will put you in charge of many things. Come and share your master's happiness" (Matthew 25:21)?

SECTION IV—*The Servant's Meekness*

"He will not shout or cry out,/ or raise his voice in the streets" (Isaiah 42:2).

The first element in the training of a good servant is discipline, subjection, self-suppression and self-restraint. How beautifully we behold this in the meek and lowly Christ! "I am among you as one who serves" (Luke 22:27). In this age of loud and noisy people, when even Christian work is blazoned, advertised and flaunted before the eyes of the multitude, how restful to turn to this picture of Him who is our great Example of service. The Hebrew word here literally means loud and screamy. He was not loud and screamy, but His Spirit was very chastened and self-suppressed. We get a little conception of how the Deity within Him was pressing out for expression in that scene in the temple when He was 12 years old and when His heart gave utterance to that deep cry, "Didn't you know I had to be in my Father's house?" (2:49). And yet He went back for 18 years to the quiet drudgery of the workbench at Nazareth and held within that bursting heart that longing to glorify His Father and save and help His fellow men. At length the devil came to Him to His highest longings, and whispered, "Now is your chance to reveal yourself and glorify your Father by a stupendous miracle. Cast yourself down from the pinnacle of the temple, throw yourself upon the protecting arms of omnipotence, let the people see who you are." But He only said, "Away from me, Satan!" (Matthew 4:10). "Do not put the Lord your God to the test" (Luke 4:12). Yet again the adversary tried to tempt Him to accept a throne among the kingdoms of the world, and all the glory, urging no doubt, not His selfish ambition and personal glory so much as the opportunity it would give Him to be a blessing to the world and alleviate the miseries of mankind. But again He refused the tempting offer and went forth on His path of lowly suffering.

During His earthly ministry how often we find Him giving up His rights. Just before Matthew quotes this passage from our text he tells us that,

. . . the Pharisees went out and plotted how they might kill Jesus.

Aware of this, Jesus withdrew from that place. Many followed him, and he healed all their sick, warning them not to tell who he was. This was to fulfill what was spoken through the prophet Isaiah:

> "Here is my servant whom I have chosen,
>   the one I love, in whom I delight;
> I will put my Spirit on him,
>   and he will proclaim justice to the nations.
> He will not quarrel or cry out;
>   no one will hear his voice in the streets." (12:14–19)

A little later, they tried to take Him by force and make Him a king, but He gently took Himself out of their hands. The Samaritans refused to receive Him and the ardent disciples insisted that He should call down fire from heaven and consume them, but He quietly answered, "Ye know not what manner of spirit ye are of" (Luke 9:55, KJV); and He went to another village.

To the very close of His earthly ministry, we see the spirit of self-restraint. In the judgment hall, He answered not a word. Even after His resurrection, His appearances to the disciples were of the most simple and quiet character. All the glory which He had won by His great redemption He kept in reserve, giving to His followers rather than assuming to Himself the victories of Pentecost. He is waiting for the reward of His sufferings until the end of the age while He still ministers in sympathy and tenderness to His suffering church. He is content to be the rejected Nazarene and let the present age have its day, while He is slowly gathering in from the lowly children of sin the members of His body and His Bride.

Oh, that our service were more like His, hidden "in the shadow of His hand" (Isaiah 49:2) with less of self and more of Christ and with that "hiding of His power" which is the very triumph of power divine.

The power which today controls the tremendous machinery of our age was hidden deep in the bowels of the earth thousands of years ago by the fire that consumed primeval forests and stored the coal mines of our mountains with the real material of all physical force. The mighty battleship, the swift Atlantic flyer, the trains that sweep across the myriad tracks of transportation are all moved by the coal mines of the mountains.

So the force which God uses in the great process of the spiritual world comes forth from the hidden depths of lives where perhaps long ago the natural and the earthly were burned away by the fire of the Holy Spirit and God was starting up the power which today is leading some great revival or evangelizing some heathen land.

God help us to learn the silent sources of spiritual power and the ministry of waiting as well as working.

SECTION V—*The Servant's Gentleness*

"A bruised reed he will not break,/ and a smoldering wick he will not snuff out" (Isaiah 42:3). We need not seek far in the story of His life to find the illustrations of this blessed portrait.

Look at that crushed life which kneels weeping at His feet condemned by the Pharisees, condemned by her own sense of right, a broken reed. What is there left for a woman who has thus lost all? But listen to Him: "Neither do I condemn you. Go now and leave your life of sin" (John 8:11).

Look again at the disciple that has denied and blasphemed Him. Alas, Peter, it does seem to be all over with you this time. The Master is going now to come back no more. Many a time have you blundered and He has been there to take you back again, but that is all over. Look, they are taking Him away, bound and fettered, and in a little while He will be crucified and dead. It is too late, Peter. But just at the last moment that loving, yearning face of Christ turns back and looks on Peter and that look was a volume. It said, "No, Peter, it is not over. I forgive you and I trust you still." And Peter remembered and wept bitterly. But for that look He would not break the bruised reed, and from that hour Peter was bound to his Master with a love that could never die, and his restored life was given to comfort tempted ones.

There is no life so crushed, there is no heart so discouraged but He has still some look of love, some word of cheer, some touch of victorious help.

The smoldering wick refers rather to the feeble beginnings which others might think scarcely worth the trouble of treasuring, but He will take the feeblest beginning and fan the flame to a glorious fire. Look at that cowardly inquirer who comes sneaking in at the back door of the Master's lodging at night. He is a member of the Jewish council. His name is Nicodemus; and were it known that he was here, it would be as much as his reputation is worth. Why does not the Lord disdain to meet him in this clandestine way? Why does He not say. "Nicodemus, I will have no followers that do not come out in the open and confess me without reserve." Ah, no! Jesus is glad to see him. It is only a little smoke, but some day this man will stand up in that great council and defend the Master before His enemies. And so the Lord meets him and tells him the story of the new birth and the wondrous love of the Father in giving His only Son, and that man goes out with a new life that can never die.

And Thomas, the doubting disciple, with scarcely faith enough to come to the meeting with his brethren; Thomas, the agnostic, demanding ocular demonstration and making his own terms of faith. "All right, Thomas you can come too. If you want to put your hand in the wound of the spear, you are welcome. It is the nearest way to my heart." The Lord meets him on his own terms; but Thomas falls at his feet astonished, overwhelmed, ashamed, a thousand times convinced, crying, "My Lord and my God" (20:28).

Are there any reading these lines who feel that they have but a weak will, a timid faith and a worthless life to bring to Christ? Bring what you have. Better come blundering to His feet than not at all. He will not quench the smoking flax; He will not break the bruised reed.

SECTION VI—*The Servant's Strength*

But His gentleness is not weakness. Oh no! "He will not falter or be discouraged/ till he establishes justice on earth" (Isaiah 42:4). The words translated "falter" and "discouraged" are the same as translated just before "break" and "snuff out." While He will not despise the weak, He is not weak. What a mighty evidence the prophet gives us of His glorious and victorious strength. There is nothing in ancient prophecy more sublime than this prophetic vision of what someone has called the passion of God, as it rises to its climax and as He comes forth to the world in His last manifestation to beat down his adversaries and bring in His kingdom. "The LORD will march out like a mighty man,/ like a warrior he will stir up his zeal;/ with a shout he will raise the battle cry/ and will triumph over his enemies" (42:13). And then, like a great spasm of inward conflict, He continues,

> For a long time I have kept silent,
> I have been quiet and held myself back.
> But now like a woman in childbirth,
> I cry out, I gasp and pant.
> I will lay waste the mountains and hills
> and dry up all their vegetation;
> I will turn rivers into islands
> and dry up the pools.
> I will lead the blind by ways they have not known,
> along unfamiliar paths I will guide them;
> I will turn the darkness into light before them
> and make the rough places smooth.
> These are the things I will do;
> I will not forsake them.
> (42:14–16)

Space will not permit us to dwell on this sublime picture of the conflict of

Christ and the passionate intensity with which we should be ready to enter into that conflict in the victories of faith and prayer. We are reading today of men of God who stand in front of a great religious movement whose very souls seem rent asunder in agonies of prayer as they plead for perishing souls, and we have also been told how the Holy Spirit has come in tidal waves of victory and blessing just through such spiritual conflicts and agonizing prayers. It is Gethsemane repeated in the body of Christ as once it was experienced by the Head. It is through His people the Master is to fight these final battles and win these millennial triumphs.

Oh, that we might enter into His throbbing heart. Oh, that we might share the anguish of His love and the joy of His triumph. Oh, that each of us might say:

> Lord, kindle in this heart of mine
> The passion fire of love divine.

CHAPTER 20

THE SERVANT OF THE LORD

(Part 2)

He said to me, "You are my servant,
Israel, in whom I will display my splendor."
(Isaiah 49:3)

W e have already seen that the expression, "servant of the LORD," is used in three senses in the book of Isaiah. The first has reference to Israel, the second to the Lord Jesus and the third to the individual believer. Israel having failed to meet the conditions of His high commission, Christ took His place as the Father's Servant and has transferred to us, the members of His body, the fellowship of service. It is in this latter sense that we are to consider the expression at this time. We find very much in this prophetic book about service.

SECTION I—*The Names Given to the Lord's Servants*

SERVANT

1. Servant is the first term applied to us. It is used throughout the Scriptures in the strong sense, not merely of an employee, but of a bond slave. The Bible servant is the property of his master. The very principle of Christian service is that we first belong to Him ourselves, and then we give Him our service, just as in a royal palace every vessel bears the monogram of the king. He will not use any vessel that is not exclusively His own. So the Lord wants us to bear His monogram before He employs us on His commissions. The watchword of the true servant of the Lord is, "whose I am and whom I serve" (Acts 27:23). This is the source of constant weakness and failure in Christian work: the attempt to do things for the cause of Christ by people who do not

themselves belong to Christ. This is all untempered mortar and worthless work.

"Whose pocketbook is that?" was asked of a Christian gentleman. "Why, mine of course." "To whom do you belong?" "I belong to the Lord." "Ah, you belong to the Lord and the pocketbook belongs to you." That is about the measure of the average Christian service.

Paul gloried in calling himself the bond slave of Jesus Christ. Oh, that we might better learn his message to the Corinthians: "Do you not know that your body is a temple of the Holy Spirit, who is in you, whom you have received from God? You are not your own; you were bought at a price. Therefore honor God with your body" (1 Corinthians 6:19–20).

Are you a true servant of God? Have you ceased to own yourself? Are you His property, and do you recognize yourself and all you own as absolutely at His disposal, and are you letting Him shape your plans, direct your will and control your life? This is to be a servant of the Lord. "Therefore, I urge you, brothers, in view of God's mercy, to offer your bodies as living sacrifices, holy and pleasing to God—this is your spiritual act of worship" (Romans 12:1).

PRIESTS AND MINISTERS

2. Next, the Lord's servants are called priests and ministers of God (Isaiah 61:6). The word "minister" also means a servant, but not in the extreme sense of the slave. It represents rather an official servant, one who holds an office in the public service. In this passage the two expressions "priests and ministers," undoubtedly refer to the two classes among the ancient Hebrews, namely the priests and Levites. These together comprised the official servants of Jehovah, but they were quite different in their functions. The priests represented the idea of worship; the Levites, work. The first ministered directly to God; the second, to their brethren. The business of the priests was to offer sacrifice and incense in the holy place. The business of the Levites was to set up the tabernacle, to take it down, to carry it on its wilderness journeys, to teach the people to perform the manual duties connected with the camp and the service of the sanctuary.

In the Christian Church there are not any longer two classes of servants, but two kinds of service are combined in the life in each of us. We are to be both priests and Levites. One part of our ministry is to worship God, to love Him, to pray to Him, to praise Him, to pour forth continually the sacrifice of a loving, reverent heart in praise, communion and prayer as "a fragrant offering" (Philippians 4:18). The other part is to be active, useful, helpful, practical, to serve one another by love, to work for the cause of Christ, to build up His Church, to seek and save the lost, to supply the means by which His work is carried on, to be teachers of His people and the active promoters of His work in every proper way. We are to be at once busy and devout, faithful in every earthly trust, yet "keep your spiritual fervor serving the Lord" (Romans 12:11).

Are we thus ministering in His Church, a holy priesthood, true ministers of the sanctuary which God has built and not man?

WITNESSES

3. " 'You are my witnesses,' declares the LORD" (Isaiah 43:10). A witness is one who bears personal testimony of what he knows. We are to know God so that we can make Him real to men. We are to know Christ and be able to communicate Him to others. This we are to do not only by what we say, but our whole life should be an object lesson of witness-bearing for God. Is it truly so? Do we constantly reflect Him? Do we make Him real to the people who know us and see us from day to day? Do we make Him attractive to them so that they are hungry for the Christ that we have found? Do we always act as though we were on the witness stand for Him? Do we bring credit and honor to His name? Or are we sometimes like the man who had forgotten his sacred trust and, although a prominent member of the Church of Christ, had allowed himself to be drawn into compromising friendships, fellowships and amusements, and was often found in the company of the ungodly, countenancing things which God could not approve. One of his truest friends had long tried to draw him away from this false life, but failed to impress him. One day he sent a card in to him as he sat at a worldly entertainment with a lot of godless companions, and on the other side of the card were these simple words, "Ye are my witnesses, saith the Lord." As he read it, he flushed crimson. He looked at the friends around him. He realized how out of keeping the whole surroundings were with his high calling as a witness for God, and he soon excused himself on the plea of an emergency call and left the forbidden world in which he had been betraying his Master, never to return again.

Are you a witness for Christ or against Him?

SECTION II—*The Qualifications of the Servants of the Lord*

FIRE-TOUCHED LIPS

1. The first qualification is that we have fire-touched lips (6:7). It was thus that Isaiah's own service for God had begun. It is thus that all true Christian service must begin, in the baptism of the Holy Spirit and the cleansing of heart and tongue by God's consuming fire. Then his ears were opened to hear the voices of heaven. Then his eyes were opened to see the needs of the world. Then the message was understood. "Whom shall I send? And who will go for us?" (6:8a). And the answer came springing from his lips, "Here am I. Send me!" (6:8b).

It is not your natural abilities that can equip you for the service of the Lord. You must receive the definite baptism of the Holy Spirit. Have you received Him? If you have, the first place where it will be evident will be your tongue. It will show its reality and power by what you say, and still more by what you do not say. Oh, has it burned up the frivolousness, the flippancy, the folly of unholy speech and burned in God's messages to your trembling lips as in the days of old?

OPENED EARS

2. The second qualification is that we have opened ears. "The Sovereign LORD has given me an instructed tongue,/ to know the word that sustains the weary./ He wakens me morning by morning,/ wakens my ear to listen like one being taught" (50:4). We must first hear our own messages from His lips before others can hear them from ours with any profit. The true servant of the Lord has a quickened ear. He knows the voice of his Master. He hears the word from His mouth. His messages are not merely reasoned out and gathered up from the newspapers and the current religious literature of the time, but they are echoes of a heavenly voice, and back of them the speaker and the hearer recognize, "Thus saith the LORD." Fellow workers, do you know His voice? Do you wait for His messages and do you speak as one that has been instructed "to know the word that sustains the weary" (50:4)? It is not a great many words that help. It is not a whole sermon or talk. It is one single word that falls into one heart and another message into another. This is God's way of warning, quickening, convicting, comforting and inspiring His people.

Those who can thus hear God's voice and bring His message are the true prophets of every age. God give to us the prophetic spirit and the God-touched ears and tongues of Pentecost.

FOCUSED EYES

3. The third qualification is that the servant have eyes blinded to all else but His work. "Who is blind but my servant,/ and deaf like the messenger I send?/ Who is blind like the one committed to me,/ blind like the servant of the LORD?" (42:19).

God's true servants have to be blind to everything else but their business for Him. Like a driving horse, whose eyes are shaded from all side views and can only look straight on, so God would have us go with eyes concentrated on His work and will. How many things there are by which the adversary would side-track us or distract us. The world's attractions—the people about us, the things they say about us or do not say about us—all these we must be blind to and our watchword be, "But one thing I do" (Philippians 3:13).

SWIFT AND WILLING FEET

4. Swift and willing feet to run His errands is the servant's fourth qualification. "How beautiful on the mountains/ are the feet of those who bring good news,/ who proclaim peace,/ who bring good tidings,/ who proclaim salvation,/ who say to Zion,/ 'Your God reigns!' " (Isaiah 52:7). The Lord's servant must not only know, but he must go. His work will call him to the mountains, the hard place of service; but his feet will be "fitted with the readiness that comes from the gospel of peace" (Ephesians 6:15), and he will leave behind him a shining track of beauty and of light.

There is another fine passage about consecrated feet in Isaiah 32:20. "How blessed you will be,/ sowing your seed by every stream,/ and letting your cattle and donkeys range free." Sowing beside every stream has reference to the irrigated valleys of the Orient and the planting of our seed where the waters have prepared the soil. We are to follow the Holy Spirit as He opens our way and prepares the hearts of men. "Letting your cattle and donkeys range free" is very suggestive of true Christian service.

The ox is the toiling beast, the ass, the burden-bearer. The one works, the other suffers. Both suggest the fine symbol used by the Baptist Missionary Society as its trademark: an ox standing between a plough on the one hand and an altar on the other with the inscription over him, "Ready for either or both." The true servant of the Lord is ready for service or suffering as the Lord may call for the plough or the altar. This is finely worked out in the Gospel of Mark, which is a picture of Jesus Christ as the Father's servant. There we see Him as the toiling Christ first and then as the suffering Christ.

Are our feet following His footprints, going forth "by every stream" in ministries of loving service and patient suffering?

HIDDEN

5. One more qualification for the true servant is found in our context. "He made my mouth like a sharpened sword,/ in the shadow of his hand he hid me;/ he made me into a polished arrow/ and concealed me in his quiver" (49:2). It is to be hidden in the shadow of His hand, while His hand alone is seen, and we are out of sight.

The bane of much service is the blaze of publicity, the blowing of the trumpet of the worker and the bid that is so often made for the popular sensation, applause and admiration. God can only use His hidden workers. The seraphim used four of their six wings to cover their faces and their feet, and the true servant of the Lord will always seek to be out of sight himself that Jesus may be glorified.

Are we thus divinely equipped and consecrated for the service of our Lord?

SECTION III—*The Ministries of True Service*

THE LIGHT OF THE GOSPEL

1. Our first ministry is to give the light of the gospel to the world. In Isaiah 42:6 and 7 we have the commission of the Master which has been passed on to His servants. "I, the LORD, have called you in righteousness;/ I will take hold of your hand./ I will keep you and will make you/ to be a covenant for the people/ and a light for the Gentiles,/ to open eyes that are blind,/ to free captives from prison/ and to release from the dungeon those who sit in darkness." This is our supreme service: to give the light of His gospel to the world and set free the prisoners of sin and Satan. Are we doing this? Is the chief business of our lives to spread the Gospel and save our fellowmen?

EDIFICATION OF HIS PEOPLE

2. "The Sovereign LORD has given me an instructed tongue,/ to know the word that sustains the weary" (50:4). This is for the comfort and edification of His people.

It is just as important that we minister to Christians as that we save sinners. God's people need much comfort, quickening and spiritual help. They are often weary. Hearts are fainting all around us and we do not at all seem to care. Oh, for the men and women that are ready to speak a word in season! If you are much with your Master, your lives will drop the oil of joy for mourning, and your hands will bring balm for broken hearts. The social call, the chance meeting on the street, the journey on the railway train, the call of some burdened business man for counsel and advice—all these will give you opportunities quite as valuable as the inquiry room, the Sunday school class and the religious meeting to speak such words for Christ and the comfort of your fellows. God help us, beloved, to be true to this wayside ministry.

THE AGE TO COME

3. We are called to work for the age to come. There is a very sublime passage in Isaiah 51:16 which appeals to the highest feelings of the earnest Christian. "I have put my words in your mouth/ and covered you with the shadow of my hand—/ I who set the heavens in place,/ who laid the foundations of the earth,/ and who say to Zion, 'You are my people.' "

What a superb figure! "Set the heavens in place." "Laid the foundations of the earth." The trees of righteousness and the amaranthine flowers that are filling the paradise of God are planted by our hands. Oh, some day to find in your home above innumerable souls that have been brought there through your instrumentality to be your joy and crown of righteousness forever. Thus we may "set the heavens in place" and we may lay "the foundations of the earth." That is the future millennial earth.

The work we are doing in calling out a people for His name, in evangelizing the world and in preparing for His coming—truly this is laying the foundations of that new earth where Christ shall reign and we shall sit with Him upon His throne.

Is there any earthly ambition that can compare with this? Is there any sort of hope that shines with so bright a luster? Is every recompense that earth can offer you worthy of comparison? Oh, turn from the tinsel baubles of a vain and passing world and begin to lay up treasure beyond. Come into that splendid partnership with Him where we receive our wages now, but our dividends by and by and the dividend shall be the whole inheritance. "The reaper draws his wages, even now he harvests the crop for eternal life" (John 4:36). Shall we "set the heavens in place" and lay "the foundations of the earth," and invest our lives in the age to come?

RESTORATION

4. We are called to restore the things that have been lost by a faithless church. Here is a fine description of the ministry to which God is calling many today. "Your people will rebuild the ancient ruins/ and will raise up the age-old foundations;/ you will be called Repairer of Broken Walls,/ Restorer of Streets with Dwellings" (Isaiah 58:12).

How much has been lost since Pentecostal days! How much has been missed from the full heritage of His will! Thank God, His faithful servants today are being used to repair the breaches, to restore the old paths and show us that Jesus Christ is the same yesterday, today and forever.

GLORIFY THE MASTER

5. The supreme business of the servant is to glorify His Master. "You are my servant,/ Israel, in whom I will display my splendor" (49:3). Are we glorifying Him? Is it our supreme aim to do so?

At a railway station, an officer of the company was very strictly carrying out the instructions of his chief and excluding many from the gates. All sorts of devices were used by the knowing ones to get through, but he was inexorably firm both to flatteries and frowns. At last one man said to him, "You seem to be absolutely indifferent to what anybody thinks of you in this crowd." "Well," he said, "my one business and my only ambition is to please the man that employs me, and he is the only man I am trying to please."

Oh, that loyalty to Christ might be as true! Are we glorifying Him?

SECTION IV—*Promises to the Servants of the Lord*

UPHOLDING

1. "I, the LORD, have called you in righteousness;/ I will take hold of your hand./ I will keep you and will make you/ to be a covenant for the people/ and a light for the Gentiles" (42:6). The servant of the Lord is held and upheld by Him who holds the seven stars in His right hand.

ALL NECESSARY RESOURCES

2. "I will go before you/ and will level the mountains;/ I will break down gates of bronze/ and cut through bars of iron./ I will give you the treasures of darkness,/ riches stored in secret places,/ so that you may know that I am the LORD,/ the God of Israel, who summons you by name" (45:2–3). His mighty providence will go before us and prepare our way. His infinite riches will open to us the treasures of darkness and He will supply the means and resources we require as we go forward and trust Him for His work.

PROTECTION

3. " 'No weapon forged against you will prevail,/ and you will refute every tongue that accuses you./ This is the heritage of the servants of the LORD,/ and this is their vindication from me,'/ declares the LORD" (54:17). It is not because of our righteousness that He does this, but because He gives us His righteousness and guards us for His own name's sake that our reputation is safe in His keeping and our lives are immortal till our work is done.

EFFICIENCY AND SUCCESS

4. "So is my word that goes out from my mouth:/ It will not return to me empty,/ but will accomplish what I desire/ and achieve the purpose for which I sent it" (55:11). The fruit may tarry long, the work may seem in vain, but nothing that His Spirit has prompted can ever fall to the ground.

COMPENSATION FOR SEEMING FAILURE

> And now the LORD says—
>   he who formed me in the womb to be his servant
> to bring Jacob back to him
>   and gather Israel to himself,
> for I am honored in the eyes of the LORD
>   and my God has been my strength—
>
> he says:

"It is too small a thing for you to be my servant
   to restore the tribes of Jacob
   and bring back those of Israel I have kept.
I will also make you a light for the Gentiles,
   that you may bring my salvation to the ends of the earth."
   (49:5–6)

5. Our work may seem to fail as the great Servant's did in one direction, but we shall still be glorious in the eyes of the Lord. As He promised Christ, so to us He will also give a new and larger ministry in some other direction and make glorious compensation for every hard place and seeming failure.

THE RECOMPENSE OF JOY

6. Here are some of the recompenses of the sorrowing and toiling servant. "Therefore this is what the Sovereign LORD says:/ 'My servants will eat,/ but you will go hungry;/ my servants will drink,/ but you will go thirsty;/ my servants will rejoice,/ but you will be put to shame./ My servants will sing/ out of the joy of their hearts,/ but you will cry out/ from anguish of heart/ and wail in brokenness of spirit' " (65:13–14). Such is the joy of true service. Such is the recompense the Master holds for all that follow Him. He is a good Master. Let us be true and faithful servants. He was the great Servant Himself. Let us follow in His footsteps and count it our highest honor to say, "I serve." Will He have our lives? Will He have them wholly, gladly and forevermore?

Give me a faithful heart,
   Likeness to Thee,
That each departing day
   Henceforth may see
Some work of love begun,
Some deed of kindness done,
Some wanderer sought and won,
   Something for Thee.

CHAPTER 21

THE SUFFERING SAVIOR

Just as there were many who were appalled at him—
  his appearance was so disfigured beyond that of any man
  and his form marred beyond human likeness—
so will he sprinkle many nations,
  and kings will shut their mouths because of him.
For what they were not told, they will see,
  and what they have not heard, they will understand.

After the suffering of his soul,
  he will see the light of life and be satisfied;
by his knowledge my righteous servant will justify many,
  and he will bear their iniquities.
  (Isaiah 52:14–15; 53:11)

The 53rd chapter of Isaiah should begin with our first text, including the last paragraph of the 52nd chapter. It is all one combined picture of the suffering Messiah.

Jewish writers have tried hard to apply it to Israel as a nation and to show that it demands no other fulfillment in the life of an individual sufferer. But after the utmost strain of the natural force of language, such a construction utterly fails to carry conviction to an unprejudiced reader. We are constrained to recognize this marred face of suffering, this Man of sorrows, this victim of sacrifice, this Conqueror of Satan and sin as no less a person than the Man of Galilee and the Man of Calvary, who in the fullness of time appeared on earth and fulfilled every one of those minute predictions in His own person and in His passion and death.

The prophet commences the 53rd chapter with a wail of complaint against the indifference and unbelief that rejected this momentous message and refused to recognize the arm of the Lord. He gives a picture of the sufferings of the Savior and the fruits that grow from the blood-stained soil of Calvary.

SECTION I—*The Sufferer*

Many details make up this tragic picture.

HIS LOWLY BIRTH

1. The first is His lowly birth. "He grew up before him like a tender shoot,/ and like a root out of dry ground./ He had no beauty or majesty to attract us to him,/ nothing in his appearance that we should desire him" (53:2). This great sufferer began His career amid circumstances of the deepest humiliation. He was born of a maiden mother with a cloud of reproach upon His name. His lot was that of poverty. His cradle was a manger. His home was Nazareth, whose very name stood for all that was despicable and was a play upon the words of the text, for its root word *Nastar,* just means a dry sprout, "a root out of dry ground." There seems to have been no natural attractiveness about the person of Jesus Christ in a purely human way. He was a contradiction of the ideals of the flesh, and a disappointment to every form of human pride.

HIS REJECTION

2. Second is His rejection by His own people. "He was despised and rejected by men,/ a man of sorrows, and familiar with suffering./ Like one from whom men hide their faces/ he was despised, and we esteemed him not" (53:3).

What a bitter trial it was to Moses to come to his nation with high enthusiasm and patriotic devotion, prepared to stand up for them against their oppressors, and then to find that they refused to appreciate his services and failed to understand his mission. Likewise, Jesus "came unto his own, and his own received him not" (John 1:11, KJV). That too must have been one of the great sorrows of Jesus' life—to be conscious of the intense love which was sacrificing itself for His people and their utter inability to understand Him, appreciate Him or let Him save them.

HIS EARTHLY LIFE

3. Jesus also suffered through the privations and sorrows of His earthly life. All the elements which constitute man's cup of sorrow filled His bitter draught of earthly pain. He was poor and had to toil for His own livelihood and that of His mother. He was lonely and felt Himself a stranger in a strange world. His life was one of constant self-denial, repression and intense toil. He walked on foot again and again over all the land, working incessant-

ly and often with wearied frame from dawn till darkness, teaching, healing, helping His fellowmen. And suffering was so strange to Him. He had never known sorrow before. It was a new world of experience. He was like a land bird far at sea and out of its element. He was like a naked man fighting His way through thickets of thorns. His whole being was open to a thousand sensitive sufferings that our coarser natures know nothing of. He was indeed "familiar with suffering." Others left Him, His disciples forsook Him, but sorrow never left His side.

HIS SACRIFICIAL SUFFERINGS

4. Perhaps the keenest element in His sorrow was His sacrificial sufferings. "God made him who had no sin to be sin for us" (2 Corinthians 5:21). "The LORD makes his life a guilt offering" (Isaiah 53:10). "He bore the sin of many" (53:12). The terrible sting of sin entered His soul. We know something of what it is to be crushed with a single sin and perhaps agonize and pray for hours before we rise above it and find forgiveness and victory; but on Him there rested all the sins of all the world. They were imputed to Him and counted as His own, and He had to bear their penalty and their poison.

A great writer has said that there are three things in the story of Jesus that are utterly above all human experience. The first is that an innocent Man suffered as no one else suffered before. The second is that an Almighty One was crushed, defeated, destroyed by forces that He could easily have overcome. And the third is that through this very paradox He has won His victory and accomplished His great purpose of the world's redemption.

The question is often asked, "Is it right for an innocent person to suffer for the guilt of sinners?" In answer we may say first that God has so permitted, and therefore, it must be right. Secondly, vicarious suffering is the law of the universe. The vegetable world lives by absorbing the mineral. The animal world lives by absorbing the vegetable. The lower animals sacrifice themselves that the higher may live, and even the human race suffers and dies that it may give place to and propagate the next generation. Thirdly, He was voluntary in thus suffering vicariously for others. It would be wrong to compel an innocent person to suffer for the wrong of others. But if he chooses to be a substitute on the higher plane of heroism we have no right to prevent it. Fourthly, the One who suffered for us was not a stranger, but really One of our own race, its federal Head and entitled to represent us. And finally, it was on this principle that the human race fell through the sin of one man, Adam, our federal head. It is therefore in keeping that the race should be redeemed by their new Head, Jesus Christ.

There is no doubt that Isaiah's picture of the Savior's sufferings represent them as vicarious. "But he was pierced for our transgressions,/ he was crushed for our iniquities;/ the punishment that brought us peace was upon him,/ and by his wounds we are healed./ We all, like sheep, have gone astray,/ each of us has turned to his own way;/ and the LORD has laid on him/ the iniquity of us all" (53:5–6).

What a picture of concentrated suffering. It is as though one man were suddenly compelled to stand for all the debts of all the people in the world, and from every quarter they came in upon him until He was swamped, bankrupt and crushed. It is as though a shepherd had gone out alone to stand between the flock and the wolves, and they all set upon him until they had torn him to pieces and he fell bleeding and dying, but the sheep were saved. It is as though all the burning rays of yonder sun at its torrid noon were converged in a great burning glass into one single point of flame and one sensitive heart was placed beneath that fiery focus and burned to cinders. All our guilt and all the penalty it deserved met upon Him and He sank beneath the awful load. But not until He had met the claim, had canceled the debt and had saved the world.

HIS TRIAL AND JUDGMENT

5. Another place of suffering was His trial and judgment. "For he was cut off from the land of the living;/ for the transgression of my people he was stricken" (53:8). What a pathetic story the trial of Jesus was. Worn with a sleepless night, His clothing damp with the bloody sweat of the garden, His heart sore with the betrayal of Judas, He is hurried before the council of the Jews and there He has to face the cruel denial of Peter, His own disciple, and the false accusations of His bitter foes. Again He is hustled to the court of Pilate, dismissed to the judgment seat of Herod, marched back again amid the mockeries of the soldiers to Pilate's court once more, and there insulted, belied, stripped and scourged with cruel lashes loaded with nails, until the flesh hangs bleeding from His bones. And even Pilate, moved with a strange sympathy, points to Him as a spectacle of compassion, "Here is the man!" (John 19:5). Then amid a hideous carnival of cruelty and scorn, He is condemned and compelled to carry His heavy cross to the hill of Calvary where they crucify Him. Well might He say in the prophetic words of Jeremiah, "Look around and see./ Is any suffering like my suffering" (Lamentations 1:12).

HIS DEATH AND BURIAL

6. He suffered in His death and burial. "He was assigned a grave with the wicked,/ and with the rich in his death,/ though he had done no violence,/ nor was any deceit in his mouth" (Isaiah 53:9).

Death to Him must have had a touch more terrible than to less sensitive natures, but He gave Himself up to it as an offering and a willing sacrifice. He literally poured out His very life unto death. The one extenuating feature in it all was that, instead of being buried with the wicked, He was with the rich in His death and the tomb of Joseph was offered as the resting place of His lifeless form.

FORSAKEN BY THE FATHER

7. But the bitterest dregs of His cup of sorrow were yet to come. These were caused by the Father's stroke. "Yet it was the LORD'S will to crush him and cause him to suffer" (53:10a). For that dreadful moment He stood in place of guilty men and it was their day of judgment. Therefore upon His single head there fell the judgment stroke which the guilty world deserved. He bore our hell and in that awful moment, for an instant, His heart was crushed. When our dark hours come to us, we can bear anything if we have His presence. But when death was creeping over Him, and demons were tormenting Him and men were torturing Him, He reached out for His Father's hand, He looked up for His Father's smile, and all was darkness and wrath, and He uttered that bitter cry, "My God, My God, why have you forsaken me?" (Matthew 27:46). "God made him who had no sin to be sin for us" (2 Corinthians 5:21).

> Jehovah lifted up His rod,
>   O Christ, it fell on Thee;
> Thou wast sore stricken of Thy God,
>   Thy bruising healeth me;
> A victim led, my Savior bled,
>   Now there's no curse for me.

THE TRAVAIL OF HIS SOUL

8. Still another area of suffering was the travail of His soul. Christ's deepest anguish was inward. He was going through a great soul conflict of responsibility, desire and intense prayer for the salvation of men. The whole weight of the world's redemption was resting upon His heart. It was the birth hour of heaven. Had He failed, hope would have died for every human soul and heaven been draped in mourning. That awful weight was upon Him. All His life long He bore it, but in the last and crisis hour it absorbed His being with the anguish of a travailing woman. The 22nd Psalm gives a little picture of that conflict. There is a strange expression there, "Deliver my soul from the sword; my darling from the power of the dogs" (22:20, KJV). Who was His darling? It was His beloved Bride. It was the Church that He was holding in His arms from the fearful attack of her foe, and His one last thought was to save others, but He couldn't save Himself. (Matthew 27:42). He did save others, but oh, the awful cost—what tongue can tell!

SECTION II—*The Fruit of His Sorrow*

AS IT AFFECTS US

First let us look at the fruit of His sorrow as it affects us.

1. It brings us deliverance from sickness. "Surely he took up our infirmities" (Isaiah 53:4a).

2. It brings us victory over sorrow. "[He] carried our sorrows" (53:4b).

3. It brings us the forgiveness of our transgressions. "But he was pierced for our transgressions" (53:5a).

4. It brings us salvation from the power of sin. "He was crushed for our iniquities" (53:5b)—the power of indwelling sin.

5. It brings us peace. "The punishment that brought us peace was upon him" (53:5c).

6. It brings us justification. "By his knowledge my righteous servant will justify many" (53:11).

7. It brings us His intercession. "[He] made intercession for the transgressors" (53:12).

8. It brings salvation for the nations. "So will he sprinkle many nations" (52:15).

What a rich and glorious salvation is thus provided, covering all our temporal and spiritual needs, and large as the world itself in its boundless fullness.

AS IT AFFECTS HIM

Second, let's look at it as it affects Him.

1. God will "prolong his days" (53:10c). This refers to His resurrection, ascension and "the power of an indestructible life" (Hebrews 7:16) which has been given Him.

2. "He will see his offspring" (Isaiah 53:10c). This refers to His spiritual offspring. There are two races in the world today, the Adam race and the Christ race. The Adam race is doomed. The Christ race is redeemed. Christians are the seed of Jesus, born of His very being and partners of His own life.

3. "The will of the LORD will prosper in his hand" (53:10d). This refers to the great mediatorial work given Him by the Father which is the reward of His sufferings and which He is carrying on with victorious power until His kingdom shall have been established in all the world.

4. Next, there are the spoils of victory. "Therefore I will give him a portion among the great,/ and he will divide the spoils with the strong,/ because he poured out his life unto death" (53:12). As the reward of His conflict and suffering, He is to share the spoils of victory over Satan and all his foes.

Among them are the restitution of this lost world which Satan had captured for a time and claimed to rule as its lord. Christ has overcome him by the cross and is finishing His triumph through the power of the gospel and the Holy Spirit. The vision of prophecy has revealed to us the final triumph when the enemy shall be forever imprisoned in the lake of fire and all the things that he has wrecked shall be restored when "the time comes for God to restore everything" (Acts 3:21). Then shall that sublime vision of the Apocalypse be fulfilled,

> I saw heaven standing open and there before me was a white horse, whose rider is called Faithful and True. With justice he judges and makes war. His eyes are like blazing fire, and on his head are many crowns. He has a name written on him that no one knows but he himself. He is dressed in a robe dipped in blood, and his name is the Word of God.

On his robe and on his thigh he has this name written:

KING OF KINGS AND LORD OF LORDS.
(Revelation 19:11–13, 16)

5. "He will see the light of life and be satisfied" (Isaiah 53:11b). Tell me how much would satisfy your heart for this sin-cursed world, and there I will tell you something of what would satisfy the heart of Jesus. But you could tell me nothing, if you were to talk for a thousand years, that would even faintly approximate all the joy, the victory, the glory which these words imply for earth and heaven, for our ransomed race and our Redeemer's heart of love. All this He saw as He hung that day on Calvary and the prospect took away the bitterness of the cross.

> He could see the ransomed throng,
> He could hear their rapturous song
> Rolling through the ages long;
> He could see His glorious Bride
> Saved and seated by His side,
> And His soul was satisfied.

Will we help to satisfy His soul?

CHAPTER 22

CHRIST: CONQUEROR, SAVIOR AND SUFFERER

Why are your garments red,
like those of one treading the winepress?
I have trodden the winepress alone.
(Isaiah 63:2–3)

Three pictures of the Lord Jesus are given in this splendid poetic vision.

SECTION I—*The Conqueror*

It is a picture of the hero warrior coming back from the conflict with Edom, Israel's traditional foe. It is a picture of the Conqueror, not the warrior, that we see. The battle is over. The carnage, the struggle, the horrors of the battlefield are all behind Him. It is only as a victor that He appears, marching in splendid majesty, "robed in splendor,/ striding forward in the greatness of his strength" (63:1).

The picture is true to the whole analogy of prophecy and the whole story of redemption. It is all one long battle from Edom to Armageddon. The first promise of redemption is the prophecy of a battle between the seed of the woman and the serpent, the emissary of Satan. The conflict between Moses and Pharaoh, Israel and Amalek, Joshua and the Canaanites, David and his enemies, the wars of Jehoshaphat, Hezekiah and the kings of Judah: all these were but types of that greater battle raging in the heavenly places and leading on to the final triumph of the Son of God and the setting up of His millennial throne. The life of every Christian is but a section of this great conflict. It is renewed from generation to generation and age to age, and every Christian must be a soldier as well as a saint.

But the point of the whole prophetic picture is not so much the conflict as the Conqueror. The figure that stands in the front is the victorious Christ. The battle fought, the triumph won and the enemy destroyed. The lesson for us is that the battle is not ours, but God's; and that battle has been won for us already by Him. We go into every conflict with the prestige of victory assured. Just as David met Goliath single-handed, and as the champion of Israel defeated the army of the Philistines by defeating their leader, so the Son of God has won for us the great victory of redemption; and it is our privilege to enter into His victory and go into every conflict saying, "But thanks be to God! He gives us the victory through our Lord Jesus Christ" (1 Corinthians 15:57).

Are we thus taking His victory and entering into the triumph of His cross? It is our glorious privilege so to do. Then we need never know defeat or doubt or fear, but will meet Satan as a conquered foe and ourselves be "more than conquerors through him who loved us" (Romans 8:37).

The prominence of Edom in this conflict is very significant. Edom stands for the flesh, our greatest spiritual foe. In this connection there is a remarkable passage in the 17th chapter of Exodus describing Israel's first conflict with the race of Edom, Amalek. This was typical of the battle which God has ever been waging against the flesh and the power of sin. This battle was not won by human valor, but by divine power. Only while Moses held up his hands did Israel prevail, and when his hands grew heavy and fell down then Amalek prevailed. It was to teach us that we are to overcome our spiritual adversaries not by our energy, but by the uplifted hands of faith, claiming the supernatural power of God. This conflict was to be permanent. "The LORD will be at war against the Amalekites from generation to generation" (Exodus 17:16), and we find this true in every stage of our Christian career.

But in the marginal reading of this verse there is a striking expression which confirms the teaching that we have just been giving. "Because the hand is upon the throne of the LORD from generation to generation." The hand upon the throne of the Lord represents the hand of faith taking God Himself for the victory. When this is the case and our hand is there, then the Lord fights our battle and comes from Edom, evermore "striding forward in the greatness of his strength,/ . . . mighty to save" (Isaiah 63:1b).

Will we learn the lesson of His victory? Will we follow the Captain of our salvation, and in all these things be more than conquerors through Him that loved us?

SECTION II—*The Savior*

"It is I, speaking in righteousness, mighty to save" (63:1c). This is not a selfish conflict like most human wars, for personal ambition and earthly power and renown. Oh, how human blood has flowed and human hearts have ached that some selfish hero might be called earth's greatest conqueror. There are some wars that have been undertaken, not for ambition, but for the deliverance of an oppressed and captive people. Such is the great conflict of redemption. Our mighty Captain has come forth to fight the battle for a lost world and to rescue us from the powers of darkness, and He conquers only that He may save. He is the Champion of the oppressed and it is written of Him, "He will . . . save the children of the needy;/ he will crush the oppressor. . . . For he will deliver the needy who cry out,/ the afflicted who have no one to help" (72:4, 12).

The prophet tells us four things about His great salvation.

A RIGHTEOUS SAVIOR

1. He is a righteous Savior. He does not override the claims of justice, but He is "a righteous God and a Savior" (Isaiah 45:21). He has recognized the claims of God's law against sinful men has fully met them. He has paid the penalty of sin in His own person by His death upon the cross. He has fulfilled for us a broken law and presented to God a perfect righteousness in our stead, and the salvation He gives to us is not merely the obliterating of the record against us but a complete settlement of every claim which justifies us in the sight of God and enables us to say, "Who is he that condemns?" (Romans 8:34); "Who will bring any charge against those whom God has chosen?" (8:33).

A MIGHTY SAVIOR

2. He is a mighty Savior. He has overcome all the obstacles that interposed and there is no cause too hard for His power. He saves us from the guilt of sin and the wrath of God against it. He saves us from the fear of punishment. He saves us from the defiling power of sin in our hearts and purifies and cleanses our nature. He saves us from the physical effects of sin and is the Healer of the body as well as the Redeemer of the soul. He saves us from the consequences of our sin and restores to us "the years the locust have eaten" (Joel 2:25), and the opportunities that our folly threw away. He saves us from the fear of death and raises us to a higher glory than we could have ever known if sin had not come. He is "able to save completely (to the uttermost, KJV) those who come to God" (Hebrews 7:25). He is able to save from the uttermost, too. There is no soul too lost, there is no heart too hard for Him to conquer. He can save our loved ones and rescue the captives of the mighty from the very jaws of the destroyer.

THE ONLY SAVIOR

3. He is the only Savior. "I looked, but there was no one to help,/ I was appalled that no one gave support;/ so my own arm worked salvation for me,/ and my own wrath sustained me" (Isaiah 63:5).

SALVATION THROUGH DESTRUCTION

4. There is a strange blending here of salvation with destruction. "For the day of vengeance was in my heart,/ and the year of my redemption has come" (63:4). This is really one of the underlying principles of the plan of redemption. It is a salvation through destruction. This is the very significance of the cross. It is life through death, victory through seeming defeat, and joy through sorrow. It was thus that the antediluvian world was saved "by water" that is, through the destruction of the sin that was engulfing it. It was thus that Israel was saved from Egypt by the death stroke that smote the firstborn. It was thus that humanity was saved on the cross by the death of Christ, and all our sinful nature with Him, and it is thus that each of us is saved by going through death to life through the power of His grace. So finally, the material world is to be saved by fire and the destruction of the present economy is to usher in "a new heaven and a new earth, the home of righteousness" (2 Peter 3:13).

SECTION III—*The Sufferer*

But this was a costly victory. This Conqueror has not easily won His splendid triumph and saved His captive people. "Why are your garments red,/ like those of one treading the winepress?/ 'I have trodden the winepress alone' " (Isaiah 63:2–3a). While a severe exegesis might insist upon the application of this figure wholly to the sufferings of His foes, yet the beautiful Christian sentiment that has always associated it with the sufferings of the Redeemer cannot be set aside. His grateful and ransomed people will always associate this pathetic verse with the agony of the garden and the cross.

The peculiar feature, however, of Christ's sufferings emphasized in this passage, is their solitariness. "I have trodden the winepress alone;/ from the nations no one was with me" (63:3). The very greatness of Christ and the loftiness of His nature separated Him inevitably from others both in His sufferings and in His deepest life. His lofty nature made Him peculiarly sensitive to things that we would not so deeply feel. To Him the world of sin and sorrow was wholly strange and new. On his finer sensitiveness, the rudeness, coarseness and wrongness of every earthly thing must have grated with a strange pain. Above all, the presence of sin and His identification with it, must have been a hideous agony to the holy nature of the Son of God. To be treated as a malefactor, to be counted worthy of the shame that the vilest sinner deserved, "to be sin for us, so that in him we might become the righteousness of God" (2 Corinthians 5:21), to be judged by His Father as an accursed one and to go down for a little while into the very realms of Hades, and touch for a moment our very hell; all these were elements in the peculiar sufferings of the Son of God which human hearts can never comprehend. Then, besides, He was left in utter desolation in His darkest hour. His disciples forsook Him and fled. Peter denied Him. Judas betrayed Him, and even His Father covered His face with a cloud, and for a little while poured upon His head the judgment that sinners deserved. Truly He was treading the winepress alone.

Surely it is fitting that those who love Him should often go apart and gaze upon that spectacle of sorrow while they hear Him saying, "Is it nothing to you, all you who pass by?/ Look around and see./ Is any suffering like my suffering/ that was inflicted on me/ that the LORD brought on me/ in the day of his fierce anger?" (Lamentations 1:12).

The very design of the Lord's Supper is to keep alive the tender recollection of His passion and to do this in remembrance of Him.

There are two practical lessons for us in connection with this subject.

SUFFERING IN OUR LIFE

1. The first lesson deals with the place of suffering in our life. The greatest mystery about the gospel is that Jesus, that most innocent of beings, was the greatest sufferer, and His suffering is His supremest glory. It is equally true of us that suffering must be part of our discipline and our glory too. While there were sufferings which He had to bear alone, there are others which He shares with us. We can have no part in that sacrificial offering by which He once for all redeemed us and saved us, but we can have a part in the travail of His soul which, as our great High Priest, He is forever bearing in the conflict of the ages and the accomplishment of redemption. On the heavenly throne He is still suffering in sympathy with His people and in prayer for the completion of His redemption. That is the burden which we may share with Him. It was of this Paul said, "I rejoice in what was suffered for you, and I fill up in my flesh what is still lacking in regard to Christ's afflictions, for the sake of his body, which is the church" (Colossians 1:24). Every soul that is converted, every victory that is won for the cause of Christ costs Him the travail of His soul; and we, His body, can bear that travail with Him. This is the meaning of the ministry of prayer. This is the meaning of the burden of suffering which He lays upon the hearts that are willing to watch and weep with Him. Shall we enter into this holy ministry and thus be partakers of the sufferings of Christ and the glory that shall follow?

THE SOLITARINESS OF OUR LIFE

2. The second lesson comes from the solitariness of our life. The Master was alone in the deepest tragedy of His life, and every true follower of Jesus must also learn to be often alone. There are sufferings that will come to us that no other can share. There are experiences that no other can understand.

There are confidences between us and our Lord that no human soul can share. Shall we go with Him along the solitary way? Many of us are there now. Let us not be discouraged, but remember the lone Master who went before us, saying, "The one who sent me is with me; he has not left me alone" (John 8:29).

Ah, be not sad although thy lot be cast
Far from the fold, and in a boundless waste
No shepherd's tents within thy view appear;
But the chief Shepherd even there is near.
Thy tender sorrow and thy plaintive strain
Flow in a foreign land, but not in vain
Thy tears all issue from a source divine,
And every drop bespeaks a Savior thine.

CHAPTER 23

ISAIAH'S GOSPEL

Come, all you who are thirsty,
come to the waters;
and you who have no money,
come, buy and eat!
Come, buy wine and milk
without money and without cost.
Why spend money on what is not bread,
and your labor on what does not satisfy?
Listen, listen to me, and eat what is good,
and your soul will delight in the richest of fare.
Give ear and come to me;
hear me, that your soul may live.
I will make an everlasting covenant with you,
my faithful love promised to David.
(Isaiah 55:1–3)

The 55th chapter of Isaiah naturally follows the 53rd as the proclamation of the gospel follows the cross of Calvary and the completed atonement. The chapter opens with a business note; in fact, it is like an announcement from an Oriental bargain counter. The Jews had already begun to learn from their intercourse with the Babylonians those commercial lessons which have made them ever since the great traders of the world. Like an Eastern merchant offering his wares to the passerby, the prophet cries, "Come, all you who are thirsty,/ come to the waters;/ and you who have no money,/ come, buy and eat!/ Come, buy wine and milk/ without money and without cost." It is indeed a great bargain that He is offering—everything for nothing.

SECTION I—*What He Offers*

In a word, it is the gospel in all the fullness of its blessings.

BLESSINGS

1. The waters represent the more ordinary and essential blessings of the gospel—its cleansing and satisfying streams of life and salvation.

SPECIAL PROVISIONS

2. Wine represents rather the cordials and comforts and the special provisions which Christ has made for the sick, the suffering and the feeble. "Give . . . wine to those who are in anguish" (Proverbs 31:6), is the prescription of the Hebrew sage. And so wine represents the richer, choicer things which the Holy Spirit gives to the hearts that are prepared.

MILK

3. He offers milk—food for babes. This is the gospel's provision for the little children. This is the simplicity that is in Christ Jesus whose salvation is adapted alike to the humblest child and the loftiest sage.

FEAST

4. He offers the feast of fat things. "Eat what is good,/ and your soul will delight in the richest of fare" (Isaiah 55:2b). The gospel has the choicest blessings, the supremest joys and, best of all, the power to quicken our being so that we can take in these higher blessings and our capacity for enjoyment is immeasurably enlarged as well as the means to satisfy it.

LIFE FOR THE SOUL

5. He offers life in all its deep and everlasting meaning. "Hear me, that your soul may live" (Isaiah 55:3). Life for the soul, life for the spirit, life more abundantly, life forevermore, eternal life "begun on earth and perfected in the skies."

FORGIVENESS, MERCY AND PARDON

6. He offers forgiveness of sins, mercy and pardon. "He will have mercy on him,/ and to our God, for he will freely pardon" (55:7b).

THE COVENANTED LIFE

7. He offers the covenanted life. "I will make an everlasting covenant with you,/ my faithful love promised to David" (55:3). The ungodly has no security for the future. The sinner knows not what a day may bring forth.

Life has nothing guaranteed, and eternity is still more uncertain and unsafe. The unsaved man is adrift upon a shoreless ocean, at the mercy of every wind and tide. But the believer in the Lord Jesus Christ has a covenanted life. His future is guaranteed and he knows that all is well. Of the one it is said, "remember that at that time you were separate from Christ, excluded from citizenship in Israel and foreigners to the covenants of the promise, without hope and without God in the world" (Ephesians 2:12). And of the other it is true,

> For I am convinced that neither death nor life, neither angels nor demons, neither the present nor the future, nor any powers, neither height nor depth, nor anything else in all creation, will be able to separate us from the love of God that is in Christ Jesus our Lord.

> And we know that in all things God works for the good of those who love him, who have been called according to his purpose. (Romans 8:38–39, 28)

JOY AND PEACE

8. He provides joy and peace. "You will go out in joy/ and be led forth in peace;/ the mountains and hills/ will burst into song before you,/ and all the trees of the field/ will clap their hands" (Isaiah 55:12). This is the life of triumph. The mountains stand for difficulties; the trees for the fruits of our lives. Everything shall fall in line with the triumphant future of the children of God and earth and heaven claim their abundant entrance into the everlasting kingdom of our Lord and Savior, Jesus Christ.

VICTORY OVER TRIAL AND SUFFERING

9. He offers victory over trial and suffering. "Instead of the thornbush will grow the pine tree,/ and instead of briers the myrtle will grow" (55:13). This is the promise of the transformation of evil into good and the curse into a blessing. The thornbush and the brier represent the bitter ills of life. But these shall be so overruled and so counteracted that we shall meet them in the land beyond as palms of victory and myrtles of beauty. And the very trees that shall adorn our home in paradise shall be made out of the thorns and briars of our earthly wilderness.

Oh, what a gospel this is that can turn the world upside down and transmute the darkest, saddest things into memorials of blessing and voices of everlasting praise!

SECTION II—*The Persons to Whom This Offer Is Made*

THE THIRSTY

1. "Come all you who are thirsty" (55:1). These are the souls that have grown weary of this vain and empty world and found its promises and even its pleasures "Utterly meaningless! Everything is meaningless" (Ecclesiastes 1:2). How unsatisfying are all earthly things. Their chief enjoyment consists in their pursuit. Their attainment leaves us sated, tired and ready for some new excitement. How pathetic the cry of that weary heart that had gone from flower to flower in her reckless pursuit of pleasure and yet was compelled to cry, "Sir, give me this water so that I won't get thirsty and have to keep coming here to draw water" (John 4:15).

THE POOR

2. "You who have no money,/ come, buy and eat!" (Isaiah 55:1b). This means the poor in spirit, the people that have nothing to give in return for the mercy of God. He asks nothing but our poverty, our helplessness and the opportunity of saving us, blessing us and making our lives happy, and receiving back the recompense of our joy and our praise. You are not really ready to come until you find your poverty and are willing to say:

Nothing in my hand I bring,
Simply to Thy cross I cling;
Naked, come to Thee for dress,
Helpless, look to Thee for grace;
Foul, I to the fountain fly,
Wash me, Savior, or I die.

THE DECEIVED

3. "Why spend money on what is not bread,/ and your labor on what does not satisfy?" (55:2a) You have been fooled by the tempter. You have sought, in the broken cisterns of earth, to quench your thirst, and they have all disappointed you. Perhaps you have been more cruelly deceived by wicked men, unprincipled women and a false and selfish world. Come to Him. He will never deceive you. Why should you pay so much and get so little when He has all to give and nothing to ask but your trust and love?

THE SINNER

4. "Let the wicked forsake his way/ and the evil man his thoughts" (55:7). Human societies are looking out for the people that have references and can

show their good standing. Christ is looking out for people that have no standing. Here is one place you are welcome in proportion to your unworthiness. It is passing strange indeed, but wonderful and divine. "This man welcomes sinners and eats with them" (Luke 15:2). Are you unworthy? Are you conscious of wrong? Are you tired of sinning? There is welcome for you.

SECTION III—*The Terms and Conditions on Which We Are Invited*

FREE

1. It is all free. There is nothing to pay. Even our future life of love and service is not a recompense but a grateful and loving return. We are not accepted and saved because we are going to be good, but because we are utterly bad. Our goodness is but the offering up of our grateful love. It is grace, grace alone; love for the unlovely; help for the helpless and everything for nothing.

THE FIRST STEP

2. The first step to God is to hearken. "Give ear and come to me;/ hear me, that your soul may live (Isaiah 55:3). The greatest hindrances to true life are inattention, insensibility, indifference and hardness of heart. Our cares are deafened by the voices of the world. Our minds are absorbed by the vanities of earth. We do not really give attention to the things of God. The round of fashion, the routine of daily duty, the rush of life drive us along like a great torrent and we come to the end of life before we really awake to its solemn meaning. Therefore God calls us aloud: " Give ear and come to me;/ hear me, that your soul may live," and the Holy Spirit waits, "Today, if you hear his voice,/ do not harden your hearts" (Psalm 95:7b–8a).

INVITED TO COME

3. The first thing we are invited to do is to come. This is an approach to God, a move toward Him. Anything that brings us nearer is coming: the putting forth of desire; the stretching out a hand; the kneeling in prayer of a penitent and a suppliant; the movement forward to the altar of the inquirer; or better than all, the lifting up of the heart to God and the reaching out of the soul in earnest prayer. Come any way at all, but come, and "whoever comes to me I will never drive away" (John 6:37).

BUY

4. Next, we must buy. This means to appropriate; to make it your own; to put your name in it; to claim it. The things you purchase are yours. So we must take Christ and His salvation. We must not only ask for it, but we

must say "It is mine," and we must begin to act and think as though it were ours. You don't have to pay for it, and yet you buy it. The price has been paid by another, and it becomes yours not as a charity but as a redemption right. You can look in the face of a just and holy God and claim it and know that He cannot refuse to give it to you, not only as a matter of grace, but as a matter of justice and right, inasmuch as it has been purchased for you by the precious blood of His only begotten Son.

EAT

5. Then we must eat. This is more than buying. This is beginning to enjoy your purchase. This is getting the good of it and taking into your life the comfort, the strength, the joy which you have claimed by faith, and which is your privilege to know by actual experience as well.

SEEK

6. "Seek the LORD." This is for the souls that are far away. They may not find Him at once, but they are to continue to seek, to press their suit and to wait upon Him until they receive the fullness of His blessing. He is not far from the earnest seeker. "Seek the LORD while He may be found" (Isaiah 55:6a), and found He will surely be.

CALL

7. "Call on Him." This represents prayer. It is thus that we shall find Him, on our knees and at the throne of grace. Anybody can call. It is the cry of distress. It needs no science or education, but a deep sense of need and a simple confidence that there is Someone sure to hear and answer. "Call on him while he is near" (55:6b).

TURN FROM SIN

8. Then we must turn from sin to God. "Let the wicked forsake his way/ and the evil man his thoughts./ Let him turn to the LORD" (55:7). This is repentance. There must be an actual forsaking of sin. There must be an honest turning to God. There must be an uncompromising "No" to the devil and the world and the flesh and the voice of sin and temptation; and there must be an everlasting "Yes" to God in all His good and holy will. Without this our own conscience and sense of right forbid us to expect an answer or a blessing. But acting thus, no past transgression, no record of sin, no imperfection of your faith or your prayer, no possible barrier can keep you back from His mercy and His blessing. "He will have mercy on [you],/ . . . he will freely pardon" (55:7b).

SECTION IV—*God's Appeal*

THE WASTE OF LIFE

1. "Why spend money on what is not bread,/ and your labor on what does not satisfy?" (55:2a). He pleads with us to give up the foolish waste of life on things that do not profit and to take the things that alone are worth living for. Oh, how cheaply we sell our souls!

It is said that Roland Hill, while preaching in the open air one day, was attracted by the passing of Lady Erskine, a distinguished duchess. Suddenly he stopped in his discourse and striking the pose of an auctioneer, he said, "Lady Erskine's soul is for sale. Who will have it? Ah, Satan, you are bidding. You will give the world, pleasure, honor, every earthly attraction. But I hear another voice. It is the voice of the Lord Jesus. 'I have given my life for her, and I will give to her eternal life.' Lady Erskine, who shall have your soul!" And the duchess cried out, "Mr. Hill, the Lord Jesus shall have my soul, for He has paid the greater price and offers the richer boon."

Oh, will we waste our real treasures and throw ourselves away for the tinsel of a passing world?

HIS OWN LOVE

2. He appeals by His own great love. "My thoughts are not your thoughts,/ neither are your ways my ways" (55:8). We may not be able to understand how God can give away so much for so little. It may seem too good to be true, but it is not. It is just like Him. "As the heavens are higher than the earth,/ so are my ways higher than your ways/ and my thoughts than your thoughts" (55:9).

> How Thou canst think so well of us
> And be the God Thou art
> Is darkness to my intellect,
> But sunshine to my heart.

HIS UNFAILING WORD

3. God appeals to us through His unfailing Word. "My word . . . will not return to me empty" (55:11a), He says. We can trust this promise. We can take Him at His Word and He will never, never fail us. Will we do so? Will we put our names in these great promises? Will we claim this rich inheritance? Will we accept the gospel of Isaiah which is the precious gospel of our Lord and Savior Jesus Christ?

CHAPTER 24

THE RIGHT AND THE WRONG WAY OF LIVING

Why spend money on what is not bread,
and your labor on what does not satisfy?
Listen, listen to me, and eat what is good,
and your soul will delight in the richest of fare.
(Isaiah 55:2)

This passage tells us of misdirected effort and wasted strength. There is a coarse and brutal way in which multitudes are thus spending their "money on what is not bread" and their "labor on what does not satisfy," in sensual indulgence and degrading vice. But there are also more refined and respectable ways in which multitudes are throwing away their lives and getting nothing at last but the empty shells.

One is reminded of the story told by Lord Dufferin about his Irish estate. There was a fine old castle on the land which was exposed to neglect and depredation through lack of a protecting wall. The old ruin was of great value and the noble lord desired to preserve it at a heavy cost. So before leaving for India, he gave instructions to his steward to have a fine substantial wall erected all around it. On his return from India he went to see the estate and inspect the old castle, but found to his dismay that the castle had entirely disappeared and there was just a great modern wall of solid masonry enclosing nothing but the site of the old ruin. He called and asked him what he had done with the castle that he valued so highly. "Och!" he said, "that ould thing. I just pulled it down and used the materials to build the wall."

The gifted lord used to often tell the humorous story and find in it a fine illustration of the way in which so many people were destroying the real treasures of life and putting their strength and energy into that which was but a mere shell to hold something else which had been overlooked and neglected.

Not unlike the thoughtlessness of the steward, was the conduct of a little

461

girl in England who got a half crown given her by a friend and immediately went and spent it to buy a purse to hold the money in. When she got home she found a purse but nothing to put in it.

So multitudes are spending life with its infinite possibilities in merely providing the outward forms of things, to discover at last that the real values have been quite forgotten. How often we find higher culture and education simply providing a lot of empty shells, qualities which have no practical value either in producing happiness or power. How often we see money spent lavishly in accumulating the mere materials of life—houses, lands, equipage, income and the whole machinery of life—but when it is all accomplished, it is hollow at heart. There are houses, but they are not homes, for there is not love to hallow them. There are the means of gratification, but there is no pleasure, for selfishness has destroyed the secret of true happiness.

Saddest of all is the waste of religious effort. What is ceremony and form without real devotion and love! How empty the pageant of a splendid ritual when behind it is the skeleton of a dead church and a Christless soul! Not more cold and cheerless are the marble monuments in the cemetery and the gilded spires on the cathedral above the worshiper's head. It is all like the vision of the valley of dry bones: the forms of men, but there is no life in them.

Are you spending your life in simply building walls with nothing to enclose, in buying purses that only hide their own emptiness, in making picture frames while the picture itself is absent and in spending existence in one endless round of busy toil and anxious pursuit of happiness and success? Have you found at last, like the preacher in Ecclesiastes, that your vision has faded like a dream, that your life is scaffolding and the building has not yet even been begun, and that there is nothing left but to sit in the chill winter of despair and cry, "Utterly meaningless! Everything is meaningless" (1:2)?

What then, is the real object of life? What is there that is worth living for and extending our strength to realize and accomplish?

FIND GOD

1. The first object of life is to find God and to be rightly adjusted to Him. As the flower needs the sun, as the birdling needs its mother, as the infant perishes without a parent's love and care, so the human soul was made for God and never can rest until it rests in Him. The worlds of space all circle around their proper suns. There is a center of gravitation for everything; when any planet loses this bond, it becomes a wandering star and drifts into darkness and destruction.

God is our center and our sun. Faith is the great bond that holds us to our orbit and without that we are "wandering stars, for whom blackest darkness has been reserved forever" (Jude 13). The object of the gospel is to bring man back to God; to restore the bond of confidence and bring us into our true place of trust and obedience to Him. Then we truly begin to live. Then our hearts find the source of their happiness and God pours into us that fullness of love and blessing which we were made to receive.

This must all begin by that simple trust that blots out our sin and brings us into fellowship and confidence with Him. Then the Holy Spirit reestablishes the vital bond of love and union, and God fills us with His own nature, and we blossom and bud and bear fruit like the vine that has found its congenial soil and reached the fountains from which it draws its vital support.

Until this comes to pass, everything in life is vain. Our efforts are misdirected; our toil is wasted; our struggles are vain. We are but marking time like the soldier who stands on a pivot while the army centers round him. We are making no progress, or to adopt the figure of the text, we are spending our "money on what is not bread, and [our] labor on what does not satisfy" (Isaiah 55:2).

Oh, wandering hearts, come home to God. Accept His reconciling love. Become His children. Receive His Spirit and return to your true place of rest and satisfaction. God needs you to receive His fullness, and you need Him to fill the void which no created thing can ever fill.

FIND YOURSELF

2. The second thing in life is to find yourself and rise to your true ideal of character and power.

When we find God, then we also find ourselves. How many people have never yet discovered the treasure of their own existence. It is buried like a jewel in the refuse of a filthy room. How true it is, "A man's life does not consist in the abundance of his possessions" (Luke 12:15). The prodigal first sought for happiness in dissipation, but he only lost himself. The first step in his restoration was when it could be said of him, "he came to his senses" (15:17). How many have lost themselves like him in earthly pleasure, sensual indulgence, the greed of gain, the whirl of fashion, the wild race for earthly success! Vainly too you seek for your true self in mere intellectual culture. You will not find a true man or woman there. The intellect is but the lamp that lights the chambers of the soul, but the guest is deeper and further than this. It is the immortal spirit that came from God, that belongs to eternity and that can only be filled with the infinite and everlasting. Sometimes men get a flash of the glory of the true nature which is hidden within them. How finely Victor Hugo used to say, "The winter of age is upon my head, but eternal springtime is in my heart. I feel within my soul the symphonies of the age to come. My work is only beginning. I feel in myself a future life. Heaven lights me with the sunshine of unseen worlds. I am rising, I know, toward the sky."

Have you found that glorious life? Have you brought your life into contact with Him and have you truly begun to live in the highest sense?

John Newton tells of a night that he lay in his hammock on the Adriatic Sea after a fearful spell of wild debauchery. In a lurid dream, he saw himself throwing away his soul into the sea like a precious jewel, at the daring of Satan. As it sank beneath the waves, a fiendish shout went up from the pit and a flash of angry fire seemed to light the mountain tops along the shore. His spirit sank within him and he felt that he had lost his soul, buried forever a treasure more precious than all the world.

There, in his dream, his Savior seemed to stand before him and He asked him if he wished to have that jewel recovered once more. He threw himself at His feet and earnestly pleaded for Him to save it if He could. Then the Redeemer leaped into the flood, battled with the waves, sank beneath the surges and at last wearied and panting rose and reached the deck, holding in his hand the precious gem. Eagerly the sailor reached out his hand to grasp it, but the Master held him back and said, "No, I will keep it now for you. If I gave it to you, you would but sacrifice it again; and when life is done I will have it for you at the gates of heaven forevermore."

And from that vision that drunken sailor went forth to become the sweetest of the saints of God, to write the hallowed hymns that have been singing men and women to glory for a century, and to leave behind him the lustre of a life more precious than earth's fairest gem.

Oh, men and women, each of you has such a treasure. Have you truly found it, and are you letting God keep it, polish it and prepare it for the highest possibilities of earth and the richest glories of heaven? There is nothing on earth, worth half so much as men. After Christ Himself, the things we value most are human souls. We would give the world for one of them. How beautiful are they to God—as precious as the blood He shed for them, and some time to become as glorious as He in the coming age. Each of us is such a treasure. God help us to know ourselves, to find our true value and to be God's best.

FIND OUR WORK

3. The third object of life is to find our work and be occupied with the best and highest things. Man was made for activity, and the powers of the human mind surpass all possible conception.

The Master's great business was to finish His work. The apostle's supreme motive was "I consider my life worth nothing to me, if only I may finish the race and complete the task the Lord Jesus has given me— the task of testifying to the gospel of God's grace" (Acts 20:24). Have we found our calling? Are we pouring out our life into other lives? Are we leaving behind us fruits that shall remain and work into which shall be crystalized the best that we could be and do?

Mother, perhaps your work is to leave one child, the blossom of your being, to accomplish in years to come mightier things than you could even dream. So the holy Monica loved, suffered, waited, prayed, until her one boy Augustine became the blossom of her life; and she passed away, leaving him to speak for her, to live for her and to live out her life on earth. So the century plant spends 100 years preparing for one supreme effort and at last produces a single flower, gorgeous beyond description, and blossoms and dies.

Wife, are you living out your life meekly, gently, unselfishly by love, by help, by prayer in the man to whom God has linked you as the helpmeet of his great struggle? Can there be a nobler ambition than to be the power behind the scenes, the vital force, the inspiring impulse of a life which is but the expression of your silence, your suffering and your love?

Christian worker, has your being been poured out in some great and noble work which God has given you and which you are leaving behind you to bless humanity when you yourself will have passed from earthly view?

Some time ago there passed through New York, on his way to China, an old man who for 40 years had lived but for one thing: to plant the gospel in the unopened provinces of that vast empire. From this faith and love had sprung the China Inland Mission, with its hundreds of missionaries and its thousands of converts. His last desire was to end his days in China. On his way across the Atlantic, a traveling companion later told how he used to talk every day with exulting joy of the delusions that had taken possession of his failing mind, namely, that all the passengers and crew upon the steamer were missionaries to China. Then he would laugh aloud his joy that so many hundreds of new missionaries were about to be added to the force in that land. The ruling passion was strong in death; and with this sublime enthusiasm overbalancing his weakened mind he passed on to interior China and into its furthest province, where his glorious spirit went up to be with God. He had found his life work and he has left it as a memorial more lasting than the monuments of Egypt.

God help us to find our Savior, to find ourselves, and to find our work,

> And, departing, leave behind us
> Footprints on the sands of time;
> Footprints which perhaps another
> Travelling o'er life's solemn main,
> Some forlorn and shipwrecked brother,
> Seeing, may take heart again.

CHAPTER 25

THE FOURFOLD GOSPEL IN ISAIAH

But he was pierced for our transgressions,
he was crushed for our iniquities;
the punishment that brought us peace was upon him,
and by his wounds we are healed.
(Isaiah 53:5)

The book of Isaiah provides us a marvelous picture of the fourfold gospel: Jesus Christ as Savior, Sanctifier, Healer and Coming King.

SECTION I—*Salvation*

The first picture of Isaiah begins with sin and salvation. What an indictment against the sinner is contained in the opening appeal:

Ah, sinful nation,
a people loaded with guilt,
a brood of evildoers,
children given to corruption!
They have forsaken the LORD;
they have spurned the Holy One of Israel
and turned their backs on him.

Why should you be beaten anymore?
Why do you persist in rebellion?
Your whole head is injured,
your whole heart afflicted.
From the sole of your foot to the top of your head
there is no soundness—
only wounds and welts

> and open sores,
> not cleansed or bandaged
> or soothed with oil.
>   (1:4–6)

But what a message of mercy and salvation, " 'Come now, let us reason together,'/ says the LORD./ 'Though your sins are like scarlet,/ they shall be as white as snow;/ though they are red as crimson,/ they shall be like wool' " (1:18).

Again, what a glorious gospel of salvation is contained in Isaiah 53:5–6, "But he was pierced for our transgressions,/ he was crushed for our iniquities;/ the punishment that brought us peace was upon him,/ and by his wounds we are healed./ We all, like sheep, have gone astray,/ each of us has turned to his own way;/ and the LORD has laid on him/ the iniquity of us all." How many it has brought to lay their sins upon Him and to come back to the Shepherd and the fold.

Where can we find a more complete and attractive gospel invitation than Isaiah 55:

> Come, all you who are thirsty,
>   come to the waters;
> and you who have no money,
>   come, buy and eat!
> Come, buy wine and milk
>   without money and without cost.
> Why spend money on what is not bread,
>   and your labor on what does not satisfy?
> Listen, listen to me, and eat what is good,
>   and your soul will delight in the richest of fare.
>
> Seek the LORD while he may be found;
>   call on him while he is near.
> Let the wicked forsake his way
>   and the evil man his thoughts.
> Let him turn to the LORD, and he will have mercy on him,
>   and to our God, for he will freely pardon.
>   (55:1–2, 6–7)

How rich the metaphors under which the gospel is presented: water, wine and milk! How fine the figures of buying without money because some one else has paid the price, and eating until our soul delights itself in the richest of fare! How infinite the grace that calls the wicked to forsake his way and the unrighteous man his thoughts and to return unto the Lord who will abundantly pardon!

How the call of the Jubilee rings through that splendid passage in Isaiah 61:1–2: "The Spirit of the Sovereign LORD is on me,/ because the LORD has anointed me/ to preach good news to the poor./ He has sent me to bind up the brokenhearted,/ to proclaim freedom for the captives/ and release from darkness for the prisoners,/ to proclaim the year of the LORD's favor/ and the day of vengeance of our God,/ to comfort all who mourn." This was the very text from which our Lord Himself preached His first sermon at Nazareth and it is the commission of every minister of the gospel.

And finally, how stirring and awakening is the call in Isaiah 45:22, "Turn to me and be saved,/ all you ends of the earth;/ for I am God, and there is no other." How it takes us back to the serpent in the wilderness and the third chapter of the Gospel of John, and how many eyes have turned at the call of this heavenly summons to look and live. Surely, Isaiah is the gospel for the sinner as well as for the saint.

SECTION II—*Sanctification*

The call of the prophet recorded in the sixth chapter of Isaiah is a testimony of sanctification. It began with a vision of God; and, as the result, a vision of himself in all the depths of his sinfulness, as it stood revealed in the white light of the throne. Then came the cry, " 'Woe to me!' I cried. 'I am ruined! For I am a man of unclean lips, and I live among a people of unclean lips, and my eyes have seen the King, the LORD Almighty' " (6:5). And then came the baptism of fire, the live coal upon his lips, which even the seraphim could not touch with their hands, and the glorious announcement, "See, this has touched your lips; your guilt is taken away and your sin atoned for" (6:7). Then with sanctified ears and lips and feet he was ready to hear and obey the great commission that sent him forth to his long and glorious ministry. God must have holy ears and lips and feet to carry His messages and represent Him to the world.

The same high standard of holiness is required from all the servants of the Lord. The Bible contains no finer portrait of the righteous man than Isaiah 33:15–17,

> He who walks righteously
>   and speaks what is right,
> who rejects gain from extortion
>   and keeps his hand from accepting bribes,
> who stops his ears against plots of murder
>   and shuts his eyes against contemplating evil—

> this is the man who will dwell on the heights,
>   whose refuge will be the mountain fortress.
> His bread will be supplied,
>   and water will not fail him.
> Your eyes will see the king in his beauty
>   and view a land that stretches afar.

This man who walks righteously and speaks what is right, and who not only avoids evil himself but shuts his eyes and ears from seeing and hearing evil, he will enter in to the beatific vision, which so sublimely anticipates the parallel promise of the sermon on the mount, "Blessed are the pure in heart,/ for they will see God" (Matthew 5:8).

How finely the highway of holiness is described in Isaiah 35: 8–9: "And a highway will be there;/ it will be called the Way of Holiness./ The unclean will not journey on it;/ it will be for those who walk in that Way;/ wicked fools will not go about on it./ No lion will be there,/ nor will any ferocious beast get up on it;/ they will not be found there./ But only the redeemed will walk there." How suggestive is the figure of the highway, not the broad way, not the ordinary way trodden even by the ordinary pilgrim, but the narrow path where the separated ones walk alone with Jesus. How simple their life. They do not need to be wise or strong. They are wayfaring men and often counted fools by the world, but they have learned the secret of the skies and they walk in safety with the ransomed to their everlasting home.

There is a fine passage in Isaiah 41:10 which suggests three progressive stages of our deeper life. The first is expressed in the promise, "I will strengthen you," the second by the clause, "[I will] help you," but the third, expressed by the phrase "I will uphold you," reaches a higher plane where God's strength and help are not sufficient, but, where, ceasing altogether from ourselves, we fall helpless into His almighty arms and He just upholds us with the right hand of His righteousness—that is, carries us altogether in His own everlasting arms.

There is a still finer passage in Isaiah 44:3–5: "For I will pour water on the thirsty land,/ and streams on the dry ground;/ I will pour out my Spirit on your offspring,/ and my blessing on your descendants./ They will spring up like grass in a meadow,/ like poplar trees by flowing streams./ One will say, 'I belong to the LORD';/ another will call himself by the name of Jacob;/ still another will write on his hand, 'The LORD'S,'/ and will take the name Israel."

Here there are two types of spiritual life distinctly contrasted. The first are those who say "I belong to the LORD" and call themselves by the name of Jacob. This represents the experience of conversion, the Jacob life. These people are undoubtedly God's people, but they have not yet reached their

Peniel. The second class, however, have passed with Jacob through the gates of Peniel and come forth into the higher place of victory and entire consecration, "still another will write on his hand, 'The LORD'S,'/ and will take the name Israel" (44:5). All through this book of Isaiah we can trace these two types. How differently he speaks of them. Notice for example his striking words, "the LORD has redeemed Jacob,/ he displays his glory in Israel" (44:23). Poor Jacob is not forgotten or discarded because he has not got further on. The Lord goes with His people even through the wilderness. But "he displays his glory in Israel" (44:23), the life that is wholly surrendered and transformed, and showing forth "the praises of him who called [us] out of darkness into his wonderful light" (1 Peter 2:9b).

These passages are sufficient to show the deep insight of the prophet's vision and the high and holy plane on which he himself walked and which he ever recognized as God's true pattern for all His children.

SECTION III—*Divine Healing*

There is no lack of material for the gospel of healing in the great Messianic prophet Isaiah. The foundation passage is, of course, Isaiah 53:4–5: "Surely he took up our infirmities/ and carried our sorrows,/ yet we considered him stricken by God,/ smitten by him, and afflicted./ But he was pierced for our transgressions,/ he was crushed for our iniquities;/ the punishment that brought us peace was upon him,/ and by his wounds we are healed." This is the only verse in the chapter prefixed by the word "surely." This is God's great Amen to the truth proclaimed in this passage. The Holy Spirit emphasized it because He knew it was the truth that was to be questioned by the belief of later generations. There is no doubt about the literal reference of this passage to the redemption of our bodies. The word translated "infirmities" literally means sicknesses and is so translated in scores of parallel passages in the Old Testament. The word "carried" is the same as that used in the 12th verse of this chapter with reference to Christ's atonement for sin, "he bore the sin of many." In Matthew 8:17, this passage is translated "He took up our infirmities and carried our diseases."

The fifth verse gives a catalog of the blessings of redemption. "But he was pierced for our transgressions"; that is our act of sin. "He was crushed for our iniquities"; that is our heart of sin. "The punishment that brought us peace was upon him"; that is the spiritual blessing which His death has purchased. And, finally, "by his wounds we are healed"; that is the physical effects of His redemption. Here then we have the fullness of Christ's atonement. To say that the last clause respecting healing means spiritual healing would be to make the sentence a barren repetition of what he had already said in the first part of the verse.

In Isaiah 57:18–19, we have another reference to the Lord's healing. " 'I have seen his ways, but I will heal him;/ I will guide him and restore comfort to him,/ creating praise on the lips of the mourners in Israel./ Peace, peace, to those far and near,'/ says the LORD. 'And I will heal them.' " Here it is evident that the sickness had been caused by sin and that God had been dealing with the transgressor in chastening, "I was enraged by his sinful greed;/ I punished him, and hid my face in anger" (57:17). But repentance has come and the erring one has learned his lesson and returned to God, and now God's promise is "I have seen his ways but I will heal him" (57:18a). His healing is followed by deeper spiritual experiences, "I will guide him and restore comfort to him,/ creating praise on the lips of the mourners in Israel./ Peace, peace, to those far and near" (57:18b–19a). This, in turn, is followed by further healing, "and I will heal them" (57:19b). As we know God more deeply through the teaching of the Holy Spirit, we come into a more profound experience of His healing touch and power. "Through Christ Jesus, the law of the Spirit of life set [us] free from the law of sin and death" (Romans 8:2).

There is another passage, Isaiah 58:8–11, which leads us into the deeper experiences of the Lord's life for the body. "Your healing will quickly appear" (58:8b) is a fine figure of the springing life that comes to us through union and communion with the Lord Jesus. "He will satisfy your needs in a sun-scorched land/ and will strengthen your frame./ You will be like a well-watered garden,/ like a spring whose waters never fail" (58:11). This represents that inner nourishment which the indwelling Christ supplies to all our vital being, making fat our bones, not in the sense of mere physical flesh and increased weight and muscular strength, but that inner freshness and fullness of life which lifts us above exhaustion and disease and renews our youth like the eagle's.

Isaiah has given us a striking object lesson of divine healing in the story of Hezekiah, and his remarkable healing is described in chapter 38. In considering this let us notice:

1. That Hezekiah's sickness was a fatal one. It is foolish to talk about his being healed through a mere poultice of figs of a disease that was declared by God Himself to be unto death.

2. In describing this event in the books of Second Chronicles (22) and Second Kings (20), the record shows that God performed a miracle and healed him. If it was a miracle, it was not a case of healing by remedies. A miracle is something performed by Almighty power when the case is an impossible one.

3. The figs were merely a sign to help his faith to rise from the natural to the supernatural, just as the oil of anointing is a sign of the touch of the Holy Spirit, but has not in itself any inherent healing power. It is mentioned

in Isaiah 38:21 and 22 as a "sign."

4. We have an interesting account of Hezekiah's state of mind during the time that he was waiting under the Lord's hand for the message of healing. At first he completely sank in dejection and despair, and the prayer which the Spirit has recorded is a very weak and miserable failure, not unlike some of our wretched wailings when trouble comes to us. Listen to this, "I waited patiently till dawn,/ but like a lion he broke all my bones;/ day and night you made an end of me./ I cried like a swift or thrush,/ I moaned like a mourning dove./ My eyes grew weak as I looked to the heavens" (Isaiah 38:13–14). How it reminds us of some of our chatterings and mournings, but at last he reaches a turn in the dark road of doubt and fear and suddenly exclaims, "I am troubled; O Lord, come to my aid!" (38:14). No sooner has this gasp of honest prayer reached the heart of God, than a marvelous revelation comes to him and we hear him exclaim, "But what can I say?/ He has spoken to me, and he himself has done this" (38:15). He has heard the voice of God and his faith has answered back and the night is passed and dawn has broken upon his despair.

5. How tender, subdued and inspiring is his note of praise. "The living, the living—they praise you,/ as I am doing today" (38:19).

6. But at last Hezekiah forgot God's great mercy and "he did not respond to the kindness shown him" (2 Chronicles 32:25). Because of this, in later years God's chastening fell upon him once more because of vainglory and sinful pride.

Oh, how sacred a trust the Lord's healing is! Let us not forget that the life He has redeemed belongs to Him and must be given back in humble, loving and devoted service.

SECTION IV—*The Lord's Coming*

Isaiah 11:1–16 is a picture of Messiah's reign in the millennial age, the restoration of Israel and the transformation of the material world and the whole system of nature. Righteousness, peace and universal blessedness shall pervade the world, and the "earth will be full of the knowledge of the LORD/ as the waters cover the sea" (11:9).

Isaiah 32:1–3 is a similar picture of the millennial earth when

A king will reign in righteousness
    and rulers will rule with justice.
Each man will be like a shelter from the wind
    and a refuge from the storm,
like streams of water in the desert
    and the shadow of a great rock in a thirsty land.

> Then the eyes of those who see will no longer be closed,
>   and the ears of those who hear will listen.

Isaiah 24:20–23 is strikingly parallel to the closing chapters of Revelation and the vision of the coming of the Son of Man.

> The earth reels like a drunkard,
>   it sways like a hut in the wind;
> so heavy upon it is the guilt of its rebellion
>   that it falls—never to rise again.
>
> In that day the LORD will punish
>   the powers in the heavens above
>   and the kings on the earth below.
> They will be herded together
>   like prisoners bound in a dungeon;
> they will be shut up in prison
>   and be punished after many days.
> The moon will be abashed, the sun ashamed;
>   for the LORD Almighty will reign
> on Mount Zion and in Jerusalem,
>   and before its elders, gloriously.

How vividly this describes the shaking of the powers of heaven at the coming of the Lord and the appearance of Christ in His glory!

Then comes in chapter 25:7–9, His appearing to Israel and the removing of the veil that has been upon the face of all people. Then in chapter 26:19, comes the vision of the resurrection, "But your dead will live;/ their bodies will rise./ You who dwell in the dust,/ wake up and shout for joy./ Your dew is like the dew of the morning;/ the earth will give birth to her dead." This is followed by the rapture of His saints as they are taken away from the great tribulation which is coming upon the earth. "Go, my people, enter your rooms/ and shut the doors behind you;/ hide yourselves for a little while/ until his wrath has passed by./ See, the LORD is coming out of his dwelling/ to punish the people of the earth for their sins./ The earth will disclose the blood shed upon her;/ she will conceal her slain no longer" (26:20–21).

Finally in chapter 27:1 we have the binding of Satan, described so vividly in Revelation 20:1–3: "And I saw an angel coming down out of heaven, having the key to the Abyss and holding in his hand a great chain. He seized the dragon, that ancient serpent, who is the devil, or Satan, and bound him for a thousand years. He threw him into the Abyss, and locked and sealed it over him, to keep him from deceiving the nations anymore until the

thousand years were ended. After that, he must be set free for a short time."
Then comes the reign of Israel through the millennial years, Isaiah 27:6, "In
days to come Jacob will take root,/ Israel will bud and blossom/ and fill all
the world with fruit." In the later chapters of Isaiah very many of the visions
concerning Judah and Jerusalem belong to the millennial age. Chapter 35 is
one of these. "And the ransomed of the LORD will return./ They will enter
Zion with singing;/ everlasting joy will crown their heads./ Gladness and joy
will overtake them,/ and sorrow and sighing will flee away" (35:10). So is
chapter 59: " 'The Redeemer will come to Zion,/ to those in Jacob who
repent of their sins,'/ declares the LORD" (59:20). The whole of the 60th
chapter belongs to this glorious time. So also Isaiah 65:17–25:

"Behold, I will create
   new heavens and a new earth.
The former things will not be remembered,
   nor will they come to mind.
But be glad and rejoice forever
   in what I will create,
for I will create Jerusalem to be a delight
   and its people a joy.
I will rejoice over Jerusalem
   and take delight in my people;
the sound of weeping and of crying
will be heard in it no more.

"Never again will there be in it
   an infant who lives but a few days,
   or an old man who does not live out his years;
he who dies at a hundred
   will be thought a mere youth;
he who fails to reach a hundred
   will be considered accursed.
They will build houses and dwell in them;
   they will plant vineyards and eat their fruit.
No longer will they build houses and others live in them,
   or plant and others eat.
For as the days of a tree,
   so will be the days of my people;
my chosen ones will long enjoy
   the works of their hands.
They will not toil in vain
   or bear children doomed to misfortune;

for they will be a people blessed by the LORD,
   they and their descendants with them.
Before they call I will answer;
   while they are still speaking I will hear.
The wolf and the lamb will feed together,
   and the lion will eat straw like the ox,
   but dust will be the serpent's food.
They will neither harm nor destroy
   on all my holy mountain,"
        says the LORD.

And Isaiah 66:18–23:

> "And I, because of their actions and their imaginations, am about to come and gather all nations and tongues, and they will come and see my glory.
>
> "I will set a sign among them, and I will send some of those who survive to the nations—to Tarshish, to the Libyans and Lydians (famous as archers), to Tubal and Greece, and to the distant islands that have not heard of my fame or seen my glory. They will proclaim my glory among the nations. And they will bring all your brothers, from all the nations, to my holy mountain in Jerusalem as an offering to the LORD—on horses, in chariots and wagons, and on mules and camels," says the LORD. "They will bring them, as the Israelites bring their grain offerings, to the temple of the LORD in ceremonially clean vessels. And I will select some of them also to be priests and Levites," says the LORD.
>
> "As the new heavens and the new earth that I make will endure before me," declares the LORD, "so will your name and descendants endure. From one New Moon to another and from one Sabbath to another, all mankind will come and bow down before me," says the LORD.

Only the fulfillment of these glorious passages can bring their full interpretation. We can complete the broken links in Isaiah's imperfect chain from the writings of Daniel and John, and the prophetic messages from the Master Himself. No other key will solve Isaiah's vision but the coming of the Lord, the restoration of Israel, the millennial reign of Christ and the glorious realities of the blessed hope which has grown so much clearer and nearer in the light of the New Testament and the events in the days in which we live. When that glorious day shall come, Isaiah's splendid songs and visions of glory shall have a significance and a grandeur which even he but dimly comprehended when he wrote, as the apostle expresses it, "trying to find out the time and circumstances to which the Spirit of Christ in them was pointing when he predicted the sufferings of Christ and the glories that would follow" (1 Peter 1:11).

CHAPTER 26

THE "FEAR NOTS" OF ISAIAH

T his little message "fear not" is almost one of the keynotes of Isaiah. The chord of his later messages was struck in the opening of the fortieth chapter by the word "Comfort, comfort my people" (Isaiah 40:1), and in keeping with this message He again and again reassures His troubled people in these words of comfort and encouragement, "Do not fear." We find the phrase in five passages and repeated several times in some of them.

ISAIAH 41:10–14

"So do not fear, for I am with you;
    do not be dismayed, for I am your God.
I will strengthen you and help you;
    I will uphold you with my righteous right hand.

"All who rage against you
    will surely be ashamed and disgraced;
those who oppose you
    will be as nothing and perish.
Though you search for your enemies,
    you will not find them.
Those who wage war against you
    will be as nothing at all.
For I am the LORD, your God,
    who takes hold of your right hand
and says to you, Do not fear;
    I will help you.
Do not be afraid, O worm Jacob,
    O little Israel,
for I myself will help you," declares the LORD,
    your Redeemer, the Holy One of Israel.

479

Three times the command to not fear or be afraid is repeated in this passage and five reasons are given why we should not fear.

1. The first is God's presence with us: "Do not fear, for I am with you" (41:10a). His companionship under all circumstances and in all places guarantees our safety and may well charm away our fears.

2. The second is God's relation to us as our God: "Do not be dismayed, for I am your God" (41:10b). He gives Himself to us. He gives us the right to use Him against every possible need in His infinite resources. What need we fear with such a God?

3. The third reason given is the strength He promises to give us: "I will strengthen you" (41:10c). That is actual imparted strength to us. This comes in connection with the reassurance, "Do not be afraid, O worm Jacob,/ O little Israel" (41:14a). It stands over against their unworthiness and weakness. Jacob was indeed a worm and Israel was weak, but God says, "I will strengthen you."

4. The fourth reason is His promise of help: "For I myself will help you" (41:14b). Not only does He give us actual strength, but He adds His strength to us. This is very much more.

5. The fifth reason given is His upholding: "I will uphold you with my righteous right hand" (41:10d). This is more than strength, more than help. It is God undertaking the entire responsibility of our case. Our strength will fail; even His help will be insufficient, for when God only helps us and we stand in front responsible for the conflict, we will not be sufficient. But there comes a time when we completely fall into His almighty hand, and then He takes us up bodily and carries us altogether; and it is no longer a man doing his best and God helping him, but God all in all and the man letting Him be all.

In this paragraph there is a beautiful reassurance: "who takes hold of your right hand,/ and says to you" (41:13b), or more literally, "I will keep saying to you." It is not enough for Him to say it once. We need to hear it over and over again, and He never tires saying it to His troubled children until He has cheered away our fears and sorrows.

ISAIAH 43:1–7

> But now, this is what the LORD says—
>   he who created you, O Jacob,
>   he who formed you, O Israel:
> "Fear not, for I have redeemed you;
>   I have summoned you by name; you are mine.
> When you pass through the waters,
>   I will be with you;

and when you pass through the rivers,
   they will not sweep over you.
When you walk through the fire,
   you will not be burned;
   the flames will not set you ablaze.
For I am the LORD, your God,
   the Holy One of Israel, your Savior;
I give Egypt for your ransom,
   Cush and Seba in your stead.
Since you are precious and honored in my sight,
   and because I love you,
I will give men in exchange for you,
   and people in exchange for your life.
Do not be afraid, for I am with you;
   I will bring your children from the east
   and gather you from the west.
I will say to the north, 'Give them up!'
   and to the south, 'Do not hold them back.'
Bring my sons from afar
   and my daughters from the ends of the earth—
everyone who is called by my name,
   whom I created for my glory,
   whom I formed and made."

Here is a new group of fear nots and new reasons for our confidence.

1. "Fear not, for I have redeemed you;/ I have summoned you by name" (43:1b). The fact that He has purchased us with the precious blood of Christ should be enough to guarantee every other blessing we need. "He who did not spare his own Son, but gave him up for us all—how will he not also, along with him, graciously give us all things?" (Romans 8:32). After Calvary, anything. Then He says, "you are mine" (Isaiah 43:1c). We are His property and He will take care of His property. It is His interest even more than ours to guard and bless us.

2. He promises to go with us through the waters and the fires. It is in the dark hour that we know His consolations. That hour will surely come and come often; but it will give us cause to say, "for you saw my affliction" (Psalm 31:7). Indeed, we are often most truly happy in such trying hours, for God's consolation more than outweighs the pressure of our troubles.

3. "Since you are precious and honored in my sight,/ and because I love you,/ I will give men in exchange for you,/ and people in exchange for your life" (Isaiah 43:4). There is something inexpressibly tender about these words. God loves us with a jealous love that puts everything aside that would

hurt us or hinder us. There is a suggestion here of the infinite pains and trouble that He has had with us, and after all this, He is not likely to fail us. Therefore we should not fear, for nothing can work against His will.

4. He promises spiritual fruit. Whatever our troubles may be, it is an infinite comfort if they are overruled for His glory and the good of men. He tells us here that He will bring our seed to the north and south and east and west, and that the fruit of our life shall not be permitted to fail. The seed we sow may seem to perish, but we will doubtless come again rejoicing, bringing our sheaves with us (Psalm 126:6)!

ISAIAH 44:1–5

> But now listen, O Jacob, my servant,
> Israel, whom I have chosen.
> This is what the LORD says—
> he who made you, who formed you in the womb,
> and who will help you:
> Do not be afraid, O Jacob, my servant,
> Jeshurun, whom I have chosen.
> For I will pour water on the thirsty land,
> and streams on the dry ground;
> I will pour out my Spirit on your offspring,
> and my blessing on your descendants.
> They will spring up like grass in a meadow,
> like poplar trees by flowing streams.
> One will say, 'I belong to the LORD';
> another will call himself by the name of Jacob;
> still another will write on his hand, 'The LORD'S,'
> and will take the name Israel.

Here He comforts His troubled children by the promise of a great spiritual blessing and widespread and lasting revival. He will pour out His Spirit upon the thirsty land and streams on the dry ground. He will revive His languishing cause and make the drooping plants of grace to spring up like grass and like poplars by the water courses. He will send the comforting power of His grace so that here and there one shall say, " 'I belong to the LORD';/ another will call himself by the name of Jacob;/ still another will write on his hand 'The LORD'S,'/ and will take the name Israel" (44:5).

The Holy Spirit is the best antidote to our fears. When He comes all the interests of His good cause are safe and all fears are turned to rejoicings and thanksgivings.

ISAIAH 51:12–13

I, even I, am he who comforts you.
  Who are you that you fear mortal men,
    the sons of men, who are but grass,
  that you forget the LORD your Maker,
    who stretched out the heavens
    and laid the foundations of the earth,
  that you live in constant terror every day
    because of the wrath of the oppressor,
    who is bent on destruction?
For where is the wrath of the oppressor?

This passage shows us the sin of fear. It is an act of unbelief. It leads us to forget the Lord, our Maker. It comes from not remembering His power and faithfulness. All our depressions and discouragements are direct reflections upon Him who has always loved and cared for us. We are also reminded in this passage of the folly of our fears. "Who are you that you fear mortal men,/ the sons of men, who are but grass/ . . ./ that you live in constant terror every day/ because of the wrath of the oppressor,/ who is bent on destruction?/ For where is the wrath of the oppressor?" (51:12b, 13b). How very empty are all our anxious cares. How many things we allow to worry us that really never come to pass. How sad and needless the waste of life through such foolish frets and fears.

ISAIAH 54:4–17

Four great reasons are given in this splendid passage why God's trusting children should not fear.

1. The first is His tender personal relation to them. "For your Maker is your husband—/ the LORD Almighty is his name—/ the Holy One of Israel is your Redeemer;/ he is called the God of all the earth" (54:5). This figure of the marriage relation was familiar in all ancient religions, but it was polluted by the grossest abuses. God purifies it and lifts it up to the highest spiritual meaning. There is no suggestion of physical coarseness. It is merely the love of the husband to the wife and the love of the bride that are expressed in the divine marriage. But there is such a love, intense, tender and peculiar which God recognizes in His more intimate relations to His consecrated people. And that fellowship and that love guarantee all possible blessings and safeguards. The husband cherishes his wife even at the cost of his own life and the love of a true wife is stronger than death. How infinitely condescending it is on the part of God to stoop to such a fellowship with

mortal and sinful beings and with such a love how little cause have we to fear.

2. Next is His covenant and oath. "Now I have sworn," He says, "not to be angry with you,/ never to rebuke you again" (54:9b). There is a reference here to the covenant made with Noah of which the rainbow was the symbol and the seal, and God tells us with equal certainty that He has sworn to His eternal love to Israel. But these great promises are not exclusively the property of Israel any more than the epistles to the Ephesians and Galatians belong exclusively to those churches. God spake through His ancient people to every heart in every language, that can still appropriate His promises, and this is true for you and me if we will claim it and live up to it. Many Christians are constantly under the law, and they look to God as though they ever expected a frown and a blow. Rather, we should live in such perfect love that we could not even imagine His failing or forgetting us. There are some human friendships that have never had a cloud upon them. It is very beautiful to have a love that never was shaken. This is the love that God wants us to have for Him. There is a suggestion here of a time when there was a cloud. "For a brief moment I abandoned you" (54:7a). But this is all over now since Christ has died for us. God is ever striving by His great love to make us forget that there ever was such a thing as sin between His heart and ours. Beloved, have we been wholly delivered from the law, and are we living in His perfect love that casts out fear?

3. The third reason is He promises us His protecting care. "No weapon forged against you will prevail,/ and you will refute every tongue that accuses you" (54:17). There will be enemies. There will be temptations and trials; but God will protect us, preserve and vindicate us and we need fear no foe if we are trusting in Him. "Who is going to harm you if you are eager to do good?" (1 Peter 3:13).

4. Finally we don't need to fear, because He promises us His own righteousness. He does not vindicate us and protect us because we are worthy. Let us not flatter ourselves with any self-righteousness. " 'This is their vindication from me,'/ declares the LORD" (Isaiah 54:17b).

This is the mystery of His love—that He treats us as if we were faultless although we are full of blame. He accepts us in Jesus Christ, His beloved Son, clothes us with His imputed righteousness and treats us and loves us as if we were as perfect and faultless as He. What need we fear with such a defense?

> If God is for us, who can be against us? . . . Who will bring any charge against those whom God has chosen? It is God who justifies. Who is he that condemns? Christ Jesus, who died—more than that, who was raised to life—is at the right hand of God and is also interceding for us. (Romans 8:31, 33–34)

Such are some of the "fear nots" of Isaiah. Let us add one or two concluding considerations to save us from our fears.

1. It will help us to remember that the devil's fears are always falsehoods. If fear comes from Satan, then we may invariably conclude that there is nothing to fear, because his suggestions are always lies; and if lies, they cannot harm.

2. Fear is dangerous. It turns into fact the things we fear. It creates the evil just as faith creates the good. "What I feared has come upon me" (Job 3:25), is the solemn warning of Job. Let us therefore be afraid of our fears lest they should become our worst foes.

3. The remedy for fear is faith and love. "When I am afraid, I will trust in you" (Psalm 56:3). "Perfect love drives out fear" (1 John 4:18). "In this way, love is made complete among us so that we will have confidence on the day of judgment, because in this world we are like him" (4:17).

Let us no longer dishonor Him by our doubts and fears but trust Him and honor Him by our confidence, even when everything is most dark and trying. Very beautiful was the answer of that grand old sea captain, who so long commanded a stately ship on the coast line service of the Atlantic. In a violent storm off Hatteras, a trembling woman hastened up to him on the rocking deck and the spray-swept bridge and asked, "Is there any fear, Captain?" "No," he replied; "no fear, but there is considerable danger." There was peril, but no doubt or anxious care; and when he came through that danger through the providence of God, he could witness that God was able to keep in perfect peace.

CHAPTER 27

FOUR AWAKENINGS

The book of Isaiah presents four "awakenings."

SECTION I—*Isaiah 51:9*

"Awake, awake! Clothe yourself with strength,/ O arm of the LORD;/ awake, as in days gone by,/ as in generations of old./ Was it not you who cut Rahab to pieces,/ who pierced that monster through?" (51:9).

This sublime passage is a call from Jerusalem to Jehovah to awake, as in the might of ancient days, for her defense and deliverance. It seemed to her that He must be asleep, so long had He appeared to be deaf to her cries and silent to her prayers.

So the disciples thought the Master cared not for them, as He lay "in the stern sleeping on a cushion" (Mark 4:38); but the heart that was unmoved by the raging of the storm instantly responded to the faintest cry of their distress and woke to rebuke the storm and speak their hearts to peace.

And so God was not asleep. It was but the suppressed strength of His waiting and longsuffering love. It grew by waiting, and would at length burst forth as "the cry of a travailing woman" (Hosea 13:13, KJV) rending the heavens, making the mountains to flow down at His command and overcoming all His people's foes.

SECTION II—*Isaiah 51:17*

"Awake, awake!/ Rise up, O Jerusalem,/ you who have drunk from the hand of the LORD/ the cup of his wrath,/ you who have drained to its dregs/ the goblet that makes men stagger" (Isaiah 51:17).

The second passage quoted above is in answer to the first call. It is a summons from Jehovah to Jerusalem to wake. He turns her own question back upon her and cries, "Awake, awake!/ Rise up, O Jerusalem." Like the disciples in the garden, she has been sleeping for sorrow.

Yes, it is true that the heart can be drugged by grief and anguish until the fiber of our being is poisoned and paralyzed with sorrow.

Not always is suffering sanctifying. Suffering without faith, love and hope corrodes every fiber of the soul, depresses, discourages and destroys. There is nothing on earth so tragic as the case of those who weep life's bitterest tears in unavailing grief, who get nothing out of their distress but bitterness, despair and at last self-destruction, turning first against God and man and then at last, like the scorpion that stings itself to death, against themselves. Thousands of people are going wrong and going down just through heartbreak and discouragement. They say "there is no hope," and they go on from worse to worse. Oh, if you are sunk in the stupor or sleep of hopeless sorrow, hear the voice of God calling "Awake, awake." Rise up above the hideous nightmare of your gloom, throw off the spell of Satan's hate, and go forth into the clear light of truth and God, and you will find that it was but a nightmare of your heart and brain and the sun is shining around you in the heavens, the birds are singing in the branches and there is still left to you the love of God, the sweetness of life and the hope of a bright tomorrow. Awake, awake from the sleep of despairing sorrow. God lives. Christ loves and there is a whole heaven waiting for every heart that can receive it.

SECTION III—*Isaiah 52:1–2*

Awake, awake, O Zion,
 clothe yourself with strength.
Put on your garments of splendor,
 O Jerusalem, the holy city.
The uncircumcised and defiled
 will not enter you again.
Shake off your dust;
 rise up, sit enthroned, O Jerusalem.
Free yourself from the chains on your neck,
 O captive Daughter of Zion.
  (52:1–2)

The third passage in our series is another call to Zion to wake, this time not from sorrow, but from the stupor of sin. It is symbolic of the hideous sight that we sometimes behold in our great cities: a wretched woman who has fallen in the streets under the power of drunkenness and vice. Her hair is matted, her garments are dishevelled and spattered with the mire of the street and her whole frame is bound by the fearful fetters of long habits of sin. Once she was innocent and beautiful and happy; but oh, how degraded now—and as you gaze upon her with compassion, you summon her to awake, to put on her strength, to change her garments, to shake herself from the dust and then to loose herself from the bands of sin and rise and sit down once more in her womanly dignity and glory.

Thank God, many a fallen one has thus risen and is sitting "with him in the heavenly realms in Christ Jesus" (Ephesians 2:6). There are several clauses here.

AWAKE

1. The figure of slumber is often used, not only for the sinner, but for the Christian and the church. The condition of sleep is one in which we are blind to the conditions around us. The flames may be creeping through our home, the burglar may be stealing our treasures, the frowning cliff may be yawning just beneath our feet, but we are asleep and see it not. The fact that you are indifferent or unconcerned about your soul is no evidence that you are safe, but rather that you are asleep.

Then again, the sleeper lives in an unreal world. The thoughts that come to him are vain dreams and false visions of unreal things, while the world is going on around him, and he knows nothing about it. Thousands of people are living as in a dream, passionately striving for the vain things of this little day which will soon vanish and be forgotten, while the great realities of time and eternity are to them as dreams.

Oh, you that are living in a false world and for the perishing things of time, awake, awake!

Again, sleep is a condition of idleness and ease. Your belt is laid down. Your work is put aside, and you are doing nothing in the activities of life. Thousands of God's children are idle because they are asleep. The cause of the Master needs them. The claims of the work need them. The great interests of eternity need them, but they are asleep.

The sleeper is defenseless and exposed to the attacks of the enemy. It is when you sleep that the thief comes to steal your property. It was "while everyone was sleeping, his enemy came and sowed weeds among the wheat" (Matthew 13:25). It was while he slept that Bunyan's pilgrim lost his roll and had to go back afterwards and spend long and weary hours in recovering what he had lost.

How many opportunities have been lost by sleep? How pathetic the appeal of Christ to His three disciples, "Stay here and keep watch with me" (26:38), and how touching His reproach afterwards when He found them sleeping. "Could you men not keep watch with me for one hour?" (26:40). And how unspeakably mournful His final words to them as He came back at last, spent with agony and treading the winepress alone, and said, "Are you still sleeping and resting?" (26:45). It is too late to help me. You have lost your opportunity. "The Son of Man is betrayed into the hands of sinners" (26:45).

Oh, children of God, how much you are missing! Souls are perishing. Opportunities are going by. Eternal recompense is being lost while you sleep on in your dull and stupid insensibility. Awake, Awake!

When a Roman sentinel slept at his post, he lost his uniform and was publicly dishonored and disgraced. It is to this the Master refers when He says, "Blessed is he who stays awake and keeps his clothes with him, so that he may not go naked and be shamefully exposed" (Revelation 16:15).

God's awakening call is a very loud and repeated one. Not gently does the summons come when it is necessary that we must be wakened. This is the meaning of the alarms that have been rung in your heart and your life, the blows that have struck you in your home, your business and your own person. God is calling you. Oh, awake, before He will have to call so loudly that you will never forget the shock!

CLOTHE YOURSELF WITH STRENGTH

2. Sometimes we go to sleep from weakness and weariness. God is calling us to rise and let Him clothe us with His strength. This is not inherent strength of our own. It is a strength that we put on. It is the robe of fire with which the Holy Spirit is waiting to endue every willing, consecrated soul. Oh, the weakness of Christians, afraid of their own voices, afraid of the faces of men, conscious of their impotence and inefficiency, unable to speak to a soul, unable to pray a prevailing prayer, unfruitful and passing on to judgment with "nothing but leaves" (Mark 11:13) to bring before the Master.

God has provided for our strength. The Spirit of Pentecost is waiting to come upon every willing heart. He will give you power to pray, power to witness, power to live, power to bring things to pass for His cause and the world's need. God wants no imbeciles or invalids in His army. You have no business to be a baby. "Awake, awake . . ./ clothe yourself with strength" (Isaiah 52:1a). Receive the Holy Spirit.

PUT ON YOUR GARMENTS OF SPLENDOR

3. This refers to the robes of purity and practical righteousness. The Holy Spirit is given to us, not merely for power, but for all the help we need to live pure, sweet victorious lives. We have no more business to be wicked than we have to be weak. We have no business to go on sinning and failing. We have no business to go into the wedding feast, not having the wedding garment on. It is all provided, and we have but to be willing to wear His robes of purity and He will put them on us. The question is: Will you choose to be sweet, to be kind, to be holy, instead of indulging yourself in your temper, your irritation, your hasty word of retaliation? The Holy Spirit will give you all the grace, all the love, all the patience you are willing to

wear. You must take it by faith; and then wait to put it on and prove it in the real tests of actual life and in the hard places where your human nature will break down, and His divine grace will come to triumph.

This expression covers more than a mere ordinary experience of holiness. These beautiful garments include the finer touches of grace, the finishing touches of holy character, the beautiful array which the bride is to wear in order to be ready for the coming of her Lord.

Will we awake and put on our strength and our beautiful garments?

SHAKE OFF YOUR DUST

4. Every woman knows how to shake the dust from her robes when she has been sitting in an open car or by some dusty highway. The dust here refers to the entanglements with the world into which the children of God so often fall. John Bunyan describes it by the picture of a muck rake with which the miserable worldling was raking together all the dust and grime of the roadside for the sake of the little bits of shining gold he found among it, while at the same time he was refusing a golden crown which the hand of an angel was holding out to him from above.

Yes, "the thick clay," as Job expresses it, is all over us. Go into a fashionable church and angel eyes can see it upon the clothes of the vain and frivolous women, who are thinking much more about their array than about the Word of God. Or, look a little deeper behind the waistcoats of the men and you will see hearts filled with the plans of the week's business and the cares of this sordid world, and all higher thoughts shut out by mammon.

God calls us to shake ourselves from all these things, to be separated from the world and only to use it as a servant and instrument for His glory, counting all our means and possessions as His property and spending them as stewards for His service and glory. The only way to be saved from the world is to give everything to Christ and then to administer the trust as His servants and stewards.

FREEDOM FROM OUR CHAINS

5. "Free yourself from the chains on your neck" (Isaiah 52:2). We are fettered. We are bound. Sometimes it is by the fear of men; sometimes it is by the power of evil habits; sometimes it is by the restraining hand of sickness; but God bids us claim our freedom and stand forth in the glorious liberty of the children of God. We must loose ourselves. He has set us free. We have but to assert our liberty and we shall be free.

SIT DOWN

6. This speaks of rest and quietness and peace. She is first to rise from her prostrate and helpless condition and then sit down as a queen in her royal

seat. Our place is to be "seated . . . with him in the heavenly realms" (Ephesians 2:6), in the "peace of God, which transcends all understanding" (Philippians 4:7), and the rest which quiets every anxious care and fits us to bless and help the troubled hearts around us.

Have we entered into His rest? Have we "sat down under His shadow with great delight" (Song of Songs 2:3, KJV). Have we taken our place of blessing and privilege and "entered into rest"?

SECTION IV—*Isaiah 60:1*

"Arise, shine, for your light has come,/ and the glory of the LORD rises upon you" (60:1).

The splendid figure here is that of one sleeping after sunrise. The sun is up, the light has come, the glory of the Lord has risen, but we are still sleeping as if it were night. His voice bids us rise, step out into the light that is filling all the earth and heaven, and shine in its radiance for His glory.

This applies to the people that are waiting for salvation instead of rising and claiming the salvation which has come and is waiting their acceptance. This applies also to the people that are waiting for the Holy Spirit instead of recognizing the fact that the Spirit has come and that it is ours to receive Him, count upon Him and to go forth and act in dependence upon His presence and victorious power.

And this applies to all who are living below their privileges; who are waiting for some great thing to come to them, instead of recognizing that God has given us everything, and that He is waiting for us to step out and enter into our full inheritance. This word "glory" stands for the highest and the best that God has for His children. It is more than the ordinary grace which saves us. It is the life "more abundantly" (John 10:10, KJV); it is the "inexpressible and glorious joy" (1 Peter 1:8); it is "the riches of his glorious inheritance in the saints" (Ephesians 1:18). It is for us here and now. "I have given them the glory that you gave me, that they may be one as we are one" (John 17:22).

God is waiting to come into your life with a touch of sublimity that will transfigure the common things into the sunlit mountain tops of a celestial vision. It does not mean that our lives shall be on some high plane of circumstances and earthly conditions. Just as the sun can light up a little bit of glass till it glows like a diamond, just as the windows of yonder village sometimes blaze like celestial palaces when the rays of the setting sun fall upon them at a distance, so the commonest trials and duties of life grow elevated when touched by the grace of God and the victory of faith and love.

The other day Mrs. Alexander told in Albert Hall how a few nights before, as she talked with a besotted woman and told her of the love of God, that wretched being asked her if she loved her well enough to kiss her. For a moment she shrank from the new experience, but there came such a tide of God's love into her heart that she leaned over and kissed those foul lips and said, "Yes, I will kiss you, because God loves you." Then she told how that woman, begrimed and defiled with every kind of sin, broke down and gave her life to God and is now working in the meetings, bringing others to the Savior. What a touch of glory that little thing shed upon a very simple act.

And sometimes we have seen God come to some quiet Christian in the hour of overwhelming sorrow when others were crushed in despair, and yet this child of faith was enabled to rise up with face illumined and eyes that refused to weep and lips that could only praise, until all that watched wondered at the glory of His grace.

Yes, and sometimes, too, we have seen a modest, quiet Christian, after a life unmarked by religious emotion or any great experience, but filled up with simple duties, patient suffering and faithful service—we have seen such a life pass down into the dark valley, and we have wondered perhaps if there was a deep enough experience for that last great test. But the heavens have opened, the glory of God has shone upon that dying bed, and those lips have been opened to utter words of inspiration and revelation, words of peace, words of triumph, words of unutterable joy, words of sweet and solemn warning to the living, words of power in the Holy Spirit, and that chamber of mourning has become like a mount of transfiguration, and we have said, "Death has been swallowed up in victory" (1 Corinthians 15:54).

> Is that a death bed where a Christian dies?
> Yes, but not his; 'tis Death himself that dies.

This glory is for you and for me; oceans of it, ages of it are waiting for us, but God will anticipate the eternal years and give us an earnest of it now. Will we take it? Will we rise and shine, for our light has come and the glory of the Lord is risen upon us?

> Shine on, shine on,
> Ye children of the light, shine on;
> shine as the beacon light,
> Shine as the sunrise bright,
> shine as the children of the light,
> shine on, shine on.

CHAPTER 28

THE MYSTERY OF PRAYER

What does Isaiah teach us about prayer?

GOD HEARS AND ANSWERS

1. The first thing Isaiah teaches us is that God is the Hearer and Answerer of prayer. "Then you will call, and the LORD will answer;/ you will cry for help, and he will say: Here am I" (Isaiah 58:9). "Before they call I will answer;/ while they are still speaking I will hear" (65:24).

These verses assure us that our God is no isolated despot, indifferent to the needs and conditions of His creatures, but a loving Father, sensitive to every want and sorrow of His suffering children. How beautiful these promises of prayer! First He says He will answer. Then not only will He answer, but He will come. "He will say, Here I am." Next, "Before they call I will answer," He tells us. And "while they are still speaking, I will hear." Not only will He wait and listen to our appeal, but He will anticipate our need and put the prayer Himself upon our hearts or send the blessing before we ask it. How beautifully this is illustrated in the Savior's thoughtful love toward Simon Peter. Fretting about their taxes which Peter had not the means to pay, we are told that the Lord "prevented him" (Matthew 17:25, KJV) and sent him down to the sea to find a fish with a golden coin in its mouth and then bring and pay the claim for Him and them. He did not wait for Peter to ask for it. He did not allow him to be embarrassed, but His loving forethought anticipated the need. So He is ever loving and caring for us, and as the Psalmist expresses it, "you welcomed him with rich blessings" (21:3a).

The last of these promises, "While they are still speaking I will hear," finds a striking illustration in the message of God to Daniel during his long fast and prayer. "As soon as you began to pray," the angel says, "an answer was given" (Daniel 9:23). God does not wait until we have teased or coaxed Him into compliance with our wishes, but the answer comes with the prayer. It is our privilege to believe that when we ask we do receive the things for which we pray. Indeed, prayer is as much a receiving as an asking, and in the very

495

exercise of our communion with heaven, our hearts are comforted and filled and the blessing comes while we wait.

HINDRANCES AS WELL AS ENCOURAGEMENT

2. Isaiah teaches us that prayer has hindrances as well as its encouragements. The first of these is sin. "Surely the arm of the LORD is not too short to save,/ nor his ear too dull to hear./ But your iniquities have separated/ you from your God;/ your sins have hidden his face from you,/ so that he will not hear" (Isaiah 59:1–2). God cannot recognize sin or hear us if we regard iniquity in our hearts. A willful indulgence in and tolerance of sin destroys every feeling of confidence and renders it impossible for us truly to pray. Let us see to it that every forbidden and doubtful thing is put aside, and "if our hearts do not condemn us, we have confidence before God and receive from him anything we ask, because we obey his commands, and do what pleases him" (1 John 3:21–22).

Indolence is also a hindrance to prayer. "No one calls on your name/ or strives to lay hold of you;/ for you have hidden your face from us/ and made us waste away because of our sins" (Isaiah 64:7). Prayer is recognized here as an intense and active energy of the soul. It is called in James "the effectual fervent prayer" (5:16, KJV). It has real force in it. Many of us are too easy, too self-complacent and content to know much of the power of prayer. It means the waking up of all our being and the intense earnestness of our spirit in pressing through difficulties to God and fighting the good fight of faith with perseverance and power. We often misinterpret the incident of Jacob at Peniel as though the wrestling were all by the angel. It is true that the angel was wrestling with Jacob, to break down his self-sufficiency and subdue his carnal strength, but Jacob was wrestling with the angel, too, and crying out, "I will not let you go unless you bless me" (Genesis 32:26b). Both experiences are true. Each has its place. The truth lies between the two extremes of passive waiting for God and actively taking hold of God and stirring up ourselves in the victorious conflict of prevailing prayer. There is no such intense exercise of soul as real prayer, and it wakes up every dormant faculty of our being and puts us in the place where God can pour His life into us and use us as the instruments of His power.

THE OBJECT LESSON

3. Isaiah teaches us about the great object lesson of prayer. Isaiah gives a picture of the great Intercessor, the Lord Jesus Christ, "He saw that there was no one,/ he was appalled that there was no one to intervene;/ so his own arm worked salvation for him,/ and his own righteousness sustained him" (Isaiah 59:16). Here we find our great High Priest entering upon His mighty ministry of intercession and a little later, in Isaiah 62:1, we hear Him devot-

ing Himself to the long conflict which was not to cease till Zion's deliverance was complete. "For Zion's sake I will not keep silent,/ for Jerusalem's sake I will not remain quiet,/ till her righteousness shines out like the dawn,/ her salvation like a blazing torch" (62:1). Have we duly considered that the supreme ministry of the Lord Jesus Christ is prayer? He spent three and one-half years in active work and suffering, but He has spent 1,900 years in intercession for His people. What a significance, what a majesty, what a power, this gives to the ministry of prayer! The reason is that the spiritual creation is not like the natural. The worlds of space are made by the hand of God, but the church is born of His heart. He had but to put forth a single command and the sun and stars sprang into being. But before a soul can be restored to His image and the work of redemption be consummated, His own heart has to travail in birth in agonies of love. One by one each of us has to come forth from His very being, born of love, travail and pain. This is the ministry that Christ is carrying on. Therefore, it comes to pass that prayer is the secret force of everything in the spiritual kingdom. This great ministry of prayer begins in the bosom of Jesus, but is by Him transferred through the Holy Spirit to the heart of His church and carried on by us in the ministry of prayer on earth.

THE CONFLICT OF PRAYER

4. This brings us to the conflict of prayer. "I have posted watchmen on your walls, O Jerusalem;/ they will never be silent day or night./ You who call on the LORD,/ give yourselves no rest,/ and give him no rest till he establishes Jerusalem/ and makes her the praise of the earth" (62:6–7). Here we find the same language employed by Christ in the first verse re-echoed by His people. His prayer is passed on to us and by us passed back to Him. Like His, our conflict is to be deep and long. We are to "give [ourselves] no rest/ and give him no rest till he establishes Jerusalem/ and makes her the praise of the earth" (62:6–7).

Why this unceasing prayer? Why cannot we ask and then believe it has come and change our prayer to praise? Because it is through the very agency of prayer that the forces are set in motion which accomplish the answer. Natural science tells us that all the effects of light, heat and sound are produced by constant motion in the atoms and elements of matter.

The ether is in intense vibration, and forth from this come the blue sky of heaven, the tinted clouds, the glorious sunshine, the harmonies of music, the waves of heat. Look through a microscope at a drop of water and you will behold every particle and atom in constant circulation moving and moving evermore; and as it moves, developing into new forms of life, the very movement is the process of each new development. So it is in spiritual activity that God works. The stagnant heart is like a corpse or a cemetery. It is the active, intense cooperating spirit through whom He works and moves. Prayer, therefore, is that spiritual law of the fitness of things which puts our spirit in touch with the activities of the Holy Spirit. Prayer, therefore, is an actual force in the spiritual world. It not only moves God, but it moves things.

Science tells us how a single chord of music prolonged without cessation will crumble to dust a stone wall. The old myth of the fiddler fiddling down the bridge is not a fancy. There are musical chords which, if sustained, will break to pieces the strongest material forms. Therefore, passing through the Alps, every voice is hushed; a single sound would dislodge the avalanche and hurl it upon the traveler's head.

So in the spiritual world, prayer is a potency that shakes the foundations of the kingdoms of darkness, that moves the hearts of men and that works out the will of God.

Oh, praying ones, ring out the bells, prolong the notes, let the trumpets resound around the walls of Jericho and they will surely fall. This is the prayer of which the Master speaks when He says, "Knock and the door will be opened to you" (Matthew 7:7). If we let Him teach us this mystery and ministry of spiritual power, then indeed the weapons of our warfare will be mighty, pulling down strongholds and fulfilling God's majestic promise, "Call to me and I will answer you and tell you great and unsearchable things you do not know" (Jeremiah 33:3).

THE CONFIDENCE OF PRAYER

5. Next, Isaiah teaches us the confidence of prayer. "This is what the LORD says—/ the Holy One of Israel, and its Maker;/ Concerning things to come,/ do you question me about my children,/ or give me orders about the work of my hands?" (Isaiah 45:11). Prayer is here connected with the vision of God's plan for His people and His work.

First we are to ask of things concerning His sons. We are to look to Him for a revelation of His purpose for His work and the world. God does give such visions of faith to waking souls. He does forecast the things He is waiting to do for us, and then He bids us claim its actual fulfillment, and adds this mighty command: "about the work of my hands" (45:11). In the name of Jesus we are to not only ask, but claim and pass in the orders of faith to the bank of heaven. The Master Himself has said, "If you remain in me and my words remain in you, ask whatever you wish, and it will be given you," (John 15:7) or, as one has translated it, "Ye shall ask what ye command and it shall be done unto you."

This is a very high place to give to prayer, but we may take it in fellowship with Jesus.

Fear not to take thy place with Jesus on the throne,
And bid the powers of earth and hell His sovereign scepter own;
Your full redemption rights with holy boldness claim,
And to His utmost fullness prove the power of Jesus' name.

THE COMMUNION OF PRAYER

6. "But those who hope in the LORD/ will renew their strength./ They will soar on wings like eagles;/ they will run and not grow weary,/ they will walk and not be faint" (Isaiah 40:31).

This is not the prayer that asks for things, but silently receives from Him His life and strength until the spirit soars with eagle's wings and then goes forth to "run and not grow weary" and "walk and not be faint." This is the kind of prayer that comforts the sorrowing, rests the weary, refreshes the thirsty soul and brings heaven down to fill our hearts here below. It is the fellowship of prayer, the silence of prayer, the secret place of the Most High. Happy are they who have found the key and learned the secret and whose life is "hidden with Christ in God" (Colossians 3:3).

THE SINNER'S PRAYER

7. "Seek the LORD while he may be found;/ call on him while he is near./ Let the wicked forsake his way/ and the evil man his thoughts./ Let him turn to the LORD, and he will have mercy on him,/ and to our God, for he will freely pardon" (Isaiah 55:6–7).

This is the only prayer which the sinner may offer. All other prayers are useless until we begin here. God does not want your worship, your ceremonies, your many prayers. There is but one prayer for you, and that is, "Seek the LORD while he may be found;/ call on him while he is near" (55:6). Bring the prayer of the penitent sinner, "God have mercy on me, a sinner" (Luke 18:13). Until you offer that, all your other prayers are vain. Not until you accept the Savior and come to God in His name can you worship Him acceptably and pray effectually.

Come, therefore, in penitence for mercy and salvation and enter in through the door, and then you will have access to the Father's house and all the privileges and promises of the throne of grace. But come now, while He is near. Seek Him at once, while He may be found. Do not put aside the gentle hand that is touching your shoulder. Do not refuse to grasp the silken cord that is dropped down to you from heaven, and if you seize it, has power to lift you to the skies. Do not trifle with the impressions that God has given you, for impressions are solemn things, but meet the touch that is drawing you to Him; answer to the call which is breathing on your heart; pray the prayer which He has prescribed for such as you and you will find that "he will have mercy on him/ and to our God, for he will freely pardon" (Isaiah 55:7). He will lead you on to those higher ministries of prayer which will enable you to give to others the blessing that has made God so real to you.

"Lord, teach us to pray" (Luke 11:1).